The theory of [illegible] used to explain what it cannot explain!

Does light in itself here age markers? Does light grow old?

Light is used as a distance measuring stick. Not in itself a timed aging indicator.

If you "think" that your life has meaning and purpose, then you are not really an evolutionist nor atheist — a false and contradictory claim, assertion.

$55. Definition of design.

Do you believe in absolute Truth? No!

then what your answer is does not hold to absolute Truth, correct? Yes!

By recognising its inherent
fuzziness can we begin to
understand evolution more clearly
No tree of life — not isolation Ro
Interconnections of species

"In this accessible and engaging introduction, [John Lennox] guides us through the great debates about science and faith, and offers incisive assessments of the issues."
Alister McGrath, Professor of Science and Religion, University of Oxford

Complicated and tw.sty!

"In a century when all the fields of science and technology converge in biology, the effort to confront the deeper meaning of life from a historical and philosophical perspective is more relevant than ever before. This book is a timely and excellent contribution to the conversation."
Sonia Contera, Professor of Biological Physics, University of Oxford

Genetic incompatibilities

"John Lennox has a unique ability to integrate theology, philosophy, biology, physics and mathematics into one coherent unity, and a gift of explaining complicated matters in a simple and pedagogical way. [Cosmic Chemistry] is highly topical and most likely it will become an apologetic classic."
Ola Hössjer, Professor of Mathematical Statistics, Stockholm University

Genes may code for more than one trait.

"... a lucid rationalization that modern scientific discoveries offer […] ample support that God and science not only mix, but that belief in a creator God is entirely consistent with, and the best explanation for, all that science teaches us about the universe and life."
Tony Futerman, Professor of Biomolecular Sciences, Weizmann Institute of Science

Praise for *God's Undertaker*

"An excoriating demolition of Dawkins's overreach from biology into religion."
Melanie Phillips, *The Spectator*

"There is no more important debate than this – science versus religion. But it needs to begin again, with clear understanding of what science and religion actually are. Lennox has done this wonderfully."
Colin Tudge, *The Guardian*

COSMIC
CHEMISTRY

JOHN C. LENNOX

LION

Published by **Lion Books**
www.lionhudson.com
Part of the SPCK Group
SPCK, 36 Causton Street, London, SW1P 4ST

Hardback ISBN 978 0 7459 8142 0
Paperback ISBN 978 0 7459 8140 6
eISBN 978 0 7459 8141 3

First edition 2007 under the title *God's Undertaker*
This edition 2021

Acknowledgments

Unless otherwise marked Scripture quotations are taken from the Holy Bible, New International
Version Anglicised. Copyright ©1979, 1984, 2011 Biblica, formerly International Bible Society.
Used by permission of Hodder & Stoughton Ltd, an Hachette UK company. All rights reserved.
"NIV" is a registered trademark of Biblica. UK trademark number 1448790.

Scripture quotations marked ESV are from The Holy Bible, English Standard Version® (ESV®)
copyright © 2001 by Crossway, a publishing ministry of Good News Publishers. All rights reserved.

p. 159 cell diagram courtesy of Genome Research Limited

p. 161 bacterial flagellum from 'Steps in the Bacterial Flagella Motor' by Mora T., Yu H., Sowa Y.,
Wingreen N.S., in *PLoS Computational Biology* (2009) https://doi.org/10.1371/journal.pcbi.1000540
under CreativeCommons Attribution 4.0 International (CC By 4.0)

p. 172 double-helix structure © Zvitaliy / Shutterstock; p. 349 diagram of a neuron © Tefi / Shutterstock

p. 176 RNA codon table courtesy of NHGRI and in the public domain

p. 177 diagram of ribonucleic acid (public domain)

Extracts pp. 37, 127-28, 357 taken from *Miracles* by C.S. Lewis; extract p. 104 taken from
Mere Christianity by C. S. Lewis; extract p. 238 taken from *Christian Reflections* by C. S. Lewis,
all © C.S. Lewis Pte. Ltd. 1947. Extracts reprinted by permission.

Extract pp. 266, 269 taken from *Letter from J. D. Hooker to Charles Darwin*, 26 November 1862
© Cambridge University Press, reproduced with permission.

Extract p. 29 taken from 'Teleological arguments for God's existence' by Del Ratzsch and
Jeffrey Kpperski (2009) on https://plato.stanford.edu/entries/teleological-arguments/

Epigraph p. 112 taken from 'ET and God' by Paul Davies on https://www.theatlantic.com/author/
paul-davies/. Reproduced by permission.

Epigraph p. 79 taken from *One World*, John Polkinghorne (London: SPCK, 1986), p. 80.
Reproduced by permission.

Epigraph p. 140 taken from *Cosmos, Bios and Theos*, eds Henry Margenau and Roy Varghese
(La Salle, IL: Open Court, 1992), p.83. Reprinted with permission.

Epigraph p. 207 taken from 'An open letter to my colleagues' by James Tour on
https://inference-review.com/ 3 (2), 2017. Reproduced by permission.

Epigraph p. 315 taken from Hans Christian von Baeyer 'In the beginning was the bit' in
New Scientist, 17 February 2001. Reproduced by permission.

Extracts pp. 235-236 taken from 'Questioning evolution is neither science denial',
The Guardian, 5 September 2017. Reproduced by permission.

A catalogue record for this book is available from the British Library

CONTENTS

Preface

To Sally, without whose love, encouragement,
and support this book – and much else –
would never have been completed.

Preface

My book *God's Undertaker: Has Science Buried God?* was first published in 2007 and updated in 2009, and I have been very gratified to see it continuing to attract interest around the world in many languages. Major developments both in science and in the science-religion debate in the intervening years mean that the book was in need, not only of major revision and reorganization, but of rewriting. Hence this book, *Cosmic Chemistry*.

I am especially indebted to my lifelong friend Professor Nigel Cutland, a mathematical logician from the University of York, for his meticulous attention to the entire manuscript and for the many hours of work he put in to making constructive suggestions and discussing them with me. They have saved me from many a logical pitfall and inaccuracy.

I am also grateful for comments from Professor David Galloway, former President of the Royal College of Physicians and Surgeons in Glasgow, Scotland, Professor Tony Futerman, from the Department of Biomolecular Sciences at the Weizmann Institute of Science in Israel, and Dr David Glass of the School of Computing at Ulster University. I also hope that my response to the criticisms of the previous editions that I have received over the years, together with much new material, will be a stimulus in the ongoing discussion.

John C. Lennox
Oxford, January 2021

PART 1

Surveying the Landscape

Why is there something rather than nothing?
What is the meaning of it all?

1

Introduction

This book is intended as an introduction to the ongoing science–religion debate. I have spent many years thinking about the issues involved and have tried to find a way, not only of navigating the terrain myself, but also of helping others to do the same. The questions that arise are the big questions that have exercised the human mind for thousands of years. The first one, said to have been asked, among others, by mathematician Gottfried Wilhelm Leibniz, philosopher Ludwig Wittgenstein, and theologian Martin Heidegger, is: Why is there something rather than nothing? Heidegger called it the 'fundamental question of metaphysics'. It then rapidly spawns many other questions: Why, in particular, does the universe exist? Where did the cosmos come from, and where, if anywhere, is it heading? Is it the ultimate reality beyond which there is nothing, or is there something more? Can we expect an answer to physics Nobel laureate Richard Feynman's question: 'What is the meaning of it all?' Another Nobel laureate, Albert Einstein, once said: 'To know an answer to the question, "What is the meaning of human life?" *means* to be religious.'[1] And Wittgenstein said: 'To believe in God means to see that life has a meaning.'[2] Or, was philosopher and mathematician Bertrand Russell right when he said: 'The universe is just there, and that's all. No purpose, no meaning, just the brute fact of existence?' And many today will say that science has buried God: there is no need for God any more, even if he does exist, which looks increasingly unlikely.

These questions have lost none of their attraction, as is evidenced by the vast literature to which they continue to give rise. It is virtually impossible to keep up with the topic, let alone digest and condense all its various ramifications. It is also completely impossible to squeeze it into the confines of a single book, however large.

As a result I cannot go into full detail at every stage of our discussions but will try to recommend further reading in order to help the reader who wishes to pursue matters in more depth. The subject matter can be complicated at times, but then all interesting things tend to be complicated – as some of us will have learned when we graduated from a toy car to a real one. I shall make every effort, however, to make myself intelligible. As C.S. Lewis put it: 'I will be understood!'

I have developed my arguments advanced in this book in lectures, seminars, and discussions in many countries, and, although I feel that there is still much work to be done, it was at the urging of many of those present on such occasions that I originally made the attempt to write a book that would introduce the main issues and be a springboard for further discussion and exploration. I am grateful for the many questions, comments, and criticisms that have helped me in my task but, of course, I hold myself alone responsible for the remaining infelicities in this now revised and, I fear, much extended version.

Some comments about procedure are in order. I shall attempt to set the discussion in the context of the contemporary debate as I have followed it. I shall make frequent use of quotations from leading scientists and thinkers with a view to getting a clear picture of what those in the forefront of the debate are actually saying. I am, however, aware that there is always a danger of quoting out of context and in consequence not only ceasing to be fair to the person being quoted but also distorting the true picture. I hope that I have succeeded in avoiding that particular danger.

My mention of truth leads me to fear that some people of post-modernist persuasion may be tempted not to read any further, unless of course they are curious to read (and maybe even attempt to deconstruct) a text written by someone who actually believes in truth. For my part I confess to finding it curious that those who claim that there is no such thing as truth expect me to believe that what they are saying is true! Perhaps I misunderstand them, but they seem to exempt themselves from their general rubric so that what they are really saying is that there is no truth apart from what they say. They turn out to believe in truth after all.

In any case, scientists have a clear stake in truth. That is the one important point on which Richard Dawkins and I actually agree, as we made clear at the press conference that followed our debate on the topic of this book in the Oxford Natural History Museum in 2008. Why, otherwise, would we bother to do science? And it is precisely because I believe in the category of truth that I have tried only to use quotations that seem to represent an author's general position fairly, rather than cite some statement which he or she made on some 'off' day. Any of us can be guilty of that kind of infelicity. In the end I must leave it to the reader to judge whether I have succeeded.

What about bias? No one can escape it, neither author nor reader. We are all biased in the sense that we all have a worldview that consists of our answers, or partial answers, to the questions that the universe and life throw at us. Our worldviews may not be fully, or even consciously, formulated, but they are there nonetheless. Our worldviews are of course shaped by experience and reflection. They can and do change – on the basis of sound evidence, one would hope.

The concern that is central to this book is, in its essence, a worldview question: Which worldview sits most comfortably with science – theism or atheism? Has science buried God or not? Let us see where the evidence leads.

God will be understood as in the Judaeo-Christian biblical tradition though we shall be mainly interested in the scientific aspects of the underlying question. That is, we shall focus on:

Question A. *Does science – its history, presuppositions, and findings – provide evidence of a designing intelligence involved in the universe and life?*
rather than:
Question B. *What is the nature of that designing intelligence, if it exists?*

Differentiating between these two questions has been the intellectual motivation behind the Intelligent Design (ID) movement, though the distinction has often not been clearly grasped resulting in a great deal of unnecessary and unhelpful misunderstanding. We shall say something about ID at the end of Chapter 3.

Tackling Question A will take us to the history and philosophy of science as well as the demarcation between science and philosophy. It will also involve consideration of research results from physics, chemistry, biology, computer science, and mathematics. We shall necessarily be paying careful attention to the philosophical implications of that research. The danger of doing this is that the reader may get the impression that I do not sufficiently appreciate the research that has produced those results in itself. I would like to reassure you that the very opposite is the case. I have spent a lifetime in research-level mathematics and, to take two further examples, I think that some of the work in physics on self-organizing systems and work in systems biology on the role of DNA, reductionism, and teleology in the living cell is impressive, sophisticated, and ground-breaking science. After all, Nobel Prizes have been awarded for some of this work.

The big questions mentioned at the commencement of this chapter were included in Stephen Hawking's list of questions in his 2010 bestselling book *The Grand Design*,[3] co-authored with Leonard Mlodinow, and they have lost nothing of their power to fire human imagination. Spurred on by the desire to climb the mountain peaks of knowledge and understanding, scientists have already given us spectacular insights into the nature of the universe we inhabit. On the scale of the unimaginably large, the Hubble telescope, from its orbit high above earth's atmosphere, transmits stunning images of the heavens of hitherto unimaginable quality. At a much more modest level, down on earth in my tiny observatory in my garden, I am moved to wonder by seeing the Andromeda Galaxy, the Orion Nebula and the Ring Nebula, many other Messier objects, the planets and the moon, through my 10-inch telescope. On the scale of the unimaginably small, scanning tunnelling microscopes uncover the incredibly complex molecular structure of the living world with its information-rich macromolecules and its micro-miniature protein factories whose complexity and precision make even advanced human technologies look crude by comparison.

Are we and the universe, with its profusion of galactic beauty and subtle biological complexity, nothing but the products of irrational forces acting on mindless matter and energy in an unguided way, as those scientists who are atheists, still led by Richard Dawkins, constantly insist? Is human life ultimately only one, admittedly improbable, but nevertheless fortuitous, arrangement of atoms among many? In any case, how could we be in any sense special since we now know that we inhabit a tiny planet orbiting a fairly undistinguished star far out in an arm of a spiral galaxy containing billions of similar stars, a galaxy that is only one of billions distributed throughout the vastness of space?

What is more, say some, since certain basic properties of our universe, like the strength of the fundamental forces of nature and the number of observable space and time dimensions, are the result of random effects operating far back at the origin of the universe, then, surely, other universes, with very different structures, might well exist. Is, then, our universe only one in a vast array of parallel universes forever separated from each other? Is it not therefore absurd to suggest that human beings have any ultimate significance? Their measure in a multiverse would seem effectively reduced to zero.

Many scientists, therefore, think it would be an intellectually stultifying exercise in nostalgia to hark back to the early days of modern science when scientists such as Bacon, Galileo, Kepler, Newton, and Clerk Maxwell, for example, believed in an intelligent Creator God whose brainchild the cosmos is. Science has surely moved on from such primitive notions, squeezed God into a corner, killed, and then buried him by its all-embracing and satisfying explanations. God has, in the end, turned out to be no more substantial than the smile on a cosmic Cheshire cat. Unlike Schrödinger's cat, God is no ghostly superposition of dead and alive – he is certainly dead. Furthermore, the whole process of his demise shows that any attempt to reintroduce gods of any kind – especially as a 'god of the gaps'– is likely to impede the progress of science as it did in the time of the ancient Greeks. We can now see more clearly than ever before that naturalism (the view that nature is all that there is, that there is no transcendence) has no serious challengers, reigns supreme.

Peter Atkins, Emeritus Professor of Chemistry at Oxford University, while acknowledging the religious element in the historical development of science, defends the naturalistic view with characteristic vigour:

> Science, the system of belief founded securely on publicly shared reproducible knowledge, emerged from religion. There is no reason to suppose that science cannot deal with every aspect of existence. Only the religious – among whom I include not only the prejudiced but the under-informed – hope there is a dark corner of the physical universe, or of the universe of experience, that science can never hope to illuminate. But science has never encountered a barrier, and the only grounds for supposing that reductionism will fail are pessimism on the part of scientists and fear in the minds of the religious.[4]

The idea that 'science can deal with every aspect of existence' is called scientism. It sounds impressive but it is actually not only false but logically incoherent. For the statement just quoted is not itself a statement of science and so if it is true it is false. We shall have occasion to explore scientism in more detail later as, in spite of its illogicality, it is deeply ingrained in the thinking of some leading scientists.

As an example of its reach, a conference at the Salk Institute for Biological Studies in La Jolla, California in 2006 discussed the theme: 'Beyond belief: science, religion, reason and survival'. Addressing the question of whether science should do away with religion, Nobel laureate Steven Weinberg said: 'The world needs to wake up from the long nightmare of religion... Anything we scientists can do to weaken the hold of religion should be done, and may in fact be our greatest contribution to civilization.' Unsurprisingly, Richard Dawkins went even further: 'I am utterly fed up with the respect we have been brainwashed into bestowing upon religion.' As I am writing now there is no evidence that either Weinberg or Dawkins have changed their opinions.

And yet, and yet... I still wish to ask: Are they right? Are all religious people to be written off as prejudiced and under-informed? Indeed not as, for example, it turns out that in the twentieth century 65.4 per cent of all Nobel laureates stated that Christianity was their religious preference.[5] Some of them still do, like William Phillips, a physics Nobel Prize winner. So not all scientists who believe in God nowadays pin their hopes on 'finding a dark corner of the universe that science can never hope to illuminate' as Atkins rather wildly suggests. It would appear that he himself may belong to the group of the prejudiced and uninformed that he criticizes. Also, and most importantly, the majority, if not all of the early pioneers in science maintained that it was precisely their belief in a Creator that inspired their science to ever greater heights. For them it was the dark corners of the universe that science *did* illuminate that provided ample evidence of the existence and ingenuity of God.

And what of the biosphere? Is its intricate complexity really only *apparently* designed, as asserted by Richard Dawkins, Peter Atkins' staunch ally in faith? (Yes, you read me correctly, atheism is a faith, a belief system, as we shall see.) Can rationality really arise through unguided natural processes working under the constraints of nature's laws on the basic materials of the universe in some random way? Is the solution of the mind–body problem simply that rational mind 'emerged' from mindless body by undirected mindless processes?

Questions about the status of this naturalistic story do not readily go away, as the level of public interest still shows. I have been interested in such questions since I was a teenager. My parents were unfortunately not able to benefit from the kind of advanced education that they generously enabled me to have, but they were nevertheless remarkably intelligent people. Their Christian faith was lived out daily and, for me, formed a highly credible introduction to it. Not only that, my father was a questioner, a fact that was responsible for me eventually regarding Socrates, that most famous questioner of all, as an intellectual hero. Dad was prepared to question his own faith in God and interpretations of the Bible and he encouraged me to do the same. He even went so far, unusual in those days in Northern Ireland, to encourage me to read views hostile to Christianity, like Marxism, for example.

When I was in upper school I had friends a little older than me who were already studying science at university and through them I was introduced to the writings of Dr R. E. D. Clark, who lectured in chemistry. His books *Christian Belief and Science – A Reconciliation and a Partnership* and *The Universe: Plan or Accident* proved very stimulating, as did his *Darwin, Before & After*. I also confess that, at the time, I found them easier to digest than some other books I tackled, like, for instance, Alfred North Whitehead's *Science and the Modern World*. I did, however, glean more from it later. I sought Robert Clark out not long after I arrived as a student in Cambridge and thereafter visited him a number of times for very stimulating conversations. He was a voracious reader and told me that each week he attached a small wooden tea chest to his bicycle that he would fill with books from the university library, returning the next week for another load.

One key question to which Clark drew my attention was whether a naturalistic worldview was actually demanded by science, as Atkins and Dawkins were later to insist so strongly. Or, was it conceivable that their naturalism is *a priori*, that is, as a set of beliefs that they brought to bear on their science, rather than a faith system that is entailed by their science? Could it even be, as some have suggested, more like a religious faith for them? One might at least be forgiven for entertaining such thoughts from the manner in which those scientists that risk questioning the naturalism that dominates the academy are sometimes treated. Like religious heretics of a former age they may suffer a form of academic martyrdom by the practical expedient of cutting their grants – or, in extreme cases, even losing their jobs.

Aristotle is reputed to have said that in order to succeed we must ask the right questions. It turns out, however, that there are certain questions that it is risky to ask in a scientific context and even more risky to attempt to answer if they seem to threaten a reigning paradigm. Yet, surely taking that kind of risk is in both the spirit and interests of science. From a

[handwritten annotations at top of page:]

Strength of light — light loses its brightness as it is further from its source.

Speed of light — constant / Time varies, changes, View.i reference

historical perspective this is not a controversial point in itself. In the Middle Ages, for instance, science had to free itself from certain aspects of Aristotelian philosophy before it could investigate the world as it actually was. Aristotle had taught that from the moon and beyond all was perfection and, since perfect motion, in his view, had to be circular, the planets and stars moved in perfect circles. Beneath the moon motion was linear and there was imperfection. This view dominated thought for centuries. Then Galileo looked through his telescope and saw the ragged edges of lunar craters. The universe had spoken and part of Aristotle's deduction from his *a priori* concept of perfection lay in tatters.

But Galileo was still obsessed with Aristotle's circles: 'For the maintenance of perfect order among the parts of the Universe, it is necessary to say that movable bodies are movable only circularly.'[6] Yet the circles, too, were doomed. It fell to Kepler, on the basis of his analysis of the direct and meticulous observations of the orbit of Mars made by his predecessor as Imperial Mathematician in Prague, Tycho Brahe, to take the daring step of suggesting that astronomical observations were of more evidential value than calculations based on the *a priori* theory that planetary motion must be circular. The rest, as they say, is history.

Kepler made the ground-breaking suggestion that the planets moved in equally 'perfect' ellipses around the sun that was situated at one focus of the ellipse, a view later brilliantly illuminated by Newton's inverse-square law theory of gravitational attraction, which compressed all of these developments into one stunningly brief and elegant formula. Kepler had changed science forever by unleashing it from the inadequate philosophy that had constrained it for centuries. It would perhaps be presumptuous to assume that such a liberating step will never have to be taken again. Indeed, I think it is highly likely.

To this it will be objected that, since the time of the pioneers Galileo, Kepler, and Newton, science has shown exponential growth and there is no evidence that the philosophy of naturalism, with which science is now so closely related (at least in the minds of many), is inadequate. Indeed, in their opinion, naturalism only serves to further science, which can now proceed unencumbered by the kind of mythological baggage that held it back so often in the past. The great merit of naturalism, it will be argued, is that it cannot possibly inhibit science for the very simply reason that it believes the scientific method to be supreme. It is the one philosophy that is absolutely compatible with science, essentially by definition.

But is that really the case? For most of the great scientific figures who contributed to the meteoric rise of science at that time, belief in a Creator God was not inhibiting but rather positively stimulating, precisely because it did not specify how the universe had to be – that is, the universe is contingent. The conviction that the universe was the work of a divine intelligence was therefore a prime motivation for scientific investigation of that contingent universe. That being the case, the vehemence of the atheism of some contemporary writers spurs me to ask: Why are they now so convinced that atheism is the only intellectually tenable position? Is it really true that everything in science points towards atheism? Are science and atheism such natural bedfellows? Or, does science give any evidence of design?

2

Matters of Evidence and Faith

'All my studies in science… have confirmed my faith.'
Sir Ghillean Prance FRS

In this chapter we show that there is considerable confusion not only in the public space but also among scientists regarding faith and what it is. We argue that the common 'New Atheist' view that faith is a religious word that means 'belief without evidence' is false. We also describe the results of some surveys on the attitudes of scientists to faith in God. Finally, we point out the important principle that statements by scientists are not always statement of science.

The last nail in God's coffin?

It is a widespread popular impression that each new scientific advance is another nail in God's coffin. It is an impression fuelled by influential scientists. Chemist Peter Atkins writes: 'Humanity should accept that science has eliminated the justification for believing in cosmic purpose, and that any survival of purpose is inspired only by sentiment.'[1] Now, how science, which is traditionally thought not even to deal with questions of (cosmic) purpose, could actually do any such thing is not very clear, as we shall later see. What *is* very clear is that Atkins reduces faith in God at a stroke, not simply to sentiment but to sentiment that is inimical to science. Atkins does not stand alone. Not to be outdone, Richard Dawkins goes a step further. He regards faith in God as an evil to be eliminated:

> It is fashionable to wax apocalyptic about the threat to humanity posed by the AIDS virus, 'mad cow' disease and many others, but I think that a case can be made that *faith* is one of the world's great evils, comparable to the smallpox virus but harder to eradicate. Faith, being belief that isn't based on evidence, is the principal vice of any religion.'[2]

More recently, faith, in Dawkins' opinion, has graduated (if that is the right term) from being a vice to being a delusion. In his book *The God Delusion*[3] he quotes Robert Pirsig, author of *Zen and the Art of Motorcycle Maintenance*: 'When one person suffers from a delusion, it is called insanity. When many people suffer from a delusion, it is called Religion.' For Dawkins, God is not only a delusion, but a pernicious delusion.

Such views are at one extreme of a wide spectrum and it would be a mistake to think that they were typical. Many atheists are far from happy with the militant aggression, not to mention the repressive, even totalitarian, overtones of such so-called 'New Atheist' views, and in more recent years have largely rejected them. However, as always, it is the extreme views that receive public attention and media exposure, with the result that many people are aware of those views and have been affected by them. It would, therefore, be unwise to ignore them. We must take them seriously.

From what he says it is clear that one of the things that has generated Dawkins' hostility to faith in God is the impression he has (sadly) gained that, whereas 'scientific belief is based upon publicly checkable evidence, religious faith not only lacks evidence; its independence from evidence is its joy, shouted from the rooftops'.[4] In other words, he takes all religious faith to be blind faith. If that is what it is, perhaps it does deserve to be classified with smallpox. However, taking Dawkins' own advice we ask (him): Where is the evidence that religious faith is not based on evidence?

Admittedly, there unfortunately are some people who profess faith in God and take an overtly anti-scientific and obscurantist viewpoint. Their attitude brings faith in God into disrepute and is to be deplored. Perhaps Richard Dawkins has had the misfortune to meet disproportionately many of them.

Religion is a very broad term and it would be impossible in a book of this size to discuss the whole range of religious attitudes to these questions. However, in 1896, William James usefully defined religious faith as 'faith in the existence of an unseen order of some kind in which the riddles of the natural order can be found and explained.'[5]

In my view, each religion has the right to, and should, if it so desires, speak for itself. In any case, I cannot credibly represent any viewpoint other than the one I espouse, which is Christianity.

It is the fact, however, that science has buried many gods – the gods of the ancient world, for instance, and rightly so, for belief in them held up progress in the rational understanding of the world, as we shall see in Chapter 3. For instance, you would not be much inclined to study the moon if you believed it was a god whose influence on you might well be baleful. However, the God that will concern us in this book is the God of the Judaeo-Christian biblical tradition – the supernatural Creator and Upholder of the cosmos.

The topic of science and a *supernatural* God will inevitably raise for us the question of God's interaction with the universe.

But back to the matter of evidence. Christianity will insist that faith in God is evidence-based. For, faith, as presented in the New Testament is a considered response to evidence, not a rejoicing in its absence. In his biography of Jesus the Christian apostle John clearly expresses this point: 'These things are written that you might believe... .'[6] That is, he understands, that the collection of supernatural 'signs' that he records Jesus as having performed (we often call them 'miracles') form evidence on which faith can be based. That is, faith that Jesus is God incarnate is evidence-based. The apostle Paul says what many pioneers of modern science believed, namely, that nature itself is part of the evidence for the existence of God: 'For since the creation of the world God's invisible qualities – his eternal power and divine nature have been clearly seen, being understood from what has been made, so that people are without excuse.'[7] It is no part of the biblical view that things should be believed where there is no evidence. *Just as in science, faith, reason, and evidence belong together.* Dawkins' definition of faith as what most of us understand as 'blind faith' turns out, therefore, to be the exact opposite of the biblical one. Curious that he does not seem to be aware of the discrepancy. Could it be as a consequence of blind faith of his own? For, Dawkins' idiosyncratic definition of faith provides a striking example of the very thing he claims to abhor – thinking that is not evidence-based. In an exhibition of breath-taking inconsistency, evidence is the very thing he himself fails to supply for his claim that independence of evidence is faith's joy. And the reason why he fails to supply such evidence is not hard to find – there is none. It takes no great research effort to ascertain that no serious biblical scholar or thinker would support Dawkins' definition of faith. Francis Collins, former Head of the Human Genome Project and current Director of the National Institutes of Health (NIH), says of Dawkins' definition that it 'certainly does not describe the faith of most serious believers in history, nor of most of those in my personal acquaintance.'[8]

Collins' point is important for it shows that those who reject all faith as blind are destroying their own credibility. Theologian John Haught says:

'Even one white crow is enough to show that not all crows are black, so surely the existence of countless believers who reject the new atheists' simplistic definition of faith is enough to place in question the applicability of their critiques to a significant section of the religious population.'[9]

Professor of Science and Religion at Oxford, Alister McGrath, points out in his highly accessible assessment[10] that Dawkins has signally failed to engage with any serious Christian thinkers. What then should we think of Dawkins' excellent maxim: 'Next time that somebody tells you that something is true, why not say to them: "What kind of evidence is there for that?" And if they can't give you a good answer, I hope you'll think very carefully before you believe a word they say'?[11] One might well be forgiven for giving in to the powerful temptation to apply Dawkins' maxim to him – and just not believe anything he says.

In light of their erratic and inconsequential pronouncements, I am inclined to hope, with philosopher Alvin Plantinga, Emeritus Professor at the University of Notre Dame, that: 'the new atheists are but a temporary blemish on the face of serious conversation in this crucial area.'[12]

Dawkins is not alone in holding the erroneous notion that faith in God is not based on any kind of evidence. I am disappointed to find that it is relatively common among members of the scientific community, even though it may well be formulated in a somewhat different way. I am often told, for example, that faith in God 'belongs to the private domain, whereas scientific commitment belongs to the public domain', that 'faith in God is a different kind of faith from that which we exercise in science' – in short, faith in God is 'blind faith'. We shall have occasion to look at this issue more closely in Chapter 4 in the section on the rational intelligibility of the universe.

First of all, though, let us get at least some idea of the state of belief/ unbelief in God in the scientific community. One of the most interesting surveys in this regard is that conducted in 1996 by Edward Larsen and Larry Witham and reported in *Nature*.[13] Their survey was a repeat of a survey conducted in 1916 by Professor Leuba in which 1,000 scientists (chosen at random from the 1910 edition of *American Men of Science*) were asked whether they believed both in a God who answered prayer and in personal immortality – that is, a supernatural God, rather than some vague divinity. The response rate was 70 per cent of whom 41.8 per cent said yes, 41.5 per cent no, and 16.7 per cent were agnostic. In 1996, the response was 60 per cent of whom 39.6 per cent said yes, 45.5 per cent no, and 14.9 per cent[14] were agnostic. These statistics were given differing interpretations in the press on the half-full, half-empty principle. Some used them as evidence of the survival of belief, others of the constancy of unbelief. Perhaps the most surprising thing is that there has been relatively little change in the proportion of believers to unbelievers during those eighty years of enormous growth in scientific knowledge, a fact that contrasts sharply with prevailing public perception.

A similar survey showed that the percentage of atheists is higher at the top levels of science. Larsen and Witham showed in 1998[15] that, among the top scientists in the National Academy of Sciences in the USA who responded, 72.2 per cent were atheists, 7 per cent believed in God and 20.8 per cent were agnostics. Unfortunately we have no comparable statistics from 1916 to see if those proportions have changed since then or not, although we do know that over 90 per cent of the founders of the Royal Society in England were theists.

That is no longer the case. In 2018 a survey was done of Fellows of the Royal Society who were asked what level of agreement or disagreement they had with each of a set of statements. The first statement was: 'I believe that there is a strong likelihood that a supernatural being such as God exists or has existed'; 78 per cent strongly disagreed and 8 per cent strongly agreed.

Perhaps the most interesting set of responses were to the statement: 'I believe that science and religion occupy non-overlapping domains of discourse and can peacefully co-exist (NOMA).'[16] The researchers concluded from the answers that the majority of these mainly atheist scientists see tensions but do not see religion as in overt conflict with science.

A more recent survey of a different type was conducted by sociologist Elaine Howard Ecklund of Rice University, Texas, in 2014. Here is a summary of her results: 'We found that nearly 50 percent of evangelicals believe that science and religion can work together and support one another', Ecklund said. 'That's in contrast to the fact that only 38 percent of Americans feel that science and religion can work in collaboration.'[17]

Of course, how one interprets such (indeed, any!) statistics is a complex business and, in any case, the matter is not going to be settled by statistics. Yet, whatever their ramifications, these surveys provide evidence enough to show that Dawkins may well be right about the difficulty of accomplishing his rather ominously totalitarian-sounding task of eradicating faith in God among scientists. For, in addition to the nearly

40 per cent of believing scientists in the general survey, there have been and are some very eminent scientists who do believe in God – notably the aforementioned Templeton Prize winner Dr Francis Collins, Professor William (Bill) Phillips, winner of the Nobel Prize for Physics in 1997, Sir Brian Heap FRS, former Vice President of the Royal Society, and the late Sir John Houghton FRS, former Director of the British Meteorological Office, co-Chair of the Intergovernmental Panel on Climate Change, and Director of the John Ray Initiative on the Environment, and Sir Ghillean Prance FRS, former Director of Kew Gardens in London.

Here are two examples of what they say. Sir John Houghton wrote: 'Our science is God's science. He holds the responsibility for the whole scientific story... The remarkable order, consistency, reliability and fascinating complexity found in the scientific description of the universe are reflections of the order, consistency, reliability and complexity of God's activity.'[18]

Sir Ghillian Prance gave equally clear expression to his faith: 'For many years I have believed that God is the great designer behind all nature... All my studies in science since then have confirmed my faith. I regard the Bible as my principal source of authority.'[19]

Again, of course, the statements just listed are not statements of science either, but statements of personal belief. It should be noted, however, that they contain hints as to the evidence that might be adduced to support that belief. For instance, Sir Ghillean Prance explicitly says that it is science itself that confirms his faith. By contrast, Peter Atkins thinks that there is simply no question of reconciling science and religion, since religion has failed and science reigns supreme.[20]

This is triumphalist language, much of it pure assertion. But has the triumph really been secured? Which religion has failed, and in what regard? Although science is certainly a delight, is it really the supreme delight of the intellect? Do music, art, literature, love, and truth have nothing to do with the intellect? I can hear the rising chorus of protest from the humanities – and I will happily join in as I believe that the humanities have a vast amount to teach us, particularly about things that really matter, like meaning and truth and the human condition that are beyond the reach of science as commonly understood.

What is more, the fact that there are *scientists* who appear to be at war with God is emphatically not the same thing as *science* itself being at war with God. For example, some musicians are militant atheists. But does that mean music itself is at war with God? Hardly. The point here may be expressed as by saying that *statements by scientists are not necessarily statements of science*.

Nor, we might add, are such statements necessarily true or necessarily false; although the prestige of science is such that they are often taken to be true without further enquiry. For example, the assertions by Atkins and Dawkins cited above, fall into that category. They are not statements of science but rather expressions of personal belief, indeed, of faith – fundamentally no different from (though noticeably less tolerant than) much expression of the kind of faith in God that Dawkins expressly wishes to eradicate.

Thus, on the one hand, naturalist thinkers tell us that science has confirmed their atheism, indeed, demands it, whereas, on the other hand, theists tell us that science confirms their faith in God and may even lead to it. These opposing positions are held by highly competent scientists. What does this mean? It certainly implies that it would be very simplistic to assume that science and faith in God are enemies. It also suggests that it could be worth exploring what exactly the relationships between science and atheism and between science and theism are. In particular, which, if any, of these two diametrically opposing worldviews of theism and atheism does science support? For answers we turn first to the history of science.

3

A Historical Perspective: The Forgotten Roots of Science and Arguments From Design

'But suppose I had found a watch upon the ground, and it should be inquired how the watch happened to be in that place... The watch must have had a maker: there must have existed... an artificer... who formed it for the purpose which we find it actually to answer; who comprehended its construction and designed its use... Every indication of contrivance, every manifestation of design, which existed in the watch, exists in the works of nature; with the difference, on the side of nature, of being greater or more, and that in a degree which exceeds all computation.'
William Paley

Thinking about whether or not the universe was designed predates modern science by a very long time. It goes back to Democritus, Socrates, Plato, and Aristotle, and, centuries before that, to the Hebrew Bible. We reflect on the important difference between the Greek worldview and the biblical worldview and trace the two streams of materialism and theism from ancient times.

We think about the famous Five Ways arguments for the existence of God put forward by Thomas Aquinas in the thirteenth century. We then explore the important connection between the rise of modern science in the sixteenth and seventeenth centuries and the biblical ideas of creation and contingency. This leads to a discussion of two iconic incidents that have fuelled the idea that science and religion are at war. They are firstly the clash between Galileo and the Roman Catholic Church in the seventeenth century and, secondly, the clash between

Thomas Henry Huxley and Bishop Wilberforce in the Natural History Museum at Oxford in the nineteenth century. It turns out that historical analysis of these incidents does nothing to support the conflict narrative that unfortunately still garners support even today.

We backtrack a little in the nineteenth century to consider the design arguments of William Paley that were initially convincing to Charles Darwin in his early days. However, in Darwin's view, and that of many others, Paley's argument was undermined by Darwin's discovery of natural selection. We look at the criticism of Paley made by John Henry Newman and, more generally, at David Hume's earlier criticisms of design arguments. We find that Paley's argument is updatable and retains considerable force.

We finally look at the concept of Intelligent Design (ID) that stands in the tradition of Paley.

At the heart of all science lies the conviction that the universe is orderly. Without this deep conviction science would not be possible. So we are entitled to ask: Where does the conviction come from? Melvin Calvin, Nobel Prize winner in biochemistry, seems in little doubt about its provenance:

> As I try to discern the origin of that conviction, I seem to find it in a basic notion discovered 2,000 or 3,000 years ago, and enunciated first in the Western world by the ancient Hebrews: namely that the universe is governed by a single God, and is not the product of the whims of many gods, each governing his own province according to his own laws. This monotheistic view seems to be the historical foundation for modern science.[1]

We find this idea expressed in the resonant poetry of the Hebrew psalms. Psalm 19:1 says: 'The heavens declare the glory of God; the skies proclaim the work of his hands.' Psalm 94:9 says: 'Does he who fashioned the ear not hear? Does he who formed the eye not see?' This is, perhaps, something that, to borrow Dawkins' language (which he in turn borrowed from the New Testament!), ought to be 'shouted from the rooftops' as an antidote to a summary rejection of God. For it means that the foundation on which science stands, the base from which its trajectory has swept up to the edge of the universe, has a strong theistic dimension.

The first Professor of Science and Religion at Oxford was John Hedley Brooke, a historian of science. I had the privilege of attending his graduate lectures on science and religion and subsequently teaching part of the course. One of the main things I learned from John was the importance of a historical perspective on the science–religion debate which is the topic of this chapter.

Melvin Calvin's observation is very striking in view of the fact that it is common in university courses on science first to trace the roots of contemporary science back to the Greeks of the sixth century BC and then to point out that, for science to proceed, the Greek worldview had to be emptied of its polytheistic content so that atheism became the natural foundation worldview in which science originally thrived. We shall return to the latter point below.

We simply wish to point out here that, although the Greeks certainly were in many ways the first to do science in anything like the way we understand it today, as we shall see below, here is a top scientist, Melvin Calvin, telling us that it was the Hebrew view that the universe was designed, created, and upheld by God that was of greatest help to science, a view very much older than the worldview of the Greeks.

Before the sixth century BC – and, in part, after that – there was a profound difference between the Greek and Hebrew views of the universe. Commenting on Hesiod's poem *Theogony* (*The Genesis of the gods*), Oxford expert Werner Jaeger writes:

> If we compare this Greek hypostasis of the world-creative Eros with that of the *Logos* in the Hebrew account of creation, we may observe a deep-lying difference in the outlook of the two peoples. The *Logos* is a substantialization of an intellectual property or power of God the Creator, who is stationed *outside* the world and brings that world into existence by his own personal fiat.[2]

In order to set all this in context we first think in general of the types of argument we shall encounter. Design arguments come in two main forms. Firstly, the *argument to design* where the idea is that, if we believe in a Creator for whatever reason, then we would expect to find evidence of that fact in the physical world. Such evidence would then confirm the existence of God. The *argument from design* moves in the opposite direction, in taking perceived design in the universe as evidence of the existence of God. Of course there can be a mutual reinforcement cycle between the two.

The *Stanford Encyclopedia of Philosophy* entry 'Teleological Arguments for God's Existence' by philosopher Del Ratzsch is an excellent introduction to these arguments;

> It is not uncommon for humans to find themselves with the intuition that random, unplanned, unexplained accident just couldn't produce the order, beauty, elegance, and seeming purpose that we experience in the natural world around us. As Hume's interlocutor Cleanthes put it, we seem to see 'the image of mind reflected on us from innumerable objects' in nature. (Hume 1779 [1998], 35). And many people find themselves convinced that no explanation for that mind-resonance which fails to acknowledge a causal role for intelligence, intent and purpose in nature can be seriously plausible.[3]

We pause to look closer at intellectual history in light of the claim made by many contemporary scientists that atheism is a necessary presupposition for true science to be carried out. They think that any move to bring in a Designer God will prove to be the end of science. If, for example, when it thunders, we suppose, like some of the ancient Greeks, Romans etc., that it is a god who is actually making the noise, then we would not, and could not, investigate the mechanism behind the noise. Only by assuming that there are no gods can we be free to investigate the mechanisms of nature in a truly scientific manner: introduce gods at any stage, and science stops. For them, gods of any kind are science-stoppers. In order to be able to be free to study nature we need to bury gods 'inside the world' that are mere deifications of the forces of nature.

That revolutionary step in thinking began to be taken by the early Greek natural philosophers Thales, Anaximander, and Anaximenes of Miletus, a city in modern-day Turkey, over 2,500 years ago. These Milesian thinkers were not content with mythological explanations, such as those that had been written down by Homer and Hesiod around 700 BC. These philosophers looked for explanations in terms of natural processes and chalked up some notable successes.

For instance, Thales is accredited with determining the length of the year to be 365 days, accurately predicting a solar eclipse in 585 BC and using geometric methods to calculate the heights of pyramids from their shadows and even to estimate the size of the earth and the moon. Thales' student Anaximander knew that the earth floats in the sky; he invented a sundial and a weatherproof clock and made the first world and star-maps. The Milesians were therefore among the earliest 'scientists', although that word first appeared in the nineteenth century. They were also laying the foundations for a naturalistic worldview.

Yet that needs to be balanced by bringing into the picture the remarkable perspective of another pre-Socratic Greek philosopher, theologian, poet, and social and religious critic, Xenophanes (c. 570–478 BC) of Colophon, near Izmir in present-day Turkey. He is well-known for his attempts to understand the fossils of sea-creatures found in Malta. He is even more famous for his trenchant denunciation of the mythological worldviews of his time. He pointed out that behaviour was attributed to the gods that among humans would be regarded as utterly shameful: the gods were rogues, thieves, and adulterers. Indeed, he held that these gods had clearly been made in the images of the peoples that believed in them: Ethiopians have gods that are dark and flat-nosed, Thracians made them blue-eyed and red-haired. He added deridingly: 'If cows and horses or lions had hands and could draw, then horses would draw the forms of gods like horses, cows like cows, making their bodies similar in shape to their own.' Thus, for Xenophanes, these gods were but obvious childish fictions of the fertile imaginations of those who believed in them. He anticipated Freud by a very long time. Such denunciation of the gods, together with a determination to investigate the natural processes hitherto almost exclusively understood to be the activity of those gods, inevitably led to the decline of mythological interpretations of the universe and to the advance of science.[4]

Xenophanes was, however, not the only ancient thinker to criticize the polytheistic worldview. More importantly, he was not the first. Unknown to him (presumably – there does not, alas, seem to be much information on the matter) and centuries beforehand, Moses had warned against worshipping 'other gods, bowing down to them, or to the sun or the moon or the stars of the sky' (NIV).[5] The Hebrew prophet Jeremiah, for example, writing in around 600 BC, similarly denounced the absurdity of deifying nature and worshipping the sun, moon, and stars.[6] For Moses and the prophets it was absurd to bow down to various bits of the universe such as the sun, moon, and stars as gods. But they regarded it as equally absurd not to believe in and bow down to the Creator God who made both the universe and them.

And these Hebrews were not introducing a radically novel idea. They did not have to have their universe de-deified as did the later Greeks, for the simple reason that they had never believed in the gods in the first place. What had saved them from that superstition was their belief in One True God, Creator of heaven and earth. That is, the idolatrous and polytheistic universe described by Homer and Hesiod was not the original world-picture of humankind – an impression that is often gained from the fact that most books on science and philosophy start with the ancient Greeks and emphasize the importance of the de-deification of the universe, singularly failing to point out that the Hebrews had protested against idolatrous interpretations of the universe long before the time of the Greeks. This serves to obscure the fact that polytheism arguably constitutes a perversion of an original belief in One Creator God.[7] It was this perversion that needed to be corrected, by recovering, not by jettisoning, belief in the Creator.

It is, therefore, very striking that, in spite of living in a polytheistic culture, Xenophanes did not make the mistake – very common today – of confusing God with the gods and thus rejecting the former with the latter. He believed in one God who ruled the universe: 'There is one God... similar to mortals neither in shape nor in thought... remote and effortless he governs all there is.'[8] Here, then, was a thinker with a scientific bent of mind who believed in God.

There were, in fact, *two trajectories in Greek thinking from that time forward.* One, like that of Xenophanes (and the Hebrews), held that there was a divine designer who transcended the material universe. The other was atheist and materialist.

We look next at the main springboard of the atheist/materialist stream. Miletus, city of Thales, was destroyed by the Persians in 494 BC, but was reborn under the Greeks a few decades later. About 700km away across the Aegean Sea is the Greek town of Abdera, where there was a philosophical school, founded in the middle of the fifth century BC by Leucippus, who may have been Milesian by birth, though that is not certain.

He, together with his much better known student Democritus founded the atomic theory. Democritus' idea of the indivisible atom[9] was a profound insight that eventually gave rise to atomic physics. The Nobel Prize winner for physics, Richard Feynman, introduced his lessons on physics by saying:

If, in some cataclysm, all scientific knowledge were to be destroyed, and only one sentence passed on to the next generation of creatures, what statement would contain the most information in the fewest words? I believe it is the atomic hypothesis... that *all things are made of atoms – little particles that move around in perpetual motion, attracting each other when they are a little distance apart, but repelling upon being squeezed into one another.* In that one sentence you will see an enormous amount of information about the world, if just a little imagination and thinking are applied.[10]

Democritus believed that the universe was composed of two things – atoms of infinitely many kinds and irregular shapes and sizes, and the infinite void in which they move. They are equipped with tiny hooks so that they can aggregate and all the macroscopic objects in the world are formed in this way. Aristotle tells us that Democritus thought that the soul consisted of fire atoms. Democritus laid the foundations for a materialistic view of the universe.

However, this was not the only view at the time. Democritus was a younger contemporary of Socrates (469–399 BC) and is included in the influential 'School of Athens' of Plato (423–327 BC) and Aristotle (385–323 BC). In common with Xenophanes, these towering intellectuals believed in transcendence – in a rational spirit that ordered the universe. Socrates is widely regarded as the father of the design argument. In Plato's work *The Philebus* he puts the following question to Protarchus: 'Whether all this which they call the universe is left to the guidance of unreason and chance medley, or, on the contrary, as our fathers have declared, ordered and governed by a marvellous intelligence and wisdom.'[11]

As one article puts it:

For Plato, God is transcendent – the highest and most perfect being-and one who uses eternal forms, or archetypes, to fashion a universe that is eternal and uncreated... Plato is not committed to monotheism, but suggests for example that since planetary motion is uniform and circular, and since such motion is the motion of reason, then a planet must be driven by a rational soul. These souls that drive the planets could be called gods.[12]

In 387 BC Plato, who ranks as the most influential of all philosophers, founded the Academy,[13] a prototype of the university. He regarded mathematics as the finest training for the mind and with that emphasis added mathematics to the foundation stones of science. The inscription over the entrance read: 'Let no one unversed in geometry enter here'. The great mathematicians Thaetetus (417–369 BC) and Eudoxus of Cnidus (c. 395–c. 342 BC) were associated with the Academy, and Plutarch describes the destruction of it by the Roman dictator Lucius Cornelius Sulla in 86 BC.[14]

Just after the death of Plato, the influential Greek atomist philosopher Epicurus was born in 341 BC. He wished to remove the myths from explanation in order to improve understanding. Perceptively, he wrote: 'Thunderbolts can be produced in several different ways – just be sure the myths are kept out of it! And they will be kept out of it if one follows rightly the appearances and takes them as signs of what is unobservable.'[15] He gave his name to Epicurean philosophy that was given its most famous expression by the Roman philosopher and poet Lucretius (94–55 BC) in his influential book, *De Rerum Natura* (*On the Nature of the Physical Universe*). This book was based on the (prolific) writings of Democritus that, unfortunately, have not survived. Lucretius' book was rediscovered in Europe in the fifteenth century and had profound influence in using Democritus' atomism to promote atheism during the Enlightenment. Benjamin Wiker, in a detailed study, calls Lucretius 'the first Darwinian' and points out that his philosophy was enthusiastically revived at the time of the Renaissance to such an extent that he should be regarded as the intellectual progenitor of contemporary naturalistic philosophy.[16]

A very different view from that of Lucretius is expressed in the New Testament in Romans 1:19–21. Paul (c. 56 AD), building on the foundation of the Hebrew scriptures, states: 'since what may be known about God is plain to them, because God has made it plain to them. For since the creation of the world God's invisible qualities – his eternal power and divine nature – have been clearly seen, being understood from what has been made, so that people are without excuse.' According to Paul, therefore, design is a perception.[17]

Plutarch (45–120 AD), a first-century historian, was, like many Greek thinkers, interested in the tension between design and chance. With perceptive wit he wrote:

Hebrew Greek

But can it be that those things which are most important and most essential for happiness do not call for intelligence, nor have any part in the processes of reason and forethought? Nobody wets clay with water and leaves it, assuming that by chance and accidentally there will be bricks, nor after providing himself with wood and leather does he sit down with a prayer to Chance that they turn into a cloak and shoes for him.[18]

The fact that for a very long time there were two streams – the theistic in Hebrew culture and both the theistic and atheistic in Greek culture – raises the interesting question of the relationship of Hebrew and Greek thought. Lord Jonathan Sacks, former Chief Rabbi in the UK, gives a helpful and measured assessment, pointing out that although the Greeks and not the Jews were not the first scientists it was Judaism, in particular the first chapter of Bereshit (Genesis), that carried out the first act of demythologizing the universe and helped sweep away the mythological idea that the universe was the product of unpredictable cosmic forces so that people could see the universe for what it was. Sacks goes on to say that Jewish philosopher Maimonides held that science was one of the routes to the love and fear of God. He adds that Jews were for a long time not involved in the mainstream of science for the simple reason that they were peripheral socially: it was not until the Renaissance in the fifteenth century that contact between Jewish and Christian scholars was established. Sacks concludes, 'The seventeenth century is really the birth of modern science. Here the influence was of Judaism, not of Jews. The Christians who read the Bible understood that the Bible was giving us a warrant to understand the universe. The study of the natural universe was as holy a task as studying the Bible.'[19]

1400's
1600's

The highly influential work of Thomas Aquinas in the thirteenth century is also relevant to our discussion. Aquinas put forward his famous 'Five Ways' collection of logical arguments for the existence of God in his magisterial work *Summa Theologiae*. They are based on the thinking of Aristotle who, in Aquinas' day was regarded as a supreme intellectual authority. They are:

1200's

- the argument from first cause, the 'unmoved mover', of the sequence of cause and effect changes in the universe
- the argument from causation of things coming into existence

First Cause — Outside Nature
Laws & mechanisms Inside nature upheld
The Forgotten Roots of Science and Arguments From Design / 35

- the argument from contingency and the existence of a necessary being
- the argument from values and degrees of goodness
5ᵗʰ the argument from final causes (teleological argument).

It is the Fifth Way that is of main interest to us here but it is important first to say something about Aquinas' ideas on causation. He held that God is the primary cause but that he works through a multitude of secondary causes. That is, initial creation had been endowed with potentialities that work themselves out without any further direct intervention from God, except that Christians would reserve the right to believe in occasional miracles. This view means that God is the author of 'the whole show' but in two distinct ways, as Creator and Upholder: it is all God's work. Aquinas regarded God as the First Cause, the ultimate cause of all things. God directly caused the universe to exist and it was thus dependent on him. This is what we might call direct causation.

Aquinas also held that there was a second level of causation, often called secondary causation, that operated within the universe. It was the cause–effect web that is spun out of the vast interlocking and interdependent system that is the universe. Thus, the fact that explanations of secondary causation can be given in terms of laws and mechanisms does not imply the non-existence of the Creator on which the very existence of the cause–effect web depends.

The notion that belief in the biblical Creator God who created (direct causation) and who upholds the universe (indirect causation) would bring science to an end is fallacious. Indeed, it is rather perverse in light of the role that this conviction has played in the rise of science, for if it were true, science might never have started. Believing that the engine of the car had been designed by Mr Ford would not stop anybody from investigating scientifically how the engine worked; in fact it might well spur them on to do so.

However, and this is crucial, if they came to superstitiously believe that Mr Ford *was* the engine, that would stop their science dead. This is the key issue: there is a great difference between God and the gods, and between a God who is a Creator distinct from his creation, and a god who is the universe.

Here is how Aquinas states his Fifth Way:

Handwritten annotation at top of page:
Causes 1) material 2) formal - shape
3) efficient 4) final - purpose
creator

We see that things which lack knowledge, such as natural bodies, act for an end, and this is evident from their acting always, or nearly always, in the same way, so as to obtain the best result. Hence it is plain that they achieve their end, not fortuitously, but designedly. Now whatever lacks knowledge cannot move towards an end, unless it be directed by some being endowed with knowledge and intelligence; as the arrow is directed by the archer. Therefore some intelligent being exists by whom all natural things are directed to their end; and this being we call God.[20]

Oxford theologian and philosopher Keith Ward FBA says:

the Five Ways can be seen as articulations of the idea of ultimate mind as the final personal explanation of the universe. If that idea is dismissed at the outset, the proofs cannot succeed. But if the idea is accepted as a real possibility, then the proofs both provide more detailed specifications of the idea, and provide good reasons that the idea corresponds to reality – that there is a God.[21]

The Fifth Way goes back to the last of the famous four causes postulated by Aristotle. They are: the material cause (what something, say a vase, is made of); the formal cause (the form that determines the shape of the vase); the efficient cause (what brings the vase into being – a potter); and a final cause (the purpose for which the vase was made – to adorn a dining table).

Aristotle held that everything has a goal to which it is directed by its nature. He was not thinking primarily of a design argument for God as his gods were uninterested in the world. In his Fifth Way, Aquinas took the argument further by saying that things could only have a goal if that goal were ultimately intended by a conscious being, namely God. It was therefore a design argument.

All this is very different from the atheistic atomism of Democritus and Lucretius. Perhaps most importantly of all, Sir Isaac Newton (1642–1727), the greatest scientist of all time, demonstrated that *the profound insights of the atomic theory did not need to be shrouded in atheism.* He wrote: 'All these things being considered, it seems probable to me that God, in the beginning, formed matter in solid, massy, hard, impenetrable, movable particles, of such sizes and figures, and with such other properties, and in such proportions to space as most conduced to the end for which he form'd them.'[22]

Carlo Rovelli, one of the most stimulating writers on physics these days, says that this was 'the world of Democritus reborn' and 'rendered mathematical'. His comment is revealing: 'Reference to ancient atomism is clear in Newton, even if still formulated in conventional terms.'[23] I presume that, by 'conventional terms', Rovelli means the theistic worldview and by 'even if' he shows his antipathy to that position – without giving any real grounds for it. We might as well say that Rovelli expresses his own view in 'conventional atheist' terms. This seems to me to be a very superficial assessment and a great pity in light of the weight that Rovelli gives to the immense legacy of Newton. Nevertheless, reading Rovelli is a real treat!

The verdict of the eminent historian of science and mathematician Sir Alfred North Whitehead is very different from that of Rovelli. He observed that medieval Europe in 1500 knew less than Archimedes in the third century BC and yet by 1700 Newton had written his masterpiece, *Principia Mathematica*. Whitehead asked the obvious question: How could such an explosion of knowledge have happened in such a relatively short time? His answer: 'modern science must come from the medieval insistence on the rationality of God... My explanation is that the faith in the possibility of science, generated antecedently to the development of modern scientific theory, is an unconscious derivative from medieval theology.'[24] C. S. Lewis' succinct formulation of Whitehead's view is worth recording: 'Men became scientific because they expected Law in Nature and they expected Law in Nature because they believed in a Legislator.'[25] It was this conviction that led Francis Bacon (1561–1626), regarded by many as the father of modern science, to teach that God has provided us with two books – the book of Nature and the Bible – and that to be really properly educated, one should give one's mind to studying both.

Rovelli has chosen to read history through the lens of Democritus which is perhaps why, although he mentions that Einstein was Jewish, he passes over the fact that the great pioneers of modern physics to whom he refers, like Newton, were theists who agreed with Bacon. Men such as Galileo (1564–1642), Kepler (1571–1630), Pascal (1623–62), Boyle (1627–91), Faraday (1791–1867), Babbage (1791–1871), Mendel (1822–84), Pasteur (1822–95), Kelvin (1824–1907), and Clerk Maxwell (1831–79) all believed in God; most of them, in fact, were Christians.

Their faith in God, far from being a hindrance to their science, was often the main inspiration for it and they were not shy of saying so. The driving force behind Galileo's science was his conviction that the Creator who had 'endowed us with senses, reason and intellect' intended us not to 'forgo their use and by some other means to give us knowledge which we can attain by them'. Such discovery, for Johannes Kepler, amounted, in his famous phrase, to saying 'I was merely thinking God's thoughts after him. Since we astronomers are priests of the highest God in regard to the book of nature, it benefits us to be thoughtful, not of the glory of our minds, but rather, above all else, of the glory of God.' Democritus' atomic theory influenced them all but they did not believe that it had to be associated with atheism.

When I put this to Richard Dawkins he replied that it was not surprising that Galileo, Kepler, and Newton believed in God since everybody believed in God in those days. However, Dawkins was thinking only of the West. China was different. For, although China developed sophisticated technology e.g. fireworks and printing, they never discovered abstract science. Why was that? Chemist Joseph Needham at Cambridge was an expert in Chinese technology and wrote the definitive histories of technology in that country. He recorded the reaction of the Chinese in the eighteenth century when news about the great developments in science that had taken place in the West was brought to them by Jesuit missionaries. For the Chinese, the idea that the universe could be governed by simple laws which human beings not only could, but had discovered, was foolish in the extreme. Their culture simply was not receptive to such notions.[26] The interesting thing here is that Needham, a neo-Marxist, tried for years to explain in Marxist terms why the Chinese did not discover abstract science. He failed to do so and came to the conclusion that what made the real difference was the fact that the Chinese lacked the idea of a single creator, who had created the universe to run according to laws that could be described by mathematics. This finding serves to substantiate the connection between Christianity and the rise of modern science.

Lack of appreciation of the precise point we are making here can lead to confusion. We are by no means claiming that *all* aspects of religion in general and Christianity in particular have contributed to the rise of science. What we are suggesting is that the biblical doctrine of a unique Creator God, who is responsible for the existence of and order in the universe, has played an important role in the history of science.

Furthermore, we are not suggesting that there never has been any religious antagonism to science. Indeed, T. F. Torrance,[27] commenting on Whitehead's analysis, points out that science was often 'seriously hindered by the Christian church even when within it the beginnings of modern ideas were taking their rise'. As an example he states that the Augustinian theology that dominated Europe for 1,000 years led to great contributions to the arts in the Middle Ages, but its 'eschatology which perpetuated the idea of decay and collapse of the world and of salvation as redemption out of it, directed attention away from the world to the super-terrestrial, while its conception of the sacramental universe allowed only a symbolic understanding of nature and a religious, illustrative use of it' thus 'taking up and sanctifying a cosmological outlook that had to be replaced if scientific progress was to be made'.

Torrance also says that what often discouraged the scientific mind was a 'hardened notion of authority and its relation to understanding that went back to Augustine... which first gave rise to bitter complaints against the church'.[28] Galileo is a case in point, as we shall see below. Sadly, we find even today professing Christians with an obscurantist, anti-scientific attitude which does nothing to support their message and tells us more about them than about science.

Torrance, nevertheless, gave strong support to the general tenor of Whitehead's thesis:

> In spite of the unfortunate tension that has so often cropped up between the advance of scientific theories and traditional habits of thought in the church, theology can still claim to have mothered throughout long centuries the basic beliefs and impulses which have given rise especially to modern empirical science, if only through its unflagging faith in the reliability of God the Creator and in the ultimate intelligibility of his creation.[29]

John Hedley Brooke, Oxford's first Professor of Science and Religion, is more cautious than Torrance:

> In the past religious beliefs have served as a presupposition of the scientific enterprise insofar as they have underwritten that uniformity... a doctrine of creation could give coherence to scientific endeavour insofar as it implied a dependable order

Go + Look

behind the flux of nature. ...this need not entail the strong claim that without a prior theology, science would never have taken off, but it does mean that the particular conceptions of science held by its pioneers were often informed by theological and metaphysical beliefs.[30]

More recently, Brooke's successor in the Oxford Chair of Science and Religion, Peter Harrison, made an impressive case that one of the dominant features in the rise of modern science was the Protestant attitude to the interpretation of biblical texts, which spelt an end to the symbolic approach of the Middle Ages.[31]

It is, of course, notoriously difficult to know 'what would have happened if...', but it is surely not too much to say that the rise of science would have been seriously retarded if one particular biblical doctrine, the doctrine of creation, had not been present. Brooke issues a healthy warning against overstating the case: just because a religion has supported science does not prove that the religion is true. Quite so, and the same can, of course, be said of atheism.

The doctrine of creation was not only important in the rise of modern science because of its entailment of order in the universe. It was important for another reason which we hinted at in the introduction. In order for science to develop, thinking had to be freed from the hitherto widespread Aristotelian attempt to derive from fixed (philosophical) principles how the universe ought to be. The radically new approach was to allow the universe to speak as directly as possible – to go and see what it looked like as far as possible without deciding in advance what you felt it had to look like. That fundamental shift in perspective was facilitated by the notion of a *contingent* creation – that is, that God the Creator could have created the universe any way he liked. Hence, in order to find out what the universe is really like and how it works, there is no alternative to going and looking. You cannot deduce how the universe works simply by reasoning from *a priori* philosophical principles. That is precisely what Galileo and, later, Kepler and others thought and so they went and looked – and revolutionized science.

Newtonian mechanics and materialism

We have seen how the work of Newton and the other pioneers of modern

[Handwritten annotation at top: "Determinism: fixed, predestined | Value based intentional efforts behaviours by choice"]

science owed much to their theistic worldview. However, in a twist of historical irony, the mechanistic view of the universe that arose from it, as well as from the earlier thinking of Descartes, which formed the core of classical physics, contributed a great deal to the atheist-materialist worldview during the Enlightenment and subsequently up to the present, exemplified, as we saw, in the case of physicist Carlo Rovelli.

Newton's laws applied universally to the stars and planets as well as to apples and particles and readily lent themselves to a deterministic view of the universe – that is, that the time evolution of the universe is fixed by the initial conditions and the laws. There was no room for any influence of (or even existence of) mind. This had major implications for understanding human beings for it seemed that science was reducing human beings to automata. Determinism also destroyed the rational foundations of human moral responsibility: How could anyone be held responsible for actions that were determined at the origin of the universe?[32] Quantum physicist Henry Stapp spells out the implications of the classical physics that reigned from the time of Newton until the twentieth century: 'This conception of man undermines the foundations of rational moral philosophy, and science is doubly culpable. It not only erodes the foundations of earlier value systems, but also acts to strip man of any vision of himself and his place in the universe that could be the rational base for an elevated set of values.'

Stapp explains how all this changed when this morally corrosive mechanical view of nature failed because it was fundamentally flawed. It was replaced by a new conceptual framework by the brilliant, Nobel prize-winning physicists, Heisenberg, Bohr, Pauli, and others. They replaced the then dominant ideas of Newton that matter consisted of 'solid, massy, hard, impenetrable, moveable particles' with a completely radical perspective that: 'swept away the meaningless billiard-ball universe, and replaced it with a universe in which we human beings, by means of our value-based intentional efforts, can make a difference first in our own behaviours, thence in the social matrix in which we are imbedded, and eventually in the entire physical reality that sustains our streams of conscious experiences.'[33]

However, at this stage in our book, we are still a long way from the quantum mechanics revolution of the twentieth century to which we shall return in Chapter 21. We now revert to classical times to explore two iconic incidents that are still used to promote a conflict view of science against religion.

Doctrine of Creation | Separate issue | Church politics / RCC Galileo

Huxley vs Rutherforce

Myths of Conflict: Galileo and the Roman Catholic Church, Huxley, and Wilberforce

Everyone knows that Galileo got into trouble. We need, therefore, to turn to his story to see what is to be gleaned from it. One of the main reasons for distinguishing clearly between the influence of the doctrine of creation and the influence of other aspects of religious life and, in particular, religious politics, on the rise of science is so that we can better evaluate those iconic accounts from history that are often used to maintain the widespread public impression that science and religion are mutual enemies – a notion often referred to as the conflict thesis, or conflict metaphor. These accounts concern two of the most famous confrontations in history: the first, just mentioned above, between Galileo and the Roman Catholic Church; and the second, the debate between Huxley and Wilberforce on the subject of Charles Darwin's famous book *The Origin of Species*.

Upon investigation, however, these two incidents fail to support the conflict thesis, a conclusion that comes as a surprise to many, but a conclusion, nonetheless, that has history firmly on its side. History Professor Peter Harrison in his magisterial work, *The Territories of Science and Religion*, which is regarded as one of the most important books on the whole area of the alleged science–religion conflict, says of the Galileo affair:

> But to cite this as an instance of science–religion conflict is to misconstrue the context. For a start, the Catholic Church endorsed the scientific consensus of the period, which, on the basis of the available evidence, held that the earth was stationary in the middle of the cosmos. To this extent it might be better to characterise the episode as a conflict within science... rather than between science and religion. Second, the first use of the Galileo affair for propaganda purposes was by Protestants seeking to discredit Catholics, so that it was initially given a role in conflicts within religion.[34]

We recall that Galileo himself appeared in our list of scientists who believed in God. He was no agnostic or atheist, at loggerheads with the theism of his day. Dava Sobel, in her brilliant, entertaining, and informative biography *Galileo's Daughter*,[35] effectively debunks this mythical impression of Galileo as 'a renegade who scoffed at the Bible'. It turns out in fact that Galileo was a firm believer in God and the Bible, and remained so all of his life. He held

Conflict thesis, mutual enemies, conflict metaphor

that 'the laws of nature are written by the hand of God in the language of mathematics' and that the 'human mind is a work of God and one of the most excellent'.

There are, however, many myths surrounding Galileo. Arthur Koestler referred to some of them in his book, *The Sleepwalkers*:

> Contrary to statements in even recent outlines of science, Galileo did not invent the telescope, nor the microscope, nor the thermometer, nor the pendulum clock. He did not throw down weights from the leaning tower of Pisa, and did not prove the truth of the Copernican system. He was not tortured by the Inquisition, did not languish in its dungeons, did not say '*eppur si muove*' ['but it moves']; and he was not a martyr of science. What he *did* was to found the modern science of dynamics...'.[36]

His first scientific publication, which appeared in March 1610, was a 24-page booklet written in Latin, entitled 'Starry Messenger'. In it he pointed out that the moon's surface was rough with mountains and valleys, that the Milky Way consisted of nothing but countless stars, that nebulae like Orion were star clusters, and that four planets were in orbit around Jupiter. The booklet contained the first published evidence that he accepted Copernicus' view that the planets were in orbit round the sun.

In his later work (c. 1611), *Three Letters on Sunspots*, Galileo made his support even clearer when he said that his Saturn discovery: 'harmonises with the great Copernican system, to the universal revelation of which doctrine propitious breezes are now seen to be directed towards us, leaving little fear of clouds or crosswinds.'

Galileo enjoyed a great deal of support from religious intellectuals, at least at the start. The astronomers of the powerful Jesuit educational institution, the Collegio Romano, initially endorsed his astronomical work and fêted him for it during a visit to Rome. However, things began to turn sour and in December 1614 a Dominican friar, Tommaso Caccini, denounced, in the church of Santa Maria Novella in Florence, Copernicanism, Galileo, and all mathematicians.

The next year, in his famous 'Letter to the Grand Duchess Christina', Galileo claimed that some academics were so opposed to him that they were trying to influence the church authorities to speak out against him.

Furthermore, at that time the Protestant Reformation was challenging the authority of Rome and thus, from Rome's perspective, religious security was under increasing threat. It was therefore a very sensitive time from a cultural perspective.

Biographers of Galileo differ widely in their assessments of his character. In his book *Great Astronomers in European History* historian of science Dr Paul Marston gives an appreciative description of Galileo's science with its ups and downs and also of his increasingly difficult character that was often the main reason for the trouble he got into.[37]

Galileo's own lack of a sense of diplomacy, were contributing factors. He irritated the elite of his day by his attempts to give some intellectual empowerment to ordinary people by publishing in Italian as well as in Latin. He seems to have been committed to what later would be called the public understanding of science.

Galileo also developed an unhelpfully short-sighted habit of denouncing in vitriolic terms those who disagreed with him. Neither did he promote his cause by the way in which he handled an official directive to include in his 'Dialogue Concerning the Two Principal Systems of the World' the argument of his erstwhile friend and supporter Pope Urban VIII (Maffeo Berberini).

That argument was essentially that, since God was omnipotent, he could produce any given natural phenomenon in many different ways. Hence, it would be presumptuous of the natural philosophers to claim that they had found the unique solution. Galileo dutifully obliged but he did so by putting this argument into the mouth of a dull-witted character in his book, whom he called Simplicio ('buffoon'). One might see this as a classic case of shooting oneself in the foot. As Marston wryly comments, not a good career move!

There is, of course, no excuse for the Roman Catholic Church subsequently dragging its feet for centuries before it 'rehabilitated' him. It should, however, be noted that, again contrary to popular belief, Galileo was never tortured; and his subsequent 'house arrest' was spent, for the most part, in luxurious private residences belonging to friends.[38]

There are important lessons to be gleaned from the Galileo story. First, a lesson for those who are disposed to take the biblical account seriously. It is hard to imagine that there are any today who believe that the earth is the centre of the universe, with the planets and sun revolving around it. That is, the vast majority accept the heliocentric Copernican view that Galileo defended.

What is more, they do not think that the heliocentric view conflicts with the Bible even though it was a common view before the time of Copernicus that the earth was at the physical centre of the universe and a literalistic reading of parts of the Bible was often used to support that idea.

What has happened since then to make the difference? Simply that such people now take a more sophisticated, nuanced view of the Bible,[39] and can see that when, for example, it talks of the sun 'rising', it is speaking phenomenologically – that is, giving a description as it appears to an observer, rather than implying commitment to a particular solar and planetary theory. Scientists today do just the same: they also speak in normal conversation of the sun rising, and their statements are not usually taken to imply that they are obscurantist fixed-earthers.

Another lesson is that we should be humble enough to distinguish between what the Bible says and our interpretations of it. The biblical text just might be more sophisticated than we first imagined and we might therefore be in danger of using it to support ideas that it never intended to teach. So, at least, thought Galileo in his day – and history has subsequently proved him right.

Philosophers and scientists today also have need of humility in light of facts, even if those facts are being pointed out to them by a believer in God. Lack of belief in God is no more of a guarantee of scientific orthodoxy than is belief in God. What is clear, in Galileo's time and ours, is that criticism of those in authority is fraught with risk, no matter who is engaged in it.

Marston concludes that the 'Galileo affair' does nothing to confirm a simplistic conflict view of the relationship of science to religion.[40] Citing Arthur Koestler, he says: 'As Koestler said in his classic book [*The Sleepwalkers*], we cannot see it as a kind of "showdown" between enlightened reason and blind faith. Galileo himself never wavered in his Catholic faith; he was advocating science which was at least 24 years out of date and had no proof at all that the Earth moved apart from a bogus one which contradicted his own dynamics.'[41]

The Huxley–Wilberforce Debate, Oxford 1860

Nor in fact does that other frequently cited incident, the debate on 30 June 1860 at the British Association for the Advancement of Science held in Oxford's Natural History Museum, which took place between T. H. Huxley ('Darwin's bulldog') and Bishop Samuel Wilberforce ('Soapy Sam'). The debate was occasioned by a lecture delivered by John Draper on Darwin's theory of evolution set out in *The Origin of Species* that had been published seven months earlier. This encounter is often portrayed as a simple clash between science and religion, where the competent scientist convincingly triumphed over the ignorant churchman. Yet historians of science have shown that this account is also very far from the truth.[42]

In the first place, Wilberforce was no ignoramus. A month after the historic meeting in question, he published a fifty-page review of Darwin's work (in the *Quarterly Review*), that Darwin regarded as 'uncommonly clever; it picks out with skill all the most conjectural parts, and brings forward well all the difficulties. It quizzes me most splendidly.' Secondly, Wilberforce was no obscurantist. He was determined that the debate should not be between science and religion, but a scientific debate – scientist versus scientist on scientific grounds – an intention which figures significantly in his summary of the review:

> We have objected to the views with which we are dealing, solely on scientific grounds. We have done so from the fixed conviction that it is thus that the truth or falsehood of such arguments should be tried. We have no sympathy with those who object to any facts or alleged facts in nature, or to any inference logically deduced from them, because they believe them to contradict what it appears to them is taught by revelation. We think that all such objections savour of a timidity which is really inconsistent with a firm and well-intrusted faith.[43]

The robustness of this statement might come as a surprise to many people who have simply swallowed the legendary view of the encounter. One might even be excused for detecting in Wilberforce a kindred spirit to that of Galileo.

Nor was it the case that the only objections to Darwin's theory came from the side of the church. Sir Richard Owen, the leading anatomist of the day (who, incidentally, had been consulted by Wilberforce), was opposed to Darwin's theory; as was the eminent scientist Lord Kelvin.

As to contemporary accounts of the debate, John Brooke points out that initially the event seemed to cause little or no stir:

The conflict myth

It is a significant fact that the famous clash between Huxley and the Bishop was not reported by a single London newspaper at the time. Indeed, there are no official records of the meeting; and most of the reports came from Huxley's friends. Huxley himself wrote that there was 'inextinguishable laughter among the people' at his wit and 'I believe that I was the most popular man in Oxford for full four and twenty hours afterwards.'[44]

However, the evidence is that the debate was far from one-sided. One newspaper later recorded that one previous convert to Darwin's theory was de-converted as he witnessed the debate. The botanist Joseph Hooker grumbled that Huxley didn't 'put the matter in a form or way that carried the audience' so he had had to do it himself. Wilberforce wrote three days later to archaeologist Charles Taylor: 'I think I thoroughly beat him.' *The Athenaeum*'s report gives the impression that honours were about even, saying that Huxley and Wilberforce 'have each found foemen worthy of their steel'.

Frank James, historian at the Royal Institution in London, makes the suggestion that the widespread impression that Huxley was victorious may well have arisen because Wilberforce was not well-liked, a fact that is missing from most of the accounts: 'Had Wilberforce not been so unpopular in Oxford, he would have carried the day and not Huxley.'[45] Shades of Galileo!

On careful analysis, then, two of the main props commonly used to support the conflict thesis crumble. Indeed research has undermined that thesis to such an extent that historian of science Colin Russell came to the following conclusion: 'The common belief that... the actual relations between religion and science over the last few centuries have been marked by deep and enduring hostility... is not only historically inaccurate, but actually a caricature so grotesque that what needs to be explained is how it could possibly have achieved any degree of respectability.'[46]

It is, therefore, apparent that powerful forces must have been at play, in order to account for the depth to which the conflict myth has become embedded in the popular mind. And indeed there were. As in the case of Galileo, the real issue at stake in the Huxley–Wilberforce debate was not simply a question of the intellectual merits of a scientific theory. Once again, institutional power played a key role. Huxley was on a crusade to ensure the supremacy of the emerging new class of professional scientists against the privileged position of clerics, however intellectually gifted. He wanted to make sure that it was the scientists who wielded the levers of power. The legend of a conquered bishop slain by a professional scientist suited that crusade, and it was exploited to the full.

However, it is apparent that even more was involved. A central element in Huxley's crusade is highlighted by science educator Michael Poole. He writes,

> In this struggle, the concept of 'Nature' was spelt with a capital N and reified. Huxley vested 'Dame Nature', as he called her, with attributes hitherto ascribed to God, a tactic eagerly copied by others since. The logical oddity of crediting *nature* (every physical thing there is) with planning and creating every physical thing there is, passed unnoticed. 'Dame Nature', like some ancient fertility goddess, had taken up residence, her maternal arms encompassing *Victorian scientific naturalism*.[47]

Thus a mythical conflict was (and still often is) hyped up and shamelessly used as a weapon in another battle, the real one this time, that is, that between naturalism and theism.

I must confess that I was very aware of this historic incident and of the war between theism and naturalism when, 148 years later, on 21 October 2008, I debated Richard Dawkins in the very same place, Oxford's Natural History Museum.[48]

I have bracketed the Huxley–Wilberforce debate with Galileo since they are the most quoted cases in connection with the alleged conflict between science and religion.

However, I wish to go back to the eighteenth century to discuss one of the most famous people associated with the design argument, William Paley (1743–1805).

Paley and his watch

The watchmaker metaphor has a long history in connection with design arguments. Cicero (106–43 BC) extrapolated from his experience of intelligently designed machines to the ordered movement of the planets and stars: 'when we see some examples of a mechanism... do we doubt that it is the creation of a conscious intelligence? So when we see the movement of the heavenly bodies... how can we doubt that these too are not only the works of reason but of a reason which is perfect and divine?'[49] Cicero here anticipates by centuries the most famous (or infamous!) classic statement of the design argument, which was made by the eighteenth-century theologian and naturalist, William Paley.

> But suppose I had found a watch upon the ground, and it should be inquired how the watch happened to be in that place; I should hardly think of the answer which I had before given, that for anything I knew the watch had always been there... The watch must have had a maker: there must have existed... an artificer... who formed it for the purpose which we find it actually to answer; who comprehended its construction and designed its use....[50]

Thus far, Paley has not said anything controversial. We use design arguments all the time, for instance in archaeology, when we are talking about things that nature could not produce by any stretch of the imagination – like artefacts of human origin. So when we find a potsherd with ancient writing on it we do not face a storm of controversy when we attribute the writing to human agency. Even SETI – the Search for Extra Terrestrial Intelligence – is largely unproblematic since the implicit assumption is that if ETI exists, it is as part of physical nature as we are.

Design arguments usually become controversial when they purport to identify design of *supernatural* origin, as Paley went on to do. However, there should really be nothing controversial about this either as our discussion of Hume in Chapter 6 will show.

Before we continue with Paley's argument, however, I wish to point out that, once the discussion becomes heated, as it often does, it is easy to lose sight of the very important distinction I mentioned earlier between the recognition of design and the identification of the designer. We recognize design in the arrangements of standing stones in many places around the world, but we rarely know who designed those arrangements or even why they are thus arranged.

Paley continues: 'Every indication of contrivance, every manifestation of design, which existed in the watch, exists in the works of nature; with the difference, on the side of nature, of being greater or more, and that in a degree which exceeds all computation.'[51]

The essence, then, of Paley's argument was that if the complexity of a watch and its evident design, its adaptation to a perceived end, implies the existence of a watchmaker, how much more does a vastly more intricate biological mechanism, like the human eye, demand the existence of an intelligent Divine watchmaker? 'The marks of design are too strong to be got over. Design must have a designer. That designer must have been a person. That person is God.'[52]

Throughout history many people, including scientists, have found this kind of argument very plausible. Darwin, in his student days at Cambridge, was one of them. According to Stephen Jay Gould, Paley was the 'intellectual hero of Darwin's youth'.[53] Darwin himself wrote that Paley's work

> gave me as much delight as did Euclid. The careful study of these works, without attempting to learn any part by rote, was the only part of the Academical Course which, as I then felt and as I still believe, was of the least use to me in the education of my mind. I did not at that time trouble myself about Paley's premises; and taking these on trust I was charmed and convinced of the long line of argumentation.

However, this was all to change. In his autobiography Darwin pinpoints his difficulty: 'The old argument of design in nature, as given by Paley, which formerly seemed to me so conclusive, fails, now that the law of natural selection has been discovered. We can no longer argue that, for instance, the beautiful hinge of a bivalve shell must have been made by an intelligent being, like the hinge of a door by a man.'[54]

So Paley came under attack. So much so that for many today he is simply a figure of fun, a sad and tragic reminder of the absurd and facile attempts that have been made in the past to make belief in God credible by linking it somehow with science. But, as is often the case with figures who have become part of the rhetoric of science in that they stand as icons for a particular constellation of (often extreme) ideas, the reality is much more subtle and, indeed, more interesting, than the myth. Admittedly, Paley attracted legitimate criticism because of his over-concentration on specific adaptations and the fanciful way in which he sometimes embellished the watchmaker argument using 'just-so' stories to explain various specific animal features.

The upshot of these and other criticisms of Paley, and his iconic association with all that is regarded as suspect in design arguments, is that his core inference from the nature of a watch to its intelligent origin is itself sometimes dismissed out of hand, even though such criticisms do not really affect it. No less a mind than that of Bertrand Russell, not known for sympathy to theism, found the design argument logically impressive:

> This argument contends that, on a survey of the known world, we find things which cannot plausibly be explained as the product of blind natural forces, but are much more reasonably to be regarded as evidences of a beneficent purpose. This argument has no formal logical defect; its premises are empirical and its conclusion professes to be reached in accordance with the usual canons of empirical inference.
>
> The question whether it is to be accepted or not turns, therefore, not on general metaphysical questions, but on comparatively detailed considerations.[55]

Russell is making a reasonable inference to the best explanation in comparing the plausibility of blind forces with beneficent purpose.

Before we leave Paley we must briefly comment on the claim that his arguments were demolished by David Hume's earlier onslaught against design.[56] One element in that attack was the allegation that such arguments tended to be arguments from analogies that did not always hold.[57] Hume's work is cast in the form of a discussion, one protagonist of which was a certain Cleanthes (mentioned earlier), who is addressed thus:

> If we see a house, Cleanthes, we conclude, with the greatest certainty, that it had an architect or builder; for this is precisely that species of effort that we have experienced to proceed from that species of cause. But surely you will not affirm, that the universe bears such a resemblance to a house, that we can with the same certainty infer a similar

cause, or that the analogy is here entire and perfect. The dissimilitude is so striking, that the utmost you can pretend to is a presumption concerning a similar cause....[58]

Hume also argued that, in order to infer that our world had been designed, we would have to have observed other worlds, both designed and not designed, in order to compare. It is clear from this that Hume is formulating his argument against design as an inductive argument dependent for its force on the sample space of observed universes. Thus, Hume concludes, the argument is very weak since the only universe we have observed is this one.

Induction However, as philosopher Elliott Sober points out, the objection dissolves once we move from the model of inductive sampling to that of likelihood: 'You don't have to observe the processes of Intelligent Design and chance at work in different worlds in order to maintain that the two hypotheses confer different probabilities on your observation.'[59]

The point here is important. As we said earlier, not all science is inductive, because we do not always have the luxury of repeated observation or experimentation. We cannot repeat the Big Bang, or the origin of life, or the history of life, or the history of the universe. Does the fact that no historical event is repeatable mean that we can say nothing about what happened in the past? It would, if we followed Hume.

abduction or inference There is, however, another methodology that can be applied to such situations, well known to historians. It is the method of abduction, or inference to the best explanation. An argument that does explain a given effect is always better than one that does not. Hume's argument leaves abduction untouched. We shall discuss abduction in Chapter 4.

It might, therefore, just be more than a trifle premature to conclude that Hume has even shut the lid on Paley's coffin, let alone nailed it down. Elliott Sober says that 'Although Hume's criticism is devastating if the design argument is an argument from analogy, I see no reason why the design argument should be construed in that way. Paley's argument about organisms stands on its own, regardless of whether watches and organisms happen to be similar. The point of talking about watches is to help the reader see that the argument about organisms is compelling.'[60]

Also, it is easy to overlook the fact that analogical argument by no means exhausts all inferences to design. The impression of design in nature is not so much argument by analogy as it is a perception: living systems simply *look* designed. Del Ratzsch says that proponents of design arguments were and are convinced that the evidences they adduced for design are the kind of thing that a mind might generate. This means that their evidential power does not depend on prior known instances of design:

> When we see a text version of the Gettysburg Address, that text says mind to us in a way totally unrelated to any induction or analogy from past encounters with written texts... Intricate, dynamic, stable, functioning order of the sort we encounter in nature was frequently placed in this category. Such order was taken to be suggestive of minds in that it seemed nearly self-evidently the sort of thing minds, and so far as was definitively known, only minds were prone to produce. It was a property whose mind-resonating character we could unhesitatingly attribute to intent.[61]

Furthermore, though Paley's argument about organisms stands on its own, it is considerably strengthened by the observation that, since his time, developments in science have shown that there are many kinds of systems within living organisms for which the term 'molecular machine' is entirely appropriate. Among these are to be found biological clocks that are responsible for the vital molecular timekeeping function within the living cell and which are of vastly greater sophistication than Paley's illustrative watch. Indeed, 'machine' language is ubiquitous in cutting-edge molecular biology as we shall see.

Hume might have been astonished to learn that it would one day be possible in laboratories in this world for human intelligence to design biochemical systems and construct proteins, and even simple organisms from their molecular components.[62] What would Hume have to say then? The design argument has turned out to be very much more robust than Hume thought, though it is important to keep his caution about analogies in mind even though much of the force of his objection has been dissipated by more recent progress in biology – and progress in the philosophical analysis of Hume's writings.

Sadly, it is rather difficult to separate the design argument from the negative image with which unwarranted rhetoric about Paley has surrounded it. Yet, Paley's excursion into natural theology, now seen by many as an argument too far, should not obscure the basic point that is now, more than ever, valid: as more of the workings of life and the universe are discovered, the more this points to a designer.

There is, however, a further reason why design arguments have not been taken seriously in more recent years. This has to do with the fact that the very mention of the word 'design' to some people immediately conjures up the powerful clockwork image that figured prominently in older design arguments.

The result is that 'design' became associated, whether consciously or unconsciously, with the clockwork universe of Newton.[63] Likening the workings of the universe to the smooth running of a master-clock had understandable appeal in the heyday of Newtonian mechanics, but that appeal began to wane especially for those engaged in the biological sciences for the simple reason that the biological world did not look much like a clock. It also waned somewhat for theologians as it could easily be used to support a deistic view of God – the notion that God wound up the universe like a clock and left it to run – rather than the vibrant biblical view of God as Creator and Sustainer of the universe.

The situation since then has changed dramatically. For the biosphere is now known to contain endless clocks and hitherto unimaginable clock-like structures. That means that design arguments cannot so easily be dismissed. However, it would be a mistake to use them with a reductionist spin in order to give the impression that the universe was nothing more than clockwork.[64] Consequently, in order to avoid potentially misleading associations of ideas, it might well be better to talk about arguments inferring intelligent origin, than about design arguments.

Del Ratzsch's aforementioned article concludes with an important non-inferential approach to design by asking the following very reasonable question: 'Why do design arguments remain so durable if empirical evidence is inferentially ambiguous, the arguments logically controversial, and the conclusions vociferously disputed?'

Ratzsch gives two answers. The first is that the arguments are better than most critics of design are prepared to grant. The second is the interesting possibility that intuition of design does not rest on inference at all – a situation that parallels our convictions that there is an external world and that there are other minds. Ratzsch cites Thomas Reid, the important eighteenth-century Scottish 'common sense' philosopher, that we human beings are so constituted that we simply find that in normal experience we

① What are the explanations of the origin of life and the complexity of nature?
② Which is the best explanation?

have such convictions. Ratzsch suggests that this may well be the reason that led to the abject failure of efforts to reconstruct that arguments that led to such beliefs in the first place.

He concludes: 'If a similar involuntary belief-producing mechanism operated with respect to intuitions of design, that would similarly explain why argumentative attempts have been less than universally compelling but yet why design ideas fail to disappear despite the purported failure of such arguments.'[65]

Physicist Sir John Polkinghorne sums up the position as he sees it: 'So where is natural theology today, two centuries after William Paley? The short answer is, "Alive and well, having learned from past experience to lay claim to insight rather than to coercive logical necessity, and to be able to live in a friendly relationship with science, based on complementarity rather than rivalry."'[66]

Intelligent Design *ID*

Eminent British philosopher Anthony Flew was for many years a leading intellectual champion of atheism; he was the Richard Dawkins of his day. However, he eventually came to find the design argument convincing. Accordingly, in a BBC interview he announced that the existence of a super-intelligent cause is the only good explanation of the origin of life and of the complexity of nature.[67] He had come to believe that the universe was intelligently designed.

Such an announcement by an intellectual of Flew's calibre gave a new twist of interest to the vigorous, if sometimes heated, contemporary debate on 'intelligent design', for which we shall use the common acronym ID. At least some of this heat may arise from the fact that the term 'ID' unfortunately conveys to many people a relatively recent, crypto-creationist, anti-scientific attitude that is chiefly focussed on attacking evolutionary biology. The result is that ID has changed its meaning in many peoples' minds to the detriment of serious debate on the issue.

We must now ask what is meant by the concept of 'design' itself. Del Ratzsch, in his excellent book, *Science and its Limits*, offers the following definition: 'A design is an intentionally produced (or exemplified) pattern, where a pattern is an abstract structure that resonates, matches or meshes with mind, with cognition.'[68] In light of that definition, the expression 'intelligent design' strikes some as curious, since design is usually

Definition of design

perceived to be the result of intelligence. The adjective 'intelligent' is therefore technically redundant, though it can still serve a useful purpose in highlighting the association of design with mental intention. If we simply replace the phrase with 'design' or 'intelligent causation', then we are speaking of a very respectable notion in the history of thought.

Is ID crypto-creationism, as is often suggested? Here we need first to flag up a potential misunderstanding. For the meaning of 'creationism' has changed. It used to denote the belief that there was a Creator, full stop. It carried no implications of how the creating was done. However, it has subsequently accreted a great deal of extraneous baggage and come to denote, not only belief in a Creator, but also a commitment to a whole additional raft of ideas. By far the most dominant among them is a particular interpretation of Genesis that holds that the earth is only a few thousand years old. One of its main proponents was a certain Archbishop Ussher (1581–1656), who, I now openly confess, was Archbishop of Ireland and lived in my home city of Armagh! I sincerely hope that this confession will not stop you reading at this point as you will rapidly learn that I must, albeit respectfully, beg to disagree with the learned archbishop on the issue.

This radical shift in the meaning of 'creationism' and 'creationist' has had three very unfortunate effects. First of all, it polarizes the discussion and gives an apparently soft target to those who reject out of hand any notion of intelligent causation in the universe. Secondly, it fails to do justice to the fact that there is a wide divergence of opinion on the interpretation of the Genesis account even among those Christian thinkers who ascribe final authority to the biblical record.[69] Finally, it obscures the (original) purpose of using the term 'intelligent design', which was to make the crucial distinction between the recognition of design and the identification of the designer. That issue has absolutely nothing to do with the age of the earth.

The point of insisting on this distinction was to clear the way to ask whether there is any way in which science can help answer the first question. It is therefore unfortunate that the radical difference between these questions is often obscured by the accusation that 'ID' is shorthand for 'crypto-creationism'. Some time ago, at a 'professors' forum' dinner meeting in Oxford attended by a number of senior members of the university's scientific community, I was surprised and intrigued to find that the subject tabled for the meeting was Intelligent Design. I assure the reader that I was not responsible for this choice of topic. After quite a bit of discussion in which participants asserted that ID was crypto-creationism, I

Intelligent origin.

asked the following question: 'Suppose we scientists are given a black box to investigate. Is it legitimate for us to ask and investigate whether there is any scientific evidence for an informational input into the design and function of the box?' All present agreed that this was completely legitimate. I then said that this question is the key to understanding ID. There was a chorus of: 'No it is not!' But it is, and the negative chorus shows just how careful we must be to avoid people getting the wrong end of the stick.

Because the term ID for many people has unfortunately become freighted with many misleading ideas it might therefore be wiser, as I suggested above, to speak instead, as I tend to do, of intelligent causation or of intelligent origin, rather than use the term 'ID'.

In this connection, I profited greatly in my youth from the following advice: when you write a book or a lecture, do not only ask yourself how you will be understood; also ask yourself how you could be misunderstood. In light of this advice, I often introduce the topic of intelligent causation in nature by saying straight up that I believe that there is an Intelligent Designer God who created and who upholds the universe. I then add that the issue that I wish to address, however, has nothing to do with the _identity_ of a putative creator. It is the entirely different matter as to whether there can be scientific evidence for an intelligent input, from whatever source or sources unknown, into, or in the structure and function of any entity, including the universe.

I approach this matter in the same spirit as an archaeologist would when having to decide (rationally and scientifically) whether something found in a dig is an artefact or simply the product of natural forces – weathering, volcanic activity, wind, or fire, and so on. It is the forensic method of that of Hercule Poirot investigating whether a person accidentally fell from a roof or was pushed.

Another oft-repeated question is whether ID is science or not. To say that it is without further qualification can be rather misleading, certainly if we understand the term 'intelligent design' in its original sense: that certain features of the universe and of living things are best explained by an intelligent cause, not an undirected natural process.

Let me explain what I mean. When some people ask: Is X science? they simply mean: Is X rational? Well, ID is certainly rational. But the question usually means: Is X part of the natural sciences? Suppose we were to ask the parallel questions: Is theism science? or Is atheism science? Most people would, I hope, say that both were rational but not part of the natural sciences. If we were now to say that what we meant by the question is whether there is any scientific evidence for theism (or for atheism), then we are likely to be faced with the reply: If that is what you meant, why did you not say so?

One way to make sense of the question whether ID is science or not is to reinterpret it as I did in my question to my fellow professors in Oxford: Is there any scientific evidence for design? If this is how the question should be understood, then it should be expressed accordingly, in order to avoid the kind of misunderstanding exhibited by the statement made in the Dover trial in 2005. This was the first direct challenge brought in the United States federal courts testing a public school district policy that required the teaching of intelligent design. The assertion was that: 'ID is an interesting theological argument, but that it is not science.'[70] Indeed, in the film *Expelled* (April 2008), Richard Dawkins himself appears to concede that one could scientifically investigate whether the origin of life reflected natural processes or whether it was likely to be the result of intervention from an external, intelligent source. And that really would be science!

In his article 'Public Education and Intelligent Design',[71] Thomas Nagel of New York, a prominent professor of philosophy and a strong atheist who does not even want there to be a God, understands the crucial point here: 'The purposes and intentions of God, if there is a god, and the nature of his will, are not possible subjects of a scientific theory or scientific explanation. But that does not imply that there cannot be scientific evidence for or against the intervention of such a non-law-governed cause in the natural order.'[72] Based on his reading of books, such as Michael Behe's *Edge of Evolution* (Behe was a witness in the Dover trial), Nagel reports that ID: 'does not seem to depend on massive distortions of the evidence and hopeless incoherencies in its interpretation'.[73] Nagel's considered assessment is that ID is not based on the assumption that it is 'immune to empirical evidence' in the way that believers in biblical literalism believe the Bible is immune to disproof by evidence. Nagel thinks that: 'ID is very different from creation science.'[74]

Nagel also says that he 'has for a long time been sceptical of the claims of traditional evolutionary theory to be the whole story about the history of life'.[75] He reports that it is 'difficult to find in the accessible literature the grounds' for these claims. It is his view that the 'presently available evidence' comes 'nothing close' to establishing 'the sufficiency of standard evolutionary mechanisms to account for the entire evolution of life'.[76]

It was R. E. D. Clark who first suggested to me over fifty years ago that this was the case. However, Clark was a Christian; Nagel is an atheist, and so he cannot be accused of pre-judging the issue in favour of theism. I cited Nagel's comments on evolution since, as is well known, authors such as Peter Atkins, Richard Dawkins, and Daniel Dennett argue that evolutionary biology yields strong scientific support for atheism. They are evidently happy to make a scientific case for what is, after all, a metaphysical position. They, of all people, therefore, have no grounds for objecting to others using scientific evidence to support the opposing metaphysical position, that of theistic (or, as with Flew, deistic) design. I am well aware that the immediate reaction on the part of some will be that there is no alternative case to be put. I hope to show, however, that such a judgment might just be a little premature.

We could also rephrase the question of whether ID is science by asking whether the ID hypothesis can lead to scientifically testable hypotheses. We shall see later that there are two major areas in which such a hypothesis has already yielded results that are acceptable to the overwhelming majority of scientists: the rational intelligibility of the universe and the beginning of the universe. In fact, the first of these turns out to be a necessary prior belief for all wishing to do science and the second is almost universally accepted.

PART 2

Science and Explanation

4

Science, its Presuppositions, Scope, and Methodology

'Men became scientific because they expected Law in Nature and they expected Law in Nature because they believed in a Legislator.'
C. S. Lewis

One of the great features of science is its internationality with researchers from every conceivable background of culture, philosophy, and religion. Yet that fact can make some scientists nervous of raising metaphysical issues: we point out that very little of science raises such questions.

What then is science? Answers prove rather more difficult than one might first think and philosophers of science find it more helpful to give a list of activities that are associated with the concept of science. We examine some possible definitions. Science explains and we describe some of its main methods: explanation by repeated experimentation (induction); inference to the best explanation (abduction); explanation in terms of reduction; explanations in terms of mechanism and agency. We introduce the idea of paradigm and conclude the chapter by discussing the limits of science.

The international character of science

For many of us, one of the highlights of being a scientist is that of belonging to a truly international community transcending all kinds of frontiers: race, ideology, religion, political conviction, and the myriad other things that can divide people from one another. All of these things are forgotten as we together try to get to grips with the mysteries of mathematics, make sense of quantum mechanics, fight against debilitating disease, investigate the properties of strange materials, formulate theories about the interiors of stars, develop new ways of producing energy, or study the complexity of proteomics.

It is precisely because of this ideal of an international community, free to get on with its scientific work untrammelled by extraneous and potentially divisive intrusions, that scientists understandably begin to get nervous when metaphysics threatens to rear its head, or worse still when the God question appears. Surely, if there is one area that can (and should) be kept religiously and theologically neutral, it is science? And, for the most part, it is so. Vast tracts of the natural sciences, in fact, probably by far and away the major part, are just like that. After all, the nature of the elements, the periodic table, the values of the fundamental constants of nature, the structure of DNA, the Krebs cycle, Newton's laws, Einstein's equations, and so on have essentially nothing to do with metaphysical commitment. Isn't it all like that? It is time for us to think about what science is.

Defining science

Science (in the sense of the natural sciences – physics, chemistry, biology, astronomy, and the like) is associated in all of our minds with finding things out about the natural world by making observations, doing experiments, and studying natural history. It turns out, however, that giving a precise definition of science is surprisingly difficult. In order to get into the spirit of things I recommend the reader to have a look at the first chapter of Nobel laureate Richard Feynman's delightful little book, *The Meaning of it All*:

> What is science? The word is usually used to mean one of three things, or a mixture of them. I do not think we need to be precise – it is not always a good idea to be too precise. Science means, sometimes, a special method of finding things out. Sometimes it means the body of knowledge arising from the things found out. It may also mean the things you can do when you have found something out, or the actual doing of new things.[1]

In another of his books, *The Pleasure of Finding Things Out*, Feynman fleshes this out:

If I do this, what will happen?
Try it and see!

> As a matter of fact, science can be defined as a method for, and a body of information obtained by, trying to answer only questions which can be put into the form: If I do this, what will happen? The technique of it, fundamentally, is: Try it and see. Then you put together a large amount of information from such experiences. All scientists will agree that a question – any question, philosophical or other – which cannot be put into the form that can be tested by experiment... is not a scientific question; it is outside the realm of science.[2]

For many people this implies that science and religion have nothing to do with each other so that science by definition simply cannot adjudicate on the existence or non-existence of God – a matter to which we shall return.

More prosaic but slightly wider is the definition produced by the Science Council: 'Science is the pursuit and application of knowledge and understanding of the natural and social world following a systematic methodology based on evidence.'[3]

Philosophers of science are often reluctant to try to give a precise definition of science and prefer, for example, to list various activities that we associate with science. Again, the Science Council suggests in the article just cited that scientific methodology includes the following:

- objective observation: measurement and data (possibly although not necessarily using mathematics as a tool);
- evidence;
- experiment and/or observation as benchmarks for testing hypotheses;
- deduction and induction: reasoning to establish general rules or conclusions drawn from facts or examples;
- repetition;
- critical analysis;
- verification and testing: critical exposure to scrutiny, peer review, and assessment.

It is surprising that they do not mention inference to the best explanation, or abduction (see below), so the list excludes the very important historical dimension to science. In addition, such definitions can give the impression that science is a completely rational and logical process where a train of reasoning based on observations leads to the result. However, this is far from the case. Very often great discoveries start with an intuition or hunch that a person believes to be true without any particular reason but sticks doggedly at it until they can show it to be true. Imagination can play an important role. Scientists can have flashes of insight when they are dreaming, when out for a walk, or not even thinking of their problem at all. For instance, Dmitri Mendeleev was half-asleep at his desk in 1869 when he had a vision of the elements arranged in what became his periodic table. After four years' work on a mathematical problem Carl Friedrich Gauss describes the solution as follows:

> At last I succeeded, not by painful effort, but so to speak by the grace of God. As a sudden flash of light the enigma was solved. For my part I am not in a position to point to the thread which joins what I knew previously to what I succeeded in doing... I have my results but I do not yet know how I arrived at them.[4]

Aesthetics can be an important factor in mathematics. The Nobel laureate Paul A. M. Dirac once wrote: 'This result is too beautiful to be false; it is more important to have beauty in one's equations than to have them fit experiment.'[5]

We have two hemispheres in our brain: the left, which is the more analytical, and the right, which is the more integrative; both get involved in science. There are also vigorous contemporary discussions among philosophers of science as to whether science is observation-and-prediction-based, or problem-and-explanation-based. And also, when we set up our theories, they tend to be underdetermined by the data: for instance, infinitely many curves can be drawn through a given finite set of points. By its very nature, therefore, science inevitably possesses a certain degree of tentativeness and provisionality. Science is not so much about truth as about probability – what we think is most likely and why we think it.

Richard Feynman is characteristically clear on this:

> All scientific knowledge is uncertain. This experience with doubt and uncertainty is important. I believe it is of very

great value and one that extends beyond the sciences. I
believe that to solve any problem that has not been solved
before, you have to leave the door to the unknown ajar.
You have to permit the possibility that you do not have it
exactly right. Otherwise, if you have made up your mind
already, you might not solve it... So what we call scientific
knowledge today is a body of knowledge of varying degrees
of certainty.[6]

We hasten to add that this is far from granting that science is some kind
of subjective and arbitrary social construct, as is held by some thinkers of
postmodern persuasion.[7] It is probably fair to say that many scientists are,
like myself, 'critical realists', believing in an objective world which can be
studied and who hold that their theories, though not amounting to 'truth'
in any final or absolute sense, give them an increasingly firm handle on
reality, as exemplified, say, in the development of the understanding of the
universe, from Galileo via Newton to Einstein.[8]

Repeated experimentation

When attempting to understand how science works, the first thing that
comes to mind is probably that of finding things out by observation and
experiment. Most of us are familiar with this from school and are aware
that the experiments had been done thousands of times giving the same
results. That is, the results were established by repetition. For example,
the hypothesis that water is made up of hydrogen and oxygen can be
repeatedly tested by a classroom experiment. Chemists will then say that
the result has been established by induction – or perhaps, more accurately,
by hypothetico-deductivism.[9] They reason that if the hypothesis is true,
we can expect a certain outcome when we carry out the experiment.
Observing that outcome in turn confirms the hypothesis. Of course, the
assumption is that no matter how many times, or in how many places, we
test the hypothesis under the same conditions we will get the same result.

The element of repeatability is such an important aspect of science
that some think it essentially defines what science is. An example is
given by well-known philosopher of biology, Michael Ruse, who says that
science 'by definition deals only with the natural, the repeatable, that
which is governed by law'.[10] On the positive side this definition of science

would certainly allow us to distinguish between astronomy and astrology. However, it is too restrictive in the sense that many of the phenomena studied by scientists are not repeatable and yet are still regarded as part of science. Ruse's definition of science would rule out most of contemporary cosmology. It is hard to see how the standard model for the origin of the universe can be describing anything other than unique events – the origin of the universe is not (as yet!) repeatable. Cosmologists might understandably protest at being told that their activities did not qualify as science. For, even though much of what cosmologists study is not repeatable, nevertheless repeatability plays an important role in their work. For example, repeated observations of the galaxies and stars, repeated measurements of their radiation spectra are essential to shaping our ideas about the cosmos.

In addition, however, there is another approach that is an essential part of the methodology of contemporary science that applies to unrepeatable events like the origin of the universe. It is based on the ability of scientific hypotheses to explain the phenomena and is known as abduction.

Abduction: Inference to the best explanation[11]

Of course, with repeatable events, we trust that our explanations of them are the best explanation in that they have predictive power. With unrepeatable events we ask: What is the best explanation of this phenomenon?

Inference to the best explanation is often called abduction and it is interesting that the word *Obduktion* in German means a post-mortem. That conveys the idea exactly, as a post-mortem attempts to ascertain the best explanation as to cause of death. Abduction is probably even more familiar to most people as the method used by those brilliant detectives Sherlock Holmes, Hercule Poirot, and Miss Marple to solve their mysteries. A murder cannot be re-run to determine what happened. The forensic method is certainly not one of repeated experimentation! Forensic science proceeds as follows: Poirot observes A and reasons: if X did the murder then A would probably follow, so X is a suspect. Poirot then notices B. He sees at once that if X did the murder then B would not have happened. So X is off the hook. However, if on the other hand Y did the dastardly deed then both A and B would follow. Hence Y is a better candidate for the murderer than X. And so on. The final dénouement is, of course, a masterly inference to the best explanation. Many results in cosmology are like this: think of the inferences that were made in the twentieth century that led to scientists accepting that space time had a beginning.

One challenge for abduction is what is meant by 'best' explanation. This can involve a subjective judgment, especially when wider issues, dependent on worldview, come into play. What I mean is that in certain cases the best naturalistic explanation will be looked for which may well be the answer. However, there are some situations, particularly when we are trying to assess what results mean, where the issue may be whether we are prepared to contemplate other sources of meaning outside the limitations of science. Here, for ideological reasons, some will hold that the best explanation must be a naturalistic one; others will be prepared to look beyond this limitation.

In summary, repeatability plays an important role in science and can lead to well-confirmed scientific hypotheses, but scientific reasoning can also deal with unrepeatable events via inference to the best explanation and this too can lead to well-confirmed hypotheses, if there is good evidence. Moreover, inference to the best explanation can also be applied outside of science to history or religious beliefs, for example. While subjective judgments can come into play, the crucial thing is the quality of the evidence in a given case.

Explanation in terms of reduction

The object of *explaining* something is to give an accessible and intelligible description of its nature and function. One obvious thing to try to do is to split the problem up into separate parts or aspects, and thus 'reduce' it to simpler components that are individually easier to investigate. For instance, water is a mixture of hydrogen and oxygen – although there is more to water than we can readily see by investigating separately the hydrogen and oxygen of which it is composed. This kind of procedure, *methodological reduction*, is a major part of the normal process of science, and, indeed of many other activities in everyday life. It has proved very effective – so effective, indeed, that many scientists are convinced that it is the only methodology we need. This leads to the worldview of reductionism which we shall discuss in Chapter 5.

Explanation in terms of mechanism and agency

Science has been, and still is, proving spectacularly successful in probing the nature of the physical universe and elucidating the mechanisms by which the universe works. Scientific research has also led to the eradication of many horrific diseases, and raised hopes of eliminating many more. And science has had another effect in a completely different direction: it has served to relieve a lot of people from superstitious fears. For instance, people need no longer think that an eclipse of the moon is caused by some frightful demon, which they have to placate. For all of these and myriad other things we should be very grateful.

But in some quarters the very success of science has also led to the idea that, because we can understand how the universe works without bringing in God, we can safely conclude that there was no God who designed and created the universe in the first place. However, such reasoning involves a logical fallacy, which we can illustrate as follows.

Take a Ford motor car. It is conceivable that someone from a remote part of the world, who was seeing one for the first time and who knew nothing about modern engineering, might imagine that there is a god (Mr Ford) inside the engine, making it go. He might further imagine that when the engine ran sweetly it was because Mr Ford inside the engine liked him, and when it refused to go it was because Mr Ford did not like him. Of course, if he were subsequently to study engineering and take the engine to pieces, he would discover that there is no Mr Ford inside it. Neither would it take much intelligence for him to see that he did not need to introduce Mr Ford as an explanation for its working. His grasp of the impersonal principles of internal combustion would be altogether enough to explain how the engine works. So far, so good. But if he then decided that his understanding of the principles of how the engine works made it impossible to believe in the existence of a Mr Ford who designed the engine in the first place, this would be patently false – in philosophical terminology he would be committing a category mistake. Had there never been a Mr Ford to design the mechanisms, none would exist for him to understand.

It is likewise a category mistake to suppose that our understanding of the impersonal principles according to which the universe works makes it either unnecessary or impossible to believe in the existence of a personal Creator who designed, made, and upholds the universe. In other words, we should not confuse the mechanisms by which the universe works either with its cause or its upholder.

The basic issue here, so far as I can determine, is that those, like Atkins and Dawkins who are wedded to *scientism*, the idea that science is the only way to discover truth, which we shall look at in the next chapter, rather inexplicably, fail to distinguish between *mechanism* and *agency*. In philosophical terms they make a very elementary category mistake when they argue that, because we understand a mechanism that accounts for a particular phenomenon, there is no agent that designed the mechanism. Sir Isaac Newton did not make this mistake.

In the *General Scholium*[12] to his *Philosophiæ Naturalis Principia Mathematica* (*Mathematical Principles of Natural Philosophy*), the most famous book in the history of science, Newton wrote:

> This most beautiful System of the Sun, Planets, and Comets, could only proceed from the counsel and dominion of an intelligent and powerful being. And if the fixed Stars are the centres of other like systems, these being form'd by the likewise counsel, must be all subject to the dominion of One. And lest the systems of the fixed Stars should, by their gravity, fall on each other mutually, he hath placed those Systems at immense distances one from another.[13]

In a letter to his friend Bentley on 10 December 1692 he explained one of his motives in writing *Principia*: 'When I wrote my treatise about the system, I had an eye upon such principles as might work with considering men for the belief in a Deity and nothing can rejoice me more than to find it useful for that purpose.'[14]

Michael Poole, in his published debate with Richard Dawkins,[15] points out why Newton's stance makes perfect sense: 'there is no logical conflict between reason-giving explanations which concern mechanisms, and reason-giving explanations which concern the plans and purposes of an agent, human or divine. This is a logical point, not a matter of whether one does or does not happen to believe in God oneself.'

In total disregard of this logical point, a famous statement made by the French mathematician Laplace (1749–1827) is constantly misused to buttress atheism. On being asked by Napoleon where God fitted into his mathematical work, Laplace, quite correctly, replied: 'Sir, I have no need of that hypothesis.' Of course God did not appear in Laplace's mathematical description of how things work, just as Mr Ford would not appear in a scientific description of the working of a Ford car.

But what would that prove? That Henry Ford did not exist? Of course not. Neither does such an argument prove that God does not exist. Austin Farrer comments on the Laplace incident as follows:

> Since God is not a rule built into the action of forces, nor is he a block of force, no sentence about God can play a part in physics or astronomy... We may forgive Laplace – he was answering an amateur according to his ignorance, not to say a fool according to his folly. Considered as a serious observation, his remark could scarcely have been more misleading. Laplace and his colleagues had not learned to do without theology; they had merely learned to mind their own business.[16]

Quite so. But suppose Napoleon had posed a somewhat different question to Laplace: 'Why is there a universe at all in which there is matter and gravity and in which projectiles composed of matter moving under gravity describe the orbits encapsulated in your mathematical equations?' It would be harder to argue that the existence of God was irrelevant to that question. But then, that was not the question that Laplace was asked. So he did not answer it.

The issue in the foregoing is that certain phenomena are not only capable of being explained in more than one way, but also that both (or more) explanations are necessary. We do not have to choose between them for in doing so we lose some aspect of the reality we are trying to explain. In other words, we are thinking of a situation in which multiple explanations are better than one in the sense that they have more explanatory power. The term 'conjunctive explanation' is now used to capture this idea. The main contention of this book is that science has not buried God but rather theology and science join together in a conjunctive explanation that has more explanatory power than either on its own.

The presuppositions of science ⹀ Convictions
The existence of the universe

Presuppositions are, as the name implies, convictions – beliefs that we bring to science. They are prior to science. They are not the results of science although we use science to confirm them so far as possible. They are unavoidable beliefs and their existence shows that science starts with faith – a matter to be investigated below.

The first presupposition in science is the conviction that the universe is there to study. This is so self-evident that we can easily take it for granted. And that is a pity. For one of the fundamental problems of existence is: Why is there a universe at all, why is there something rather than nothing? Now there are some scientists and philosophers who think that we should not even ask this question. For them there is no point in looking for a reason for the existence of the universe since, according to them, there simply isn't one. Their view is that, since any chain of reasoning must start somewhere, we might as well start with the existence of the universe.

Echoing Bertrand Russell, Edward P. Tryton writes: 'Our universe is simply one of those things which happen from time to time.'[17] However, that answer sounds about as scientific as answering the question of why apples fall to the ground, by saying that they just do. In addition, it would be distinctly odd, as Keith Ward points out, 'to think that there is a reason for everything, except for that most important item of all – that is, the existence of everything, the universe itself'.[18] The insatiable human desire for explanation will not let that question rest there.

Richard Dawkins confesses he does not know what caused the universe to exist, but he believes[19] that there will one day be a naturalistic explanation of it. As he said in his Oxford debate with me, he did not need to resort to magic to explain the universe. However, in the press conference after the debate he responded to a question from Melanie Phillips by saying that he believed that the universe could have just appeared from nothing. 'Magic,' she said. She later reported that Dawkins told her afterwards that an explanation for the universe in terms of LGM (little green men) made more sense than postulating a Creator. Anything but God, it would seem.

Others maintain that the universe is self-explanatory. For instance, Peter Atkins believes that 'Space-time generates its own dust in the process of its own self-assembly.'[20] He calls this the 'Cosmic bootstrap', referring to the ludicrous idea of a person lifting himself by pulling on his own bootlaces. Keith Ward is surely right to say that Atkins' view of the universe is as blatantly self-contradictory as the name he gives to it, pointing out that it is 'logically impossible for a cause to bring about some effect without already being in existence'. Ward concludes: 'Between the hypothesis of God and the hypothesis of a cosmic bootstrap, there is no competition. We were always right to think that persons, or universes, who seek to pull themselves up by their own bootstraps are forever doomed to failure.'[21] Atkins' 'self-generation' explanation is demanded from him by his materialism, not his science.

Stephen Hawking, on the other hand, seemed to think that science cannot answer the question of why there is a universe. He wrote: 'The usual approach of science of constructing a mathematical model cannot answer the questions of why there should be a universe for the model to describe. Why does the universe go to all the bother of existing? Is the unified theory so compelling that it brings about its own existence? Or does it need a Creator, and, if so, does he have any other effect on the universe?'[22]

Hawking's first suggestion here is, not that the universe is self-generating, but that it is brought into existence by a theory. Physicist Paul Davies says something similar in an interview: 'There's no need to invoke anything supernatural in the origins of the universe or of life. I have never liked the idea of divine tinkering: for me it is much more inspiring to believe that a set of mathematical laws can be so clever as to bring all these things into being.'[23]

It is strange that a scientist of Davies' standing is prepared to decide how things started on the basis of likes or dislikes. Furthermore, he is here ascribing intelligence (if not personality) to a set of mathematical laws – and believing that they could be intelligent on the basis that he finds it inspiring! Is this wishful thinking, or what? Leaving aside Davies' dubious-sounding motivation we might well ask what could possibly be meant by a theory or laws bringing the universe into existence. We certainly expect to be able to formulate theories involving mathematical laws that describe natural phenomena, and we can often do this to astonishing degrees of precision. However, the laws we find cannot themselves cause anything. Newton's laws can describe the motion of a billiard ball,[24] but it is the cue wielded by the billiard player that sets the ball moving, not the laws. The laws help us map the trajectory of the ball's movement in the future (provided nothing external interferes), but they are powerless to move the ball, let alone bring it into existence.

And, if one dare say so, the much maligned William Paley (of whom we shall say more in Chapter 5) said as much long ago. Speaking of the person who had just stumbled on a watch on the heath and picked it up he says that such a person would not be

> less surprised to be informed, that the watch in his hand
> was nothing more than the result of the laws of metallic
> nature. It is a perversion of language to assign any law,
> as the efficient, operative cause of anything. A law

Agent - power to do..

presupposes an agent; for it is only the mode, according
to which an agent proceeds: it implies a power; for it is the
order, according to which that power acts. Without this
agent, without this power, which are both distinct from
itself, the law does nothing; is nothing.[25]

In the world in which most of us live the simple law of arithmetic, $1 + 1 = 2$, never brought anything into being by itself. It certainly has never put any money into my bank account. If I first put £1,000 into the bank and then later another £1,000, the laws of arithmetic will rationally explain how it is that I now have £2,000 in the bank. But if I never put any money into the bank myself and simply leave it to the laws of arithmetic to bring money into being in my bank account, I shall remain permanently bankrupt. The world of strict naturalism, in which clever mathematical laws all by themselves bring the universe and life into existence, is pure (and, one might add, poor) fiction. To call it science-fiction would besmirch the name of science. Theories and laws simply do not bring anything into existence. The view that they nevertheless somehow have that capacity seems a rather desperate refuge (and it is hard to see what else it could be but a refuge) from the alternative possibility contained in Hawkings' final question cited above: 'Or does it need a Creator?'

Allan Sandage, widely regarded as one of the fathers of modern astronomy, discoverer of quasars and winner of the Crafoord Prize, astronomy's equivalent of the Nobel Prize, is in no doubt that the answer to that question is positive: 'I find it quite improbable that such order came out of chaos. There has to be some organizing principle. God to me is a mystery but is the explanation for the miracle of existence – why there is something rather than nothing.'[26]

2nd The rational intelligibility of the universe

The second presupposition for any scientist is that she believes that science can be done. This means that she believes that the universe itself is rationally intelligible – that is, accessible, at least in part, to the probing of the human mind. It was Albert Einstein's astonishment at the intelligibility of the cosmos that prompted him to make the famous statement, 'The most incomprehensible thing about the universe is that it is comprehensible.'[27] What is more, the very concept of the intelligibility of the universe presupposes the existence of a rationality capable of recognizing that intelligibility. Indeed, confidence that our human mental processes possess some degree of reliability and are capable of giving us some information about the world is fundamental to any kind of study, not only the study of science. This involves believing that we can capture nature and its workings in language – something quite wonderful and even awe-inspiring. It is a reduction since the language of mathematics gets mapped onto the universe, but it isn't the universe. It also involves believing the laws of logic. None of these things can be deduced from science – we must accept them to start with.

These convictions are so central to all thinking that we cannot even question their validity without assuming them in the first place, since we have to rely on reason and the laws of logic in order to do the questioning. It is the bedrock belief upon which all intellectual inquiry is built. I shall argue that theism gives it a consistent and reasonable justification whereas naturalism fails to do so.

Indeed, rational intelligibility is one of the main considerations that have led thinkers of all generations to reject ontological reductionism and conclude that the universe must itself be a product of intelligence. Keith Ward sums up:

> To the majority of those who have reflected deeply and written about the origin and nature of the universe, it has seemed that it points beyond itself to a source which is non-physical and of great intelligence and power. Almost all of the great classical philosophers – certainly Plato, Aristotle, Descartes, Leibniz, Spinoza, Kant, Hegel, Locke, Berkeley – saw the origin of the universe as lying in a transcendent reality. They had different specific ideas of this reality... but that the universe is not self-explanatory, and that it requires some explanation beyond itself, was something they accepted as fairly obvious.[28]

Thus the inference to the best explanation from the origin and nature of the universe to an underlying non-physical intelligence has a long and impressive pedigree.

For Albert Einstein the comprehensibility of the universe was something to be wondered at:

> You find it strange that I consider the comprehensibility
> of the world... as a miracle or as an eternal mystery. Well, *a
> priori*, one should expect a chaotic world, which cannot be
> grasped by the mind in any way... the kind of order created
> by Newton's theory of gravitation, for example, is wholly
> different. Even if man proposes the axioms of the theory,
> the success of such a project presupposes a high degree
> of ordering of the objective world, and this could not
> be expected a priori. That is the 'miracle' which is being
> constantly reinforced as our knowledge expands.[29]

For, as the example of Newton's theory shows, it is not only the fact that the universe is intelligible which is amazing; it is the mathematical nature of that intelligibility which is remarkable. We tend to take the usefulness of mathematics as obvious because we are so used to it. But why?

Paul Davies is among those not satisfied with the glib response of people who say that the fundamental laws of nature are mathematical simply because we define as fundamental those laws that are mathematical. One of the main reasons for his dissatisfaction is that much of the mathematics found to be successfully applicable 'was worked out as an abstract exercise by pure mathematicians, long before it was applied to the real world. The original investigations were entirely unconnected with their eventual application.'[30] It is very striking that the most abstract mathematical concepts that seem to be pure inventions of the human mind can turn out to be of vital importance for branches of science, with a vast range of practical applications.[31] It needs saying that mental abstractions in general, and mathematics in particular, since they are immaterial, show that materialism is not a viable worldview. In any case, as we shall see in Chapter 21, quantum mechanics spells the end of materialism.

Science involves faith

Davies here echoes a famous essay entitled *The Unreasonable Effectiveness of Mathematics* written in 1961 by physics Nobel laureate Eugene Wigner in which he said: 'The enormous usefulness of mathematics in the natural sciences is something bordering on the mysterious, and there is no rational explanation for it... it is an article of faith.'[32] The relationship between mathematics and physics goes very deep and it is very hard to think of it as some random accident. Oxford mathematician Sir Roger Penrose FRS OM, whose understanding of that relationship is unquestioned, has this to say about it:

> It is hard for me to believe... that such SUPERB theories could have arisen merely by some random natural selection of ideas leaving only the good ones as survivors. The good ones are simply much too good to be the survivors of ideas that have arisen in a random way. There must be, instead, some deep underlying reason for the accord between mathematics and physics.[33]

Certainly science itself cannot account for this phenomenon. Why? Because, in the words of John Polkinghorne: 'Science does not explain the mathematical intelligibility of the physical world, for it is part of science's founding faith that this is so.'[34]

Thus, we have two leading physicists, Wigner and Polkinghorne, explicitly drawing our attention to the foundational role that faith plays in science. Yes, faith. This may come as a surprise, even as a shock, to many, especially if they have been exposed to the very common fallacy mentioned at the beginning of this book and spread with memetic speed by Richard Dawkins and others, that the word 'faith' denotes 'blind faith' and belongs exclusively to the domain of religion, whereas science does not involve faith at all. Dawkins is simply wrong on all counts: faith – belief and intellectual commitment based on evidence – is at the heart of any scientific endeavour. Gödel's second incompleteness theorem (to be discussed in Chapter 5) gives further evidence for this: you cannot even do mathematics without faith in its consistency. You cannot do science without belief in its presuppositions.

But there is more. Think of Newton's inverse square law of gravitational attraction. Because we are so familiar with it as an explanation of how the planets orbit the sun in ellipses, and use it (or rather, the experts do) to predict all kinds of astronomical events, eclipses and such like, we often fail to realize that there is a hidden faith dimension even here. It is betrayed by our belief that what happened today will happen again tomorrow. This is the well-known problem of induction in philosophy that was memorably illustrated by Bertrand Russell in his story of the 'inductivist turkey'. The hero of the story is a turkey that, because it had been regularly fed in the days

or The principle of the uniformity of nature
= The rational intelligibility of the Universe.

preceding Christmas, reasoned that it would be fed every day. However, it hit a serious crisis on Christmas Day that, for a split-second at least, might just have revealed to it the perils of induction! Paul Davies comments: 'Just because the sun has risen every day of your life, there is no guarantee that it will rise tomorrow. The belief that it will, that there are indeed dependable regularities of nature, is an act of faith, but one which is indispensable to the progress of science.'[35] This aspect of the rational intelligibility of the universe is often referred to as the principle of uniformity of nature. It is an article of any scientist's faith.

The challenge to straighten out!

Unfortunately the two ideas – that all religious faith is blind faith and that science does not involve faith – are so widely disseminated in atheist literature that we constantly need to protest vigorously that they are wrong. John Haught points out that what he calls a 'leap of faith' is always involved at some stage in the validation of truth claims and hypotheses. The (scientific) search for understanding involves trust at an essential level. Haught perceptively says that if we doubt what he is saying our very doubt shows that we are trusting our minds sufficiently to express that doubt. In addition, we only raise such concern if we believe that truth is worth searching for. He concludes: 'Faith in this sense, and not in the sense of wild imaginings and wishful thinking, lies at the root of all authentic religion – and science.'[36] Haught rightly concludes that this 'shows clearly that the new atheistic attempts to cleanse human consciousness of faith are absurd and doomed to failure'.[37]

My only quibble with Haught is his use of the expression 'leap of faith' which may convey to some people the idea of a wild jump into the completely unknown. I do not think Haught intends it that way and was rather thinking of that step of trust that is required in order to reach out to something new, but which is a step grounded in all the evidence that we have had up to that moment that would justify trusting that next step. If there is no such evidence, it might be wise not to take the step as, for instance, when people we scarcely know say, 'Just trust me!' Trust must be earned.

Our answer to the question of why the universe is rationally intelligible will in fact depend, not so much on whether we are scientists or not, but on whether we are theists or naturalists. Theists like myself will argue that Wigner is wrong when he says there is no rational explanation for that intelligibility. On the contrary, the intelligibility of the universe is grounded in the nature of the ultimate rationality of God: both the real

False (2)

"Blind Faith", Science - no faith required.

The intelligibility of the universe is grounded in the nature of the ultimate rationality of God. Traceable to the mind of God.

world and mathematics are traceable to the Mind of God who created both the universe and the human mind with all its potentiality for observation and abstract thought. It is, therefore, not surprising when the mathematical theories spun by human minds created in the image of God's Mind, find ready application in a universe whose architect was that same creative Mind.

Keith Ward supports this view: 'The continuing conformity of physical particles to precise mathematical relationships is something that is much more likely to exist if there is an ordering cosmic mathematician who sets up the correlation in the requisite way. The existence of laws of physics... strongly implies that there is a God who formulates such laws and ensures that the physical realm conforms to them.'[38] Or, is it that God creates the physical realm in a certain way and the laws of physics are our formulations of the way it works? The difference – if there is one – is not relevant to the important point Keith Ward is making here. The upshot of it is that the rational intelligibility of the universe makes sense in a theistic framework; whereas, as we saw earlier, the (ontological) reductionist thesis undermines it and dissolves it into meaninglessness.

Far from science burying God, there is, therefore, a substantial case for saying that it is the existence of a Creator that gives to science its fundamental intellectual justification. Even the late Stephen Hawking, an atheist, admitted in a television interview: 'It is difficult to discuss the beginning of the universe without mentioning the concept of God. My work on the origin of the universe is on the borderline between science and religion, but I try to stay on the scientific side of the border. It is quite possible that God acts in ways that cannot be described by scientific laws.'[39] Rather oddly, this statement conflicts with Hawking's scientism since what he says opens up the possibility that science cannot explain everything.

It is for this kind of reason that we may see a certain consonance between scientific and religious ways of thinking about the universe. In his debate on atheism and theism with J. J. C. Smart, J. J. Haldane makes precisely this point, arguing that scientific and religious approaches are similar:

> Thus science is faith-like in resting upon 'creedal' presuppositions, and inasmuch as these relate to the order and intelligibility of the universe they also resemble the content of a theistic conception of the universe as an

ordered creation. Furthermore it seems that the theist carries the scientific impulse further by pressing on with the question of how perceived order is possible, seeking the most fundamental descriptions-cum-explanations of the existence and nature of the universe.[40]

Paradigms — an agreed intellectual frameworks

As famously observed by Thomas Kuhn,[41] scientists tend to work within what is called a *paradigm* – from the Greek *paradeigma* = pattern, example, sample. It is used to denote an agreed intellectual framework of concepts, procedures, results, and theories that define a scientific theory at a particular time. In a paradigm there are certain permitted core concepts; others are excluded. For instance, Aristotle's geocentric model, Copernicus' heliocentric model, Newtonian mechanics, Einstein's relativity, and the standard model of physics are all paradigms.

Paradigms can and do change as the above examples show and such changes sometimes happen as a result of tensions arising when empirical evidence conflicts with the paradigm reigning at the time.[42] The notorious refusal of some churchmen to look through Galileo's telescope is a classic expression of that kind of tension. For those clerics, the implications of the physical evidence were too much to face, since there was no way in which they could accept that their favoured Aristotelian paradigm was false.

Yet, it is not only churchmen who can be guilty of such obscurantism. In the early twentieth century, for example, Mendelian geneticists were persecuted by Marxists because Mendel's ideas on heredity were regarded as inconsistent with Marxist philosophy, and so the Marxists refused to allow the Mendelians to follow where the evidence led.

As in the case of the overthrow of Aristotelianism, entrenched attitudes may mean that it can take a long time before an accumulation of evidence favouring a new paradigm leads to the replacement of the existing one. For a scientific paradigm does not necessarily immediately crumble the moment some inconsistent evidence is found, although it must be said that the history of science throws up noteworthy exceptions. For example, when Rutherford discovered the nucleus of the atom he at once overthrew a dogma of classical physics and an immediate paradigm shift resulted. And DNA replaced protein as the basic genetic material virtually overnight. In these cases, of course, no deep-lying, uncomfortable, worldview issues were involved.

A comment from Thomas Nagel is apposite:

> Of course belief is often controlled by the will; it can even be coerced. The obvious examples are political and religious. But the captive mind is found in subtler form in purely intellectual contexts. One of its strongest motives is the simple hunger for belief itself. Sufferers from this condition find it difficult to tolerate having no opinion for any length of time on a subject that interests them. They may change their opinions easily when there is an alternative that can be adopted without discomfort, but they do not like to be in a condition of suspended judgement.[43]

However, alternatives cannot always be adopted without discomfort and particularly in cases where worldviews may be, or appear to be, threatened by contrary evidence there can be enormous resistance and even antagonism shown to anyone who wishes to follow where the evidence appears to lead. It takes a strong person to swim against the tide and risk the opprobrium of his peers. And yet, some of impressive intellectual stature do precisely that. 'My whole life has been guided by the principle of Plato's Socrates,' writes the late Anthony Flew, an eminent philosopher and expert on David Hume, in connection with his conversion from atheism to deism. 'Follow the evidence wherever it leads.' And what if people don't like it? 'That's too bad,' he says.[44]

There would seem, then, to be two extremes to be avoided. The first is to see the relationship between science and religion solely in terms of conflict. The second is to see all science as philosophically or theologically neutral.[45] The word 'all' is important here, since it is easy to lose sight of it, get things out of proportion and see the entire scientific enterprise as a hostage to philosophical fortune. We cannot emphasize too much that vast tracts of science remain unaffected by such philosophical commitments.

Instead of begging the question and defining science to be essentially applied naturalism which worldview is, therefore, metaphysically *a priori*, suppose we take it to be investigation of and theorizing about the natural order, so that we give weight to what is surely of the essence of true science – a willingness to follow empirical evidence, wherever it leads. The key question now arises as to what happens if our investigations turn up evidence that conflicts with our worldview commitment.

The limits of science

An everyday illustration can help us see that science has its limits. Let us imagine that my Aunt Matilda has baked a beautiful cake and we take it along to be analysed by a group of the world's top scientists. I, as master of ceremonies, ask them for an explanation of the cake and they go to work. The nutrition scientists will tell us about the number of calories in the cake and its nutritional effect; the biochemists will inform us about the structure of the proteins, fats etc., in the cake; the chemists, about the elements involved and their bonding; the physicists will be able to analyse the cake in terms of fundamental particles; and the mathematicians will no doubt offer us a set of elegant equations to describe the behaviour of those particles.

Now that these experts, each in terms of his or her scientific discipline, have given us an exhaustive description of the cake, can we say that the cake is completely explained? We have certainly been given a description of *how* the cake was made and *how* its various constituent elements relate to each other; but suppose I now ask the assembled group of experts a final question: *Why* was the cake made? The grin on Aunt Matilda's face shows she knows the answer, for she made the cake, and she made it for a purpose. But all the nutrition scientists, biochemists, chemists, physicists, and mathematicians in the world will not be able to answer the question – and it is no insult to their disciplines to state their incapacity to answer it. Their disciplines, which can cope with questions about the nature and structure of the cake, that is, answering the 'how' questions, cannot answer the 'why' questions connected with the purpose for which the cake was made.[46]

The only way we shall ever get an answer is if Aunt Matilda reveals it to us. But if she does not disclose the answer to us, no amount of scientific analysis will enlighten us. To say, with Bertrand Russell that, because science cannot tell us why Aunt Matilda made the cake, we cannot know why she made it, is patently false. All we have to do is ask her to reveal it to us.

Erwin Schrödinger, a physics Nobel laureate and one of the pioneers of quantum mechanics, made himself very clear on the limits of science:

> I am very astonished that the scientific picture of the real world around me is very deficient. It gives us a lot of factual information... but it is ghastly silent about all

How did everything begin?
what are we all here for?
what is the point of living?

and sundry... that really matters to us. It cannot tell us a
word about red and blue, bitter and sweet, physical pain
and physical delight; it knows nothing of beautiful and
ugly, good or bad, God and eternity. Science sometimes
pretends to answer questions in these domains but the
answers are very often so silly that we are not inclined to
take them seriously.[47]

He was right, for the claim that science is the only way to truth is a claim
ultimately unworthy of science itself. Nobel laureate Sir Peter Medawar
points this out in his excellent book *Advice to a Young Scientist*:

There is no quicker way for a scientist to bring discredit
upon himself and upon his profession than roundly to
declare – particularly when no declaration of any kind
is called for – that science knows, or soon will know, the
answers to all questions worth asking, and that questions
which do not admit a scientific answer are in some way
non-questions or 'pseudo-questions' that only simpletons
ask and only the gullible profess to be able to answer.[48]

Medawar goes on to say that there is a limit to science that is shown by the
fact that there are questions that science cannot now, and will never be
able to, answer – the so-called 'ultimate questions' of the philosopher Karl
Popper that even children ask. How did everything begin? What are we all
here for? What is the point of living?
    Medawar adds that it is not to science but rather to imaginative
literature and religion that we must turn for answers to such questions.[49]
Francis Collins also emphasizes this: 'Science is powerless to answer
questions such as "Why did the universe come into being?" "What is the
meaning of human existence?" "What happens after we die?".'[50] There
is clearly no inconsistency involved in being a passionately committed
scientist at the highest level while simultaneously recognizing that science
cannot answer every kind of question, including some of the deepest
questions that human beings can ask.
    It is only fair to say also that Russell, in spite of the fact that he wrote
the very scientistic sounding statement we cited above, indicated elsewhere
that he did not subscribe to full-blown scientism. He did, however, think

[handwritten: Is there a way of living noble and any way of living base?]

[handwritten: Matter — Mind]

that all definite knowledge belongs to science, which certainly sounds like incipient scientism, but then he immediately goes on to say that most of the interesting questions lie outside the competence of science:

> Is the world divided into mind and matter, and, if so, what is mind, what is matter? ... Has the universe any unity or purpose? Is it evolving towards some goal? ... Is man what he seems to the astronomer, a tiny lump of impure carbon and water impotently crawling on a small and unimportant planet? Or is he what he appears to Hamlet? Is there a way of living that is noble and another that is base, or are all ways of living merely futile? ... To such questions no answers can be found in the laboratory.[51]

Richard Feynman captures this idea very well:

[handwritten: "Should do ---"]

[handwritten: Making]

> Scientists take all those things that *can* be analysed by observation, and thus the things called science are found out. But there are some things left out, for which the method does not work. This does not mean that those things are unimportant. They are in many ways the most important. In any decision for action, when you have to make up your mind what to do, there is always a 'should' involved and this cannot be worked out from: 'If I do this, what will happen?' alone.[52]

[handwritten: Ethical Values]

He later says 'ethical values lie outside the scientific realm'.[53]

What we are saying here has been familiar since the time of Aristotle, who distinguished between what he called four causes: the material cause (the material of which the cake is made); the formal cause (the form into which the materials are shaped); the efficient cause (the work of Aunt Matilda the cook); and the final cause (the purpose for which the cake was made – someone's birthday). It is the fourth of Aristotle's causes, the final cause, which is outside the scope of natural science.

Austin Farrar writes: 'Every science picks out an aspect of things in the world and shows how it goes. Everything that lies outside such a field lies outside the scope of that science. And since God is not a part of the world, still less an aspect of it, nothing that is said about God, however truly, can be a statement belonging to any science.'[54]

[handwritten: M – F – E – P]

Purpose?

Scientism self-destructs

In light of this, Peter Atkins' statements 'There is no reason to suppose that science cannot deal with every aspect of existence' (cited above) and 'There is nothing that cannot be understood'[55] seem to be completely off the wall. Not surprisingly, there is a high price to pay for attribution of such omni-competence to science: 'Science has no need of purpose... all the extraordinary, wonderful richness of the world can be expressed as growth from the dunghill of purposeless interconnected corruption.'[56] One wonders what Aunt Matilda would make of that as an ultimate explanation for the fact that she made the cake for her nephew Jimmy's birthday, indeed as an ultimate explanation of why she, Jimmy, and the birthday cake existed in the first place. She might even prefer a 'primeval soup' to a 'dunghill of corruption', if she were offered the choice.

It is one thing to suggest that science cannot answer questions of ultimate purpose. It is quite another to dismiss purpose itself as an illusion because science cannot deal with it. And yet, Atkins is simply taking his materialism to its logical conclusion – or perhaps not quite. After all, the existence of a dunghill presupposes the existence of creatures capable of making dung! Rather odd then to think of the dung as creating the creatures. And if it is a 'dunghill of corruption' (in line with, one might suppose, the second law of thermodynamics) one might wonder how the corruption gets reversed. The mind boggles.

But what undermines scientism is the fatal flaw of self-contradiction that runs through it. Scientism does not need to be refuted by external argument: it self-destructs. It suffers the same fate as in earlier times did the verification principle that was at the heart of the philosophy of logical-positivism. For, the statement that only science can lead to truth is not itself deduced from science. It is not a scientific statement but rather a statement about science, that is, it is a meta-scientific statement. *illogical* Therefore, if scientism's basic principle is true, the statement expressing scientism must be false. Scientism refutes itself. Hence it is incoherent.

Medawar's view that science is limited is, therefore, no insult to science. The very reverse is the case. It is those scientists who make exaggerated claims for science who make it look ridiculous. They have unintentionally and perhaps unconsciously wandered from doing science into myth-making – incoherent myths at that.

Before we leave Aunt Matilda we should note that her simple story helps to sort out another common confusion to which we hinted earlier. We have seen how unaided scientific reasoning cannot find out why she made the cake; she must reveal it to us. But that does not mean reason is from that point on either irrelevant or inactive. The contrary is the case. For, understanding what she says when she tells us for whom the cake was made requires the use of our reason. We further need our reason to assess the credibility of her explanation. If she says she made the cake for her nephew Jimmy and we know that she has no nephew of that name, we will doubt her explanation; if we know she has a nephew of that name then her explanation will make sense. In other words, reason is not opposed to revelation – it is simply that her revelation of the purpose for which she made the cake supplies to reason information that unaided reason cannot access. But reason is absolutely essential to process that information. The point is that in cases where science is not our source of information, we cannot automatically assume that reason has ceased to function and evidence has ceased to be relevant.

When theists claim that there is Someone who stands in the same relationship to the universe that Aunt Matilda stands to her cake and that that Someone has revealed why the universe was created, they are not abandoning reason, rationality, and evidence at all. They are simply claiming that there are certain questions which unaided reason cannot answer and to answer them we need another source of information – in this instance, revelation from God. However, in order to understand and evaluate that revelation, reason is still absolutely essential. It was in this spirit that Francis Bacon talked of God's Two Books – the Book of Nature and the Bible. Reason, rationality, and evidence apply to both.

5

Worldviews and Their Relation to Science: Naturalism and its Shortcomings

*'If cows and horses or lions had hands and could draw,
then horses would draw the forms of gods like horses,
cows like cows, making their bodies similar in shape to
their own.'*
Xenophanes, 500 BC

We have already alluded to the fact that worldview presuppositions play a role in science and in this chapter we explore this matter more deeply. We concentrate on the two main worldviews of naturalism and theism and their relationship with science. It turns out that, though there is no real conflict between science and God, there is a conflict between the worldviews of naturalism and theism. That leads us on to consider the worldviews of reductionism and scientism, each of which has a fatal flaw in comparison with theism. Scientism, or scientific fundamentalism, is the notion that science can, at least potentially, explain everything. We shall show that it is not only false but logically incoherent.

Worldview families

A worldview can be likened to a pair of coloured glasses through which we look at the world. They impose their colour on everything we see. Each one of us has such glasses. They consist of what we believe about the world. They contain our set of answers to all kinds of questions including the big questions of existence. It forms a reference frame that shapes our thinking. Questions like: What is the nature of reality? Is the universe a product of matter, plus time, plus chance – or is it a creation? Does life have a meaning?

Is there life after death? Worldviews are belief systems and fall into three main families: theism, atheism, and pantheism that can be roughly thought of as follows. **Theism** believes that there is a God who created and upholds the universe but is distinct from it; **atheism** believes that the universe exists but God doesn't; and **pantheism** tends to fuse god(s) with universe into something impersonal.

As we have already seen, the two worldviews that tend to be of greatest interest in the science–religion debate, particularly in the West, are:

- atheism in the form of naturalism and materialism
- theism in the form of Judaism, Christianity, and Islam.

Here we reach one of the major points we wish to make in this book. I believe that there is a conflict, but it is not really a conflict, between science and religion in the sense that not all scientists are atheists – belief in God is not confined to non-scientists, as we have seen.

The real conflict is in fact between atheism and theism – two *worldviews* that conflict, indeed, are mutually exclusive, by definition. Philosopher Alvin Plantinga has written an important book dedicated to the thesis that: 'there is superficial conflict but deep concord between science and theistic religion, but superficial concord and deep conflict between science and naturalism'.[1] For the sake of clarity, we note that naturalism is related to, but not identical with, materialism; although sometimes they are difficult to tell apart. *The Oxford Companion to Philosophy* says that the complexity of the concept of matter has meant that 'the various materialist philosophies have tended to substitute for "matter" some notion like: "whatever it is that can be studied by the methods of natural science", thus turning materialism into naturalism; though it would be an exaggeration to say the two outlooks have simply coincided'.[2]

Materialists are naturalists. But there are naturalists who hold that mind and consciousness are to be distinguished from matter. They regard the former as 'emergent' phenomena; that is, dependent on matter, but occurring on a higher level which is not reducible to the lower-level properties of matter. There are also other naturalists who hold that the universe consists purely of 'mind stuff'. Naturalism, however, in common with materialism, stands opposed to supernaturalism, insisting that: 'the world of nature should form a single sphere without incursions from outside by souls or spirits, divine or human'.[3] Whatever their differences, materialism and naturalism are, therefore, intrinsically atheistic.

Furthermore, materialism/naturalism comes in different versions. For example, E. O. Wilson, in an article in *Harvard Magazine*, distinguishes two. The first is what he calls political behaviourism:

> Still beloved by the now rapidly fading Marxist–Leninist states, it says that the brain is largely a blank slate devoid of any inborn inscription beyond reflexes and primitive bodily urges. ... Because there is no biologically based 'human nature', people can be moulded to the best possible political and economic system, namely, as urged upon the world through most of the twentieth century, communism. In practical politics, this belief has been repeatedly tested and, after economic collapses and tens of millions of deaths in a dozen dysfunctional states, is generally deemed a failure.[4]

The second, Wilson's own view, he calls scientific humanism, a worldview that he thinks 'drains the fever swamps of religion and blank-slate dogma'. He defines it as follows:

> Still held by only a tiny minority of the world's population, it considers humanity to be a biological species that evolved over millions of years in a biological world, acquiring unprecedented intelligence yet still guided by complex inherited emotions and biased channels of learning. Human nature exists and it was self-assembled. It is the commonality of the hereditary responses and propensities that define our species.[5]

Further, Wilson asserts that it is this Darwinian view that 'imposes the heavy burden of individual choice that goes with intellectual freedom'.[6] It goes beyond the scope of this book to consider the various nuances of these and other views. We wish here to concentrate on what is essentially common to all of them, something that astronomer Carl Sagan expressed with elegant economy in the opening words of his acclaimed 1980 television series *Cosmos: A Personal Voyage*: 'The cosmos is all there is, or was, or ever shall be.' This is the essence of naturalism.

Sterling Lamprecht's definition is longer but nevertheless worth recording. He defines naturalism to be: 'a philosophical position, empirical method that regards everything that exists or occurs to be conditioned in its existence or occurrence by causal factors within one all-encompassing system of nature'.[7] In other words, there is nothing but nature. It is a closed system of cause and effect. There is no realm of the transcendent or supernatural. There is no 'outside'.

Diametrically opposed to naturalism and materialism is the theistic view of the universe that finds clear expression in the opening words of Genesis: 'In the beginning God created the heavens and the earth.'[8] Here is an assertion that the universe is not a closed system but a creation, an artefact designed and produced by the mind of God, maintained and upheld by him. It is an answer to the question: Why does the universe exist? It exists because God causes it to be.

The Genesis statement is a statement of belief, not a statement of science, in exactly the same way as Sagan's assertion is not a statement of science, but of his personal belief. Thus the key issue is, we repeat, not so much the relationship of the discipline of science to that of theology, but the relationship of science to the various worldviews held by scientists, in particular to naturalism and theism. Thus, when we ask if science has buried God, we are talking at the level of the interpretation of science. What we are really asking is: Which worldview does science support, naturalism or theism?

E. O. Wilson is in no doubt of the answer: scientific humanism is 'the only worldview compatible with science's growing knowledge of the real world and the laws of nature'.[9] Quantum chemist and Nobel Prize nominee Henry F. Schaeffer III is in no doubt of his answer either: 'A Creator must exist. The Big Bang ripples and subsequent scientific findings are clearly pointing to an *ex nihilo* creation consistent with the first few verses of the book of Genesis.'[10]

Natural science and naturalism

As we have seen the word 'science' is often qualified by the adjective 'natural'. This means first of all that the things studied by science are the things found in nature. But it may also imply that the explanations to be given of such things can count as scientific only if they are couched solely in terms of physics, chemistry, and natural processes. Certainly this is a very common view.

For example, Professor of Ecology and Evolution Massimo Pigliucci states that 'The basic assumption of science is that the world can be explained entirely in physical terms, without recourse to godlike entities.'[11]

This is a remarkable statement to make when quantum mechanics shows that this is not the case. Yet the view persists. In a similar vein Nobel laureate Christian de Duve writes:

> Scientific enquiry rests on the notion that all manifestations in the universe are explainable in natural terms, without supernatural intervention. Strictly speaking, this notion is... a *postulate*, a working hypothesis that we should be prepared to abandon if faced with facts that defy every attempt at rational explanation. Many scientists, however, do not bother to make this distinction, tacitly extrapolating from hypothesis to affirmation. They are perfectly happy with the explanations provided by science. Like Laplace, they have no need for the 'God hypothesis' and equate the scientific attitude with agnosticism, if not with outright atheism.[12]

Here is a clear admission by a world-class scientist that, for many, science is practically inseparable from a metaphysical commitment to an agnostic or atheistic viewpoint. We notice in passing the subtle implication that 'supernatural intervention' is to be equated with 'defying every attempt at rational explanation'. In other words, 'supernatural' implies 'non-rational'. To those of us who have engaged in serious theological reflection, this will seem quite wrong-headed: the notion that there is a Creator God is a rational notion, not a non-rational one. To equate 'rational explanation' with 'natural explanation' is at best an indicator of a strong prejudice, at worst a category mistake. To think that rational is co-extensive with scientific is just as wrong-headed. Universities are devoted to rational thought and to equate rationality with science would lead to the absurd exclusion of the humanities as rational disciplines.

Yet, De Duve's view was shared by the judge in *Kitzmiller et al. vs Dover Area School District* (2005) in deciding that 'Intelligent Design' is a religious and not a scientific view. Judge Jones states forthrightly:

> Expert testimony reveals that since the scientific revolution of the sixteenth and seventeenth centuries, science has been limited to the search for natural causes to explain natural phenomena... While supernatural explanations may be important and have merit, they are not part of science...

> This self-imposed convention of science which limits inquiry
> to testable, natural explanations about the natural world, is
> referred to by philosophers as 'methodological naturalism'
> and is sometimes known as the scientific method ... which
> requires scientists to seek explanations in the world around us
> based upon what we can observe, test, replicate, and verify.[13]

This 'ground rule' assumes that God, if he exists, *does* nothing in the world. By definition, it has nothing to say about God's existence. One can understand why such an approach is attractive. In the first place it makes for a clear distinction between good science and superstition, between astronomy and astrology, or between chemistry and alchemy.

Philosopher Paul Kurtz goes much further: 'What is common to naturalistic philosophy is its commitment to science. Indeed, naturalism might be defined in its more general sense as the philosophical generalizations of the methods and conclusions of the sciences.'[14] This means that, in his view, science leads to atheism, as naturalism is by definition atheistic. That is a quantum leap beyond *methodological* naturalism into a worldview, indeed an ideology.

However, there is at least one serious down-side to Kurtz's view. His suggestion of such a close relationship between science and naturalism could – and indeed often does – mean that any data, phenomena, or interpretations of such, that did not comfortably fit the naturalistic worldview might experience resistance. Now, of course, this is only a down-side if naturalism is false as a philosophy. If naturalism is true, then such problem will never arise, even if the naturalistic explanation of a given phenomenon takes many years to discover. The question that needs to be faced, though, is whether or not naturalism is actually true.

Notice further that Kurtz defines naturalism as a philosophy that *arises out of* the natural sciences. That is, in his view, the scientist first studies the universe, formulates her theories, and then sees that a naturalistic or materialistic philosophy is demanded by them. However, as we have already pointed out, the picture of a scientific 'tabula rasa', of a completely open mind, free of philosophical pre-commitment brought to the study of the natural world, is seriously misleading. For some scientists admit that what may actually happen is precisely the reverse of what Kurtz suggests.

For instance, immunologist George Klein, states categorically that his atheism is *not* based on science, but is an *a priori* faith commitment.

[handwritten: prior commitment]

[handwritten: Natural vs Supernatural]

Commenting on a letter in which one of his friends described him as an agnostic, he writes: 'I am not an agnostic. I am an atheist. My attitude is not based on science, but rather on faith... The absence of a Creator, the non-existence of God is my childhood faith, my adult belief, unshakable and holy.'[15] We notice in passing the idea that Klein, in common with Dawkins, holds that faith and science are in opposition, a notion to which we shall take exception.

Similarly, in his review of Carl Sagan's last book, the distinguished Harvard geneticist Richard Lewontin explicitly states that his materialism is *a priori*. He not only confesses that his materialism does not derive from his science, but he also admits, on the contrary, that it is his materialism that actually consciously determines the nature of what he conceives science to be. That means, he tells us, that the key to grasping the 'struggle between science and the supernatural' lies in the fact that scientists are prepared to accept constructs that are clearly absurd. They are willing to put up with 'unsubstantiated just-so' stories because of their prior commitment to the materialist worldview. Then he makes a stunning admission:

> It is not that the methods and institutions of science somehow compel us to accept a material explanation of the phenomenal world but, on the contrary, that we are forced by our *a priori* adherence to material causes to create an apparatus of investigation and a set of concepts that produce material explanations, no matter how counter-intuitive, no matter how mystifying to the uninitiated.[16]

This statement is as astonishing as it is honest.[17] And it is poles apart from Kurtz's assertion that naturalism (or materialism) derives from science. Moreover, Lewontin claims that there is a struggle between 'science and the supernatural', and yet at once contradicts himself by admitting that science carries no compulsion within itself to force materialism upon us.

This supports our contention that the real battle is not so much between science and faith in God, but rather between a materialistic or, more broadly, a naturalistic worldview and a supernatural, or theistic, worldview. After all, Lewontin's faith (= trust = belief) in materialism, like that of Klein, is self-confessedly *not* rooted in his science but on something completely different, as becomes clear from what he says next: 'Moreover, that materialism is absolute, for we cannot allow a Divine foot in the door.'[18]

I am not so sure that Dawkins would be as enthusiastic about eradicating this kind of 'blind faith' in materialism as he is about eradicating faith in God, though consistency would argue that he should. And what, in any case, is the precise force of the word 'cannot' in connection with allowing a Divine foot in the door? If, as Lewontin says, science does not force us to be materialists, then his use of the word 'cannot' clearly does not imply that science is incapable of indicating the existence of a Divine foot. It must simply mean that 'we materialists cannot allow a Divine foot in the door'. Well, of course, it is a tautology to say that 'materialists cannot allow a Divine foot in the door'. That assertion has nothing whatsoever to do with science.

Materialism rejects both the Divine foot and, come to think of it, anything else that might be attached to it as well, since the idea of a door into something bigger is more than atheism can cope with. There is after all, no 'outside' for a materialist – the 'cosmos is all that is, was, or ever shall be', a closed system of cause and effect. But that rejection carries no implications whatsoever about the existence of such a foot or door beyond the mere unsubstantiated assertion that Lewontin personally does not believe in either of them.

After all, if a physicist deliberately designs a machine that is capable of detecting radiation only within the visible spectrum, then, however useful her machine is, it would be absurd for her to try to use it to deny the existence of, for example, X-rays, that it cannot, by construction, see. Also, how Lewontin can hold to his materialistic views in light of quantum mechanics is a complete mystery (see Chapter 21).

Methodological naturalism

It would, of course, be as false to deny that good science can be done by scientists committed to materialistic or naturalistic assumptions as it would be to deny that good science can be done by theists. What is more, lest we lose our sense of proportion, we should bear in mind that, by and large, science done on atheistic presuppositions will lead to the same results as science done on theistic presuppositions.[19] For example, when trying to find out in practice *how* an organism functions, it matters little whether one assumes that it is *actually* designed, or only *apparently* designed – referring to Richard Dawkins' characterization of biology as: 'the study of complicated things that give the appearance of having been designed for a purpose'[20] – a descriptor that we shall discuss later.

Here the assumption of either 'methodological naturalism' (sometimes called 'methodological atheism') or what we might equally reasonably call 'methodological theism' will lead to essentially the same results. This is so for the very simple reason that the organism in question is being treated methodologically as if it had been designed in both cases.

This consideration should lessen whatever tensions may exist between scientists of different worldview persuasions, at least when it comes to the practical doing of their work. For, the design hypothesis – apparent or real – has been very fruitful in scientific research. Historian of science Timothy Lenoir points out that: 'Teleological thinking has been steadfastly resisted by modern biology. And yet, in nearly every area of research biologists are hard pressed to find language that does not impute purposiveness to living forms.'[21] These days, texts on biology are full of words like 'design', 'machine', and 'purpose'.

The danger of terms such as 'methodological atheism' or 'methodological naturalism' is that they might be understood as lending support to an atheistic worldview, and therefore giving the impression that atheism had something to do with the success of the science – which might not be the case at all. To see this point even more clearly, just imagine what would happen if the term 'methodological theism' were to be employed in the literature instead of the term 'methodological atheism'. It would be howled down at once on the basis that it could give the impression that it was the theism that had contributed to the success of the science.

And yet we find, rather incongruously, that there are scientists with *theistic* convictions who insist on defining science in explicitly naturalistic terms, thus bringing worldviews directly into their science. Ernan McMullin writes:

> methodological naturalism does not restrict our study of nature, it just lays down which sort of study qualifies as science. If someone wants to pursue another approach to nature – and there are many others – the methodological naturalist has no reason to object. Scientists have to proceed in this way; the methodology of science gives no purchase on the claim that a particular event or type of event is to be explained by invoking God's creative action directly.[22]

There is an important difference between Lewontin and McMullin. Lewontin will not allow a Divine foot – full stop. For McMullin there may well be a Divine foot but science has nothing to say about it. For him there are other approaches to nature, but they do not qualify as scientific and so they may inevitably be regarded as less authoritative. They may, however, be rational approaches. We would like to suggest that neither the expression 'methodological naturalism' nor the expression 'methodological theism' is particularly helpful: better to avoid both.

However, it is one thing to eschew the use of certain unhelpful terminology. What no scientists can avoid is having their own *a priori* philosophical commitments. Those commitments, as we have just said, are not likely to figure very largely, if at all, when we are studying *how things work*, but they may well play a much more dominant role when we are studying *how things came to exist in the first place*, or when we are studying things that bear on our understanding of ourselves as human beings.

Reductionism – put into a firmula.

One very useful explanatory method used in the natural sciences is that of expressing complex things in terms of simpler things – for instance, water in terms of its constituent elements: hydrogen and oxygen. We say that water can be *reduced* to hydrogen and oxygen. This procedure is called (methodological) *reductionism*. That there are limits to its explanatory power is borne out by the history of science, which teaches us that it is important to balance our justifiable enthusiasm for reduction in the contexts where it works, by bearing in mind that there may well be, and often is, more to a given whole than what we obtain by adding up all that we have learned from the parts.

For instance, studying all the parts of a watch separately will not necessarily enable you to grasp how the complete watch works as an integrated whole. There are many composite systems in which understanding the individual parts of the system is impossible without an understanding of the system as a whole. One of the prime examples of this is the living cell.

The place to start, however, is with something that is fundamental to all of science – mathematics. No one can fail to be impressed by the way in which the language of mathematics is used to reduce or compress the description of often very complex phenomena into short and elegant equations. Think of the phenomenal achievement of Kepler in taking Tycho Brahe's many observations of the motion of Mars and compressing them into the single statement that it and the other planets moved in elliptical orbits with the sun at one focus. Or take Newton's further compression or reduction of Kepler's work in his law of gravitation.

Similarly, the equations of Maxwell, Einstein, Schrödinger, and Dirac are among the most famous iconic examples of the triumph of mathematical reduction, and the ongoing quest for a TOE (Theory of Everything) is driven by the desire to achieve the ultimate mathematical compression by uniting the four fundamental forces of nature.

The great mathematician David Hilbert, spurred on by the remarkable achievements of mathematical compression, proposed a programme to reduce all of mathematics to a collection of formal statements in a finite set of symbols together with a finite set of axioms and rules of inference. The hope was to show that such a system could encapsulate all of mathematics in a way that is provably consistent and such that the truth or otherwise of all mathematical statements could be settled. It was a seductive thought with the ultimate in 'bottom-up' explanation as the glittering prize.

In a little more detail, Hilbert's Programme involved using mathematical symbols or letters in a precisely defined language, in which the basic truths or axioms of mathematics could be expressed. The symbols are to be regarded as marks on the paper without any meaning attached; they are then used to write mathematical statements, again without any attention to 'significance' or meaning, let alone truth. For example, the statements $x + y = y + x$ and $2 + 3 = 9$ are to be viewed as merely sequences of marks (even though we give them meaning, and see them as true and false respectively). Then, using precise rules of logical deduction, formal consequences of the axioms are deduced giving the collection of provable statements. It was hoped that in such a logical system, for every possible statement S, either S or not-S could be proved starting from the axioms, showing that the system is complete. Then, mathematical truth would have been reduced to provability and this would in turn provide a general algorithmic process for deciding the truth or falsity (in this sense) of any mathematical statement S in the language – a solution to the so-called *Entscheidungsproblem*.[23] How? By systematically working through all possible proofs and eventually finding either a proof of S or a proof of not-S. Completeness would guarantee that one or the other would be found eventually. Hilbert's programme went even further: he envisioned a proof that this formal approach to mathematics is consistent – that is, free from any inherent contradictions – and that the proof of that would be finitistic and therefore beyond dispute.

Hilbert and others felt intuitively that this programme could be achieved, but their intuition proved wrong. In 1931 the Austrian mathematician Kurt Gödel published a paper entitled 'On Formally Undecidable Propositions of *Principia Mathematica* and Related Systems'. His paper, though only twenty-five pages long, caused the mathematical equivalent of an earthquake whose reverberations are still with us. For Gödel had actually proved that Hilbert's Programme was doomed – it is unrealizable.

In a piece of mathematics that stands as an intellectual tour-de-force of the first magnitude, Gödel demonstrated that the arithmetic with which we are all familiar is incomplete: that is, in any logical system that has an explicit set of axioms and rules of inference and includes the basic rules of ordinary arithmetic, there is always a statement G (often called a Gödel statement) such that neither G nor not-G can be proved on the basis of that set of axioms and those rules of inference. This result is known as Gödel's first incompleteness theorem. However, if the notion of truth is admitted, then on an informal level G is clearly true because it is a mathematical coding of the statement 'G is not provable'. In other words, there are intuitively true mathematical facts that are unprovable.

As noted above, Hilbert's Programme also aimed to prove the essential consistency of his formulation of mathematics as a formal system. Gödel's first incompleteness theorem actually had an important assumption – namely that the system is consistent. In his second incompleteness theorem Gödel cleverly used this to deal the final blow to Hilbert's Programme. He proved that one of the statements that cannot be proved in a sufficiently strong formal system is the consistency of the system itself – provided of course that it actually is consistent. In other words, if arithmetic is consistent then that fact is one of the true things that cannot be proved in the system. It is something that we can only believe on the basis of the evidence, or by appeal to higher axioms. This has been succinctly summarized by saying that if a religion is something whose foundations are based on faith, then mathematics is the only religion that can prove it is a religion!

And this is implicitly the case with almost all practising mathematicians, who accept the modern theory of sets as the foundation for the whole mathematical enterprise. Set theory is subject to Gödel's two theorems, so is incomplete (meaning that there is still a role for mathematical discovery – thankfully mathematicians cannot be replaced by computers!); and, if it is free from contradictions, we can never know that for certain. Nevertheless, the cumulative evidence of more than a century of mathematical activity leads most mathematicians to believe that set theory is consistent.

One upshot of all this is that reduction fails in mathematics. In any bottom-up formulation of mathematics, Gödel has shown us that there will be statements whose truth cannot be settled without going outside the formulation. When these are discovered there is the option to add them as basic axioms if they seem reasonable or fruitful (and there are many examples of this in mathematics). However, no matter what is added to try to complete the system, the new system will have the same limitations. In informal terms, as the British-born American physicist and mathematician Freeman Dyson puts it, 'Gödel proved that in mathematics the whole is always greater than the sum of the parts'.[24] Thus there is a limit to reduction. Therefore, Peter Atkins' statement, cited earlier, that 'the only grounds for supposing that reductionism will fail are pessimism in the minds of the scientists and fear in the minds of the religious' is incorrect. It failed in mathematics.

In addition to methodological reduction, there are two further important types of reduction: epistemological and ontological. They both lead to reductionisms. Epistemological reductionism is the view that higher level phenomena can *always* be explained by processes at a lower level – namely that bottom-up explanations can *always* be achieved without remainder. That means, for example, chemistry can ultimately be explained by physics; biochemistry by chemistry; biology by biochemistry; psychology by biology; sociology by brain science; and theology by sociology. As the Nobel Prize-winning molecular biologist Francis Crick puts it: 'The ultimate aim of the modern development in biology is, in fact, to explain all biology in terms of physics and chemistry.'[25] This strong reductionist view is shared by Richard Dawkins: 'My task is to explain elephants, and the world of complex things, in terms of the simple things that physicists either understand, or are working on.'[26] This is ontological reductionism – from the Greek word *ontos* meaning being. All existing things can be explained in terms of physics and chemistry.

physicalism

There is No life in the matter & energy per say

Leaving aside for the moment the very questionable assertion that the subject matter of physics is simple – quantum electrodynamics and string theory are fiendishly complicated – the ultimate goal of such reductionism is evidently to represent everything in nature including all human behaviour – our likes and dislikes, the entire mental landscape of our lives – in terms of physics and chemistry. This materialist view is often called *physicalism*.

With this we come to the heart of one of the major issues to be discussed at length in this book. Reductionism is demanded by a materialist worldview, which is one reason why there is such pressure from atheist scientists to espouse it particularly in biology. Reductionism is therefore at the centre of the science–religion debate. If 'bottom-up' is the only legitimate form of explanation, then there is, by definition, no ultimate top-down causation. Therefore, God is dead and science has buried him. If, on the other hand, reductionism is provably inadequate to cover all scientific explanation, then talk of God's decease is premature.

However, ontological reductionism has been seriously undermined and that has led to a radical rethinking of fundamental questions of science that bear directly upon the science–religion debate. In fact, biology is not part of physics and chemistry as eminent evolutionary biologists like Jacques Monod[27] and Ernst Mayr[28] have pointed out. Biology is no more part of physics and chemistry, than quantum mechanics is part of Newtonian physics.

More recently, world-ranking philosopher Thomas Nagel wrote a book in 2012 with a subtitle that would, in all probability, have been rejected as politically incorrect by publishers even a few years ago: *Mind and Cosmos: Why the Materialist Neo-Darwinian Conception of the World is Almost Certainly False*. Nagel says:

> Physico-chemical reductionism in biology is the orthodox view, and any resistance to it is regarded as not only scientifically but politically incorrect. But for a long time I have found the materialist account of how we and our fellow organisms came to exist hard to believe, including the standard version of how the evolutionary process works. The more details we learn about the chemical basis of life and the intricacy of the genetic code, the more unbelievable the standard historical account becomes.[29]

Reductionism — major issue of debate

Bottom up or Top down

This is exactly what I learned from R. E. D. Clark over fifty years ago. I am glad at long last to see that it is now gaining support from some leading biologists whose increasing scepticism about neo-Darwinism, now often called the modern synthesis, has taken concrete shape, as we shall see in Chapter 19. Now Nagel is an atheist, indeed a hard atheist in the sense that he says he hopes there isn't a God, he doesn't even want there to be a God. This greatly increases the importance of his book since, as we have seen, for an atheist the presupposition of reductionism is virtually unavoidable. Nevertheless, Nagel hopes one day to come up with some alternative to theism, although he honestly admits that he has so far failed to do so.

I agree with Nagel about reductionism but, by contrast with him, I do believe that the God explanation, or, at least, the hypothesis of top-down intelligent causation behind the universe and life, is the only one that is capable of giving a satisfactory answer to the difficulties that Nagel raises.

We shall therefore need to consider various aspects of reductionism, particularly its ontological form that permeates science today to a greater depth than is sometimes realized. It is not, however, a view which commends universal support, and that is for very good reasons. As Karl Popper pointed out: 'There is almost always an unresolved residue left by even the most successful attempts at reduction.'[30] Scientist and philosopher Michael Polanyi[31] showed why it is intrinsically implausible to expect epistemological reductionism to work in every circumstance. He asks us to think of the various process levels involved in constructing an office building with bricks. First of all there is the process of extracting the raw materials out of which the bricks have to be made. Then there are the successively higher levels of making the bricks – they do not make themselves; brick-laying – the bricks do not 'self-assemble'; designing the building – it does not design itself; and planning the town in which the building is to be built – it does not organize itself.

Each level has its own rules. The laws of physics and chemistry govern the raw material of the bricks; technology prescribes the art of brick-making; brick-layers lay the bricks as directed by the builders according to the plan developed by architects who in turn are subject to regulation by town planners. Each level is controlled by the level above. But the reverse is not true. The laws of a higher level cannot be derived from the laws of a lower level, although what can be done at a higher level will, of course, depend on the lower levels. For example, if the bricks are not strong there will be a limit on the height of the building that can safely be built with them.

Or take another example, quite literally to your hand at this moment. Consider the page you are reading just now. It consists of paper imprinted with ink (or perhaps it is a series of dots on the computer screen in front of you). It is surely obvious that the physics and chemistry of ink and paper (or pixels on a computer monitor) can never, even in principle, tell you anything about the significance of the shapes of the letters on the page (or the arrangement of the pixels). This has nothing to do with the fact that physics and chemistry are not yet sufficiently advanced to deal with this question. No matter how much time we allow for these sciences to develop, it will make no difference, because the shapes of those letters demand a totally new and higher level of explanation than physics and chemistry are capable of giving.

In fact, complete explanation can only be given in terms of higher level concepts such as language and authorship, the communication of a message by a person, the existence of minds. The ink and paper are carriers of the message, but the message certainly does not arise automatically from them. Furthermore, when it comes to language itself, there is again a sequence of levels. You cannot derive a vocabulary from phonetics, or the grammar of a language from its vocabulary, etc.[32]

As is well known, the genetic material DNA found in living cells carries information. We shall discuss this fundamentally important idea in more detail in later chapters. Sufficient for the time being is the basic idea that the DNA in the human genome can be thought of as a long tape on which there is a string of letters written in a four-letter chemical alphabet. The sequence of letters contains coded instructions (information) that the cell uses to make proteins. But the *order* of the letters in the sequence is not, indeed, cannot be, generated by the chemistry of the base letters themselves, as we shall see. This is a very important further instance of the failure of physicalism.

In each of the above examples, we have a series of levels, each higher than the previous one in the sense that what happens on the higher level is dependent on, but not completely derivable from, what happens on the level beneath it. In this situation it is sometimes said that the higher level phenomena 'emerge' from the lower level.

Unfortunately, however, the word 'emerge' is easily misunderstood, and even misused, to imply that the higher level properties arise *automatically* from the lower level properties without any further input of information or organization, although this does happen sometimes. For example, the higher level properties of water emerge from combining

self-organize, self-replicate

oxygen and hydrogen. However, automatic, unaided, emergence is clearly false in general, as in the case of building and writing on paper. The building does not *emerge* from the bricks nor the writing from the paper and ink without the injection of both energy and intelligent activity.

The same argument applies to the illustration of emergence offered by Dawkins in answer to a question I asked him at a public lecture in Oxford (20 January 1999). He replied that the capacity to do word-processing is an 'emergent' property of computers. Well, yes, but only at the expense of the additional input of large quantities of information contained in an intelligently designed software package like Microsoft Word.

The British theologian and biochemist Arthur Peacocke wrote: 'In no way can the concept of "information", the concept of conveying a message, be articulated in terms of the concepts of physics and chemistry, even though the latter can be shown to explain how the molecular machinery (DNA, RNA and protein) operates to carry information....'[33]

Yet, notwithstanding the fact that writing on paper, computer software and DNA have in common the fact that they encode a 'message', those scientists committed to materialistic philosophy insist that the information-carrying properties of DNA must ultimately have emerged automatically out of matter *by a mindless, unguided, process.*

The driving force behind their insistence is obvious. For if, as materialism holds, matter and energy are all that exists, then it follows logically that matter and energy *must* possess the inherent potential to organize themselves in such a way that eventually all the complex molecules necessary for life, including DNA, will emerge. On the basis of their materialistic hypotheses no other possibility is either conceivable or allowable. Whether there is any evidence that matter and energy actually possess this 'emergent' capacity is another thing altogether.

Next, we must come back to the third type of reductionism that we have actually jumped the gun by already mentioning. That is, ontological reductionism, which is closely related to epistemological reductionism. A classic example of it is given by Richard Dawkins: 'The universe is nothing but a collection of atoms in motion, human beings are simply machines for propagating DNA, and the propagation of DNA is a self-sustaining process. It is every living object's sole reason for living.'[34] It is this sort of reductionism that excludes God by definition. The words 'nothing but', 'sole', or 'simply', are the tell-tale signature of ontological reductionist thinking. If we remove these words we are usually left with something unobjectionable.

The universe certainly is a collection of atoms, and human beings do propagate DNA. Both of these statements are statements of science. But immediately we add the words 'nothing but', the statements go beyond science and become expressions of materialistic or naturalistic belief. The question is, do the statements remain true when we add those tell-tale words? Is there really nothing more to the universe and life than that?

Scientific fundamentalism

Science explains. For many people this encapsulates the power and the fascination of science. Science enables us to understand what we did not understand before; and, by giving us understanding of nature, it gives us power over nature. We have seen some of the ways in which science explains in terms of induction and abduction. A question remains: How much does science explain? Are there any limits to its explanatory power?

C. S. Lewis was not a scientist but his books demonstrate considerable understanding of the philosophy and methodology of science. He saw clearly that there were limits to science's explanatory power. In his famous book *Mere Christianity* he gave a memorable description of how science proceeds:

> Science works by experiments. It watches how things behave. Every scientific statement in the long run, however complicated it looks, really means something like, 'I pointed the telescope to such and such a part of the sky at 2:20 a.m. on January 15th and saw so-and-so,' or, 'I put some of this stuff in a pot and heated it to such-and-such a temperature and it did so-and-so.' Do not think I am saying anything against science: I am only saying what its job is.[35]

Lewis goes on to point out the (obvious but important) fact that the question as to why there is a universe for science to study is not one that science can answer. Nor can science answer the question as to whether there is anything behind the universe – since if there is then it will remain unknown or else it must reveal itself in some other manner.

According to Lewis, then, science cannot answer the really big ultimate questions about our existence and that of the universe. However, on the materialist end of the spectrum, there are those who hold that science is the only way to knowledge and truth. Science can, in their view at least in principle, explain everything. This view is called 'scientism'. It is exemplified by the late Stephen Hawking at the beginning of *The Grand Design* where he lists the kind of big question to which Lewis refers. Hawking then says: 'Traditionally these are questions for philosophy, but philosophy is dead. It has not kept up with modern developments in science, particularly in physics. As a result scientists have become the bearers of the torch of discovery in our quest for knowledge.'[36] This is scientism with a vengeance. Ironically, having declared philosophy to be dead, Hawking and Mlodinow nevertheless proceed, clearly unaware of what they are doing, to write a book on nothing other than (the) philosophy (of science)! Sad to say, but their scientism is philosophically illiterate. They would have profited from taking on board Albert Einstein's attitude to philosophy in general and to epistemology (the theory of knowledge – how we get to know things). Einstein wrote: 'The reciprocal relationship of epistemology and science is of noteworthy kind. They are dependent upon each other. Epistemology without contact with science becomes an empty scheme. Science without epistemology is – in so far as it is thinkable at all – primitive and muddled.'[37] Einstein also wrote: 'It has often been said, and certainly not without justification, that the man of science is a poor philosopher.'[38]

Peter Atkins gives what at first sight looks like a classic expression of scientism in a statement I quoted in the introduction: 'There is no reason to suppose that science cannot deal with every aspect of existence... But science has never encountered a barrier and the only grounds for supposing that reductionism will fail are pessimism on the part of scientists and fear in the minds of the religious.'[39]

I said 'at first sight' since it is not always entirely clear what Atkins means by 'science'. Let me try to explain. In English, the word 'science' is derived from the Latin *scientia* meaning 'knowledge' and originally 'science' denoted knowledge of all kinds. Nowadays, in the English-speaking world, it means almost exclusively the natural sciences – physics, chemistry, biology, and so on, as contrasted with the humanities – literature, languages, history, philosophy, theology, and the like.

However, the older usage still exists. In German, for instance, the word *Wissenschaft* means 'science' in the old sense and is divided into *'die Naturwissenschaften'* and *'die Geisteswissenchaften'* (the natural sciences and the humanities) although, just to confuse things a bit, *Wissenschaft* is often used to denote the natural sciences. Returning to Atkins' use of the word 'science', in his book *On Being* he writes: 'I stand by my claim that the scientific method is the only means of discovering the nature of reality,

Rational Inquiry!

and although its current views are open to revision, the approach, making observations and comparing notes, will forever survive as the only way of acquiring reliable knowledge.'[40]

Note that Atkins refers here not to science as such but to the scientific method, which he defines as consisting in making observations and comparing notes. This fits in with the old meaning of science as knowledge (*Wissenschaft*), since it is essentially a description of what is involved in any sort of rational enquiry and not just the natural sciences.

If this is what he means by 'science' then, of course, science can explain everything, since by explanation we normally mean a rational account that delivers knowledge and understanding. Knowledge of history, literature, economics, ethics, philosophy, theology, etc., is gained in this way. They are all rational disciplines. In particular, Christianity is firmly based on this kind of rational approach. But none of these rational disciplines is a natural science.

Nevertheless, Atkins, whom I have encountered in public debate on several occasions,[41] usually manages to give the impression that he believes that it is the prerogative of the natural sciences to explain everything. He regards all talk of God, religion, and religious experience as outside of science, and therefore does not constitute objective knowledge. Of course, like the rest of us, he can see that many people think about God and that such thinking can have emotional and even physical effects, some of which may be beneficial. But, for Atkins, thinking about God is like thinking about Father Christmas, dragons, hobgoblins, or fairies and leprechauns at the bottom of the garden.

Richard Dawkins thinks the same way. He dedicates his book *The God Delusion* to the memory of Douglas Adams with the following quote: 'Isn't it enough to see that a garden is beautiful without having to believe that there are fairies at the bottom of it?' However, the fact that you can think about fairies and be enchanted or terrified by them does not mean that they exist. The Douglas Adams quote gives the game away. It shows Dawkins erroneously proposing false alternatives: either fairies or nothing. Fairies at the bottom of the garden may well be a delusion, but what about a gardener, to say nothing about an owner? The possibility of their existence cannot be so summarily dismissed. In fact, most gardens have both.

Many scientists, are often, but not always, as we have seen, happy to let people go on thinking about God and religion if they want to, as long as they do not claim that God has any objective existence, or that religious belief constitutes knowledge. In other words, science and religion can peacefully co-exist provided religion does not invade the realm of science. For only science can tell us what is objectively true: only science can deliver knowledge. The bottom line would therefore seem to be that science deals with physical reality, religion does not. This, as I understand it, is essentially what the late Stephen Jay Gould meant by saying that science and religion constituted NOMA (Non-Overlapping Magisteria).

Furthermore, take the claim that only science in the sense of the natural sciences can deliver knowledge. If it were true, it would at once spell the end of many disciplines in schools and universities. For the evaluation of philosophy, literature, art, music lies outside the scope of science. How could science tell us whether a poem is a bad poem or a work of genius? Scarcely by measuring the lengths of the words or the frequencies of the letters occurring in them. How could science possibly tell us whether a painting is a masterpiece or a confused smudge of colours? Certainly not by making a chemical analysis of the paint and the canvas.

The teaching of morality likewise lies outside science. Science can tell you that if you add strychnine to someone's drink, it will kill them. But science cannot tell you whether it is morally right or wrong to put strychnine into your grandmother's tea so that you can get your hands on her property.

In the *Encylopedia of Religion and Science*, philosopher Mikael Stenmark writes:

> while the doctrines that are described as scientism have many possible forms and varying degrees of ambition, they share the idea that the boundaries of science (that is, typically the natural sciences) could and should be expanded so that something that has not been previously considered as a subject pertinent to science can now be understood as part of science (usually with science becoming the sole or the main arbiter regarding this area or dimension).[42]

According to Stenmark, the strongest form of scientism states that science has no boundaries and that all human problems and all aspects of human endeavour will, in due time, be dealt with and solved by science alone. Stenmark calls this scientific expansionism. It is a form of intellectual imperialism.

scientific fundamentalism

How do you know this?

I think the term 'scientific fundamentalism' is also an accurate, perhaps even a better descriptor. Fundamentalist aggression of any kind goes hand in hand with exaggerated claims to knowledge and truth. Scientism fits this description perfectly. Ian Hutchinson, an MIT physicist, warns in this connection of the 'knowledge domination of scientism' – the view that science is the only game in town.[43] After all, it is surely obvious, as I pointed out above, that if scientism were true, half the departments in each university would have to close and the British Academy would cease to exist. It might be worth replacing the term *scientism* by *scientific fundamentalism* in order to alert a wider public to its existence and dangers.

Cosmologist George Ellis FRS says that the essential nature of scientific fundamentalism, and of all other fundamentalisms, is that: 'a partial truth is proclaimed as the whole truth. Only one viewpoint is allowed on any issue, all others are false. This dogmatism is combined with an inability to relate understanding to context. Admitting that what is important varies with the context would undermine the fundamentalist's need to see the same single issue as dominant in every situation, come what may'.[44] Ellis regards such fundamentalism as 'a major problem'.[45]

Philosopher and mathematician Bertrand Russell once wrote: 'While it is true that science cannot decide questions of value, that is because they cannot be intellectually decided at all, and lie outside the realm of truth and falsehood. Whatever knowledge is attainable, must be attained by scientific methods; and what science cannot discover, mankind cannot know.'[46] Russell says that science cannot decide questions of value. He is certainly right there. Einstein once said: 'You can speak of the ethical foundations of science but not of the scientific foundations of ethics'.

However, to assert, as Russell does, that this is because questions of value cannot be intellectually decided at all is a remarkably arrogant dismissal of the serious and important *rational* discipline of ethics.

Russell was a mathematician and philosopher well versed in logic. Nevertheless, the last part of his statement – 'what science cannot tell us mankind cannot know' – is self-contradictory. In order to see that we simply have to ask: How does Russell know this? For his statement is not itself a statement of science and so if it is true then, according to the statement itself, it is unknowable – and yet Russell believes it to be true!

However, I may have misread Russell here. For, on the last page of his magisterial *History of Western Philosophy*, he says: 'In the welter of conflicting fanaticisms, one of the few unifying forces is scientific truthfulness, by which I mean the habit of basing our beliefs on observations and inferences as impersonal, and as much divested of local and temperamental bias as is possible for human beings.'[47]

Reflecting on Russell's earlier statement in light of this, I wonder if it is just possible that he is using the word 'science' in the same way as Peter Atkins: in its older sense to denote rational enquiry that gives us knowledge. If that is the case, then Russell's statement 'what science cannot tell us, mankind cannot know', although still confusing, becomes a little less of a contradiction.

6

Theism and its Relationship to Science: God of the Gaps, Complexity of God and Miracles

'Ascribing the origin of life to a divine miracle not only is anathema to scientists but also is theologically suspect.'
Paul Davies, physicist and author

'A miracle is a violation of the laws of nature; and as a firm and unalterable experience has established these laws, the proof against a miracle, from the very nature of the fact, is as entire as any argument from experience as can be imagined.'
David Hume

Theism is the view that there is a God who created and upholds the universe. Any 'God-explanation' will sooner or later encounter objections. We first consider the 'God-of-the-gaps' objection which amounts to: 'I can't explain it, so I believe God did it'. The mistake here is to regard the God explanation as the same type of explanation as the science explanation. Secondly, we look at Dawkins' 'complexity of God objection'.

The polar opposite of materialist/naturalist reductionist explanation is the explanation that involves God and the supernatural. It raises fundamental questions about the relationship between God and the universe. We consider what it means that God both created and upholds the universe.

We then examine the implication of this for science and, in particular, for one of science's basic assumptions – the uniformity of nature. The dominant view is that nature is not only uniform but absolutely uniform, so that science and the supernatural are incompatible. It is often assumed that this was shown by the seventeenth-century philosopher David Hume. In this chapter, therefore, we investigate Hume's arguments and show that they are fallacious. This involves studying the nature and status of the laws of nature. We argue that science cannot demonstrate that miracles of the kind to be found in the New Testament are impossible. Whether or not they actually happened is another matter, but we shall see that the in-principle possibility of there being a supernatural dimension is not inimical to science. This opens the way to consider as a legitimate scientific hypothesis that super-intelligence is involved in bringing about the origin of life.

The final part of the chapter is devoted to discussing chance and randomness – ideas that are for many people irreconcilable with the existence of God.

Theism

Theism is the worldview that there is a God. In its various manifestations it is the most widespread worldview on the planet. But what do we mean by *God?* When I debated Richard Dawkins in the Oxford Museum of Natural History on the question 'Has Science Buried God?' his initial response was to say: 'Which God?' – a perfectly valid inquiry. We soon settled down to concentrate on the supernatural God who both created the universe and upholds it. We have already seen that belief in such a God played a central role in the rise of modern science. Part of the reason for that is that the theistic worldview gives a coherent account of the presuppositions of science – that the universe is rationally intelligible and orderly. In the succeeding chapters we shall also argue that theism is strongly consistent with the findings of science in the sense that it provides explanation in terms of agency that complements scientific explanations in terms of law and mechanism. We contend that there is increasing *scientific* evidence that a creative mind/intelligence is responsible for the existence and operation of the universe.

Key

Gods of the gaps

In any discussion about science and religion, sooner or later the question of the 'God of the gaps' will be raised. This is the idea that the introduction of a god or God as explanation of any phenomenon is an evidence of intellectual laziness: we cannot explain something scientifically and so we introduce an explanation in terms of a 'god or God' to cover our ignorance or laziness. Putting it simply, it sounds like saying: 'I cannot understand it, therefore God did it.'

An example of this kind of thinking that is often cited is that due to Isaac Newton in his letter to Bentley dated 11 February 1692/3. Referring to an earlier letter Newton wrote:

> In my former I represented that the diurnal rotations of the Planets could not be derived from gravity but required a divine power to impress them.... I would now add that the Hypothesis of matters being at first eavenly spread through the heavens is, in my opinion, inconsistent with the Hypothesis of innate gravity without a supernatural power to reconcile them, & therefore it infers a Deity.[1]

Thus, gravity could account for some motions but not for diurnal rotation – God had done that. This looks like classic God-of-the-gaps thinking. However, we mentioned earlier that in the *General Scholium* (the addition to the second edition of *Principia*) Newton wrote: 'This most beautiful System of the Sun, Planets and Comets, could only proceed from the counsel and dominion of an intelligent and powerful being.' This statement indicates that Newton did not think of God *only* as a God of the gaps. What Perry Marshall calls the 'evil twin' to thinking that God did it is to think that God had nothing to do with it.[2] Newton was not in that category.

We shall have more to say about this later, but at this juncture it is important to point out that Mr Ford is not to be found in the gaps in our knowledge about the workings of internal combustion engines. More precisely, he is not to be found in any reason-giving explanations that concern mechanisms. For Henry Ford is not a mechanism: yet he is the no less real agent who was responsible for the existence of the mechanism in the first place[3] so that it *all* bears the marks of his handiwork – and that means the bits we do understand and the bits we don't.

So it is with God. At the more abstract level of the explanatory power of science itself, philosopher Richard Swinburne in his book *Is there a God?* says:

Note that I am not postulating a 'God of the gaps', a god merely to explain the things that science has not yet explained. I am postulating a God to explain why science explains; I do not deny that science explains, but I postulate God to explain why science explains. The very success of science in showing us how deeply ordered the natural world is provides strong grounds for believing that there is an even deeper cause for that order.[4]

Swinburne is using inference to the best explanation and saying that God is the best explanation for the explanatory power of science.

The point to grasp here is that, God is not to be understood merely as a God of the gaps since he is not an alternative to science as an explanation. On the contrary, he is the ground of all explanation. It is his existence which gives rise to the very possibility of explanation, scientific or otherwise. It is important to stress this because influential authors such as Richard Dawkins will insist on conceiving of God as an explanatory alternative to science, an idea that is nowhere to be found in theological reflection of any depth. Dawkins is therefore tilting at a windmill in dismissing a concept of God that no serious thinker believes in anyway. Such activity is not necessarily to be regarded as a mark of intellectual sophistication. The brilliant scientist James Clerk Maxwell, who discovered the mathematical equations governing electromagnetism, understood this well when he had inscribed over the door of the famous Cavendish Physics laboratory in Cambridge the words: 'Great are the works of the Lord; they are pondered by all who delight in them.'[5]

As we look back over the history of science we have every reason to be grateful to those who took the brave step of questioning the mythological view of nature that endowed various bits of the universe with divine powers that they did not possess. We have seen that some of them did so, not only without rejecting the concept of a Creator, but in the very name of that Creator. Perhaps there is a subtle danger today that, in their desire to eliminate the concept of a Creator completely, some scientists and philosophers have been led, albeit unwittingly, to re-deify the universe by endowing matter and energy with creative powers that they cannot be convincingly shown to possess. Banishing the One Creator God, they would end up with what has been described as the ultimate in polytheism – a universe in which every particle has god-like capacities.

Dawkins' complexity of God objection

I hope that the reader will by now realize that the materialist, ontological-reductionist explanation is not convincing as an inference to the best explanation of the provenance of the universe. However, I am aware that heavy fire is to be expected from that quarter against any suggestion that there is an ultimate top-down explanation in terms of an intelligence that is not already part of the universe. Richard Dawkins thinks that considerations of complexity actually clinch his case against top-down explanations involving God. He writes: 'Any God capable of designing a universe... must be a supremely complex and improbable entity who needs an even bigger explanation than the one he is supposed to provide.'[6] In other words, Dawkins thinks that the God 'explanation' is not a meaningful explanation, since, by definition, God is more complex, and therefore less probable, than the thing for which you are using him to explain.

He spells it out as follows: 'To explain the origin of the DNA/protein machine by invoking a supernatural Designer is to explain precisely nothing, for it leaves unexplained the origin of the Designer. You have to say something like "God was always there" and if you allow yourself that kind of lazy way out, you might as well just say "DNA was always there", or "Life was always there", and be done with it.'[7] This is illogical, indeed, rather silly. Firstly, we know that DNA was not always there, nor was life – nor indeed, come to think of it, was the universe. This is one of the main reasons why scientists seek explanations for their existence.

But the underlying issue is Dawkins' inadequate understanding of what explanation means. It would seem from this that he imagines that the only kind of explanation that is worthy of the adjective 'scientific' is *explanation that proceeds from the simple to the complex*. As we saw earlier, his express desire is to explain everything in terms of the 'simple things that physicists understand'.[8] In other words the only valid kind of explanation is a reductionist explanation.

Let us think, however, of a physicist's attempt to explain the falling of an apple. This is surely a 'simple' event in the sense that it is readily grasped by ordinary people. However, its explanation in terms of Newton's law of gravitation is already complicated enough for most people, and a deeper relativistic explanation in terms of Einstein's curved space-time leaves all but the expert behind. If we were to reject explanations on the basis that they were, or seemed to be, more complex than the thing being explained, we would reject a great deal of science.

Again, atoms are simpler than living creatures since living creatures are complex structures made up of atoms. On the other hand, atoms are far from simple, which is one of the reasons elementary particle physics continues to attract some of the most powerful minds in science. The deeper you probe into the ultimate nature of the structure of the universe, the more complex it becomes. The 'simple things that physicists understand' are not so simple after all.

There is something odd here: if Richard Dawkins objects to the complexity of God as ultimate explanation, he ought also to object to the complexity of the structure of the universe of particle physics and be totally dissatisfied with ultimate explanations in terms of concepts like 'energy', since we do not really understand them.

The point is that Dawkins is mistaken. Firstly, the things he takes to be simple are not; and secondly, the reason that such complex physical theories are accepted by scientists is not because of their simplicity; it is because of their *explanatory power*. Explanatory power is just as important, if not more important than simplicity, for the validity of a scientific theory. Sometimes simpler theories have been discarded because they did not have sufficient explanatory power. It was, after all, Einstein who said: 'Explanations should be as simple as possible, but no simpler.'[9] Explanatory power often trumps simplicity, a fact that Dawkins seems not to appreciate.

This issue is so important that we should explore it a little further. Postulating the existence of a being that is even more complex than the thing you are attempting to explain is something scientists constantly do. Take, for example, the around 400-page book entitled *The God Delusion*. Should we reject an explanation of the existence of this book in terms of the mind of a being called Richard Dawkins since it is immeasurably more complex than the book itself?

In fact we don't even need 400 pages to convince us of the validity of explanations that are more complex than the things that they are put forward to explain. For instance, imagine an archaeologist who, pointing at two scratch marks on the walls of a hitherto unexplored cave, exclaims: 'Human intelligence!'

Following Dawkins' 'reasoning' we should react: 'Don't be ridiculous. Those scratch marks are very simple. After all, there are only two of them. It is no explanation to postulate the existence of something as complex as a human brain to account for such simple scratch marks on a cave wall!' What would we then say if she patiently goes on to explain that the two

Refusing to acknowledge w hat is

Sensible because it does not fit evolution

'simple' scratches form the Chinese character for a human being – that is, they have a semiotic dimension, they carry meaning?

Would we still be prepared to maintain that explaining the scratch marks in terms of human activity 'explains precisely nothing' since the almost infinity complexity of the human mind is involved? Of course not. We would admit the archaeologist's inference to intelligent activity as perfectly legitimate.

Furthermore, we would also understand that accounting for the scratches in terms of something more complex than the scratches themselves *did not lead to the end of science*. Those scratch marks could well be important clues as to the identity, culture, and intelligence of the people that made them even though they might not tell us everything that might be known about those people.

Incidentally in passing, is it not odd that our archaeologist immediately inferred intelligent origin when faced with two scratches on a rock surface, whereas some scientists, when faced with the 3.5 billion letter sequence of the human genome, tell us, without embarrassment, that it is to be explained solely in terms of chance and necessity? The ideogram formed by the scratches and the DNA molecule each have a semiotic dimension. It is not for nothing that we speak of the DNA *code*, whose significance we shall later explore in Chapters 9 and 10.

The fact is that we all, scientists included, regularly make inferences to complex intelligent sources when we find certain structures or patterns which, though 'simple' in themselves, exhibit characteristics that we associate only with intelligent activity. Of course, it may be objected that we make such inferences because we are familiar with human beings and their propensity for designing things. But is that really a solid reason for attributing something that arguably exhibits a structure consistent with intelligent activity to a non-intelligent source, especially when there is no supporting evidence for our contention? Arguments that make sense are to be preferred to those that do not.

Remember what we would in all likelihood deduce on visiting a remote planet if we found a succession of piles of perfect cubes of titanium with a prime number of cubes in each pile in ascending order – 2,3,5,7,11, etc. We would see at once that here was an artefact produced by an intelligent agent, even though we had no idea what kind of intelligent agent it could possibly be. The piles of cubes are in themselves much 'simpler' than the intelligence that made them, but that fact does not prevent our deduction of intelligent origin as a reasonable inference to the best explanation. We instinctively infer 'upwards' to an ultimately intelligent causation rather than 'downwards' to chance and necessity.

The SETI project, as we have seen, uses precisely the same argument. If we were to receive, as featured in Carl Sagan's novel *Contact*, or the film of the same name, a signal consisting of a sequence of prime numbers, we would assume it was coming from an intelligent source. What is more, such an event, were it to happen, would dominate the world's press overnight and no scientist would ever dream of objecting that postulating intelligent origin for the sequence was not an explanation since it would be tantamount to explaining the sequence in terms of something more complex than the sequence itself.

To be sure it would raise many more questions – that of the nature of the intelligence, for instance – but at least we would have settled that there was an extra-terrestrial intelligence. As we remarked, even Dawkins would seem, from what he says in the film *Expelled*, to have moved his ground toward admitting that design is something that, in principle, could be recognized by science.

We should also note in this context that Dawkins seems to be impressed by the multiverse hypothesis and yet he realizes there is a problem: 'it is tempting to think (and many have succumbed) that to postulate a plethora of universes is a profligate luxury which should not be allowed. If we are going to permit the extravagance of a multiverse, we might as well be hung for a sheep as a lamb and allow a God.'[10] His solution to this question is that the God hypothesis is genuinely extravagant but the multiverse is only apparently extravagant. His reasoning on the basis of statistical improbability is not convincing.[11]

If there are vastly many universes then one would have thought that most of them are highly complex; and if we are ultimately the product of such a multiverse then Dawkins' acclaimed argument that things always proceed from the simple to the complex is in tatters.

In light of the weight Dawkins gives to the 'complexity of God argument', I was very surprised (as were others) at his public admission in that debate with me in the Oxford Natural History Museum in October 2008 that a case could be made for a deistic god, though he hastened to point out that he did not accept it, giving no reason why. It was surprising that he mentioned it at all, since nothing could demolish his argument more effectively than the existence of a deistic God, since a deistic God is

Nature is what God does.

Why is there something rather than nothing

precisely a complex being that is posited as an ultimate explanation for a simpler universe.

The 'complexity of God' argument collapses like a house of cards. Continued use of it serves only to increase the suspicion that the Emperor of Atheism has no clothes.

Miracles, chance, and the supernatural God and nature

The word 'miracle' conveys to most people the idea of an unusual event that lies outside the normal course of things and involves the supernatural – although the word is sometimes used colloquially in statements like: 'It was a miracle that she passed her maths test.'

However, if there is a God who not only created the universe but who also maintains it in existence, then it could be argued that the cosmos itself is a constant manifestation of the supernatural. As Augustine once said: 'Nature is what God does'.[12]

We therefore need to make some distinctions. We have already said a great deal about scientific explanations and we should now redress the balance by exploring theistic explanations. I shall approach this from the perspective of the biblical worldview according to which:

God is the reason the universe exists

He created it: 'In the beginning God created the heavens and the earth' (Genesis 1:1). 'In the beginning was the Word... and the Word was God... all things came to be [lit.] through him... without him nothing came to be that came to be' (John 1:1–3). That is, God the Word is the First Cause, the answer to the question why there is something rather than nothing. He caused the universe to be.

Gen 1:1
Jn 1:1-3

However, there would appear to be different levels of causation – primary or direct and secondary or indirect. God causing the universe to exist in the first place is primary. God 'sending' rain and snow is secondary. That is, secondary processes are built in to the created order by God and do not need his direct involvement. Furthermore, human beings are made in the image of God, one evidence of which is surely our ability to be creative and cause things directly. God has honoured us by delegating to us real responsibility for aspects of the running of the world to the extent that we shall be held accountable for the way we have gone about it.

The question now arises as to the status of the laws of nature that we associate with regularities and uniformity. How, then, can miracles fit in, if at all? Would they not break these laws, which is impossible, is it not? Yet some eminent scientists nevertheless utter the word 'miracle' on occasion. For example, the Nobel Prize winner Sir Francis Crick, who, with James Watson, discovered the double helix structure of DNA, wrote: 'The origin of life seems almost to be a miracle, so many are the conditions which would have had to have been satisfied to get it going.'[13] Crick was an atheist, hence he carefully inserted the word 'almost'. I once asked James Watson what he thought of Crick's remark. His reply was: 'It happened.' He then made it very clear that he did not wish to engage further on the topic. For, I imagine, like all atheist scientists and even some of theistic persuasion, Watson was allergic to the idea that life's origin could have been a miracle in the sense of a supernatural event. Atheists and theists often find common cause here in the name of protecting the integrity of science and it would seem that one is on a hiding to nothing if one even introduces a whiff of the supernatural to account for (aspects of) the origin of life – or, indeed, anything else.

What divides theists from atheists, however, is that they are usually prepared to ascribe some things to the direct creative activity of God. For instance, they regard God as directly responsible for the existence of space–time and mass-energy. Such divine activity for them is not part of the space-time continuum or the normal course of events but is the cause of their existence in the first place which seems to them a relatively harmless way of introducing the supernatural. What they, in common with their atheist colleagues, do not regard as harmless is introducing supernatural acts of God to account for any phenomena *within* the causal history of the universe since the Big Bang, thus disrupting the uniformity of nature as they conceive it.

Yet even at this level, further differences of opinion may be observed, in particular on the part of Christians. For, central to the Christian worldview is the claim that Christ was raised from the dead by a special act of God's power. The resurrection of Christ, they believe, was a supernatural event, indeed, the supernatural event par excellence. And it occurred in earth's unfolding history long after the creation of the universe, as did the other supernatural events recorded in the New Testament.

Many atheists react to this with scorn. For instance, Richard Dawkins claims that:

> The nineteenth century is the last time when it was
> possible for an educated person to admit to believing in
> miracles like the virgin birth without embarrassment.
> When pressed, many educated Christians are too loyal
> to deny the virgin birth and the resurrection. But it
> embarrasses them because their rational minds know that
> it is absurd, so they would much rather not be asked.[14]

This is false and Dawkins must know it, unless he is prepared to leave himself open to a charge of arrogance by denying the description 'educated person' to many scientists of much greater eminence than himself, such as Sir John Polkinghorne FRS, Dr Francis Collins ForMemRS, and Dr William Phillips, a Nobel Prize winner in physics. They all publicly, and without either embarrassment or a sense of absurdity, affirm their belief in the supernatural and, in particular, in the resurrection of Christ, which they regard as the supreme evidence for the truth of the Christian worldview. It is evident, therefore, that it is no necessary part of being a (distinguished) scientist that one should reject in principle either the possibility or the actuality of miracles of the kind to be found in the New Testament.

The upshot of all of this means that, before we even begin to consider the possibility of a supernatural dimension to any specific issue like the origin of life, we need to address the question of the relationship of science to the supernatural in principle. How is it possible for a scientist to believe in the supernatural at all? Ian Hutchinson, Professor of Nuclear Science and Engineering at MIT, lays some groundwork saying that he and millions of other scientists around the world think that the literal miracle of the resurrection of Jesus of Nazareth is not only possible but it actually happened.

He points out that many of the pioneers of the scientific revolution believed the same – among them Robert Boyle (of the ideal gas law who co-founded the Royal Society in London in 1660) and James Clerk Maxwell (whose Maxwell equations of 1862 govern electromagnetism). Coming up to the modern era, William Phillips, who won the Nobel Prize in 1997 for methods to trap atoms with laser light, holds that the resurrection of Christ is not discredited by science.

Hutchinson thinks that there is no difficulty in explaining how a scientist can be a Christian:

Miracles are supernatural events.
But not all supernatural events are miracles.

Science cannot and does not disprove the resurrection. Natural
science describes the normal reproducible working of the world of
nature. Indeed, the key meaning of 'nature', as Boyle emphasized,
is 'the normal course of events.' Miracles like the resurrection
do not fit in with the normal course of events. It does not take
modern science to tell us that humans don't rise from the dead.
People knew that perfectly well in the first century; just as they
knew that the blind from birth don't as adults regain their sight,
or water doesn't instantly turn into wine.[15]

If there is a God who created the universe then there is surely no difficulty
in believing that he could do special things. Whether he has actually done so
on a specific occasion is, of course, a different matter. Francis Collins wisely
remarks: 'It is crucial that a healthy scepticism be applied when interpreting
potentially miraculous events, lest the integrity and rationality of the religious
perspective be brought into question. The only thing that will kill the possibility
of miracles more quickly than a committed materialism is the claiming of
miracle status for everyday events for which natural explanations are readily
at hand.'[16]

An important distinction needs to be made at this juncture between
miracles and supernatural events. Miracles, genuine miracles, that is, are
supernatural events, but not all supernatural events are miracles in the
strict sense. For instance, the origin of the universe and its laws, though a
supernatural event, does not come under the rubric of miracle since miracles,
strictly speaking, are exceptions to an already recognized normal course of
things and, as such, they clearly presuppose the existence of such a 'normal
course of things'. The creation of the universe together with its regularities
that form the 'normal course of things' can scarcely be regarded as an
exception to them.

The widely held notion that science has rendered miracles impossible
was once and, unfortunately, still is thought in some quarters to have
been given its most powerful expression by the Scottish Enlightenment
philosopher, David Hume (1711–76). Hume was a sceptical naturalist
philosopher who asserted in his famous essay *An Enquiry Concerning
Human Understanding* that miracles are 'violations of the laws of nature'.
He regarded the laws as firmly established by experience and so the argument
against them based on experience is as complete as you could ask for.
He explains,

> It is no miracle that a man, seemingly in good health, should die on a sudden: because such a kind of death, though more unusual than any other, has yet been frequently observed to happen. But it is a miracle that a dead man should come to life; because that has never been observed, in any age or country. There must, therefore, be a uniform experience against every miraculous event, otherwise the event would not merit that appellation.[17]

Hume denies miracle because miracle would go against the uniform laws of nature. But elsewhere he points out that the uniformity of nature cannot be demonstrated – because of the problem of induction. Just because the sun has been observed to rise in the morning for thousands of years, it does not mean that we can be sure that it will rise tomorrow – something that physicist Paul Davies pointed out as we mentioned in Chapter 4.[18] On the basis of past experience you cannot predict the future, says Hume. But if that were true, let us see what it implies in particular. Suppose that Hume is right that no dead man has ever risen up from the grave through the whole of earth's history so far; then, by his own argument, he still couldn't be sure that a dead man will not rise up tomorrow. That being so he cannot rule out miracle. He has undermined the very basis on which he denies the possibility of miracles.

In any case, if, according to Hume, we can infer no regularities, it would be impossible even to speak of a 'law of nature', let alone the uniformity of nature with respect to those laws. And, if nature is not uniform, then using the uniformity of nature as an argument against miracles is simply absurd.

What is more, his notion that miracles are 'violations of the laws of nature' evaporates under careful analysis. Let's think of those laws for a moment. They are not simply descriptions of what happens but give us insight into the internal logic of a system in terms of cause and effect relationships between its constituent parts.

It is here that we run up against what is generally acknowledged as a surprising self-contradiction in Hume's position – he denies the very cause and effect relationships that are involved in formulating the laws of nature. He says: 'All events seem entirely loose and separate. One event follows another; but we never can observe any tie between them. They seem conjoined, but never connected... *When we say, therefore, that one object is connected with another, we mean only that they have acquired a connection in our thought....*'[19]

I have italicized the last sentence to emphasize the fact that Hume explicitly rejects the idea of necessary connection. This would undermine a great deal of modern science, since scientific laws involve precisely what Hume denies – cause-effect descriptions of the workings of a system. Just think of what would be left of atomic physics if we were not allowed to infer the existence of elementary particles from the tracks physicists observe in a bubble-chamber!

Philosopher Anthony Flew, a world authority on Hume and once a much feted atheist, radically revised his assessment of Hume, saying that his (Flew's) work on Hume needs to be re-written:

> in the light of my new-found awareness that Hume was utterly wrong to maintain that we have no experience, and hence no genuine ideas, of making things happen and preventing things from happening, of physical necessity and physical impossibility. Generations of Humeans have in consequence been misled into offering analyses of causation and of natural law that have been far too weak because they had no basis for accepting the existence of either cause and effect or natural laws... Hume's scepticism about cause and effect and his agnosticism about the external world are of course jettisoned the moment he leaves his study.[20]

Quite so. Strange that authors like Christopher Hitchens think that Hume wrote 'the last word on the subject'.[21] But then Hitchens is not a scientist. Dawkins does not have the same excuse.

To be fair, however, not all who regard miracles as violations of the laws of nature would argue like Hume, and so we must further consider this issue from the perspective of contemporary science and its thinking about the laws of nature. Scientists nowadays do not regard them as merely capable of describing what has happened in the past. Provided we are not working at the quantum level, such laws can successfully predict what will happen in the future with such accuracy that, for example, the orbits of communication satellites can be precisely calculated, and moon and Mars landings are possible.

It is understandable, therefore, that many scientists resent the idea that some god could arbitrarily intervene and alter, suspend, reverse, or otherwise 'violate' these laws of nature. For that would seem to them to contradict the immutability of those laws, and thus overturn the very basis of the scientific understanding of the universe. As a corollary to this, many such scientists would advance two arguments.

Argument 1. *Belief in miracles in general, and in the New Testament miracles in particular, arose in a primitive, pre-scientific culture in which people were ignorant of the laws of nature and so readily accepted miracle stories.*

Hume endorses this view when he says that accounts of miracles 'are observed chiefly to abound among ignorant and barbarous nations'.[22] Yet, however plausible this explanation may seem at first sight, it is in fact nonsense when applied to the New Testament miracles. For a moment's thought will show us that, in order to recognize some event as a miracle, there must be some perceived regularity to which that event is an apparent exception! You cannot recognize something as abnormal, if you do not know what is normal.

Ian Hutchinson again: 'Still, the fact that the resurrection was impossible in the normal course of events was as obvious in the first century as it is for us. Indeed that is why it was seen as a great demonstration of God's power.'[23] The early Christians were not a credulous bunch, unaware of the laws of nature, and therefore prepared to believe any miraculous story, however absurd. They felt the difficulty in believing the story of such a miracle, just like anyone else. If in the end they believed that a miracle had taken place, it was because they were forced to by the sheer weight of the direct evidence presented to them, not because of ignorance of nature's laws.

Argument 2. *Now that we know the laws of nature, belief in miracles is impossible.*

The idea that miracles are 'violations' of the laws of nature involves another fallacy, which C. S. Lewis illustrated using an analogy that can be put as follows. Suppose that I am staying in a hotel in London for four nights. On each of the first three nights I put £100 in the room safe so that, according to the laws of arithmetic, there is £300 in the safe. On the fourth day, I go out in a hurry and forget to lock the safe. Upon my return I discover only

£100 in the safe. What should I conclude? That the laws of arithmetic have been broken? Of course not. I conclude that the laws of England have been broken by an opportunist thief who has grabbed £200 and run. It would be stupid of me to say that the laws of arithmetic made it impossible for me to believe that a thief could intervene and steal my cash. On the contrary, it is my knowledge of the laws of arithmetic that tell me that that is exactly what happened.[24]

This analogy illustrates where the problem really lies. The mistake was to think that the drawer in the desk in the room formed a causally closed system. That was Laplace's view of the universe (not Newton's, by the way) – that the universe was causally closed and deterministic and therefore excluded special miraculous interaction.

The world picture of both Newton and Laplace has long since been superseded by quantum mechanics (QM) and, indeed, relativity, but that is less germane to our discussion). However, we do not really have to consider QM as the Newtonian classical picture does not present a real barrier to miracle. For an excellent discussion of the relationship between QM and divine action I recommend Alvin Plantinga's book, *Where the Conflict Really Lies*.[25]

Lewis' analogy also helps us understand that the scientific use of the word 'law' is not the same as the legal use, where we often think of a law as constraining someone's actions.[26] There is no sense in which the laws of arithmetic constrain or pressurize the thief in our story! Newton's law of gravitation tells me that if I drop an apple it will fall towards the centre of the earth. But that law does not prevent someone intervening, and catching the apple as it descends. In other words, the law predicts what will happen, provided there is no change in the conditions under which the experiment is conducted. In his highly nuanced and, in my view, extremely valuable discussion, philosopher Daniel von Wachter shows that the laws of nature do not actually entail regularities:[27]

Key

> In any case, the totality of the laws of nature also entails no regularities of succession, but only conditional prediction statements of the form: *If an event is of type x and no further things are affecting what follows, then an event of type y will follow. The laws also entail general causal statements of the form: Events of type x cause events of type y if nothing prevents them from causing.*

[Handwritten annotations in margin: "Tendencies of Nature", "laws of nature"]

The prediction statements entailed by laws leave open not only the possibility of intervention by material things but also by God.[28]

Von Wachter concludes:

> The question of miracle led us to question the general view of the laws and of the causal structure of the world, according to which laws entail regularities of succession and even every event is an instance of a regularity of succession. Against this view I have argued that laws do not entail regularities of succession but describe tendencies, e.g. Newtonian forces. Miracles are not violations of the laws because in the case of a miracle the tendencies that the laws describe remain.[29]

He continues:

> Some theists are worried that there is no room for miracles, for example Keith Ward claims that 'there must be gaps in physical causality if God is ever to do anything'... Some therefore think that quantum mechanics can help us here in that God acts by determining the outcome of probabilistic processes on the quantum level.[30] However, even if the Newtonian laws, which are deterministic, were the ultimate laws, miracles would be perfectly possible. Hence we are at fully at liberty to consider the only question that really matters... whether and which miracles have, in fact, occurred.[31]

To sum up: the (classical) laws of physics predict what is bound to happen unless something or someone else intervenes. To argue that those laws make it impossible for us to believe in the existence of God, and in the possibility of his intervention in the universe, is plainly fallacious. It would be like claiming that understanding of the laws governing the behaviour of internal combustion engines makes it impossible to believe that the designer of a motor car, or one of his mechanics, could or would intervene and remove the cylinder head. Of course they could intervene. Moreover, the intervention would not destroy those laws. The very same laws that explained why the engine worked with the cylinder head on would now explain why it did not work with the head removed.

It therefore turns out that Hume was wrong to say that miracles 'violate' the laws of nature. Again, C. S. Lewis is very helpful:

> If God annihilates or creates or deflects a unit of matter, He has created a new situation at that point. Immediately all nature domiciles this new situation, makes it at home in her realm, adapts all other events to it. It finds itself conforming to all the laws. If God creates a miraculous spermatozoon in the body of a virgin, it does not proceed to break any laws. The laws at once take over. Nature is ready. Pregnancy follows, according to all the normal laws, and nine months later a child is born.[32]

To put this another way, we could say that it is a law of nature that human beings do not rise again from the dead by some natural mechanism. But Christians do not claim that Christ rose from the dead by such a mechanism. They claim that he rose from the dead by an injection of supernatural power. By themselves, the laws of nature cannot rule out that possibility. When a miracle takes place, it is our knowledge of the laws of nature that alerts us to the fact that it is a miracle.

Christians do not deny the laws of nature. Quite the contrary is true as we pointed out at the beginning of this chapter. It is an essential part of the Christian position to believe in the laws of nature as descriptions of those regularities and cause–effect relationships built into the universe by its Creator and according to which it normally operates. If we did not know those regularities, we should never recognize a miracle if we saw one. Uniformity, even for lengthy time periods, is one thing, absolute uniformity is something entirely different.

Miracles are, of course, inherently improbable by definition. We should certainly demand strong evidence for their happening in any particular case. But this is not the real problem with miracles of the sort found in the New Testament. The real problem is that they threaten the foundations of naturalism, which is clearly Hume's worldview at this point. That is, Hume regards it as axiomatic that nature is all that there is and that there is nothing and no one outside nature that could from time to time intervene in nature. His axiom, of course, is simply a belief, and not a consequence of scientific investigation.

Ironically enough, it is surely arguable that it is only belief in a Creator that gives us a satisfactory ground for believing in the normal uniformity of nature in the first place. In denying that there is a Creator, the atheists are kicking away the basis of their own position. As Lewis put it:

> If all that exists is Nature, the great mindless interlocking event, if our own deepest convictions are merely the by-products of an irrational process, then clearly there is not the slightest ground for supposing that our sense of fitness and our consequent faith in uniformity tell us anything about a reality external to ourselves. Our convictions are simply a fact about us – like the colour of our hair. If Naturalism is true we have no reason to trust our conviction that Nature is uniform. It can be trusted only if quite a different metaphysic is true.[33]

Thus excluding the possibility of miracles, and making nature and its processes an absolute in the name of science, eventually removes all grounds for trusting in the rationality of science in the first place. On the other hand, regarding nature as only part of a greater reality, which includes nature's intelligent Creator God, gives a rational justification for belief in the orderliness of nature, a view which led to the rise of modern science, as we saw in Chapter 3.

Secondly, however, if, in order to account for the uniformity of nature, one admits the existence of a Creator, then that inevitably opens the door for a miracle in which that same Creator interacts with the course of nature. There is no such thing as a tame Creator who cannot, or must not, or dare not interact with the universe he has created. After all, if as we said at the start of this chapter God is actively involved in nature all the time then there is no reason to imagine that God in the course of sustaining the regularities cannot decide to do something special that does not fall within those regularities – it is all the activity of God.

I stress once more that one can, therefore, at least agree with Hume that 'uniform experience' shows that resurrection *by means of a natural mechanism* is extremely improbable,[34] and we may rule it out. But, and this is important, Christians do not claim that Jesus rose by some natural mechanism. They claim something totally different – that God raised him from the dead. And if there is a God, why should that be thought impossible?

Before leaving David Hume I should say that, in spite of his objections to miracles, he also, rather paradoxically, wrote: 'The whole frame of nature bespeaks an intelligent author; and no rational enquirer can, after serious reflection, suspend his belief a moment with regard to the primary principles of genuine Theism and Religion.'[35] In Hume's famous *Dialogues Concerning Natural Religion*, one of the three participants, Cleanthes, says that we seem to see 'the image of mind reflected on us from innumerable objects' in nature.[36] Many who quote Hume assiduously against miracles do not seem to be aware of his sympathy with intelligent design.

There is, therefore, no scientific, in-principle objection to the possibility of miracles. Surely, then, the open-minded attitude demanded by reason is now to proceed to investigate the evidence, to establish the facts, and to be prepared to follow where that process leads, even if it entails alterations to our *a priori*[37] views. We shall never know whether there is a mouse in the attic unless we actually go and look!

This has been a lengthy discussion but a necessary one if we are to understand what the issues are that surround any claim to miraculous intervention. Nothing of what we have said about miracles and the supernatural demands that there is any supernatural aspect to natural history, but neither does it forbid it. Hence, in that sense it at least opens up a rational consideration of the possibility of involvement of a designing intelligence.

Of course, there is a wide spectrum of opinions on the matter – even among scientists. At one extreme is the view that all that is needed for life is matter, energy and the laws of nature and time. Stephen Hawking said: 'The life we have on Earth must have spontaneously generated itself.' This is the reductionist, physicalist perspective and we should bear in mind that it is essentially eliminated by the analysis of ontological reductionism outlined in Chapter 5. At the other end of the spectrum is the view that life was created by constant divine activity. Somewhere in between are variants postulating a mixture of God's direct and indirect activity.

For instance, one idea is that God front-loaded the Big Bang event with all the potential for life and, without any further intervention on his part, the universe has been fruitful in producing life on its own through secondary causation. Others think that God has been involved all along, but only indirectly, in 'supervising' natural processes in some way to ensure that life eventually starts and subsequently evolves. How God is involved is important, but in the overall scheme of things, not as important as the

What actually happened?
How did it happened?
What are the possible causes ...

fact that he is involved. He is God of the whole show and it involves both primary and secondary causation.

Science, of course, whether done by atheists or theists, is concerned to find out what actually happened. However, the influence of *a priori* worldviews is hard to avoid, and, as we have seen, there are scientists who admit that their materialism is *a priori* and others who admit that their theism is *a priori*.

Where, then, does this leave us? That clearly depends on our worldview and it is only fair to explain where it leaves me. As a scientist and a Christian I am convinced that the universe began to exist in an event that will unavoidably appear to be a singularity from a naturalistic perspective but which is an act of God.

What happened after that initial creation event? Our discussion of miracles and the supernatural leads to the idea of a punctuated uniformity of nature. That is, nature has been mostly uniform yet that uniformity has been occasionally punctuated by a supernatural input from the outside. As a Christian I believe that the resurrection of Christ and the miracles that establish his identity fit into that category. This implies that I think that there were several (but not many) discontinuities after creation with periods where nature is uniform, in between them. I shall later give my reasons to think there may well be scientific evidence of such discontinuities, for instance, at the origin of life and of human life. My argument will be cumulative and so I would ask my readers to be gracious and patient enough not to write me off at this stage as a God-of-the-gaps man, if only for the simple reason that, in addition to believing there is evidence of discontinuities, I emphatically believe that God is the God of the whole show, the bits we do understand, and the bits we don't.

The debate My particular *scientific* question, therefore, is this: Is there evidence of the interaction of mind in the origin and subsequent spread of life, whatever material processes may also be involved? Or does the evidence show that unguided natural evolutionary processes are all that was necessary?

Rejection of the supernatural has arguably held up progress in science from time to time. Firstly, as philosopher Thomas Nagel points out: 'The priority given to evolutionary naturalism in the face of its implausible conclusions about other subjects is due, I think, to the secular consensus that this is the only form of external understanding of ourselves that provides an alternative to theism – which is to be rejected as a mere projection of our internal self-conception onto the universe, without evidence.'[38]

Is there evidence --

or does the evidence show

Secondly, in an important book entitled *Evolution: A View from the 21st Century*[39] evolutionary biologist James Shapiro[40] explains why people held on to the neo-Darwinian synthesis with its emphasis on random mutation long after that the theory had been found to be seriously defective. Related to this history there is a revealing account by New Zealand natural history science reporter Suzan Mazur in her book *The Altenberg 16*,[41] containing interviews she conducted with leading biologists on the need to rethink the modern synthesis. Her book gives an insight into the tensions and rivalries between scientists that shows that science is a very human endeavour and not the dispassionate activity it was once thought to be.

Reminiscent of Lewontin's *a priori* rejection of a 'Divine foot' in the door which we considered in Chapter 5, Shapiro writes:

> As many professional and popular press articles attest, the accidental stochastic nature of mutations is still the prevailing and widely accepted wisdom on the subject. In the context of earlier ideological debates about evolution, this insistence on randomness and accident is not surprising. It springs from a determination in the 19th and 20th centuries by biologists to reject the role of a supernatural agent in religious accounts of how diverse living organisms originated.[42]

Shapiro finds this surprising in light of strong evidence to the contrary – *particularly the now undeniable capacity of living organisms to alter their own heredity.* I have placed part of the last sentence in italics to alert the reader to the fact that there has been a massive shift in understanding of the mechanisms of heredity which has negative consequences for the status of the modern synthesis but opens up exciting new vistas of research. We shall learn more about Shapiro's work in Chapter 19.

God and chance

We have been discussing different levels of God's interaction with the world in terms of creating it, upholding it, and, from time to time, doing something miraculous by intervening in the normal course of its activity. We now need to bring in to our consideration, from both biblical and scientific perspectives, the concepts of chance and randomness. Consider the following statements:

agent - has instrumental power.

'The lot is cast into the lap, but its every decision is from the Lord' (Proverbs 16:33).

'It necessarily follows that chance alone is at the source of every innovation, and of all creation in the biosphere' (Jacques Monod, *Chance and Necessity*[43]).

'As long as chance rules, God is an anachronism' (Arthur Koestler).

'Quantum theory yields much, but it hardly brings us close to the Old One's secrets. I, in any case, am convinced He does not play dice with the universe' (Albert Einstein[44]).

These statements proceed from very different perceptions of reality. The first statement implies that God is involved in decisions that from our perspective involve chance. The statements by atheist biochemist and Nobel Prize winner Jacques Monod (1910–76) and Arthur Koestler (1905–1983) imply that God and chance are mutually exclusive. The statement by Einstein is that God is not involved in chance processes – at least so far as quantum mechanics is concerned.

Questions arise: How can God be involved in chance processes? Surely God and chance are polar opposites, as Koestler says, in that the more you ascribe to chance, the less you can ascribe to God and vice versa – so that from a theistic perspective chance is bad?

In order to tackle questions like this the first thing to ask is what we mean by chance. Chance and randomness often refer to the same thing. However, chance can simply mean 'opportunity' – 'I would love the chance to visit Rome.' You cannot replace 'chance' by 'randomness' in that sentence!

Consider the statement: 'It happened by chance' (= it happened at random). This could mean either a) it was not predictable by us; or b) it had no (known) determining cause. Statements like this one can give the impression that there is a substantive agency called chance (shades of the goddess Fortuna!) that does things. This is not the case. 'I met Fred by chance this morning' means the meeting was unplanned by either of us. It was a coincidence. Chance is neither a cause nor an agent. It has no instrumental power. That raises questions about the meaning of Monod's statement above. Note that saying the meeting was by chance does not mean that there was no cause involved. However, chance was not the cause.

The word 'chance' is very often used simply to mean ignorance of true causes. It refers to many things in everyday life that may be predictable in principle but not in practice. The famous French mathematician Pierre Laplace once wrote:

> Given an intelligence which could for one instant comprehend all the forces by which nature is animated and the respective situations of the beings who compose it – an intelligence sufficiently vast to submit this data to analysis – it would embrace in the same formula the movements of the greatest bodies of the universe and the lightest atom; for it nothing would be uncertain, and the future, as the past, would be present to its eyes.[45]

Here are some examples that involve chance:

- The fact that you exist – a particular sperm of millions penetrated the egg first. The one that won is predictable in principle.
- Weather patterns, the breaking of a wave, or falling of a leaf.
- The rolling of a die.

To say that such events are chance events means they are unpredictable by us. This is a comment on our science rather than on the event in the sense that our prediction paradigm cannot cope with it. It does not say anything about whether the event had a determinate specification before it happened. It leaves questions of causality and determinacy open. Indeterminate means that there was no prior determining or specifying factor. On the other hand, an eclipse is a determinate event in the sense it is specified by precedent, that is, on the assumption of the uniformity of nature.

We speak of chance in mathematics in terms of probability. If 100 people take part in a raffle (where someone is bound to get the prize) then we all understand what it means when we say that each person has one chance in a hundred of winning, or, equivalently that the probability of a *given person* winning is 1/100 or 1 per cent. The probability of *someone* winning is 1 = certainty.

If you toss a coin many times, in the long run you expect to get an equal number of heads and tails, so you say that the probability of getting a head on any throw is ½ or 50 per cent. Of course, the way the coin falls depends on its construction, the way it is thrown, the wind, and so on, and if we knew all these factors and could compute them accurately enough we could in principle calculate how the coin would fall. It might even land on its edge in some soft material like sand and remain vertical. But we cannot calculate all this in advance accurately enough to make predictions. Therefore, once more we are expressing our ignorance when we say the coin will be heads with probability one half.

We can sum up by noting that there are essentially three types of probability:

1.Classical

Let S=sample space which is the set of all possible distinct outcomes of a trial – say the roll of a die. Then the probability of an event =

$$\frac{\text{Number of ways the event occurs}}{\text{number of outcomes in S}}$$

If we roll a die the number of possible outcomes is six. The probability or chance of the event that a 3 appears is therefore 1/6.

2. Relative frequency

The probability of an event in an experiment is the proportion (or fraction) of times the event occurs in a very long (theoretically infinite) series of (independent) repetitions of experiment. For instance, the probability of obtaining heads in coin tossing will be nearly 1/2 if the coin is fair and unbiased.

3. Subjective probability

The probability of an event is a 'best guess' by a person making the statement of the chances that the event will happen. For example, when a weather forecaster says that there is a 30 per cent chance of rain this afternoon. In all of these cases, as above, chance is due to our ignorance.

Random numbers

Another important use of the concept of randomness is that of random numbers that are used in certain statistical trials that we wish to 'randomize'. Suppose we take a ten-sided die with sides numbered 0 to 9 and we toss it again and again, writing down the number that appears each time to get something like 5307911624850079, say. Insofar as the die is unbiased, that is, not unevenly weighted towards any particular side, this will be a random number in the sense that it has no discernible order. This is different from random in the sense of having no discernible cause. The cause is obvious in this case.

Chance in quantum mechanics[46]

It is not always the case that chance is due to our ignorance. There are events at the subatomic level that are unpredictable even in principle. Heisenberg's uncertainty principle tells us that there is a degree of fuzziness in nature, a fundamental limit to what we can know about the behaviour of particles at the quantum level. The uncertainty principle says that we cannot simultaneously measure the position and the momentum of a particle with absolute precision, in the sense that the more accurately we know one of these values, the less accurately we know the other. We can only assign probabilities to them.

Nevertheless such events do have an underlying determining cause. The uncertainty principle is a statement about the limits to our knowledge, not about absence of causes. This flags up the difference between epistemological uncertainty and ontological uncertainty. What it is very important to realize is that the uncertainty principle lies at the heart of our very existence. It tells us, for instance, why atoms don't collapse and explains the working of the nuclear decay and fission in our largest source of energy – the sun – as well as many other things in physics and chemistry that are essential to life (even in apparently mundane things like electricity transformers). If we believe that the universe was created by God, then, far from chance and uncertainty being somehow bad, it turns out that God has built fundamental uncertainty into the system in order for it to function as it does.

Chance in the sense of no purpose

However, Monod and Koestler were not thinking of chance in that sense. There is another use of the word that has worked its way into our language, and that is chance in the sense of no purpose. When people say that the

No ultimate meaning or purpose

universe happened by chance they sometimes mean that it has no ultimate meaning or purpose – and hence there is no God. This use of the word 'chance' has absolutely nothing to do with chance in the other senses above, but there is a real danger of confusion.

Chance in evolutionary biology

The concept of chance also appears in evolutionary biology. For instance, Francis Collins writes: 'Although from our perspective evolution could appear to be driven by chance, from God's perspective the outcome would be entirely specified.'[47] This statement is in keeping with the quote from Laplace above. Collins, a Christian, clearly regards this aspect of chance as good – fitting in as it does with Proverbs 16:33.

Compare that with the following extract from a conversation between Jacques Monod and a journalist about the possibility of thinking: 'of God using randomness, just so long as there was the pattern which he was imposing upon the results of the chance mutations.' Monod responds by saying: 'If you want to assume that, then I have no dispute with it, except one, which is not a scientific dispute, but a moral one. Namely, selection is the blindest, and most cruel way of evolving new species... because it is a process of elimination, of destruction. The struggle for life and elimination of the weakest is a horrible process, against which our whole modern ethics revolts. An ideal society is a non-selective society, is one where the weak is protected; which is exactly the reverse of the so-called natural law. I am surprised that a Christian would defend the idea that this is the process which God more or less set up in order to have evolution.'[48] A hefty challenge, to say the least!

PART 3

Understanding the Universe and Life

Conviction: all scientists believe that science can be done.

presuppo: that the universe is rational

7

The human mind is capable for observation and interrogation

Understanding the Universe: The Beginning and Fine-tuning

Article of faith:

> 'Astronomy leads us to a unique event, a universe which was created out of nothing, one with the very delicate balance needed to provide exactly the right conditions required to permit life, and one which has an underlying (one might say "supernatural") plan.'
>
> Arno Penzias, Physics Nobel Prize winner

Compart with Christian Worldview not Naturalist. C.

?

The way is now clear to ask the question whether or not there is any scientific evidence for a designing intelligence behind the universe? We argue that one of the most important examples of it is not a particular scientific result but rather the conviction that lies at the heart of all science: that all scientists believe that science can be done. More precisely, scientists presuppose that the universe is rationally, indeed, mathematically, intelligible, that is, it is accessible (at least in part) to observation and interrogation by the human mind.

This conviction, therefore, functions as a starting point, that is, a basic article of faith, rather than something that arises out of science. Therefore, all scientists are 'people of faith' – not that they all have faith in God, though many do, but that faith in the rational intelligibility of the universe is essential to their profession. We discuss the basis for thinking that the universe is rationally intelligible. We argue that this makes sense in a theistic worldview but not in a naturalistic one.

The next article of faith in the scientist's credo is the existence of the universe. That raises the fundamental question: Why is there anything at all? We give an initial sketch of some of the answers that are given, including the widespread notion that the universe generated itself, or that, somehow, the laws of nature brought it into being.

Fundamental Q: why is there anything at all?

Evidence for design?

In recent years science has been taking us on a journey full, not only of surprise, but also of mystery. Cosmology on an unimaginably large scale, and elementary particle physics on the incredibly small, have gradually revealed to us some of the spectacularly beautiful structure of the universe. Its sheer size makes us aware of and simultaneously amazed at our own smallness. On a linear scale, we are insignificant specks of dust in a vast galaxy, which is itself scarcely more than a speck in the universe. However, if we are mathematically minded, we could balance that statement by noticing that, on a logarithmic scale, in terms of height we are situated about half-way between the incredibly small and the incredibly large dimensions revealed to us, respectively, by nuclear physics and astronomy.

We might well ask, though: Is size the (only) criterion of value? Just what are we human beings? And what is this universe? Is it really our home, or are we just microscopic entities that the universe has happened to throw up as concoctions of chemicals, subject to the laws of nature, blindly fumbling their way through four-dimensional space-time? None of us faces these questions dispassionately. The universe is far too awe-inspiring for that. Nor do we face them disinterestedly. We cannot remain untouched by such questions – after all, we are here. Our minds insist on asking about the nature of our relationship to the universe.

There are all sorts of answers on offer. Some scientists think that we are aliens in the cosmos, 'an eczema on the face of the universe', thrown up by the vast maelstrom of chance and necessity that governs our universe's physical behaviour. We are 'the product of a mindless and purposeless natural process which did not have us in mind', said biologist George Gaylord Simpson.[1]

But there are others who do not feel like aliens in the universe. Physicist Freeman Dyson is one such. He writes: 'As we look out into the universe and identify the many accidents of physics and astronomy that have worked together to our benefit, it almost seems as if the universe must in some sense have known we were coming.'[2]

Nor is physicist Paul Davies convinced that we are mere insignificant specks of animated dust, stating: 'I cannot believe that our existence in this universe is a mere quirk of fate, an accident of history, an incidental blip in the great cosmic drama. Our involvement is too intimate... We are truly meant to be here.'[3] Davies seems to be hinting that there is a Mind behind the universe, which had humans in view when the universe was made. Why do he and Dyson take such an anti-reductionist stance and open up the God-question? Does the universe itself give us any scientific clues that would be grounds for thinking that we human beings have significance because our minds arise from the creative activity of a greater Mind?

I think it does. We recall from earlier that the very rational (mathematical) intelligibility of the universe and the uniformity of nature are strong clues. Logically, the next clue is the very existence of the universe – how it came into being and is fined-tuned for life to exist.

The question of the existence of the universe is distinct from the question of whether or not the universe had a beginning. Whether the universe had a beginning or not is a question of central importance to the history of thought. It is connected with questions about the nature of ultimate reality. For, if the universe had no beginning, it is eternal and one might argue, as some do, that it is simply a brute fact of existence. On the other hand, if it had a beginning, it is not eternal and, therefore, not ultimate.

Throughout history many ideas have been put forward to account for the existence of the universe. Plato held that the universe was made out of pre-existent matter.[4] Aristotle believed that the earth was the centre of an eternal universe. In variations on the theme of an eternal universe, other ancient cosmologies, like the Hindu cosmology, for example, thought in terms of the universe going through endlessly repeating cycles, much like the rhythm of nature but of immense duration – sometimes measured in trillions of years.

However, long before the ancient Greeks, the Hebrews believed that time was linear and that the universe had a beginning. It had been created, and the Creator was God. That is the substance of the opening sentence of the Hebrew book of Genesis: 'In the beginning God created the heavens and the earth.' This biblical view was held by leading Jewish, Christian, and Muslim thinkers. It dominated the intellectual landscape for many centuries.

In the thirteenth century Thomas Aquinas tried to reconcile this biblical position with the Aristotelian by stressing that, in his view, the concept of creation had much more to do with existence than with process. Following Augustine he held that God had created 'with time' rather than in time. According to him, therefore, creation meant simply that the universe depends on God for its existence. Aquinas thought that it was impossible to tell from philosophical considerations whether the universe was eternal or not: yet he conceded that divine revelation showed that it did indeed have a beginning.

For much of the modern scientific era following Copernicus, Galileo, and Newton, there was a general conviction that the universe was infinite in both age and extent. Thereafter, from the middle of the nineteenth century, this view began to come under increasing pressure, to the extent that belief in a beginning is once again the majority view of contemporary scientists. Evidence from the red-shift in the light from distant galaxies, the cosmic microwave background, and thermodynamics has led scientists to formulate the so-called standard 'Big Bang' model of the universe.

Antipathy to the idea of a beginning

It should at once be said, however, that not all scientists are convinced that the Big Bang model is correct. For example, there are difficulties created by possible alternative interpretations of the red-shift, and by recently discovered evidence that the expansion of the universe seems to be accelerating, a circumstance that raises the question of the existence of a hitherto unknown force that acts in the opposite direction to gravity.

Also worldview considerations evidently play a role in the antipathy to the idea of a beginning on the part of some scientists and philosophers. Friedrich Engels made a very perceptive comment on the issues at stake.

> Did God create the world, or has the world been in existence eternally? The answers which the philosophers gave to this question split them into two great camps. Those who asserted the primacy of the spirit to nature, and therefore, in the last instance, assumed world creation in some form or other... comprised the camp of idealism. The others, who regarded Nature as primary, belong to the various schools of materialism.[5]

The late Stephen Hawking adopted a similar view: 'Many people do not like the idea that time has a beginning, probably because it smacks of divine intervention.'[6]

One of them in an earlier time was Sir Arthur Eddington (1882–1944), who reacted as follows: 'Philosophically, the notion of a beginning of the present order of Nature is repugnant... I should like to find a genuine loophole.'[7] His repugnance was shared by others. In the mid-twentieth century Gold, Bondi, Hoyle, and Narlikar advanced a series of steady-state theories maintaining that the universe had always existed and that matter was continuously being created in order to keep the density of the admittedly expanding universe uniform. The creation rate they needed was incredibly slow – one atom per cubic metre in ten billion years. This meant, incidentally, that there was no real possibility of testing their theories by observation.

The motivation for their views was discussed in the prestigious weekly science journal *Nature*,[8] in which well-known science writer John Gribbin pointed out that a great deal of impetus was given to Hoyle and Bondi's steady-state theory by the philosophical and theological problems raised by the idea of a beginning to the universe, in particular, the question of what, or who, was responsible for it.

Another well-known scientist who found the idea of a beginning repugnant was Sir John Maddox, a former editor of *Nature*. He pronounced the idea of a beginning 'thoroughly unacceptable', because it implied an 'ultimate origin of our world', and gave creationists 'ample justification' for their beliefs.[9] It is rather ironical that in the sixteenth century some people resisted advances in science because they seemed to threaten belief in God; whereas in the twentieth century scientific ideas of a beginning were resisted because they threatened to increase the plausibility of belief in God.

There is another point to be made about Maddox's statement. One often hears the criticism levelled at those (scientists) who believe in a Creator that they do not have a model of the universe that leads to testable predictions. Maddox's comment shows that this is simply not true. His antipathy to the idea of a beginning arose because a creation-model of the biblical kind clearly assumes a beginning, and he did not welcome such confirmation. However, evidence of a space–time singularity in the form of the discovery of the microwave background confirmed what the biblical account implied. Science itself has shown that the hypothesis of creation is testable.

I realized the importance of this argument at a very prestigious conference in 2017 where cosmologists, physicists, mathematicians, and even a couple of philosophers and theologians, among others, gathered to discuss the possibility of finding a common language to discuss issues in the borderlands at the interface of science, philosophy, and theology.

At one point in my brief contribution I cited the Genesis creation text: 'In the beginning God created the heavens and the earth.' There was an immediate interruption from the audience by a well-known scientist who said: 'Professor Lennox, please tell us you were joking when you suggested just now that the Bible might have something useful to say to scientists today.' I replied that I was not joking and said that, of course, I agreed that the Bible is pre-scientific by definition and clearly not a text book of science – it dealt with the important questions of meaning that science cannot handle – as Lord Jonathan Sacks said: *'The meaning of a system lies outside the system. Therefore the meaning of the universe lies outside the universe.* Monotheism, by discovering the transcendental God who stands outside the universe and creates it, made it possible for the first time to believe that life has a meaning, not just a mythic or scientific explanation.'[10] However, the Bible also has some very important things to say about the same universe that scientists study, and Genesis 1:1. is one of them.

I then pointed out that Genesis had claimed that there was a beginning thousands of years before the evidence from cosmology came in that challenged Aristotle's eternal universe idea, as mentioned above. 'Now,' I said, 'suppose that scientists had taken the biblical claim that there was a beginning as a hypothesis and looked for ways of testing it, perhaps we would have got to where we are now much earlier.' No response was forthcoming. The fact is that there is a remarkable convergence between Genesis 1:1 and contemporary thinking about the origin of space-time.

There are considerable theoretical difficulties surrounding the beginning. In the so-called 'standard model', the universe near the beginning was both incredibly massive and incredibly small. At the level of the very small, quantum theory comes into its own. Physicists say that a quantum cosmology is required in order to discuss the first split-second of the universe's existence, where 'split' means an almost inconceivably short period of time, the so-called Planck time, of 10^{-43} seconds (0.00...001 with 42 zeros between the decimal point and the 1), which forms a theoretical limit to the smallest time interval for which events can be distinguished. For, at the level of the extremely small, there are unavoidable uncertainties, governed by Heisenberg's uncertainty principle. It places a limit on our ability to determine the values of measurable quantities, like the position and momentum of atomic and subatomic particles. Thus, an element of indeterminacy is introduced, so that, although we can calculate the probability that a certain quantum event will happen, like the radioactive decay of a particle, we cannot fix it precisely. There is a fuzziness in behaviour that cannot be removed. The claim is that, in some way, this fuzziness creates a possibility for the universe to spring into being as a fluctuation in a quantum vacuum.[11]

In their theoretical investigations of this idea, Hawking and Hartle developed a mathematical model of the early universe involving a concept of 'imaginary time',[12] which, they claimed, removed the need for singularities, and thus avoided the question of a Creator. But it doesn't. Apart from the admitted highly speculative nature of such explanations, saying that the universe arises from a fluctuation in a quantum vacuum simply pushes the origins question one step further back, to asking about the provenance of the quantum vacuum.

More importantly, it leaves unanswered the question: What is the origin of the laws governing such a vacuum? However, Hawking admitted that: 'In real time, the universe has a beginning and an end at singularities that form a boundary to space–time and at which the laws of science break down.'[13] There is, then, a consensus of opinion nowadays, that the universe had a beginning.[14]

That inevitably raises the question of obtaining a universe from 'nothing'. Since I have addressed this question in detail in the revised edition of my book *God and Stephen Hawking*,[15] I shall only make a few observations here. The main point is that attempts to argue that the universe is self-explanatory turn out to be self-contradictory. For example, cosmologist Lawrence Krauss makes the following extraordinarily ludicrous statement: 'For surely "nothing" is every bit as physical as "something," especially if it is to be defined as the "absence of something."'[16] Distinguished cosmologist George Ellis FRS, a co-author with Stephen Hawking, in an interview with John Horgan, is asked if he agrees with Krauss' claim that physics has basically solved the mystery of why there is something rather than nothing. Ellis replies:

> Certainly not. He is presenting untested speculative theories of how things came into existence... He does not explain in what way these entities could have pre-existed the coming into being of the universe, why they should have existed at all, or why they should have had the form they did. And he gives no experimental or observational process whereby we could test these vivid speculations... How indeed can you test what existed before the universe existed? You can't.

Logic requires being sensible

Thus what (Krauss) is presenting is not tested science:

> And above all Krauss does not address why the laws of physics exist, why they have the form they have, or in what kind of manifestation they existed before the universe existed (which he must believe if he believes they brought the universe into existence)... He does not begin to answer these questions.[17]

However, Hawking and Atkins do not seem to fare any better. Hawking's often quoted statement is: 'Because there is a law like gravity, the universe can and will create itself from nothing...'[18]; Atkins' is (as mentioned earlier): 'Space-time generates its own dust in the process of its own self-assembly.'[19] Atkins dubs this the 'Cosmic Bootstrap Principle', referring to the self-contradictory idea of a person lifting himself by pulling on his own bootlaces. Another Oxford colleague, philosopher of religion Keith Ward, is surely right to say that Atkins' view of the universe is as blatantly self-contradictory as the name he gives to it, pointing out that it is: 'logically impossible for a cause to bring about some effect without already being in existence'. Ward concludes: 'Between the hypothesis of God and the hypothesis of a cosmic bootstrap, there is no competition. We were always right to think that persons, or universes, who seek to pull themselves up by their own bootstraps are forever doomed to failure.'[20]

What this all goes to show is that nonsense remains nonsense, even when talked by world-famous scientists. What often serves to obscure the illogicality of such statements is the fact that they are made by scientists; and the general public, not surprisingly, assumes that they are statements of science and takes them on that authority. That is why it is important to point out that they are not statements of science, and any statement, whether made by a scientist or not, should be open to logical analysis. Immense prestige and authority does not compensate for faulty logic.

The more we get to know about our universe, the more the hypothesis that there is a Creator God, who designed the universe for a purpose, gains in credibility as the best explanation of why we are here. Charles Townes, who won the Nobel Prize for Physics in 1964 for his discovery of the maser, the forerunner of the laser, writes: 'In my view, the question of origin seems to be left unanswered if we explore it from a scientific point of view. Thus, I believe there is a need for some religious or metaphysical explanation. I believe in the concept of God and in his existence.'[21]

The fine-tuning of the universe

Copernicus was responsible for a revolution in scientific thinking. By overturning the idea that the earth was fixed at the centre of the universe he began a process of diminishing the earth's significance that has resulted in the widespread view that the earth is a fairly typical planet orbiting a fairly typical sun which is positioned in one of the spiral arms of a fairly typical galaxy, which, the multiverse theorists will add, is in a fairly typical universe. This cutting of earth down to size is sometimes known as the 'Copernican Principle'.

However, several avenues of research combine to call this principle into question. For, the remarkable picture that is gradually emerging from modern physics and cosmology is one of a universe whose fundamental forces are amazingly, intricately, and delicately balanced or 'fine-tuned' in order for the universe to be able to sustain life. Many of the fundamental constants of nature, from the energy levels in the carbon atom to the rate at which the universe is expanding, turn out to have exactly the right values for life to be possible. Change any of them a little, and the universe would become hostile to life and incapable of supporting it. The constants are precision-tuned, and it is this fine-tuning that many scientists (and others) think demands an explanation.

Of course, by the very nature of things, we can only refer to the current state of affairs in the awareness that there are, as always, disagreements among scientists as to the validity of some of the assumptions that underlie fine-tuning calculations and that some views may well change. Scientists do not (usually) claim to deliver final truth. Nevertheless, fine-tuning has established itself as an aspect of the universe that merits very serious consideration. Let us look, then, at some examples.

For life to exist on earth an abundant supply of carbon is needed. Carbon is formed either by combining three helium nuclei, or by combining nuclei of helium and beryllium. Mathematician and astronomer, Sir Fred Hoyle FRS, found that for this to happen the nuclear ground state energy levels have to be fine-tuned with respect to each other. This phenomenon is called 'resonance'. If the variation were more than 1 per cent either way, the universe could not sustain life. Hoyle later confessed that nothing had shaken his atheism as much as this discovery. Even this degree of fine-tuning was enough to persuade him that it looked as if: 'a super-intellect has monkeyed with physics as well as with chemistry and biology', and that 'there are no blind forces in nature worth talking about'.[22]

However, in terms of the tolerance permitted, this example pales into insignificance when we consider the fineness of the tuning of some of the other parameters in nature. Theoretical physicist Paul Davies tells us that, if the ratio of the nuclear strong force to the electromagnetic force had been different by 1 part in 10^{16}, no stars could have formed. Again, the ratio of the electromagnetic force-constant to the gravitational force-constant must be equally delicately balanced. Increase it by only 1 part in 10^{40} and only small stars can exist; decrease it by the same amount and there will only be large stars. You must have both large and small stars in the universe: the large ones produce elements in their thermonuclear furnaces; and it is only the small ones that burn long enough to sustain a planet with life.

To use Paul Davies' illustration, that is the kind of accuracy a marksman would need to hit a coin at the far side of the observable universe, twenty billion light years away.[23] If we find that difficult to imagine, a further illustration suggested by astrophysicist Hugh Ross may help.[24] Cover America with coins in a column reaching to the moon (380,000 km or 236,000 miles away), then do the same for a billion other continents of the same size. Paint one coin red and put it somewhere in one of the billion piles. Blindfold a friend and ask her to pick it out. The odds are about 1 in 10^{40} that she will.

Although we are now in realms of precision far beyond anything achievable by current human technology, the cosmos has even more stunning surprises in store. It is said that an alteration in the ratio of the expansion and contraction forces by as little as 1 part in 10^{55} at the Planck time (just 10^{-43} seconds after the origin of the universe), would have led, either to too rapid an expansion of the universe with no galaxies forming, or to too slow an expansion with consequent rapid collapse.[25]

Yet even this level of precision is trumped by what is perhaps the most mind-boggling example of all. Our universe is one in which entropy (a measure of disorder) is increasing; a fact which is enshrined in the second law of thermodynamics. Eminent mathematician Sir Roger Penrose asks us to try to picture in our minds the phase space of the entire universe in which each point represents a different way in which the universe might have started.

> We are to picture the Creator, armed with a 'pin' – which is to be placed at some point in the phase space... Each different positioning of the pin provides a different

universe. ... But in order to start off the universe in a state
of low entropy – so that there will indeed be a second law
of thermodynamics – the Creator must aim for a much
tinier volume of the phase space. How tiny would this
region be, in order that a universe closely resembling the
one in which we actually live would be the result?[26]

Penrose's calculations lead him to the remarkable conclusion that the
'Creator's aim' must have been accurate to 1 part in 10 to the power 10^{123},
that is 1 followed by 10^{123} zeros, a 'number which it would be impossible to
write out in the usual decimal way, because even if you were able to put
a zero on every particle in the universe there would not even be enough
particles to do the job'.[27] Faced with not one, but many such spectacular
examples of fine-tuning, it is perhaps not surprising that Paul Davies says,
'The impression of design is overwhelming.'[28]

Up to this point we have mainly been considering fine-tuning at the
large-scale cosmological level. When we think of the specific conditions
that are needed nearer home in our solar system and on earth, we find that
there is a host of other parameters that must be just right in order for life to
be possible. Some of them are obvious to us all. The distance from the earth
to the sun must be just right. Too near and water would evaporate, too far
and the earth would be too cold for life. A change of only 2 per cent or so
and all life would cease. Surface gravity and temperature are also critical to
within a few per cent for the earth to retain the right mix of atmospheric
gases necessary for life. The planet must rotate at the right speed: too slow
and temperature differences between day and night would be too extreme;
too fast and wind speeds would be disastrous. Astrophysicist Hugh Ross[29]
lists many such parameters that have to be fine-tuned for life to be possible,
and makes a rough but conservative calculation that the chance of one such
planet existing in the universe is about 1 in 10^{30}.

An intriguing angle on this theme has been opened up in the *The
Privileged Planet*, by Guillermo Gonzalez and Jay W. Richards.[30] The
authors draw attention to the earth's remarkable suitability as a place
on which to do science. Their thesis is that, of all possible places in the
universe, earth enjoys conditions that not only allow for habitability but
simultaneously are extremely congenial to the making of 'a stunning
diversity of measurements, from cosmology and galactic astronomy to
stellar astrophysics and geophysics'.[31]

Once one begins to think about it, examples are abundant, some of them very obvious. We might easily have found ourselves in a part of the universe where we could not see into deep space because of too much starlight; our atmosphere might have been opaque or simply translucent rather than transparent. Others are less obvious: witness the fact that the sizes of the moon and the sun and their distances from the earth are just right that a perfect eclipse of the sun is possible. This occurs when the disc of the moon just barely covers the glowing disc of the sun so that the thin ring of the chromosphere (the 'atmosphere') of the sun is visible. It can therefore be investigated scientifically, as a result of which we not only know a great deal more about the sun than we otherwise would, but we have also been able to get confirmation of the bending of light by gravity predicted by Einstein's theory of general relativity.

The authors' conclusion is:

> And yet as we stand gazing at the heavens beyond our little oasis, we gaze not into a meaningless abyss but into a wondrous arena commensurate with our capacity for discovery. Perhaps we have been staring past a cosmic signal far more significant than any mere sequence of numbers, a signal revealing a universe so skilfully crafted for life and discovery that it seems to whisper of an extra-terrestrial intelligence immeasurably more vast, more ancient, and more magnificent than anything we've been willing to expect or imagine.[32]

Arno Penzias, who used the propitious position of the space-platform of earth to make the brilliant discovery of that 'echo of the beginning' – the cosmic background microwave radiation – sums up the position as he sees it: 'Astronomy leads us to a unique event, a universe which was created out of nothing, one with the very delicate balance needed to provide exactly the right conditions required to permit life, and one which has an underlying (one might say 'supernatural') plan.'[33]

We should note once more that the preceding arguments are not 'god of the gaps' arguments; it is advance in science, not ignorance of science, that has revealed the fine-tuning. There is no 'gap' in the science. The question is rather: How should we interpret the science?

The anthropic principle

The conviction that the universe has to be fine-tuned for life, has been called the 'anthropic principle' (Greek: *anthropos* = man). In its weak form (the weak anthropic principle), it runs like this: 'the observable universe has a structure which permits the existence of observers'. Clearly, the precise status of such a statement is open to debate: Is it a tautology? Is it a principle, in the sense that it helps provide explanations, etc.? Whatever the answer, at the very least its formulation draws attention to the fact that viable theories of the cosmos must clearly take into account the existence of observers.

Some scientists and philosophers[34] maintain that we ought not to be surprised at the order and fine-tuning we see in the universe around us, since if it did not exist then carbon-based life would be impossible, and we would not be there to observe the fine-tuning. In other words, they use the anthropic principle against the inference of design. In fact, Richard Dawkins, in *The God Delusion*, tells us that the anthropic principle and God function as alternative explanations.[35] The logic here is doubly false. Dawkins is not only presenting us with false alternatives, but the former of these does not belong to the category of explanation at all. All the anthropic principle says is that for life to exist, certain necessary conditions must be fulfilled. But what it does not tell us is why those necessary conditions are fulfilled, nor how, granted they are fulfilled, life arose. Dawkins is making the elementary mistake of thinking – inexcusable in a scientist – that necessary conditions are sufficient. But that is not always the case: in order to get a first class degree at Oxford it is necessary first to get into the university; but, as many students know, it is certainly not sufficient. *The anthropic principle, far from giving an explanation of the origin of life, is an observation that gives rise to the need for such an explanation.*

Philosopher John Leslie illustrates this point by using his famous 'firing squad' analogy. He asks us to imagine that we are facing a fifty-gun firing squad and says that using the anthropic principle against design is like arguing that:

> ...you should not be surprised to find that you were alive after they had fired. After all, that is the only outcome you could possibly have observed – if one bullet had hit you, you would be dead. However, you might still feel that there is something which very much needs explanation;

namely why did they all miss? Was it by deliberate design? For there is no inconsistency in not being surprised that you do not observe that you are dead, and being surprised to observe that you are still alive.[36]

Leslie argues that the fine-tuning argument presents us with a choice between, at most, two possibilities. The first of these is that God is real. The only way to avoid that conclusion, according to Leslie, is to embrace the 'many worlds' or 'multiverse' hypothesis, popularized in David Deutsch's book *The Fabric of Reality*.[37] It postulates the simultaneous existence of many, possibly infinitely many, parallel universes in which (almost) anything which is theoretically possible will ultimately be actualized, so that there is nothing surprising in the existence of a universe like ours.

This is the view opted for by UK Astronomer Royal Lord Rees. His book *Just Six Numbers*[38] discusses the six fine-tuned numbers that he regards as the most significant controllers of the characteristics of the universe.

Deutsch based his theory on the interpretation of quantum mechanics due to Hugh Everett III in which the basic idea is that at each act of quantum measurement the universe splits into a series of parallel universes, in which all of the possible outcomes occur. Although the Everett interpretation holds out certain advantages over other theories – for example, by obviating the necessity of faster than light signalling – many scientists feel that an explanation which involves undetectable universes and represents in addition an extreme violation of the Occam's Razor principle of searching for theories that do not involve unnecessary multiplication of hypotheses, goes well beyond science into metaphysics. There is much speculation and very little evidence.

John Polkinghorne, for instance, himself an eminent quantum theorist, rejects the many-worlds interpretation:

Let us recognize these speculations for what they are. They are not physics, but in the strictest sense, metaphysics. There is no purely scientific reason to believe in an ensemble of universes. By construction these other worlds are unknowable by us. A possible explanation of equal intellectual respectability – and to my mind greater economy and elegance – would be that this one world is the way it is, because it is the creation of the will of a Creator who purposes that it should be so.[39]

Philosopher Richard Swinburne goes even further: 'To postulate a trillion-trillion other universes, rather than one God, in order to explain the orderliness of our universe, seems the height of irrationality.'[40]

Cosmologist Edward Harrison reacts in a very similar way. 'Here is the cosmological proof of the existence of God – the design argument of Paley – updated and refurbished. The fine-tuning of the universe provides prima facie evidence of deistic design. Take your choice: blind chance that requires multitudes of universes, or design that requires only one... Many scientists, when they admit their views, incline towards the teleological or design argument'.[41] Arno Penzias puts the argument the other way round: 'Some people are uncomfortable with the purposefully created world. To come up with things that contradict purpose, they tend to speculate about things they haven't seen.'[42]

Leslie's suggestion that fine-tuning implies either a God or a multiverse does not convince everyone. Logically these two options are not mutually exclusive, since parallel universes could all be the work of a Creator. Furthermore, Philosopher of Physics the late Michael Lockwood, once an intellectual sparring partner of mine in our Oxford college, observed that Leslie's firing squad argument for this universe is not actually negated by postulating a multiverse. The element of surprise and need for explanation exists within whichever universe fine-tuning is being observed. After all, the probability that a given person obtains a run of ten sixes in throwing a dice is not altered by the fact that there may be many people throwing dice in different places in the same city at the same time.

In a similar vein Christian de Duve writes:

Even if the theory turns out to be correct, the deduction drawn from it by Rees and Weinberg strikes me as what is called in French 'drowning the fish'. Whether you use all the water in the oceans to drown the animal, it will still be there affirming its presence. However many universes one postulates, ours can never be rendered insignificant by the magnitude of this number... what appears to me as supremely significant is that a combination capable of giving rise to life and mind should exist at all.[43]

Therefore the multiverse argument does not in fact weaken the design arguments advanced above.

It is interesting that Lord Rees concedes that the fine-tuning of the universe is compatible with theism but says that he *prefers* the multiverse theory: 'If one does not believe in providential design, but still thinks the fine-tuning needs some explanation, there is another perspective – a highly speculative one, so I should reiterate my health warning at this stage. It is the one I much prefer, however, even though in our present state of knowledge any such preference can be no more than a hunch.'[44] This reminds us of Paul Davies' likes and dislikes mentioned earlier. Preferences, likes and dislikes, are personal attitudes to which, of course, we are all entitled, but they take us beyond the boundary of what most people would understand science to be.

One interesting objection to multiverse theory is made by philosopher Alvin Plantinga. He says that if every logically possible universe exists, then, there must be a universe in which God exists, since his existence is logically possible. Since God is omnipotent, he must therefore exist in every universe. Hence there is only one universe, this universe, of which he is the Creator and Upholder. The concept of many worlds is clearly fraught with logical, and not only scientific, difficulties.[45] It can also present moral difficulties. If every logically possible universe exists, then presumably there is one in which I exist (or a copy of me?), and in which I am a murderer – or worse. The concept seems therefore also to lead to moral absurdity.

Finally, Arno Penzias reminds us that the conviction that there is a teleological dimension in the universe goes back millennia. He writes: 'The best data we have (concerning the Big Bang) are exactly what I would have predicted, had I nothing to go on but the five books of Moses, the Psalms and the Bible as a whole.'[46] We notice in passing Penzias' use of the word 'predicted'. Here is another major counter-example to the commonly held notion that there is no element of predictability (and thus no scientific dimension) in the theistic account of creation. For Penzias, as for many other scientists, the majestic words with which Genesis begins have lost none of their relevance or power: 'In the beginning God created the heavens and the earth.' It is perhaps not surprising, therefore, that the idea of the Big Bang was first mooted (in *Nature* in 1931) by a physicist and astronomer, Georges Lemaître, who was also a priest[47] So much then for the views of physicists and cosmologists.

We must presently turn to the biologists. But before doing so we need to emphasize the fact that the arguments we have used from cosmology and physics are arguments based on standard contemporary science that enjoys widespread acceptance. They are not arguments that involve challenging any of the mainstream claims of science. It is for this reason that fine-tuning arguments gain a ready hearing from many, if not most, scientists. They have the ring of being compatible with authentic scientific activity.

The beginning of space-time and subsequent development of the physical universe according to the standard model in cosmology is one thing; the beginning and subsequent development of biological life is quite another. The very mention of God as a designing intelligence appears to many biologists to call in to question the central pillars of the whole subject: chemical evolution and the neo-Darwinian or modern (evolutionary) synthesis. God-talk generates fear of anti-scientific religious obscurantism.

We are about to enter stormy waters and the reader may wonder why we should even bother. Why should we not simply rest content with presenting the case from physics and cosmology that science has not buried God? The answer is not hard to find. There are influential thinkers with a high public profile who insist that it is biology, of all the academic disciplines, that gives most support to the contention that science has buried God. For them, evolution proves that there is no God. To fail to discuss their arguments would, in their eyes, be to admit defeat. We must therefore take them seriously and so into the storm we must go. It is up to the reader to decide whether we manage to stay afloat. At least, if the waters are turbulent, they are surrounded by a fascinating landscape which we might even get a chance to admire.[48]

Living cell - complexity : build from scratch
Life's origin - biogenesis
Information theoretic considerations

8

The Wonder of the Living World

'No vital forces propel evolutionary change. And whatever we think of God, his existence is not manifest in the products of nature.'
Stephen Jay Gould

All seem to be agreed that the biosphere looks as if it was designed – overwhelmingly so. In order to decide whether or not it is actually designed we first spend some time exploring some of the wonders of the living world, starting with the phenomenal complexity of a living cell. We illustrate that complexity by giving two examples of superbly engineered molecular machines: the bacterial flagellum and kinesin.

We then turn to the question of life's origin, biogenesis. One approach to it is to try to use our human intelligence and ingenuity to build a cell from scratch. Another is to see how life might have arisen through natural processes. We look at the famous Miller-Urey experiment in 1952 simulating what was then thought to be a primitive earth atmosphere. It produced some amino acids, the building blocks of life. However, one of the biggest difficulties is not so much getting the building blocks, but using them to construct the essential proteins that are involved in making the cell. For, proteins are built out of an 'alphabet' of twenty amino acids that in order to function have to be arranged in precise order in very long chains. That is, they are, like the DNA used in their construction, information rich. It is that informational structure that so far has presented an insuperable barrier to scientific explanation. Information theoretic considerations will play a major role as the book progresses.

Nevertheless, a prodigious amount of effort has been put into trying to solve the 'hard problem' as to whether biogenesis occurred by natural unguided processes alone. Evolution in the Darwinian sense is a non-starter here, since it makes no sense to try to *explain* the origin of life in terms of something (natural selection and mutation) whose functioning self-evidently *depends* on life's prior existence.

humans: 50-70 trillion cells

The fact that the universe revealed to us by physics and cosmology is fine-tuned and rationally intelligible leads many to think that it has been designed with us in mind. We humans are truly 'meant to be here'. That puts us in a position now to turn from the non-living world, to the living, to investigate whether it also gives evidence of a designing intelligence, or whether it puts the final nail in God's coffin.

Earth is not a dead planet like Venus. It is a thriving biosphere teeming with living things. Yet life itself turns out to be remarkably difficult to define. We recognize it relatively easily and can identify certain characteristics we associate with it – like the capacity to reproduce,[1] the ability to metabolize, etc. Still, answering the question of what life is remains problematic, to say nothing of how we solve the really big questions as to how it began and how it developed.

From time immemorial, the living world has been a source of never-ending wonder. The more science uncovers, the more the wonder grows. Who can fail to be amazed at the homing instinct of the pigeon, the migratory instinct of the Bewick swan, the echo-locator system of the bat, the blood pressure control centre in the brain of a giraffe and the muscles in the neck of a woodpecker, to mention just a few of countless examples? The living world is replete with mechanisms of mind-bending complexity. At first sight, the biosphere has 'design' written all over it. In his *Royal Institution Christmas Lectures* broadcast in 1991 Richard Dawkins said: 'Living objects... look designed, they look overwhelmingly as though they're designed.' However, Dawkins does not think life was designed. What he thinks is therefore at loggerheads with what he perceives. That raises the interesting question of the status of perception, especially of a very strong perception. When we see a complex piece of engineering, even if we don't know its purpose or function, we perceive it is designed because it is designed. Why would someone reject the same perception regarding a vastly more complex living organism? Dawkins claims that for him it is science – yet he pushes his atheist worldview. Others claim that it is their atheist worldview that has priority. That means that we shall eventually have to look at the relationship between science and worldviews.

First of all, we need to get some sense of just how complex life is. What is it that we see? The obvious place to start is with the mind-boggling structure of even the 'simplest' living cell, the basic constituent of any organism. We humans are composed of somewhere between 50 and 70 trillion cells that go to make up a vast range of different, highly specialized tissues and organs. The first amazing thing about them is that they are all derived from a single cell called the zygote, which is formed from a single sperm merging with a single egg. The zygote divides into two cells which each divide again and so on, and, as the organism continues to grow, cells begin to differentiate from each other in order to fulfil their varied functions in the body – from a cell in a toe nail to a neuron in the brain. We can at once see that this is a phenomenally complicated process. Even a single cell is incredibly complex. Here is a highly simplified diagram to give us some idea:

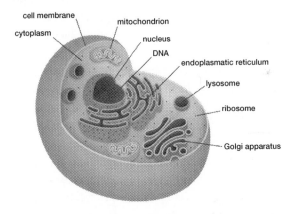

The living cell, 0.01 – 0.10 mm. The smallest thing you can see with the eye is 0.05mm. A couple of hundred cells could be placed on the dot in this letter 'i'.

A cell is made of biological molecules: proteins, lipids, carbohydrates, and nucleic acids. Most of us first encounter proteins in connection with our food. In this context proteins together with fats and carbohydrates form the three macronutrients. However, the proteins in a living cell are large, complex molecules that play many critical roles including functioning as antibodies, enzymes, transmission of signals, etc. In fact, nearly every major process in a cell is carried out by assemblies of ten or more protein molecules. And, as it carries out its biological functions, each of these protein assemblies interacts with several other large complexes of proteins. Indeed, the entire cell can be viewed as a factory that contains an elaborate network of interlocking assembly lines, each of which is composed of a set of large protein machines. They do most of the work in cells and are required for the structure, function, and regulation of the body's tissues and organs.

Geneticist Michael Denton says that the gulf between the non-living and the living world: 'represents the most dramatic and fundamental of all the discontinuities of nature. Between a living cell and the most highly ordered non-biological systems, such as a crystal or a snowflake, there is a chasm as vast and absolute as it is possible to conceive.' For instance, even the tiniest of bacterial cells, weighing less than a trillionth of a gram, is a: 'veritable micro-miniaturized factory containing thousands of exquisitely designed pieces of intricate molecular machinery, made up altogether of 100 thousand million atoms, far more complicated than any machine built by man and absolutely without parallel in the non-living world.'[2]

Furthermore, and interestingly in our context, according to Denton, there seems to be little evidence of evolution among cells as research in molecular biology has demonstrated that the basic design of cells is essentially the same in all living systems. Not only that but:

> In all organisms the roles of DNA, mRNA and protein are identical. The meaning of the genetic code is also virtually identical in all cells. The size, structure and component design of the protein synthetic machinery is practically the same in all cells. In terms of their basic biochemical design, therefore, no living system can be thought of as being primitive or ancestral with respect to any other system, nor is there the slightest empirical hint of an evolutionary sequence among all the incredibly diverse cells on earth.[3]

This view was supported by Nobel Prize winner Jacques Monod, whom Denton cites:

> We have no idea what the structure of a primitive cell might have been. The simplest living system known to us, the bacterial cell... in its overall chemical plan is the same as that of all other living beings. It employs the same genetic code and the same mechanism of translation as do, for example, human cells. Thus the simplest cells available to us for study have nothing 'primitive' about them... no vestiges of truly primitive structures are discernible.[4]

Thus the cells themselves exhibit a kind of 'stasis' similar to that which is found in the fossil record. 'We have always underestimated cells,' says Bruce Alberts, President of The National Academy of Sciences of the USA.

> The entire cell can be viewed as a factory that contains an elaborate network of interlocking assembly lines, each of which is composed of a set of large protein machines... Why do we call the large protein assemblies that underlie cell function, protein machines? Precisely because, like machines invented by humans to deal efficiently with the macroscopic world, these protein assemblies contain highly co-ordinated moving parts.[5]

It is hard for us to get any kind of grasp of the seething, dizzyingly complex activity that occurs inside a single living cell, let alone the equally mind-bending epigenetic activity that controls the switching on and off of genes that enables cell differentiation and placement at exactly the right places to form the complete organism. The concept of epigenetics (epi = upon or above) was originally introduced and defined by the highly influential British developmental biologist Conrad Waddington FRS (1905–75) to refer to the role of networks in organisms in interpreting and controlling their genetic inheritance.

That single cell contains maybe 100 million proteins of 20,000 different types and yet the whole cell is so tiny that a couple of hundred could be placed on the dot in this letter 'i'. The cell is restlessly active as its many micro-miniature assembly lines produce their unending quotas of protein machines.

Here is a highly simplified diagram of one of those machines – the bacterial flagellum that is found, for instance, in E. coli.

This is a tiny motor, discovered in 1973, that powers the bacterial flagellum, a propeller-like device that enables bacteria to swim. It is driven by the ion-motive force that is generated

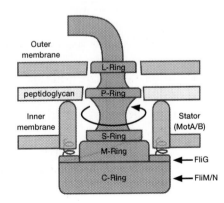

by the transit of ions (protons, in the case of the commonly studied Escherichia Coli Flagellum) across the cellular membrane.

It is so small that 35,000 laid end to end would take up only 1 mm. Indeed, it is so difficult to see, even with an optical microscope, that, although the swimming had already been observed in the seventeenth century, it took 300 years before the means of propulsion was discovered. And that means it is incredibly sophisticated. It consists of some forty protein parts including a rotor, a stator, bushings, and a drive-shaft. What is more, it can rotate at over 18,000 rpm, whereas the upper range for a car engine is around 6,000 rpm. The propeller enables the bacterium to move at a rate of 100 body lengths per second. The work that went into determining its structure was prodigious.[6]

Another fascinating example of a molecular machine is the so-called 'work-horse of the cell', kinesin.[7]

A typical cell contains microtubules, all pointing from the centre of the cell outwards to the surface. Kinesins are used to drag large objects, like lysozomes or endoplasmic reticulum, outwards away from the nucleus and towards the cellular surface. They have an ATP[8] driven motor that imparts to them a walking motion along the microtubules, placing one foot at a time 8 nanometres ahead of the other at a rate of up to 100 steps per second. Not only that but these machines have to operate in a pretty hostile environment where they are constantly assaulted by high-speed water molecules whizzing past in all directions.

The science that has revealed these processes to us is simply stunning, the processes themselves even more so, and, not surprisingly, many scientists and others, whatever their worldviews, react like me with a deep sense of wonder, indeed, awe, when they see it. It is surely very important at a time when there is a move away from science in schools to try to convey some of that wonder to young people in the hope of encouraging them to do science.

For me, the overwhelming impression on watching the kinesin simulation is that of unbelievably sophisticated design. Science is uncovering the design, but not simultaneously revealing any convincing natural process to account for it – as one would expect if the design is real and not merely apparent.

Let us now think of what is involved. Molecular machines, like the flagellum and kinesin, are made from proteins which are themselves made out of the basic building blocks of living systems, the organic compounds

All organisms — 20 Amino acids

called amino acids.[9] Twenty of these occur in living organisms. For adult humans eight have to be provided through diet and are therefore regarded as essential. They are: leucine, isoleucine, valine, threonine, methionine, phenylalanine, tryptophan, and lysine. The amino acids are assembled in long chains called polypeptides; short chains are called peptides and the amino acids are strung together by peptide bonds.

Biogenesis

Molecular machines are themselves made up of cells and some of the hardest questions in biology have to do with their origin. How did cells arise in the first place? How did all their building blocks come to exist and get put together?

Physicist Richard Feynman once said that if he couldn't build something, he couldn't understand it. So, one way of trying to answer these questions involves attempting to build a cell from scratch. The prestigious scientific periodical *Nature* reported in 2018:

2027

> In September 2017, researchers from 17 laboratories in the Netherlands formed the group *Building a Synthetic Cell* (BaSyC), which aims to construct a 'cell-like, growing and dividing system' within ten years, according to biophysicist Marileen Dogterom, who directs BaSyC and a laboratory at Delft University of Technology. The project is funded by an €18.8-million (US$21.3-million) Dutch Gravitation grant. In September, the US National Science Foundation (NSF) announced its first programme on synthetic cells, funded to the tune of $10 million... Bottom-up synthetic biologists predict that the first fully artificial cells could spark to life in little more than a decade.[10]

Research on life's origin has an interesting backstory. We shall start in the 1920s when the famous Russian biochemist A. I. Oparin suggested that the atmosphere of the primeval earth was composed essentially of methane, ammonia, hydrogen, and water vapour; and that life had arisen as a result of chemical reactions occurring between this atmosphere and the chemicals found in the earth with the aid of ultraviolet radiation from the sun and other naturally occurring sources of energy such as lightning.

In 1953, 23-year-old graduate student Stanley Miller conducted a famous experiment to test Oparin's suggestion. As a laboratory experiment, he passed electrical discharges through a mixture of water vapour, ammonia, methane, and hydrogen as suggested by Oparin. After two days Miller found a 2 per cent yield of amino acids. Subsequent experimentation has produced all but one of the twenty amino acids necessary for life.[11]

Such results were hailed as a solution for the problem of life's origin. It seemed for a time as if the building blocks of life could be relatively easily obtained by fairly unsophisticated, natural, unguided processes. However, the euphoria has vanished in the face of subsequent major difficulties raised by deeper understanding of chemistry.

First of all, geochemists now think that earth's early atmosphere did not contain the quantities of ammonia, methane, or hydrogen needed to produce a strongly reducing atmosphere as required by the Oparin hypothesis, but was much more likely to have consisted of nitrogen, carbon dioxide, and water vapour. There is also evidence of significant amounts of free oxygen.[12]

This alters the picture completely, for there are theoretical and practical reasons why amino acids could not be formed in such an atmosphere, as has been confirmed experimentally. The presence of oxygen, for example, would inhibit the production of the crucial biomolecules, and indeed even degrade such that did exist. In short then, the evidence suggests that the atmosphere of the early earth would actually have been hostile to the formation of amino acids.[13]

The test tubes used in the original work were preserved and the experiment revisited over fifty years later, leading to a publication with the title: 'The Miller Volcanic Spark Discharge Experiment'.[14] There were six authors, led by physicist Jeremy England of MIT. Here is the abstract of that paper:

Miller's 1950s experiments used, besides the apparatus known in textbooks, one that generated a hot water mist in the spark flask, simulating a water vapour rich volcanic eruption. We found the original extracts of this experiment in Miller's material and reanalysed them. The volcanic apparatus produced a wider variety of amino acids than the classic one. Release of reduced gases in volcanic eruptions accompanied by lightning could have been common on the early Earth. Prebiotic compounds synthesized in these environments could have locally accumulated, where they could have undergone further processing.[15]

However, Hubert Yockey, a physicist and information theorist who worked with Robert Oppenheimer on the Manhattan Project, in his book *Information Theory and Molecular Biology*, argues that there is scant evidence that there ever was a 'primeval soup' so that the probability of its existence is near to zero.[16] He laments the fact that it is nonetheless still presented as an established fact in many undergraduate texts.

In any case, getting the amino acid building blocks would only be the beginning of the difficulties in the way of would-be cell-constructors. Suppose, for instance, that we want to make a protein that involves 100 amino acids (this would be a short protein – most are at least three times as long). Amino acids exist in two chiral forms that are mirror images of each other, called L and D forms. These two forms appear in equal numbers in prebiotic simulation experiments, so that the probability of getting one or other of the forms is roughly 1/2. However, the great majority of the proteins found in nature contain only the L-form. The probability of getting 100 amino acids of L-form is, therefore, $(1/2)^{100}$, which is about 1 chance in 10^{30}.[17]

Next, the amino acids have to be joined together. Functional protein requires all the bonds to be of a certain type – peptide bonds – in order for it to fold into the correct three-dimensional structure. Yet in prebiotic simulations no more than half of the bonds are peptide bonds. So the probability of a peptide bond is about 1/2, and again the probability of getting 100 such bonds is 1 in 10^{30}. Thus the probability of getting 100 L-acids at random with peptide bonds is about 1 in 10^{60}.[18] In the absence of such complex information processing molecules in the prebiotic state, variable chirality, bonding, and amino acid sequence would not lead to reproducible folded states which are essential to molecular function. Of course, a short protein is much less complicated than the simplest cell for which the probabilities would consequently be very much smaller.

Paul Davies explains that matters get more complicated when one considers the thermodynamic problems that arise in connection with the production of peptide chains of amino acids. The second law of thermodynamics describes the natural tendency of closed systems to increase their entropy – that is to degenerate by losing information, order, and complexity. For instance, heat flows from hot to cold, water flows downhill, cars rust, etc. Now, the second law has a statistical character – it does not absolutely forbid physical systems going against the flow 'uphill', but it stacks the odds very much against it. Davies says: 'It has been estimated that, left to its own devices, a concentrated solution of amino acids would need a volume of fluid the size of the observable universe, to go against the thermodynamic tide, and create a single small polypeptide spontaneously. Clearly, random molecular shuffling is of little use when the arrow of directionality points the wrong way.'[19]

Also, the time available for such 'random molecular shuffling' to occur is much shorter than many people think. According to current estimates there is relatively little time, less than a billion years after the formation of the earth – roughly 4.5 billion years ago – for life to 'emerge'. This is evidenced by the fact that remains of single-celled organisms have been found in the very oldest rocks.

The major problem: the origin of the informational structure of proteins

In a written exchange between physicists Brian Miller and Jeremy England on the possible origins of life we read that:

> A minimally complex free-living cell requires hundreds of tightly regulated enzyme-enabled reactions... Both the proteins... and enzymes represent sequences of amino acids... The amino acids must be arranged in the right order in the same way the letters in a sentence must be arranged properly to convey its intended meaning. This arrangement is crucial for the chains to fold into the correct three-dimensional structures to... perform their assigned functions. This information is essential for constructing and maintaining the cell's structures and processes. *Until origins researchers address the central role of information, the origin of life will remain shrouded in mystery* [italics mine].[20]

Blind chance = chaotic mess.

Paul Davies puts it graphically: 'Making a protein simply by injecting energy is rather like exploding a stick of dynamite under a pile of bricks and expecting it to form a house. You may liberate enough energy to raise the bricks, but without coupling the energy to the bricks in a controlled and ordered way, there is little hope of producing anything other than a chaotic mess.'[21]

It is one thing to produce bricks; it is an entirely different thing to organize the building of a house or factory. If you had to, you could build a house using stones that you found lying around, in all the shapes and sizes in which they came due to natural causes. However, the organization of the building requires something that is not contained in the stones. It requires the skill of the builder, of course, but it also requires the information contained in the architect's plan for the house which is a product of the architect's intelligence. It is the same with the building blocks of life. Blind chance just will not do the job of putting them together in a specific way. Organic chemist and molecular biologist A. G. Cairns-Smith puts it this way: 'Blind chance... is very limited... he can produce exceedingly easily the equivalent of letters and small words, but he becomes very quickly incompetent as the amount of organization increases. Very soon indeed long waiting periods and massive material resources become irrelevant.'[22]

The analogy of letters and words is exactly right since the crucial feature that characterizes proteins is that the amino acids which comprise them *must be in exactly the right places in the chain*. For proteins are not made simply by mixing the right amino acids together in the correct proportions, as we might mix an inorganic acid with an alkali to produce a salt and water. Proteins are immensely specialized and intricate constructions of long chains of amino acid molecules in a specific linear order. The amino acids may be thought of as the twenty 'letters' of a chemical 'alphabet'. Then the protein is an incredibly long 'word' in that alphabet. In this word every amino acid 'letter' must be in the right place. That is, the order in which the amino acids are arranged in the chain is the vital thing, not simply the fact that they are there – just as the letters in a word, or the keystrokes in a computer program, must be in the correct order for the word to mean what it should mean, or for the program to work. A single letter in the wrong place, and the word could become another word or complete nonsense; a single incorrect keystroke in a computer program, and it will probably cease to function.

The point of this argument is made very clear from elementary probability calculations. The probability of getting the correct amino acid at a specific site in the protein is 1/20. Thus the probability of getting 100 amino acids in the correct order would be $(1/20)^{100}$, which is about 1 in 10^{130}, and therefore unimaginably small.[23] Yockey has done detailed calculations based on an actual protein iso-1-cytochrome c. His results are presented in a memorable way: 'Let us see how the Fates could go about selecting an iso-1-cytochrome c sequence from a primeval soup. Lachesis, the caster of lots, casts her 110 icosahedral dice, suitably weighted to reflect the probabilities of each amino acid. Clotho, who spins the web of life, polymerizes them. Atropos watches the progress of the spinning of iso-1-cytochrome c and cuts it when Lachesis assigns an amino acid to a site that is not among those that are functionally equivalent.

In the case that all amino acids (except Gly, which is symmetrical) are of the same optical isometry, what is the probability that Lachesis and Clotho will complete a chain of 110 amino acids in the iso-1-cytochrome c homologous family without having it cut by Atropos? Accepting the values for the concentrations of amino acids in the primeval soup from those who believe in it (as did Nobel laureate Manfred Eigen (1927–2019), a biophysical chemist), Yockey's calculations yield: 'Using the Poisson probability distribution, It is easy to calculate that Lachesis must throw her icosahedral dice selecting one from all $\sim10^{44}$ amino acid molecules in the primeval soup for 10^{23} years to have a probability of 0.95 that her nimble-fingered sister Clotho will complete *one iso-1-cytochrome c molecule* [italics added]. If this were the correct scenario, the fatal sisters would be just beginning since the universe is only about 1.5×10^{10} years old.' Yockey concludes: 'And so we see that even if we believe that the building blocks are available, they do not spontaneously make proteins, at least not by chance. The origin of life by chance in a primeval soup is impossible in probability in the same way as a perpetual motion machine is impossible in probability.'[24]

But that is only the start, and a very modest start at that. For these calculations concern only a single protein. Yet life as we know it requires hundreds of thousands of proteins, and it has been calculated that the odds against producing these by chance is more than $10^{40,000}$ to 1. Sir Fred Hoyle famously compared these odds against the spontaneous formation of life with the chance of a tornado sweeping through a junkyard and producing a Boeing 747 jet aircraft.[25] For more calculations of this type see Chapter 18.

Hoyle's observation here is but an updated version of that made by Cicero around 46 BC where he cites the Stoic Balbus who saw the difficulty of a chance-origin of a language-like structure very clearly: 'If a countless number of copies of the one-and-twenty letters of the alphabet, made of gold or what you will, were thrown together into some receptacle and then shaken out on to the ground, [would it] be possible that they should produce the *Annals of Ennius*? I doubt whether chance could possibly succeed in producing a single verse.'[26] Precisely. Blind chance will not do. Mind will do, and even simple considerations like this one show that avoiding that conclusion on scientific as distinct from worldview grounds is not going to be easy.

But, as we Irish might say, we are now getting ahead of ourselves. For the order in which the amino acids have to be arranged to form a functional protein is determined at a fundamental level by yet another miracle of engineering that is to be found in the nucleus of the cell. It is the most famous molecule in the world – Deoxyribose Nucleic Acid, or DNA for short.

9

The Genetic Code

'The problem of the origin of life is clearly basically equivalent to the problem of the origin of biological information.' Bernd-Olaf Küppers

We now look at the *genetic code* and the way in which it is carried by the DNA macromolecule that resides in the nucleus of the living cell. The discovery of the double helix structure of DNA by Crick and Watson arguably ranks as one of the greatest achievements of science. We learn that *genes*, though tricky to define, can sometimes be thought of as stretches of DNA that are used by the cell to produce proteins. However, the replication of DNA itself cannot proceed without the prior existence of a number of other proteins already in the cell. At least 100 other proteins are involved, without which the genome, which is a complete set of genes, would express nothing.

It was once thought that the genome accounted completely for an organism's inherited characteristics. This was called 'the central dogma' of biology by Francis Crick. It regarded the genome as a 'read-only' memory. We now know that this is not the case. DNA does not contain all the information to construct an organism and, on its own, DNA does not process information.[1] The genome is now understood as a much more sophisticated 'read-write' memory. This has the effect of killing genetic determinism. It also spells the end of the modern synthesis as a viable paradigm covering all aspects of life. In addition, it presents a new and substantial raft of difficulties to the theory that unguided natural processes can account for life.

Information in the cell

One of the greatest scientific discoveries of all time was the elucidation of the structure and significance of the information-bearing macromolecule

DNA. For a living cell is not merely matter. It is matter replete with information. According to Richard Dawkins, 'What lies at the heart of every living thing is not a fire, warm breath, nor a "spark of life". It is information, words, instructions... Think of a billion discrete digital characters... If you want to understand life think about digital technology.'[2]

Since living matter is digital, scientists bring to bear on it all the understanding and language of digital computing and the encoding, decoding, and transmission of messages. We might just pause to reflect on the fact that there is no trace of a digital system, or of messages controlling chemical activity, in non-living matter. The gulf between non-living and living is profound – a fact that creates the immense problem of the origin of the latter.

The information content of DNA is fundamental to life, but we need at once to be alerted to the fact that there is much more to life than DNA. For a start, DNA is not itself alive. But Dawkins is nevertheless right that we need to think about the information DNA carries as playing a fundamental role. The DNA is contained in a tight coil in the nucleus of a living cell. In itself it is inactive but one of its principal functions is to store the instructions needed for and used by the cell to build functional protein out of the amino acids. Like a computer hard disc, DNA contains a database of information that the cell can utilize to produce specified products. Every one of the 10 to 100 trillion cells in the human body contains this database, which is larger than the *Encyclopaedia Britannica*.

Over the last few decades we have witnessed the development from what was at first a somewhat reluctant acceptance on the part of molecular biologists into what is now their wholesale acceptance of the language and methodology of information technology being applicable to molecular biology. That was inevitable once the nature and function of the genetic code was recognized. All scientists now talk quite happily about a living cell as an information-processing machine, since that is precisely what it is: a molecular structure with an information-processing capacity.[3]

This is an enormously exciting intellectual development because it means that the biological information can be explored using the concepts and results of information theory. However, let us not rush to do that before we get a picture in our minds of what the DNA molecule is and how it carries information.

What is DNA?

A ↔ T
G ↔ C
C
T

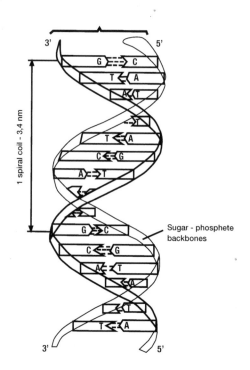

DNA double helix

DNA is a very long molecule with a double helix structure, the discovery of which gained the Nobel Prize for Francis Crick and James Watson. It resembles a spiral ladder 2 nanometres wide, made up of a chain of much simpler molecules called nucleotides. There are ten of these in each full twist of the spiral. The nucleotides consist of a sugar called ribose together with a phosphate group from which one oxygen atom has been removed (thus accounting for the prefix *deoxy-*) and a base. The bases, as they are called, are the four chemicals adenine, guanine, cytosine, and thymine, or A, G, C, T for short, and they (alone) distinguish one nucleotide from the next. The first two bases are purines and the second two are pyrimidines.

The rungs of the ladder are formed out of the base pairs, where the two base-pair molecules forming the ends of any given rung are held together by hydrogen bonds. There is a rule that A is invariably paired with T, and C with G – that is, a purine always bonds to a pyrimidine. Thus if one strand of the double helix starts AGGTCCGTAATG... then the other strand will start TCCAGGCATTAC... The two strands are therefore complementary – if you know one strand, you can work out the other. We shall see the importance of this in a moment.

Of course, the labelling of the nucleotides on the strands is arbitrary in the sense that we could, for example, assign four numbers to them, say 1, 2, 3, 4 or 2, 3, 5, 7 (or indeed any four distinct symbols), and we would then get for the start of the first strand mentioned above 133422341143... or 255733572275..., respectively. Thus a unique number could be assigned to each DNA molecule from which its sequence of bases could be read off. It would usually be an extremely long number, as we shall see below.

Just as a sequence of letters from the ordinary alphabet of one of the world's written languages can carry a message that depends on the precise ordering of the letters, so the sequence of bases on the spine of DNA (the sequence of rungs in the ladder, if you like) carries a precise message written in the four-letter alphabet consisting of the letters A, C, G, T. A gene is a long string of these letters carrying the information for making a protein so that a gene may be interpreted as a set of instructions, like a program, for making that protein.

The way the coding works is that each group of three nucleotides, called a codon, codes for an amino acid. It is this system of coding that is called the *genetic code*. Since there are four nucleotides there are $4^3 = 64$ possible triples available for coding the twenty amino acids. It turns out that one and the same amino acid can have more than one (up to six, in fact) different triples coding for it.

This is wonderful stuff for a mathematician like myself. The discovery of a code at the heart of organic life was an incredible surprise. As we shall be discussing later, it raises the big question of accounting for the existence of such a thing – so far completely intractable in terms of natural processes. As I shall argue in more detail later, irrespective of how life came into existence, the best explanation for its existence is that there is a mind behind the coding.

Another scientist who also takes this view is Marcos Eberlin, a world-renowned Brazilian chemist, prolific author of almost 1,000 research articles and winner of the Thomson Medal (2016). His book *Foresight*, endorsed by three Nobel laureates, argues that the chemistry of life points: 'beyond any purely blind evolutionary process to the workings of an attribute unique to minds – foresight.'[4] His description of the role and function of DNA is well worth reading.

The question arises as to exactly what kind of information is represented by the genetic code. It is clearly more than syntactic information since the DNA codes for the amino acids and through them it codes for the proteins. Is this semantic information? Some say no because they think that semantic information always involves a conscious mind. Since they do not believe that any mind designed the genetic coding system, in order to distinguish it from semantic information they call it 'coding' or 'shaping' information from the Latin *informare* = to give shape or form to. I suspect that this is a semantic quibble that has no real force. It also begs the question as to the existence of a mind behind the existence of DNA.

One thing that is clear is the strong analogy between the genetic code and natural human languages. Three nucleotides build a code word, comparable to a word in a natural language. The code words are joined up into functional units called genes – like a sentence in a natural language, and the genes are joined into a much longer 'text'.[5] It has been suggested to me by Professor of Mathematics, Nigel Cutland, that DNA is like the program used to control the robots that construct cars in a factory. A cell is much like modern machinery – controlled by a program on a chip – but with a cell the program also specifies the processing of the raw materials and the construction of the hardware too.

The genome

According to evolutionary biologist James Shapiro, there is 'no rigorous and consistent definition' for *gene*. One suggestion is that a gene is a 'continuous human DNA sequence encoding a specific protein'. This leads Shapiro to suggest that a better term would be *coding sequence*.[6] A consequence of genetic reductionism is that DNA is thought of as an active cause, indeed, the sole cause of heredity, when it is not. It needs to be clearly understood that DNA on its own is lifeless and produces nothing. The actual situation, as revealed by systems biology (see Chapter 19), is that the cell uses the gene to produce the proteins. Without the cell and its machinery nothing will otherwise happen.

In turn, the *genome* consists of a complete set of genes. Genomes, or rather the DNA that encodes them, are generally very large: the DNA of an E. coli bacterium is about four million letters long and would fill 1,000 pages in a book, whereas the human genome is over 3.5 billion letters long, consisting of 20 to 30,000 genes and would fill a whole library.[7] As a matter of interest the actual length of the DNA that is tightly folded into a single cell of the human body is roughly 2 metres, which is about 100,000 times longer than in most cells. We note in passing that the geometric shape of the coiling or three-dimensional folding is also a carrier of information. Since there are about 10 trillion (= 10^{13}) cells in the human body the total length of DNA is a mind-boggling 20 trillion metres.

For the sake of accuracy it should be pointed out that, although we often think of the DNA in a given organism as the genome, strictly speaking, the genome actually occupies only a part of the DNA, a relatively small part, in humans about 3 per cent. The remaining 97 per cent, called 'non-coding DNA', was for a time erroneously described as 'junk DNA'. More recent research has shown that it is far from being junk. It is responsible for the regulation, maintenance, and reprogramming of genetic processes. In addition, it contains highly mobile segments of DNA, called 'transposons', that can fabricate copies of themselves and then move to different sites on the genome with varying effects, including possibly disabling genes or activating hitherto inactive genes.[8]

The DNA resides in the nucleus of the cell, which is protected by a membrane. In order for anything to happen, the information contained in the DNA must be transported to the cytoplasm, the area of the cell outside the nucleus where the cellular machinery is working – the factory floor of the cell, if you like. That information is needed, for example, for the construction of enzymes in the cytoplasm by molecular machines called ribosomes.[9]

So how does the information on the DNA get to the ribosomes to make enzymes? It is done by means of another long nucleic acid molecule called ribonucleic acid (RNA), which is very similar to DNA except that it is not usually double stranded, though it does possess one Hydroxyl (OH) – group more than DNA. Like DNA it has four bases: three of them are our old friends A, G, and C, but the fourth is a newcomer, Uracil (U), which replaces DNA's T. What happens first is that the DNA inside the nucleus 'unzips' down the middle separating the two strands. This is facilitated by the fact that the hydrogen bonds between the strands are weak compared with the bonds that connect the bases in each strand of the DNA.

Next a strand of DNA is transcribed into RNA, so-called 'messenger-RNA' (mRNA). As a result an RNA strand emerges that is complementary to the DNA strand in which T is replaced by U throughout. The transcription proceeds at around 80 nucleotides per second. There is a correction process that checks the transcription with unbelievable precision. Occasionally errors occur that could lead to a modified protein but they are rare, perhaps one in a hundred million letters. The mRNA then travels through the wall of the nucleus to the cytoplasm where the stunningly intricate process of translation takes place. Here is the way the coding works – the amino acids are listed at the bottom.

RNA codon Table

CAC AGU

1st position	2nd position				3rd position
	U	**C**	**A**	**G**	
U	Phe	Ser	Tyr	Cys	U
	Phe	Ser	Tyr	Cys	C
	Leu	Ser	stop	stop	A
	Leu	Ser	stop	Trp	G
C	Leu	Pro	His	Arg	U
	Leu	Pro	His	Arg	C
	Leu	Pro	Gln	Arg	A
	Leu	Pro	Gln	Arg	G
A	Ile	Thr	Asn	Ser	U
	Ile	Thr	Asn	Ser	C
	Ile	Thr	Lys	Arg	A
	Met	Thr	Lys	Arg	G
G	Val	Ala	Asp	Gly	U
	Val	Ala	Asp	Gly	C
	Val	Ala	Glu	Gly	A
	Val	Ala	Glu	Gly	G

Amino Acids

Ala: Alanine	Gln: Glutamine	Leu: Leucine	Ser: Serine
Arg: Arginine	Glu: Glutamic acid	Lys: Lysine	Thr: Threonine
Asn: Asparagine	Gly: Glycine	Met: Methionine	Trp: Tryptophane
Asp: Aspartic acid	His: Histidine	Phe: Phenylalanine	Tyr: Tyrosisne
Cys: Cysteine	Ile: Isoleucine	Pro: Proline	Val: Valine

Reading this we get, for example, that CAC gives histadine, AGU gives serine.

The mRNA strand can be thought of as something like a magnetic computer tape and the ribosome a machine that constructs a protein from the information contained on that tape. In order to do so the ribosome moves along the mRNA strand 'reading' the information contained in it as it goes. It is just like a magnetic tape-recording head in a computer, or the scanning head of a Turing machine, though there we tend to think of the head as fixed and the tape as moving, an insignificant difference for our purposes. Computer-like it reads the codons, which we recall are groups of three consecutive characters, in the order they appear on the tape – so, for example, GCU, ACG, GAG, ...

Ribonucleic acid

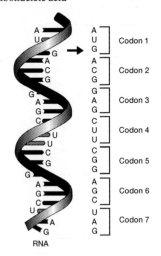

RNA

The illustration shows a typical sequence of codons in a messenger RNA (mRNA) molecule. Each of them is formed from three nucleotides that normally corresponds to a single amino acid. These nucleotides are denoted by A, U, G, and C. We note that mRNA uses U (uracil) whereas DNA uses T (thymine). An mRNA molecule instructs a ribosome to synthesize a protein using this code. The genetic code can be viewed as the set of rules used by the cell to translate information that is encoded in genetic material (DNA or mRNA).

The next task for the ribosome is to find the amino acids that correspond to these codons (in this case, asparagine, cysteine, and leucine). They turn out to be swimming around in the neighbourhood of the ribosome attached by ester bonds to molecules (called transfer RNA, tRNA) that look like crosses. If, for example, asparagine is attached to one arm of such a molecule then the other end of that arm is attached to what is called the anticodon, corresponding to the codon AAC, that is, UUG.

When the ribosome reads any particular codon it fishes around for the corresponding anticodon, nets it, and then removes the amino acid attached to it. The ribosome then joins that amino acid to those it has already assembled. Thus the new protein gradually emerges. The protein then has to be folded into a three-dimensional configuration by means of other proteins, and that folding brings with it an additional level of geometric information. These tiny mechanisms, so small that they can only be 'seen' by atomic force microscopy, not with a normal optical microscope, are of a bewildering order of sophistication, as a glance at any textbook on molecular biology will confirm. And there is a phenomenal number of them. A typical mammal cell may contain 10 billion proteins.

The nature of the complexity involved is such that even convinced evolutionary biologists such as John Maynard Smith and Eörs Szathmáry confess that: 'The existing translational machinery is at the same time so complex, so universal, and so essential, that it is hard to see how it could have come into existence, or how life could have existed without it.'[10] Nearly ten years later we find microbiologist Carl Woese lamenting that even humans with all their intelligence cannot construct such mechanisms: 'We don't understand how to create novelty from scratch – that's a question for biologists of the future.'[11]

Replication of DNA is another mind-boggling process. *Yet it cannot proceed without the prior existence of a number of other proteins already in the cell.* Robert Shapiro, expert on DNA chemistry, points out that proteins, though built following instructions encoded in DNA, are large molecules that chemically are very different from DNA: 'The above account brings to mind the old riddle: Which came first, the chicken or the egg? DNA holds the recipe for protein construction. Yet that information cannot be retrieved or copied without the assistance of proteins already in the cell. Which large molecule, then, appeared first... proteins (the chicken) or DNA (the egg)?'[12]

The answer to this is increasingly becoming clear: it is the cell that is all important. Pioneer systems biologist Denis Noble CBE FRS points us in that direction when he writes:

> After all, the genes by themselves are dead. It is only in a fertilized egg cell, with all the proteins, lipids, and other cellular machinery inherited from the mother, that the process of reading the genome to initiate development can get going. At least 100 different proteins are involved in this machinery, without which the genome would express nothing. So even at the very beginning of a new organism's life more is happening than is dreamt of in the reductionist's bottom-up model.[13]

New life therefore involves downward causation and feedback.

Casual circularity

Marcos Eberlin calls this 'chicken and egg' circumstance 'causal circularity'. It is found throughout living systems. Another fascinating example that he gives is the cell's protective membrane. Oxygen is essential for life but oxygen can be deadly, as one discovers by puncturing a cell and exposing it to the atmosphere. Cells also require nutrients so there must also be channels in the membrane. And there are protein channels in the double-layered membrane whose intricate structure is evidence of impressive foresight in its design. Eberlin puts it this way:

> No membranes, no life. And not just membranes but membranes with a myriad of phospholipids and channels that enable a cell to control its internal environment. These channels require complex and specialized proteins to function. Yet in the absence of a skilled biochemist, the necessary proteins are made only in cells – which existed long before there were biochemists. Without stable membranes loaded with protein-operated channels, there are no cells. But without cells there are no proteins to form membrane channels.[14]

There is no way out of the circularity without foresight. Mind again!

Fine-tuning in biology

In Chapter 7 we discussed the phenomenon of fine-tuning in physics and cosmology – the sensitive dependence of certain properties on the values of fundamental parameters such as the constants of nature. It is granted by almost all scientists that at this level the universe is fine-tuned for life. However, why should we stop with physics and cosmology? Is it not conceivable in light of the sophisticated nature of the protein machinery that we are now considering, that there is also some kind of fine-tuning here? Steinar Thorvaldsen, an information theoretician at the University of Tromsö and Ola Hössjer, a statistician at the University of Oslo, ask: 'Is it possible to recognize fine-tuning in biological systems at the levels of functional proteins, protein groups and cellular networks? Can fine-tuning in molecular biology be formulated using state of the art statistical methods, or are the arguments just "in the eyes of the beholder"?'[15]

The authors argue that the

> strong synergy within the protein complex makes it irreducible to an incremental process. They are rather to be acknowledged as fine-tuned initial conditions of the constituting protein sequences. These structures are biological examples of nano-engineering that surpass anything human engineers have created. Such systems pose a serious challenge to a Darwinian account of evolution, since irreducibly complex systems have no direct series of selectable intermediates, and in addition... each module (protein) is of low probability by itself.[16]

The main conclusion of their research is that it is clear that biological systems are characterized by fine-tuning even more so than in inorganic systems. They argue that this fine-tuning is ascertainable by scientific methods. Although there is a great deal more to be done they believe that they possess sufficient evidence: to demonstrate that fine-tuning and design deserve attention in the scientific community as a conceptual tool for investigating and understanding the natural world. The main agenda is to explore some fascinating possibilities for science and create room for new ideas and explorations. Biologists need richer conceptual resources than the physical sciences until now have been able to initiate, in terms of complex structures having non-physical information as input... Yet researchers have more work to do in order to establish fine-tuning as a sustainable and fully testable scientific hypothesis, and ultimately a Design Science.

Replication and cell division

There is much more to DNA than its function as the software that enables protein production. It has another vital (literally!) role in cell division. Existing cells must divide in order to make new cells and so build up an organism. Each of those new cells requires its own copy of the DNA. And there is a vast machine tool factory that sees to it that this gets done. Again, it is important for us to get some faint idea of its sophistication.

Cell division comes in two forms – meiosis and mitosis. Meiosis is the kind of division that creates egg and sperm cells. Mitosis is the process of division in which a cell duplicates all of its contents, including its chromosomes, and splits to form two identical daughter cells. These are fundamental processes of life. The replication of DNA is the only part of cell division.[17]

There are hundreds of fascinating features involved in this particular process. One amazing miniature motor, DNA polymerase, moves along the DNA strand and copies its digital information onto a new DNA strand which is constructed one 'letter' at a time at a rate of around 100 base pairs per second. I would suggest that you stop reading here and watch a video illustrating this spectacular process on YouTube.[18]

What is becoming ever more clear is that the modern synthesis, with its now rather primitive looking reductionist model, does not even begin to explain how things really work, let alone how they came to exist in the first place.

Robert Shapiro points out in his *Scientific American* article 'A Simpler Origin of Life'[19] that no trace of a hypothetical primal replicator and catalyst has been recognized so far in modern biology. He adds that even if the so-called primeval soup contained the basic building blocks of those replicators, even under favourable conditions for assembling them into a chain, they would inevitably be surrounded by defective blocks that would ruin the capacity of the chain to replicate. He helps us grasp the difficulty using an analogy:

> Picture a gorilla (very long arms are needed) at an immense keyboard connected to a word processor. The keyboard contains not only the symbols used in English and European languages but also a huge excess drawn from every other known language and all of the symbol sets stored in a typical computer. The chances for the spontaneous assembly of a replicator in the pool I described above can be compared to those of the gorilla composing, in English, a coherent recipe for the preparation of chili con carne.[20]

At this point Shapiro cites Gerald F. Joyce of the Scripps Research Institute and Leslie Orgel of the Salk Institute who concluded that the spontaneous appearance of RNA chains on the lifeless Earth 'would have been a near miracle'. Shapiro himself would extend this conclusion to all of the proposed RNA substitutes that I mentioned above.

Shapiro's conclusion (printed version) is unequivocal and illuminating: 'DNA, RNA, proteins and other elaborate large molecules must be set aside as participants of the origin of life.'[21] He proposes a 'metabolism first' scenario and actually thinks that: 'There's nothing freaky about life; it's a normal consequence of the laws of the universe.'[22]

Is it all in the genes?

In writing about the complexity of information-rich biomolecules like DNA and the genetic code, it is easy to give the impression that the genes tell us everything about what it means to be human. Indeed, as we mentioned earlier, the 'central dogma' of molecular biology was that the genome accounts completely for an organism's inherited characteristics. This inevitably fuelled genetic determinism – the idea that individual genes were responsible for a whole variety, not only of human diseases, but also for all manner of characteristics, from predisposition to violence or obesity to mathematical ability. The reductionist causal chain went inexorably from the bottom to the top: genes to proteins to pathways to sub-cellular mechanisms to cells to tissues to organs to the entire organism.[23]

Subsequent research has shown that this is not the case. The central dogma is false. James Shapiro writes:

> the view of traditional genetics and conventional evolutionary theory is that the genome is a Read-Only memory (ROM) system subject to change by stochastic damage and copying error. For over six decades, however, an increasingly prevalent alternative view has gained prominence. The alternative view has its basis in cytogenic and molecular evidence. This distinct perspective treats *the genome as a read-write (RW) memory system subject to non-random change by dedicated cell functions...*.'[24] (Italics mine.)

This development represents a long overdue major paradigm shift, that at once shows that things are much more complex than the reductionist view ever dreamed. It kills off genetic determinism with its notion that the function of the genome is simply to hold data files that determine the sequence structures of RNA and the proteins that determine the properties of the complete organism. It therefore opens up new vistas of

[handwritten annotation at top: Epigenetic: Human genome: 30K genes → 100K proteins]

research. It also clearly demonstrates that not everything is in the genes. There are higher levels of organization and inheritance that is independent of the contribution made by the DNA sequence. The term 'epigenetic' ('beyond' or 'above' genetic) is used to denote this higher level, not only of information but of information-processing and causation. Nobel laureate for Physiology (2012) Sir John Gurdon, one of the pioneers of cloning, showed the existence of this epigenetic level by demonstrating that, when cells differentiate, their genetic material is not lost or destroyed, but the original genetic material can be recovered to the extent that nuclei from specialized cells are able to create the whole animal if placed, for instance, in an unfertilized egg.[25]

The existence of such an epigenetic level is not surprising in light of the fact that the human genome turns out to contain only around 30,000 genes. This was a shock to many people. Since human cellular machinery produces somewhere around 100,000 different proteins, one might have expected at least that number of genes to encode them. This means that each gene must be involved in multiple biological functions in order to account for the incredible complexity of our inherited characteristics, let alone for the great differences between, say, plants and humans. In addition to that, there are molecules other than proteins that determine biological function – for instance, lipids that are not coded for by genes. Geneticist Steve Jones writes: 'A chimp may share 98 per cent of its DNA with ourselves but it is not 98 per cent human:[26] it is not human at all – it is a chimp. And does the fact that we have genes in common with a mouse, or a banana say anything about human nature? Some claim that genes will tell us what we really are. The idea is absurd.'

Take, for example, the crucially important fact that genes can be switched on or off at certain stages in the development of an organism. The control of such switching is mainly undertaken by sequences called 'promoters', which are usually to be found near to the start of the gene. Let us now imagine an organism with n genes, each of which can be in one of two states, on or off, expressed or unexpressed, in genetic terminology. Then there are clearly 2^n possible expression states. Suppose now we have organisms A and B with 32,000 and 30,000 genes, respectively. Then the number of expression states for A is $2^{32,000}$ and for B is $2^{30,000}$. Hence A has 2^{2000} times as many expression states as B – and 2^{2000} is a very large number, larger in fact by far than the number of elementary particles there are estimated to be in the universe (about 10^{80}).

Control mechanisms.

Suppose we are much more modest. Denis Noble writes: 'Consider, for example, the effect of adding one gene to a genome of 30,000 genes. The number of possible new potential functions is about 10^{287}. Conversely, if a function requires just one more gene, then the number of newly created possible combinations would be about 10^{292}.'[27] Noble argues that these unimaginably large numbers show the impracticability of the popular idea that it should be possible to build a living system from the bottom up, starting with the DNA code.

Thus, a relatively small difference in the number of genes could account for the very large differences in the phenotype (observable characteristics) of the organism. But that is only a beginning since the base assumption in our last calculation that genes are either on or off is too simplistic by far, especially if we are thinking of the more complex organisms. The genes of such organisms tend to be 'smarter' in the sense that they have a much wider range of molecular machines they can build and control. For instance, they may be partly expressed, that is, neither completely on nor completely off.

Such control mechanisms are capable of responding to the cellular environment in determining to what extent a gene should be switched on. Thus they are like miniature control computers in their own right. And, since the degree to which they are on or off varies, the above calculations must be drastically revised upwards. The effect of proteins working on proteins means that we are now entering a hierarchy of sharply increasing levels of complexity even the lowest level of which is difficult to grasp.

The more the living cell is studied, the more it appears to have in common with one of the most sophisticated high-tech products of human intelligence: the digital computer. Except that the cell's information-processing capacity far outstrips anything present-day computers can do. The cell is like a super-computer. The founder of the Microsoft Corporation, Bill Gates, said that 'DNA is like a computer program, but far, far more advanced than any software we've ever created.'[28] In fact DNA not only controls the computer like Windows, but has the instructions for manufacturing the hardware as well as gathering, processing and gathering the materials needed to build it.

The question of how such unbelievable complexity ever came to exist in the first place is not made any easier by the fact that this code is viewed as being extremely ancient. Werner Loewenstein, who has won world renown for his discoveries in cell communication and biological information transfer, says: 'This genetic lexicon goes back a long, long way. Not an iota seems to have changed over two billion years; all living beings on earth, from bacteria to humans, use the same sixty-four word code.'[29] The words here are called codons, of which there are $4^3 = 64$.

In his book *Gödel, Escher, Bach – an Eternal Golden Braid* mathematician Douglas Hofstadter writes:

> A natural and fundamental question to ask on learning of these incredibly, intricately interlocking pieces of software and hardware is: 'How did they ever get started in the first place?'... from simple molecules to entire cells, is almost beyond one's power to imagine. There are various theories on the origin of life. They all run aground on this most central of central questions: 'How did the Genetic Code, along with the mechanisms for its translation, originate?'[30]

Yet surely, *what* organisms *actually are* – the very nature of the complexity of organisms, the nature and extreme sophistication of their protein machinery, the coding they contain, their capacity to use programmed information, etc. is piling up evidence that there is a mind behind life, even though we have little or no idea how life itself *came to be*. It is, after all, a plain fact that the only known source of information of the type we have been studying is mind.

"You are irreducibly complex and beautifully designed by higher intelligence! marvelously"

Syntatic information — not redated to any meaning
Semantic info.

10

A Matter of Information

Up to this point we have freely referred to the concept of information. In this chapter we look more closely at what it means. We introduce the Shannon concept of syntactic information and give examples of how such information content is measured in terms of bits. We introduce semantic information and the complexity of sequences. This naturally leads us to examples of this in biology.

In ordinary language we use the word 'information' to describe something that we now know but did not know before. We say that we have received information or, that we received a message that contained information. We are familiar with many methods of transmitting information: verbally, in plain writing, in sign language, in cryptic code, etc. The problem comes when we try to quantify that information. However, the *theory of information* has made considerable progress, which is of great importance when we come to think about what we have called genetic information.

Let's start by exploring the intuitive notion that information decreases our uncertainty. For example, we arrive at a small hotel where we have made a reservation and find that there are only eight rooms. Then, on the assumption that all the rooms are similar and that we have not requested any particular room there is a probability of 1 in 8 that we will be assigned any particular room. That probability is a clear measure of our uncertainty as to which room will be ours. On being given the information that we have been assigned Room 3, say, that uncertainty disappears.

One of the ways in which we might measure this information is to work out the least number of yes or no questions we would have to ask in order to find out which room we have been assigned. A little thought should convince us that that number is 3. We say that we have received three *bits* of information, or that we need three bits of information, in order to specify our room. We notice that 3 is the power to which we have to raise 2 to get 8 (that is, $8 = 2^3$) or, putting it the other way round, 3 is the logarithm of 8 in base 2, (that is $3 = \log_2 8$). It is easy to generalize this argument to see that if there are n rooms in the hotel, then the amount of information needed to specify a particular room is $\log_2 n$ bits.

Think now of a text message written in English, which we shall regard as a language written in sentences consisting of words and spaces, so that our 'alphabet' consists of 26 letters plus a space so that 27 symbols are needed. If we are waiting for a message on our mobile phone then the probability of receiving any symbol (letter or space) is 1/27. The information added by each text symbol in bits is $\log_2 27$ (= 4.76 approx.). So the information conveyed by a text m symbols long will be $m\log_2 27$ bits (4.76m approx.).

We notice here that the amount of information conveyed is relative to the known size of the 'alphabet'. For example, if we know that our text message may contain numbers as well as letters and spaces then our 'alphabet' has now got 37 letters. Hence the information represented by each symbol received in bits is now $\log_2 37$ (= 5.2 approx.).

The number 2 clearly plays a special role here. In fact the 'alphabet' used in computing consists of the two symbols 0 and 1. It is easy to see that 2 is the minimum number of symbols necessary in order to encode any alphabet whatsoever. For example, if we think of English as needing 26 letters plus a space then binary strings of length at most 5 ($2^5 = 32 > 27$) will suffice to encode it all with room to spare: we could encode the space symbol as 00000 and put A = 00001, B = 00010, C = 00011, etc.

Syntactic and semantic information

We now introduce a very important idea that is sometimes a little tricky to grasp. Suppose we get the following 'message' on our mobile phone: UFZXXTRQ NJOPWTRP. It is 16 symbols long and so, doing the usual calculation, we get an information content of $16\log_2 27$ bits. But you say: 'Hang on a minute: that is absurd because there is no information in this gibberish.' Of course, the communication might have been encrypted but let us assume it was not. What then? We have now reached the fact that 'information' in the sense we have just been discussing has actually got nothing to do with 'meaning' at all. We call it *syntactic information*.

At first sight this seems counter-intuitive and so it needs spelling out in more detail. Suppose that you are told to expect a 'message' on your mobile phone. You are also told that there are four possible symbols you may receive (~ # * ^) and that the message will be five symbols long. You look at the screen and what you see is: ^ ^ # ~ *. How much 'information' have you received? Well, none in the sense that you have no idea what it means; indeed, you do not know if it means anything at all. But in the syntactic sense you have received information. There are four possible symbols. So the probability you will get a particular one of them is $1/4$ and the information supplied by each symbol received is two bits. The total 'message' consisting of five symbols contains ten bits. Putting it another way: if we count up how many possible 'messages' (that is strings of five symbols) you might receive, we see that it is 2^{10}. You now know what the 'message' is (not what it means!). You did not know that before. So, in that sense, you have received information.

Think again of everyday electronic communications across a channel, for example, an ordinary telephone line. At any given moment various kinds of 'information' may be flowing down it: voice communication, data communication – all kinds of streams of electronic 'symbols'. Some of it will carry meaning for some people and not for others – for instance, a person speaking Chinese will convey no information in the semantic sense to someone who speaks no Chinese. Some of it could be strings of random symbols representing noise on the line generated by random electronic effects, carrying no meaning whatsoever.

A communications engineer is not concerned with the *meaning* of what is going through the channel – the specific sequences that are being transmitted but rather in things such as: the capacity of the channel. How many telephone conversations can be carried simultaneously in a fibre-optic cable? How many symbols (of whatever kind) can be sent through it in a second? How reliable is the channel? What is the probability that a symbol will be sent in error, for example, because of noise on the channel? Can errors be corrected?

These things affect all of us. I still hold a radio amateur licence and can recall the difficulty of understanding a weak radio signal against the background of noise.

Measuring syntactic information, therefore, is very important and the theory associated with it is called the Shannon theory of information, after Claude Shannon who developed it. He established fundamental mathematical results about the capacity of channels of communication that are subject to noise and thereby laid the foundation of the theory of communication upon which our society depends today.

Let's look at another everyday example just to make sure we have got the idea. You go into a library and ask for a book on nephrology. The librarian may never have heard of nephrology. But, as a string of symbols, the word 'nephrology' contains $10 \log 27$ bits of information and if you give the library assistant those bits of information she can type them into her computer index system and come up with the fact that you should look in the section of the library labelled MedSci 46, say, where you will find three books on the subject. That is, she acts as a 'channel' to communicate the information to her index system even though, for her, the symbol string 'nephrology' has no semantic connotation at all.[1]

In this example, the word 'nephrology' is treated by the librarian at the purely syntactic level. She neither knows, nor needs to know, what the word means. The only information she needs is the string of letters of which it is composed: she simply treats the word as a meaningless string of letters from an alphabet. However for you as a medical doctor the word 'nephrology' has a meaning – the study of kidneys. That is, to you it conveys not only syntactic information but *semantic information* ('semantic' derives from the Greek word for a sign, hence 'semiotics' meaning the theory of signs).

Measuring semantic information is a much more difficult problem to get a grip of mathematically and no successful way has yet been discovered. This is hardly surprising since the meaning of a text is dependent on its context. If you see me receiving on my mobile phone the message 'YES' you may well guess that it is the answer to a question I have asked, but you will not know whether that question is 'Have you a ticket for the football game tonight?' or 'Will you marry me?'. Or, if the message is BALD its meaning is very different according to which language it is in – English 'bald', German 'soon'. The meaning of the message cannot be determined without prior knowledge of the context. Hence, additional prior information is necessary to interpret any given piece of information. The term *pragmatic information* is also used when attention is being drawn to the fact that the meaning of a message also may depend on its effect it has on the recipient. However, we can still calculate the Shannon information of a message containing semantic information and it is highly likely that whatever the measure of the semantic information it will be greater and not less than the syntactic information.

Now let us apply some of this thinking to molecular biology. Think of the string of chemical 'letters' that we find in a DNA molecule. Suppose that you are a molecular biologist and know (something about) what the string of letters 'means' in the sense that you can divide them up into genes and say what proteins those genes code for, etc. That is, for you, the string has a semantic dimension. For you, DNA exhibits precisely the same kind of specified complexity that characterizes natural languages since the order of the letters in a gene specifies the order of the sequence of amino acids in the protein.[2]

But not for me: I see the string as nothing but a lengthy list of 'meaningless' symbols like ACGGTCAGGTTCTA... . Of course, it still makes perfect sense to talk of my knowing the information content of the symbol string in the syntactical or Shannon sense. Indeed, in spite of the fact that I do not understand the 'meaning' of the string, I can work out precisely how much syntactic information you need to give me in order that I can reproduce the string accurately. The genetic alphabet consists of four letters, so each letter you read out to me, or send me by computer, involves two bits of information. Thus, for example, the DNA in a human genome which is roughly 3.5 billion letters long contains about 7 billion bits of information. If I am given them I can write out the contents of the DNA string without having any idea whatsoever of the biological significance of what I have written.

A very important aspect of research on the genome is that of 'data mining' – finding specific repeated patterns, or sequences that are common to several genomes. The reason for looking for a specific sequence may well be motivated by semantic considerations, but the actual computer search for it in the large database that is formed by the genome proceeds at the level of syntactical information.

Complexity

The fact that the human genome contains 7 billion bits of information gives us some idea of its complexity. But only some. Think, for example, of the following binary string: 001001001001001010... Let us assume that it goes on like this to total 6 billion digits – we shall want a number divisible by three. Then we can immediately see that, from our perspective so far, it contains 6 billion bits of information. Is it therefore (nearly) as complex as the human genome? Clearly not. For we see at once that it consists of a repeated pattern – the triple 001 is repeated again and again. Thus, in a sense, all of the information contained in the string is contained in the statement *repeat the triple 001 two billion times*.

This mechanical process of repetition is an example of what mathematicians call an *algorithm*.[3] This can be thought of as an automatic, step-by-step procedure or set of instructions that do not need any intelligence to carry out – in other words, the kind of process that computer programs are designed to implement. In this case we could write a simple program as follows: *For n = 1 to 2 billion, write 001. Stop.* Only 39 keystrokes are needed to type this program and it is at once obvious that if we think of 39 as the *length* of the program, this gives us a much more accurate impression of the amount of information contained in the string of binary digits than does its actual length of 6 billion digits. To put this another way, this particular string has turned out to be highly compressible in the sense that there is a program to generate it that is much shorter than the string itself. So this string is not complex and it carries little information. This idea is fundamental to algorithmic complexity theory.

11

Algorithmic Information Theory

We consider what theoretical computer science has to say about the generation of information starting with the fairly obvious fact that, whereas natural processes can transmit information, they cannot generate information additional to that which is in their input or in their own informational structure – another reason for rejecting the reductionist unguided natural processes approach to the origin of life. Algorithmic information theory (AIT) is a way of assessing the information content or complexity of a specific sequence. The idea is to calculate the size of an algorithm that could generate that sequence. We give simple examples of the different possibilities and discuss the nature of the complexity of DNA and its relevance to biogenesis.

Algorithmic information theory (AIT) was developed as a way of assessing the information content of a sequence of letters that was more refined than simply looking at its length, as in the Shannon approach. The fundamental concept behind AIT is that of 'compressing' a given string of symbols (binary digits, letters, words, etc.) into a (much) shorter space by means of a computer program. The word 'algorithm' derives from the name of the mathematician Mohammed Ibn-Musa Al-Khwarizmi, who worked in the famous House of Wisdom in Baghdad in the ninth century.

An algorithm is an effective procedure, a way of getting something done in a finite number of steps. It is purely mechanical, not requiring any thought or initiative to carry it out. For example the formula x = (–b ± sqrt(b²– 4ac))/2a gives us an effective procedure for calculating the roots of the quadratic equation ax² + bx + c = 0, where a, b, c are numbers. It is, therefore, an algorithm. Similarly, computer programs (software) are implementations of algorithms that enable the computer hardware to do its information processing. In general, computer programs will involve many algorithms, each directing its own bit of effective computation.

[handwritten annotation: Randomness means -- -incompressible. Arbitrary]

AIT was developed by the Russian mathematician Andrey Kolmogorov of Moscow State University, the founder of modern probability theory, and American-Argentine mathematician Gregory Chaitin, as a way of getting a grip on complexity. Their idea is to measure the information content or complexity of a specific sequence, by considering the size of algorithm needed to generate that sequence.[1] According to AIT, the information content of X (where X, for example, is a string of binary digits, or a string of ordinary digits or letters in any alphabet, etc.) is the size $H(X)$ in bits of the shortest program that can generate X.

As our first example, consider the string of letters ILOVEYOUILOVEY... and suppose the string contains 2 billion repetitions of the three words I LOVE YOU. Clearly the information (in the semantic sense this time) contained in the string is already contained in the first three words (although it might well be argued that the repetition carries emphasis!). In any case the full syntactic information is given by the program 'For n = 1 to 2 billion, write I LOVE YOU. Stop'. We therefore get a much better measure of the information content by counting the number of bits of syntactic information contained in the (short) program rather than in the (long) text.

Now consider a second string generated by a monkey playing with a computer keyboard: Mtl3(#8HJD[;ELSN29X1TNSP]\@... And suppose that it, too, is 6 billion letters long, i.e. the same length as the strings just considered. Then it is clear that, since the string is essentially random, any program written to generate it will be of a similar length to the string itself. That is, this string is algorithmically incompressible. Indeed, algorithmic incompressibility is a very good way of defining what randomness means. Also, this string is maximally complex on the basis of our criterion of complexity.

Finally, if we take as our third string the first 6 billion letters of the books on the shelves of a library of English books, then, although we might achieve a little algorithmic compression, it will again be negligible compared with the length of the string. That is, this string is just as algorithmically incompressible as the second string. Hence, *from a mathematical point of view*, it is random – even though the use of the word 'random' here is not intuitive as the contents of the books are far from random in the usual sense of arbitrary.

This string is clearly very complex. Yet its complexity is different from that of the string generated by the monkey. For that string had no *specified complexity ~ Context dependent notion*

Emergence requires a "how did it occur?"

meaning. The third string by contrast is replete with semantic information. We can understand the meaning of the words in the books. And the reason that the third string has meaning for us is that we have *independently* learned English and so we recognize and understand the words formed by the letters in the string. Such a string is not only complex but also exhibits what may be called specified complexity, which is easiest to think of as the kind of complexity associated with language.

This term *specified complexity* was first used by Leslie Orgel in his book *The Origins of Life*[2] and also by Paul Davies in *The Fifth Miracle*,[3] but in neither place is it made precise for the simple reason that it is difficult to do so since it is a context-dependent notion. It is evident that there is a major difference between the highly compressible string represented by the crystal type order of our first example and the essentially incompressible strings of the second two. That difference is what makes the kind of ordering processes exhibited in Rayleigh-Bénard convection or the Belousov-Zhabotinski reaction irrelevant to the origin of life. The point here is that the order generated by these processes is highly compressible.

Again, the fact that the second two strings are algorithmically incompressible means, essentially by definition, that they cannot arise as an 'emergent' property of some relatively simple algorithmic process, in the same way as beautiful fractal pictures can arise from quite simple equations. The intricate self-symmetry of the famous Mandelbrot set, computer-generated images of which adorn many a coffee-table book, is fascinating. Yet this set is traceable back to a relatively simple mathematical function of the form $f(z) = z^2 + k$ of a complex variable z. Can we not say that the complex fractal 'emerges' from the simplicity of this equation? In one sense it does, that is, if we are thinking of the fact that we can use the equation to plot the fractal curve, on a computer screen.

But it is not quite as simple as that. Firstly, the word 'emergent' is not always clearly defined. It may be used simply to indicate that the whole is greater than the sum of its parts. It may also cover hidden assumptions. For instance, when I am told that life is an emergent property of matter, I immediately ask *how* it emerges. Does it emerge purely naturally, or does it require an input of energy, or need the aid of a catalyst, or an input of information, etc. or all of these? Emergence is an empty concept in the absence of knowledge of *how* it occurs.

Consider the Mandelbrot set. If we ask how the image on the screen 'emerges' from the equation we find that there is a lot more involved than simply writing down the Mandelbrot equation. Many different iterations of the function must be calculated; colours must be assigned to corresponding pixels on the screen according to whether the trajectory of a given iteration satisfies certain properties, like local-boundedness, so that each trajectory has to be checked for this property. Thus the 'emergent' picture is only derived from the simple equation by the cost of a hefty additional input of information in terms of programming effort and intelligently designed hardware. It does not come 'free'.

A more obvious argument applies to the illustration of emergence offered by Dawkins in a public lecture in Oxford[4] that I mentioned earlier. Dawkins claimed that the capacity to do word-processing is an 'emergent' property of computers. It is; but only at the expense of the input of the information contained in an intelligently designed software package like Microsoft Word. One thing is certain: no blind-watchmaker process gives rise to the word-processing capacity of a digital computer.

To fix in our minds the importance of the difference between the second and third kinds of complexity, we give another example. If ink spills on paper a complex event occurs in the sense that, of all possible inkblots, the chance of getting just that one is infinitesimally small. But the complexity of the inkblot is unspecified. On the other hand, if someone writes a message in ink we get specified complexity. Incidentally, we ascribe the inkblot to chance and the writing to intelligent agency without a moment's thought, do we not?

Now let us apply some of these ideas to the genome. A crucial thing here is that the As, Cs, Gs, and Ts may occupy *any* given position on the DNA molecule and so they are capable of representing complex expressions that are essentially algorithmically incompressible and therefore random.

We should not, of course, imagine that this mathematical randomness implies that the DNA sequences in living cells are arbitrary. Far from it. Indeed only a very tiny proportion of all possible sequences on the DNA molecule is likely to be biologically significant, in the same way as only a very small proportion of all possible sequences of letters in the alphabet, or indeed words of any human language, form meaningful statements in the words of that language.

For example, Professor Derek Bickerton gives us an interesting linguistic insight by explaining how even a single sentence presents a prodigious problem: 'Try to rearrange any ordinary sentence consisting of ten words. There are, in principle, exactly 3,628,800 ways in which you could

A recipe to construct logic or Sentences that are NOT ungrammatical.

do this, but for the first sentence of this only one of them gives a correct and meaningful result. That means 3,628,799 of them are ungrammatical[5].'
Bickerton then asks the obvious question:

> How did we learn this? Certainly, no parent or teacher ever told us. The only way in which we can know it is by possessing, as it were, some recipe for how to construct sentences, a recipe so complex and exhaustive that it automatically rules out all 3,628,799 wrong ways of putting together a ten-word sentence and allows only the right one. But since such a recipe must apply to all sentences, not just the example given, that recipe will, for every language, rule out more ungrammatical sentences than there are atoms in the cosmos.[6]

This example shows the difficulties that lie in the way of finding a definition of meaning. But we must not allow ourselves to get diverted into the fascinating (and indeed related) issue of the origin of the human language faculty.

To give some idea of the numbers involved in the biological situation we note that the smallest proteins possessing biological function that we know of involve at least 100 amino acids and so, since there are 20 different amino acids, the DNA molecules corresponding to them have as many as 20^{100} which is approximately 1.27×10^{130} sequence alternatives, only a minute proportion of which will have biological significance. The set of all possible sequences is therefore unimaginably large. Since deoxyribose has no preference for a particular base, all base sequences of a prescribed length are equally probable. This fact entails that the probability of a purely naturalistic origin for a specified sequence of biological significance is so small as to be negligible. And that is not all. Proteins exhibit a high degree of molecular sensitivity in the sense that even the substitution of a single amino acid in a viable protein can mean catastrophic failure.[7] It could therefore be argued that the molecular biology of the cell shows the same order of fine-tuning that we saw earlier in connection with physics and cosmology.

When AIT was first developed there were high hopes that it might help to solve the riddle of the origin of the information in DNA. Chaitin made some rather extravagant claims like: 'AIT will lead to the major breakthrough

fine tuning of the cell, physical laws and cosmology.

of twenty-first century mathematics, which will be information-theoretic and complexity based characterizations and analyses of what is life, what is mind, what is intelligence, what is consciousness, of why life has to appear spontaneously and then to evolve.'[8] However, for reasons to be made clear this kind of claim seems to be very far-fetched, as pointed out for instance by Panu Raatikanen in his review of Chaitin's work, *Exploring Randomness and the Unknowable*.[9]

The inadequacy of the laws of physics to produce biological information

The key scientific question that can now be posed using the ideas of AIT is: 'Could DNA have been generated by a simple algorithm, one significantly simpler than DNA itself?' In other words, is DNA compressible? An obvious candidate would be the laws of physics, regarded as a mechanical or automatic way to produce information without any influence of chance. Could these have produced DNA in the way that a computer outputs its results? Could there have been any simpler algorithm? (And of course, if this could be established, it would simply raise the question of the source of the algorithm, that is: who or what is the programmer.)

Paul Davies points out that the fact that genomes are essentially random sequences of base pairs contradicts the notion that they could be generated by some simple, predictable law-like process. This is because laws affect algorithmic compression on data that means that they:

> boil down apparent complexity to a simple formula or procedure... A law of nature of the sort that we know and love will not create biological information or indeed any information at all. Ordinary laws just transform input data into output data. They can shuffle information about but they can't create it... Contrary to the oft-repeated claim, then, life cannot be 'written into' the laws of physics – at least not into anything like the laws of physics that we know at present.[10]

Elsewhere, Davies says: 'We conclude that biologically relevant macromolecules simultaneously possess two vital properties: *randomness and extreme specificity*. A chaotic process could possibly achieve the former property but would have a negligible probability of achieving the latter.' His next statement is remarkable: 'At first sight this appears to make the genome an impossible object, unattainable by either known laws or chance.' Nevertheless Davies then asserts: 'Clearly Darwinian evolution by variation and natural selection has what is needed to generate both randomness (information richness) *and* tightly specified biological functionality in the same system.'[11] But is it really clear? For this begs the question, since precisely what is at issue is whether natural processes of *any* kind (including Darwinian evolution[12]) have got that capacity, or whether the very thing that his argumentation is piling up evidence for is that they have not got it. Indeed, since the whole passage is about biogenesis, Davies appears to contradict what he has just said by adding: 'The problem as far as biogenesis is concerned is that Darwinism can only operate when life (of some sort) is already going. *It cannot explain how life starts in the first place.*'[13] A point that we made earlier.

Before we move on it is worth probing Davies' statement and asking why no known law could produce the specified randomness of the coding of information on the genome. Hubert Yockey, together with Dean Overman, wrote: '...the physical laws are not good candidates for the source of life's origin. By definition, a law of nature is a very short algorithm... Life requires much more information than contained in these laws. The genetic

information contained in even the smallest living organism is much larger than the information contained in the laws of physics and chemistry.'

These authors claim that Gregory Chaitin programmed the laws of physics and chemistry and found that they had very small information content. Their conclusion was that we are looking through the wrong end of a telescope if we think that the laws of physics and chemistry will explain life's origins.

However, they warn that there are implications for epistemology: 'One must be careful in drawing broad metaphysical inferences from the conclusion that we have reached. Perhaps the most that can be said is that the origin of life may be unknowable in principle.'[14] Presumably they mean unknowable from a scientific perspective. This echoes the sentiment of Nobel laureate Niels Bohr to the effect that life is consistent with, but undecidable by, human reasoning from physics and chemistry.[15]

This is a guarded attitude that springs from awareness of the danger of forcing science to say what it cannot say – for instance that it has irrefutable proof that there is mind behind the origin of life, or, by exactly

Not !, Limitations

the same token, that science has irrefutable proof that life originated through entirely natural processes and laws. This caution is of considerable importance and indicates that we have reached some kind of limit situation. We have seen that Kurt Gödel demonstrated that mathematics had inbuilt limitations. In some brilliant work on algorithmic information theory, Gregory Chaitin, using definitions of information content, randomness, and complexity has obtained Gödel-type results showing that there are limits to what can be proved about the information content of sequences such as DNA.

Let us remind ourselves that the key question here is whether DNA, which appears to be incredibly complex, could be produced by a significantly simpler algorithm – or in the terminology of AIT, whether DNA is algorithmically compressible. This has not, to date, been settled definitively. But the conviction of many workers in the field is that just as no algorithm is likely to exist to produce the works of Shakespeare, or, perhaps better in the present context, to produce a manual showing how to assemble a 747 jumbo jet from its components (each significantly smaller than those works themselves regarded as letter strings), so also DNA, as a string, would seem to be essentially incompressible and, therefore, not at all likely to be the product of a short algorithm.[16]

However, Chaitin notes[17] that there is no sharp divide between incompressible (random) and compressible for finite sequences so that there are inherent difficulties in even making the notion of incompressibility precise. The particular choice made by Chaitin in his papers is somewhat arbitrary. Nevertheless, it is clear that, whatever definition is chosen, the proportion of sequences in a given alphabet that are compressible, such as C, G, T, and A, is easily seen to be extremely small.

To return to the question – to date no one has proved that DNA is incompressible (or random) although analysis strongly suggests that it is. Workers including Paul Davies, Dean Overman, and Hubert Yockey, coming from different perspectives, all agree that DNA has more of the quality of a work of literature than the result of an algorithm. Hence, just as there would be general agreement that the works of Shakespeare could not have been generated by an algorithm, the same also applies to DNA. In light of this, there is widespread agreement that DNA is not likely to have been produced by purely natural law-like processes. As an additional twist, the Gödel-type incompleteness results of Chaitin show that:

Is there a possibility beyond ① chance and ② necessity.

① maybe a 3ʳᵈ =

(a) for any given logical system there is a number N such that there is no sequence s that can be proved to have information content greater than N (even though we know there are infinitely many);[18] and

(b) whichever precise definition of incompressible is chosen, there is no algorithm that will decide, for any given sequence, whether or not it is compressible.[19]

In consequence, to quote Michiel Van Lambalgen, a Professor of Logic and Cognitive Science at the Institute for Logic, Language and Computation in Amsterdam University: 'it is well nigh impossible to verify that *some specific string* has high complexity...' (italics mine).[20]

We therefore clearly need to be cautious in what we claim since such inferences do not belong to the realm of mathematical science but of informed beliefs, and we are dealing with just one specific sequence. Note also that AIT does not capture the additional aspect of information, namely specified complexity, otherwise known as complex functional information, or informally as 'aboutness' – all of which notions are context sensitive and so cannot be defined as an intrinsic property of the information sequence.

However, that does not mean that we should not explore the matter further. It is surely not unreasonable to ask: What other possibility is there beyond chance and necessity? Well, as Sherlock Holmes might have told us, if chance and necessity, either separately or together, are not capable of biogenesis, then we must consider the possibility that a third factor was involved. As the reader will already know, I believe that the injection of information from outside the system is a serious candidate as an inference to the best explanation for that third possibility.

This suggestion will be met by a chorus of protest that we are not talking about a detective story, and that it is in any case anti-scientific and intellectually lazy to propose what is essentially an 'intelligence of the gaps', that is, the kind of 'god of the gaps'-type solution that we discussed earlier. Of course, the charge must be taken seriously, since it is sadly possible for a theist to be intellectually lazy and say in effect 'I can't explain it, therefore God did it.'

Yet, sauce for the goose is sauce for the gander. It is also very easy to say 'natural processes did it' or, 'evolution did it' when one has not got the faintest idea how it happened, or has simply cobbled up a speculative just-so story with no evidential basis. Indeed, as we have seen, a materialist *has*

Key

to say that natural processes were solely responsible, since, for materialism, there is no admissible alternative. As a result, it is just as easy to end up with a 'naturalism of the gaps' as with a 'god of the gaps'. One might even say that it may be even easier to end up with an 'evolution of the gaps' than with a 'god of the gaps' since the former suggestion is likely to attract far less criticism than the latter.

What, then, does a theist, have to say? She can be more open than her materialist colleague and can admit, even welcome, the involvement of natural processes. But she is not committed to excluding processes that are not part of a closed cause and effect system. Indeed, she can be fully open to the possibility that the universe is an open system. This strikes me as a much more open-minded approach and therefore more in accord with the spirit of science.

Of course, some theists might, unwisely, take refuge in an unscientific god of the gaps position. I think that there is no need to do so. To explain this I turn to the realm of my own field of pure mathematics. If a conjecture, such as, say, the ancient one that any angle can be trisected using only a straight-edge and compasses, has been thought about for many years and all attempts to prove it true have failed, then, though mathematicians will not necessarily give up trying to prove it true, they may also mount an attempt to see if it is *provably false*. This, indeed, turned out to be the case with the trisection of the angle, as all students of pure mathematics (should) know.

In other words, when mathematicians fail to prove a conjecture true, they do not necessarily either give up their efforts or keep going doggedly on in the same direction as before: they may well decide alternatively (or additionally) to mount a mathematical attempt to *prove* that the conjecture is false. Now it seems to me that this is precisely the kind of thinking that we need to apply to the problem of the origin of life. What I am suggesting is similar to the seemingly endless search for perpetual motion machines. Every year articles are written by people who think they have discovered the secret of perpetual motion by inventing devices that will remain in continual motion once they have been started without any additional input of energy.[21]

Such articles are not taken seriously by scientists familiar with the fundamentals of thermodynamics. In fact most of them are never even read, and that is not because the scientists who receive them are intellectually lazy and not prepared to consider new arguments. It is because scientists believe that there is strong evidence to support the law of conservation of energy. *This law is a proscriptive law and it implies that perpetual motion machines are impossible.*

Consequently, scientists know that if they did examine the detail of any putative perpetual motion machine, they would invariably discover that it would eventually need an injection of energy from outside to keep it running. Hence, and this is the key point for our purposes, it is *science* that has shown that perpetual motion machines do not exist. Intellectual laziness does not come into it. Indeed, it would be intellectually perverse to reject this argument and keep on searching.

Why should we not apply the same kind of logic to the question of the origin of genetic information? Might not the difficulties involved in all attempts so far to give a naturalistic explanation for the origin of genetic information be sufficient reason to expend at least some of our intellectual energy enquiring if there is *something like an information-theoretic parallel to the law of energy conservation*? Such an investigation might lead to *scientific* evidence that no explanation of biogenesis *could* work that did not involve an input of information from an external intelligent source.

Admittedly, the issues at stake here are clearly of a different order of magnitude than those involved in the existence of perpetual motion machines.[22] For, if there was adequate scientific reason for thinking biogenesis cannot be adequately explained without factoring in an information input then interest would inevitably focus on finding out what the source of that information is. But it should be noted that the latter is a completely separate issue – however hard it may be to keep the two apart in our thinking. *Whether or not the source of the information can be determined is logically distinct from the question of whether an external input of information is necessary.*

After all, if we went to Mars and discovered a long line of piles of titanium cubes receding towards the Martian horizon where the piles each consisted of a prime number of cubes and the piles were in the correct ascending order 1,2,3,5,7,11,13,17,19,... then we would reasonably conclude that this arrangement involved intelligence, even if we had no idea whatsoever of the nature of the intelligence responsible for it. Yet, ironically, if we discovered something much more complex – say a DNA molecule with its clear semiotic dimension – then naturalistic scientists would presumably conclude that it was a result of chance and necessity!

Is information conserved?

Our key question now reads: *Is there any scientific evidence that information is conserved in some meaningful sense of the term?* If the answer turned out to be positive, then a lot of valuable research time and effort in connection with the origin of life could be saved by giving up the fruitless search for an information-theoretic equivalent of a perpetual motion machine. We should also observe in passing that it is no longer adequate or even sensible to object to machine-type language when referring to organisms. It is ubiquitous in molecular biology because proteins, flagella, cells, etc. are molecular machines. They may well be *more* than machines but, at the level of their information processing capability, they are certainly (digital processing) machines.

This carries with it the implication, already exploited scientifically in myriad different ways in recent years, that biological machines are open to mathematical analysis in general and information-theoretic analysis in particular. It is to this analysis that we now therefore turn to pick up ideas on the question of whether molecular machines of whatever kind can or cannot generate novel information.

The first important piece of evidence comes from the brilliant French physicist Leonard Brillouin (1889–1969), in his classic work on information theory. He has no doubt where the answer lies: 'A machine does not create any new information, but it performs a very valuable transformation of known information.'[23] Twenty years later, Nobel laureate Sir Peter Medawar wrote: 'No process of logical reasoning – no mere act of mind or computer-programmable operation – can enlarge the information content of the axioms and premises or observation statements from which it proceeds.'[24] He deduced from this observation that some kind of *law of conservation of information* must hold. His statement seems to imply that there are limits to what can be derived from a given set of physical laws that might mean certain things in science are unknowable.

Medawar did not attempt any demonstration of such a law, contenting himself with challenging his readers 'to find a logical operation that will add to the information content of any utterance whatsoever'.[25] He did, however, give a mathematical example to illustrate what he meant. He points out that Euclid's famous geometric theorems are simply a 'spelling out, or bringing out into the open, of information already contained in the axioms and postulates'.[26] After all, he adds, philosophers and logicians since the time of Bacon had no difficulty in perceiving that the process of deduction merely makes explicit information that is already there; it does not create any new information whatsoever.

Putting it another way, the theorems of Euclid are reducible to his axioms and postulates, a circumstance that should remind us of our discussion of the limits to mathematical reduction imposed by Gödel's Theorem. And, very interestingly, Kurt Gödel, who ranks as one of the greatest mathematicians of all time, thought that some kind of conservation of information was characteristic of living things. He said: 'the complexity of living bodies has to be present in the material [from which they are derived] or in the laws [governing their formation]. In particular, the materials forming the organs, if they are governed by mechanical laws, have to be of the same order of complexity as the living body'. Gödel's own formulation (in the third person) runs as follows:

> More generally, Gödel believes that mechanism in biology is a prejudice of our time which will be disproved. In this case, one disproval, in Gödel's opinion, will consist in a mathematical theorem to the effect that the formation within geological times of a human body by the laws of physics (or any other laws of a similar nature), starting from a random distribution of the elementary particles and the field, is as unlikely as the separation by chance of the atmosphere into its components.[27]

The fascinating thing here is that Gödel expected that there would one day be a mathematical proof of this – in other words that mathematics would contribute decisively to the refutation of the idea that purely natural processes were responsible for the origin of information. There is a delightful irony here. For it was Gödel himself who blazed the trail for subsequent developments on this very problem. Using algorithmic information theory, mathematician Gregory Chaitin found proofs of even stronger results related to Gödel's that bear on the question of whether algorithms generate novel information and hence, by implication, on biogenesis.

These arguments are based on the concept of a Turing machine. This is an abstract mathematical construct named after its inventor, the brilliant mathematician Alan Turing, who worked at Bletchley Park in the UK during the Second World War and led the team that built the 'Bombe'

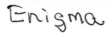
Enigma

– a machine for decrypting the messages sent by the Germans using the Enigma machine. The Enigma cipher had actually been broken by three Polish mathematicians: Marian Rejewski, Jerzy Rozycki, and Henryk Zygalski in December 1932 before Turing and his team did their brilliant work in Bletchley Park.[28]

Yockey supports Peter Medawar's notion of a law of conservation of information when he writes: 'Paradigms for the origin of life are essentially algorithms. They must contain as much or more information than the ensemble of genetic messages that they purport to generate.'[29] Bernd Olaf Küppers puts it this way: 'There is no complexity generating machine... that can generate more complexity than is contained in its input.'[30]

Küppers goes on to say: 'This fits with our fundamental experience that there is no natural process that leads to an enrichment without cause, a creation out of nothing.'[31] Hence, no Turing machine can generate any information that does not either belong to its input or its own informational structure. In fact, this would seem to be true simply by definition of the complexity of an output – which is the size, and therefore the complexity, of the smallest algorithm for generating it. Now, according to the Church–Turing Thesis, any computational device whatsoever (past, present, or future) can be simulated by a Turing machine. On this basis, any result obtained for Turing machines can be at once translated into the digital world. One implication of this would appear to be that no molecular device is capable of generating any information that does not either belong to its input or its own informational structure. Küppers considers this possibility. Referring to Schrödinger's book *What is Life?* he says that it would be 'perfectly justifiable to ask whether biological evolution, as it is usually understood, constitutes a perpetuum mobile of the third kind.'[32] In which case it would be impossible according to Küppers own work. In light of that he asks: 'Are there creative systems in nature that automatically develop to a higher complexity? Is evolution a creative process in the sense of creatio ex nihilo[33] – or must evolution be interpreted as a context-bound process of complexity generation that cannot lead beyond the threshold prescribed by that context.'[34]

I find it fascinating that, having said this, Küppers appears reluctant to abandon evolution as a complexity generator. His reason, as he says elsewhere, is that he is committed to self-organization. He regards this as part of the reductionist research programme which aims to reduce all properties and phenomena of the living to physical and chemical processes.[35] This suggests that his prior metaphysical commitment may be trumping scientific evidence.

As we have said before, the only source *we know* of the kind of language type information that we have found in the living cell is mind. Why would that fact not encourage us to do some science based on that assumption to see where it leads? Could it be that it is the naturalistic worldview, rather than science, that prevents this being done?

I am, of course, aware that there still is powerful resistance to doing this because of the alleged success of the modern synthesis to explain all of life's development subsequent to biogenesis. That is why I have felt that it was only fair for me to analyse the main arguments that have been used for years in the attempt to banish any hint of design in the biosphere. That we shall do in Part 4 where we shall argue that the modern (neo-Darwinian) synthesis with its accent on natural selection and mutation only seems to work for a very limited range of phenomena. That is the reason it is currently being replaced by a much more sophisticated systems biology approach. Paul Davies, in his 2019 book *The Demon in the Machine*, says of the modern synthesis: 'About twenty years ago this simplistic view of evolution began to crumble.'[36] Biologist Michael Denton writes: 'Nature is stubbornly discontinuous, resistant to all attempts to reduce her to a Darwinian functional continuum. The great divisions in the natural order are still profound. There is no empirical or hypothetical series of adaptive transformations among them. *Darwin's theory is a way station in the intellectual history of biology*' [italics mine].[37]

This means that the reader who is aware of such developments may wish to proceed directly to Chapter 19 on systems biology. Other readers may, nevertheless, wish to know why I agree with Denton's scepticism about the modern synthesis.

To sum up

Physicists are happy to deduce the non-existence of perpetual motion machines from the law of conservation of energy. The point of this chapter has been to sketch results from theoretical computer science that point towards the existence of something like a law of conservation of information that would preclude biogenesis by unguided processes. We shall develop these arguments in the next chapter.

12

Life's Solution: Self-organization?

'Based on what we know of chemistry, life should not exist anywhere in the universe. Life's ubiquity on this planet is utterly bizarre and the lifelessness found on other planets makes far more chemical sense.'
James Tour

Some people have attempted to explain life's origin in terms of affinities between chemical bases. Others have turned to the idea of self-organization which stands in contrast to the more familiar matter of external organization, like that of building a house to an architect's plan. Self-organization occurs when patterns are formed without the influence of external commands or restraint. We give some fascinating examples of so-called autocatalytic sets that are regarded by some scientists as potential stepping stones towards life.

However there are major difficulties looming. Paul Davies says that:

> Life is actually *not* an example of *self*-organization. Life is in fact *specified*, i.e. genetically directed, organization. Living things are instructed by the genetic software encoded in their DNA (or RNA).... The theory of self-organization as yet gives no clue how the transition is to be made between spontaneous, or self-induced organization -- which in even the most elaborate non-biological examples still involves relatively simple structures -- and the highly complex, information-based, genetic organization of living things.[1]

That is, we run once more into the barrier posed by the existence of information-rich structures.

We also make the point that, even if scientists did eventually manage to build a cell from scratch, far from that doing away with the design hypothesis, it will make that claim that there is an intelligent designer even more plausible, since the constructed 'life' will have been created by (human) intelligence working with available chemicals.

One aspect of this raft of problems is the suggestion that the original generation of genetic information is facilitated by certain chemical affinities between the molecules that carry that information. However, there is a simple logical reason that this cannot be so. Think of the alphabet. In English there is a rule that a 'q' must be followed by a 'u'. Now imagine that there are similar 'affinities' between other pairs of letters. It is immediately clear that the more such 'affinities' you have between the letters of an alphabet, the fewer expressions you can write down.

The freedom to write the letters in almost any order you like is crucial to having a rich linguistic store of words. It is the same with DNA. The whole point about the nucleotide bases (A, C, G, T) is that they may be positioned essentially randomly in a sequence. If there were any affinities between them, their information-carrying potential would be drastically reduced. The bases are bonded to the spine of the RNA by strong (covalent) bonds. But the two complementary DNA-strands are held together by comparatively weak chemical bonds, namely hydrogen bonds between the complementary bases. Michael Polanyi explained the implication of this long ago:

> Suppose that the actual structure of the DNA molecule were due to the fact that the bindings of its bases were much stronger than the bindings would be for any other distribution of bases, then such a DNA molecule would have no information content. Its code-like character would be effaced by an overwhelming redundancy... Whatever may be the origin of a DNA configuration, it can function as a code only if its order is not due to the forces of potential energy. It must be as physically indeterminate as the sequence of words is on a printed page.[2]

The operative word here is 'physically'. As we saw earlier, a message is not derivable from the physics and chemistry of paper and ink. Hubert Yockey confirms this judgment: 'Attempts to relate the idea of order...

with biological organization or specificity must be regarded as a play on words which cannot stand careful scrutiny. Informational macromolecules can code genetic messages and therefore carry information because the sequence of bases or residues is affected very little, if at all, by physico-chemical factors.'[3] Therefore the genetic text is not generated by the chemistry of the bonding between molecules.

Remarkable for the time, the brilliant physicist Erwin Schrödinger, in his famous lecture series entitled 'What is Life' given at the Institute for Advanced Study in Dublin in 1943, suggested that life would turn out to involve something like an aperiodic crystal. He was stunningly close to the truth, as an essential property of the coding on DNA is that it is precisely that – aperiodic.

If explanations in terms of chemical bonds do not work, what other possibilities are there? A simple-minded appeal to Darwinian-like processes cannot provide a solution since we are talking about biogenesis, the origin of life and, whatever Darwinian processes can do once life is there, they cannot get going in its absence. For, in order for natural selection to do anything it needs the existence of a mutating replicator. It therefore presupposes the existence of life, as Theodosius Dobzhansky said: 'Prebiotic evolution is a contradiction in terms.'

This should caution us in our use of terms like 'molecular evolution' which could be understood to imply that we are covertly assuming that we have at our disposal the very process (replication, about which alone it makes sense to talk of natural selection acting upon it) whose existence we are trying to explain. John Barrow points out that James Clerk Maxwell had observed as early as 1873 that atoms were: 'populations of identical particles whose properties were not acted on by natural selection and whose properties determined whether life could exist.'[4]

Nevertheless attempts continue to be made to solve the origin of life problem using reductionist arguments that rely solely on chance and necessity. They seem more and more doomed to failure. Self-organization is one of them. The easiest way to understand this is by contrast with external organization. A familiar example of the latter is the pattern formed by a marching band in response to the external commands of the band leader. Building a house in accordance with an architect's plan is another example. In each case the pattern formed is constrained from outside.

By contrast, self-organization involves the formation of patterns *without* external command or constraint. For instance, when wind blows over a uniform stretch of desert sand, a pattern of ridges spaced at regular intervals is formed. Nobel laureate for chemistry Ilya Prigogine and his colleague Isabelle Stengers argued that order and organization can arise spontaneously out of chaos and disorder.[5] The kind of chaos in which they are interested is that exhibited by certain thermodynamic systems that are driven far from equilibrium, as in the example of heating oil to produce the Rayleigh-Bénard convection which occurs, for instance, when a thin sheet of viscous oil is uniformly heated from below. A convection current is set up that reorganizes the liquid so that a honeycomb pattern made up of hexagonal cells appears, looking just like the famous rock formations at the Giant's Causeway in Northern Ireland.

Far from equilibrium, thermodynamic systems may begin to exhibit non-linear behaviour of such a kind that a very small change in input can trigger disproportionately large consequences. The most famous example of this phenomenon is the so-called 'butterfly effect' in which the flapping of a butterfly's wings in one part of the world sets off a chain of events that trigger a tropical storm somewhere else. Such systems, like the weather, that are exceedingly sensitive to changes in initial conditions and are therefore inherently unpredictable, are called chaotic systems. Prigogine showed that, under these kinds of condition, unexpected ordered patterns can be produced.

Autocatalytic sets are an example. Stuart Kauffman, an American polymath, medical doctor, theoretical biologist, and complex systems researcher, who studies the origin of life on earth and founded the Santa Fe Institute, defines an autocatalytic set to be a closed system containing a self-sustaining chemical reaction network in which all the molecules mutually catalyse each other's formation from a basic food source.[6] This notion is often seen as a 'counterargument' to the dominant genetics-first view of the origin of life, focusing more on metabolism instead. Of course, living cells are themselves examples of autocatalytic sets. We note that Kauffman put forward his ideas as an alternative to Darwinism whose inadequacy he had long suspected. A great deal of his work involves computer simulations and, of course, there is always the question as to how much they really do mirror the physical world. Nobel laureate Stanley Miller, when asked by John Horgan about Kauffman's work, said: 'Running equations through a computer does not constitute and experiment.'[7]

A visually impressive example of an autocatalytic reaction was discovered by the Soviet chemist Boris Pavlovich Belousov who found what

Where did the genetic code come from,
& did life come from?
Life's Solution: Self-organization? / 211

is called the Belousov-Zhabotinski reaction. It occurs, for example, when malonic acid is being oxidized by potassium bromate with the aid of two catalysts, cerium sulphate and ferroin, for instance. If the mixture is kept at about 25oC (77oF) and continuously stirred it will repeatedly change colour from red to blue[8] at approximately one-minute intervals, so that the reaction functions like a kind of chemical clock with a remarkably regular period – so that the system generates order. The reader may be interested to see simulations of this reaction by consulting the internet.[9]

In a similar vein, the late Robert Shapiro, a chemist working on the origin of life, suggested, together with others, a 'metabolism' or 'small molecule' first scenario for the origin of life, that is, one that does not initially contain a mechanism for heredity and therefore involves small molecules rather than large information-bearing molecules like DNA or RNA. Shapiro talks about the genesis of a 'kind of life... defined as the creation of greater order in localized regions by chemical cycles driven by an energy flow.'[10] It is thought by some that the study of such processes may give us an idea of how life may have started.[11]

An indicator of just how difficult experts consider getting to grips with all of this is the fact that on 31 May 2019, electrical engineer and entrepreneur Perry Marshall, together with investor Kevin Ham, announced at the Royal Society in London a $10 million Evolution 2.0 Prize, named after Marshall's book. This prize will be awarded to the first person who can discover how code can emerge from chemistry. Specifically, the prize will be awarded to the first person who creates a self-organizing digital communication system. Such a discovery would, in Marshall's opinion, bridge the gap between physics and biology and answer fundamental questions: Where did life come from? Where did the genetic code come from?

Currently, Leroy (Lee) Cronin, Regius Professor of Chemistry in Glasgow, and his group have their sights set on winning the Evolution 2.0 Prize. They are working on autocatalytic sets in an attempt to build some form of (precursor to) life. Here is part of an abstract of their research and its goal: 'Biological self-replication is driven by complex machinery requiring large amounts of sequence information too complex to have formed spontaneously... This study demonstrates how information-rich autocatalytic sets, based on simple inorganic salts, can spontaneously emerge which are capable of collective self-reproduction outside of biology.'[12]

Lack of Specificity

However, one of the most eminent origin of life experts, the late Leslie Orgel FRS, gave an analytic evaluation of such cycles, in particular the work of Kauffman, arguing from chemistry that their existence is highly implausible. He wrote:

> It is not completely impossible that sufficiently specific mineral catalysts exist for each of the reactions of the reverse citric acid cycle, but the chance of a full set of such catalysts occurring at a single locality on the primitive Earth in the absence of catalysts for disruptive side reactions seems remote in the extreme. Lack of specificity rather than inadequate efficiency may be the predominant barrier to the existence of complex autocatalytic cycles of almost any kind.[13]

He further comments: 'Why should one believe that an ensemble of minerals that are capable of catalysing each of the many steps of the reverse citric acid cycle was present anywhere on the primitive Earth, or that the cycle mysteriously organized itself topographically on a metal sulphide surface?' His conclusion is that: the prebiotic syntheses that have been investigated experimentally almost always lead to the formation of complex mixtures. Proposed polymer[14] replication schemes are unlikely to succeed except with reasonably pure input monomers. No solution of the origin-of-life problem will be possible until the gap between the two kinds of chemistry is closed.'[15]

Nevertheless, Kauffman believes that self-organization will prove to be an alternative to natural selection.

The core problem

The view that such processes, even if they did occur against all the odds that chemists put in their way, somehow give insight into the origin of life itself eventually runs into far greater difficulties that have, once more, to do with the informational complexity of proteins. For the core problem is not that of producing the kind of order that is to be seen in a crystal, honeycomb, or even an autocatalytic reaction. It is that of producing the qualitatively different, language-type arrangement of the chain of amino acids that make up a protein. We saw in Chapter 4 how Paul Davies puts

Problem: To produce the qualitatively different language-type arrangements of the chain of amino acids that make up Protein

this difference very clearly: in short, self-organization theories cannot cope with the information barrier discussed in the previous chapter. Philosopher of science Stephen Meyer confirms this: 'Self-organizational theorists explain well what does not need to be explained. *What needs explaining is not the origin of order... but the origin of information*' [italics mine].[16] This is a key statement.[17] It is the concept of language-like information that lies at the heart of the problem of life's origin.

Most of the rest of my book will be devoted to considering this. Leslie Orgel summed up the position as follows: 'There are several tenable theories about the origin of organic material on the primitive earth, but in no case is the supporting evidence compelling. Similarly, several alternative scenarios might account for the self-organization of a self-replicating entity from prebiotic organic material, but all of those that are well formulated are based on hypothetical chemical syntheses that are problematic.'[18] Orgel therefore echoes the view of Klaus Dose, also a prominent worker in origin of life research, who ten years earlier made the following assessment:

> More than thirty years of experimentation on the origin of life in the fields of chemical and molecular evolution have led to a better perception of the immensity of the problem of the origin of life on earth rather than to its solution. At present all discussions on principal theories and experiments in the field either end in stalemate or in a confession of ignorance.[19]

This is reminiscent of what we earlier quoted from Francis Crick: 'The origin of life seems almost to be a miracle, so many are the conditions which would have had to have been satisfied to get it going.'[20]

All of which would seem to support Stuart Kauffman's verdict: 'Anyone who tells you that he or she knows how life started on the earth some 3.45 billion years ago is a fool or a knave. Nobody knows.'[21] More recently, Francis Collins has confirmed this:

> But how did self-replicating organisms arise in the first place? It is fair to say that at the present time we simply do not know. No current hypothesis comes close to explaining how in the space of a mere 150 million years, the prebiotic environment that existed on planet

> earth gave rise to life. That is not to say that reasonable
> hypotheses have not been put forward, but their statistical
> probability of accounting for the development of life still
> seems remote.[22]

It would seem that the more research that is done, the greater the problem grows. James (Jim) Tour of Rice University in Houston is one of the world's leading synthetic organic chemists. A prolific researcher, he has authored nearly 700 scientific publication and holds more than 120 patents. In 2014, Thomson Reuters named him one of 'The World's Most Influential Scientific Minds', and in 2018 Clarivate Analytics recognized him as one of the world's most highly cited researchers. He writes: 'based on what we know of chemistry, life should not exist anywhere in the universe. Life's ubiquity on this planet is utterly bizarre and the lifelessness found on other planets makes far more chemical sense.'[23] So what if scientists eventually manage to build a cell from scratch? Will that finally discredit the claim that there is designing intelligence? Of course not – it will make that claim even more plausible since such a cell will have been created by human intelligence working with available chemicals. In other words, the cell will have been intelligently designed.

Tour's conclusion is that the evidence offered so far for the existence of natural processes that will generate life is very much less convincing than some scientists claim – we simply do not know. Many other distinguished scientists say the same. The origin of life remains shrouded in mystery. No one knows. This reminds us of Bohr's verdict that the answer may be undecidable, unknowable in principle and it therefore may need to be taken as an axiom as inexplicable as the axioms of quantum mechanics.

No one is in a position to claim as a *scientifically* established fact that life could or could not have originated through natural processes. We can say that science has revealed the central role played by information in living organisms and that it has failed to give any plausible, let alone convincing, explanation of the origin of that information. That failure surely increases the *plausibility* that life's origin involves an external mind.

Finally, Sara Walker and Paul Davies summarize the position as they see it:

> In our view, an explanation of life's origin is fundamentally
> incomplete in the absence of an account of how the unique

For the origin of life to be explained, requires how the physical cell was built and how the information in that cell came to be.

causal role played by information in living systems first emerged. In other words, we need to explain the origin of both the hardware and software aspects of life, or the job is only half finished. Explaining the chemical substrate of life and claiming it as a solution to life's origin is like pointing to silicon and copper as an explanation for the goings-on inside a computer.[24]

The greatest scientific minds now recognize that they have no idea how the origin of life came about by mere naturalistic processes – it is shrouded in mystery!

The plausibility is that life's origin involves an external mind.

PART 4

The Modern Synthesis

13

Life's Solution: Evolution?

We give examples of leading scientists who are convinced that evolution in the sense of the modern synthesis really has buried God. However, we show that there is a major difficulty even with the attempt to deduce the worldview of atheism from the science of biology. Firstly, such a deduction involves a philosophical category mistake and secondly it depends on the simultaneous validity of the following two assertions.

Assertion 1: *Biological evolution is incompatible with the existence of a Creator.*

Assertion 2: *Biological evolution accounts for the existence of all of life's complexity.*

In order to see that the first assertion is false we will investigate the rhetoric of Dawkins' 'Blind Watchmaker' thesis to find that he makes the mistake of arguing that the existence of a mechanism can be used as an argument for the non-existence of a designer of that mechanism. Indeed, from Darwin's time on, there have been scientists who accept evolution who also are Christian believers. As mentioned previously, Dawkins famously defined biology as: 'the study of complicated things which give the impression of having been designed for a purpose'.[1] Yet impression, say he and many other scientists, is all that it is. Biology does not give evidence of real design or teleology – a word derived from Greek telos = end or goal and logos = reason, thought, word – that is used to denote design with a goal or purpose in mind. Nobel laureate biochemist Jacques Monod went even further in asserting that: 'the cornerstone of the scientific method is... the systematic denial... of final causes.'[2]

Francis Crick warned biologists not to mistake that impression for what is, in his estimation, the underlying reality: 'Biologists must constantly keep in mind that what they see was not designed, but rather evolved.'³ Such statements provoke the age-old quip: 'If it looks like a duck, waddles like a duck and quacks like a duck, why not call it a duck?' Why are such scientists and others not prepared to draw the obvious inference, and say that living things look as if they are designed precisely because they are designed? The answer given by Crick and others is that the appearance of design is illusory since unguided evolutionary processes are capable of producing all of life's teeming complexity. And, in any case, this explanation is the only possibility allowed by their naturalistic or even materialistic worldview presuppositions.

Daniel Dennett, in his book *Darwin's Dangerous Idea*, puts it this way: 'Darwin was offering a skeptical world... a scheme for creating Design out of Chaos without the aid of Mind.'⁴ Dennett regards Darwin's idea as a kind of corrosive acid, which threatens to destroy all pre-Darwinian views of the world; in that, instead of the universe's matter being a product of mind, the minds in the universe are a product of matter. They are nothing more than the results of an undirected, mindless, purposeless process.⁵

We might well wonder at the capacity of this amazing evolutionary engine with its creative power to produce not only the vast array of different kinds of living things but also consciousness and human language. Not a divine Mind, says Richard Dawkins, but a purely natural, unguided mechanism. However tempting it is to think that nature has been designed for a purpose, he claims that there is no need for a divine watchmaker. In a much cited passage he says:

> The only watchmaker in nature is the blind forces of physics... A true watchmaker has foresight: he designs his cogs and springs, and plans their interconnections, with a future purpose in his mind's eye. Natural selection, the blind, unconscious, automatic process which Darwin discovered, and which we now know is the explanation for the existence and apparently purposeful form of all life, has no purpose in mind... It has no vision, no foresight, no sight at all. If it can be said to play the role of watchmaker in nature, it is that of the blind watchmaker.⁶

Dawkins claims that nothing but the laws of physics are needed – a very important point to which we must return later.

Palaeontologist Stephen Jay Gould, a materialist by philosophical conviction, held that after Darwin we know that: 'no intervening spirit watches lovingly over the affairs of nature (though Newton's clock-winding God might have set up the machinery at the beginning of time and then let it run). No vital forces propel evolutionary change. And whatever we think of God, his existence is not manifest in the products of nature.'[7]

Indeed, not long after the publication of *The Origin of Species* a well-known American atheist, Robert Green Ingersoll, wrote that the nineteenth century would be 'Darwin's century' when: 'his doctrine of evolution... has removed in every thinking mind the last vestige of orthodox Christianity'.[8] The point was repeated by Sir Julian Huxley when, at the 1959 Darwin Centennial in Chicago, he summed up the implications of evolution as he saw them: 'In the evolutionary scheme of thought there is no longer either need or room for the supernatural. The earth was not created, it evolved. So did all the animals and plants that inhabit it, including our human selves, mind and soul as well as brain and body. So did religion... .'[9] In Huxley's opinion evolution displaces God, giving us a purely naturalistic explanation of the origin, not only of life, but of the higher faculties of consciousness and thought.

This view, that atheism is a logical consequence of evolutionary theory, is not only to be found in popular science books but also in university texts. Take, for example, the following statement from a reputable university textbook on evolution by Monroe Strickberger of the Museum of Vertebrate Zoology, Berkeley, California: 'The fear that Darwinism was an attempt to displace God in the sphere of creation was therefore justified. To the question: Is there a divine purpose for the creation of humans? evolution answers No. According to evolution, the adaptations of species and the adaptations of humans come from natural selection and not from design.'[10]

Douglas Futuyma agrees:

> By coupling undirected, purposeless variation to the blind, uncaring process of natural selection, Darwin made theological or spiritual explanations of the life processes superfluous. Together with Marx's materialistic theory of history and society and Freud's attribution of human behaviour to influences over which we have little control, Darwin's theory of evolution was a crucial plank in the platform of mechanism and materialism –

humans desire significance.

of much of science, in short – that has been the stage of most Western thought.[11]

It is, therefore, scarcely surprising that there is a widespread feeling that the theory of evolution has swept God away as unnecessary and irrelevant, if not positively embarrassing. We shall see in Chapter 21 that around seventy years after Darwin, quantum mechanics brought the materialist edifice crashing to the ground.

So we are confronted with the following rather odd situation. On the one hand, there is the almost instinctive and overwhelming temptation to infer from the existence and nature of biological information that it has an intelligent origin. On the other hand, some of the very people who grant that the temptation is strong resist it because they are convinced that no designer is necessary: unguided, mindless, evolutionary processes did it all. It goes without saying that this is a critical issue. For, Darwinian theory has had the impact of an earthquake on the human quest for significance, an impact that extends to every aspect of human life. If life is the result of a purely naturalistic process, what then of morality? Has it, too, evolved? And if so, of what significance are our concepts of right and wrong, justice and truth?

According to William Provine: 'The destructive assumptions of evolutionary biology extend far beyond the assumptions of organized religion to a much deeper and more pervasive belief held by the vast majority of people, that non-mechanistic organizing designs or forces are somehow responsible for the visible order of the physical universe, biological organisms, and human moral order.'[12]

Daniel Dennett thinks that we have not yet really taken on board the implications of evolution and he therefore calls evolution 'Darwin's dangerous idea' because it: 'cuts much deeper into the fabric of our most fundamental beliefs than many of its sophisticated apologists have yet admitted, even to themselves.'[13]

Dawkins agrees. He has no doubt that, with Darwin, we reach an immensely significant watershed in the history of thought: 'We no longer have to resort to superstition when faced with deep problems: Is there a meaning to life? What are we here for? What is man? After posing the last of these questions, the eminent zoologist G. G. Simpson put it thus: "The point I want to make now is that all attempts to answer that question before 1859 are worthless and that we will be better off if we ignore them completely." '[14]

Dawkins' argument is that if evolutionary mechanisms can account for the apparent design in the universe, then the inference to an intelligent origin is false. He tells us that we cannot have both God and evolution. Since everything can be accounted for by evolution, there is no Creator. Evolution implies atheism.

Let us look at the logic of this position. Clearly, Dawkins' deduction of atheism from evolution depends on the simultaneous validity of the following two assertions.

> **Assertion 1.** *Biological evolution (if true) is incompatible with the existence of a Creator – in other words, gives scientific evidence for atheism.*

> **Assertion 2.** *Biological evolution accounts for the existence of all of life's complexity.*

Many people think that there is nothing to discuss here since they hold that both statements are true: the first almost self-evidently and the second as a result of scientific research. Yet two awkward facts insist that it cannot be that simple. Firstly, there are many biologists who deny the first assertion and accept the second: that is, they believe in God as well as in evolution. They would assent, not to Assertion 1 but to:

> **Assertion 1*** *Unguided biological evolution is incompatible with belief in a Creator.*

Most theists would assent to this. Like Thomas Aquinas, they regard God as the direct cause of the existence of a universe that has brought life about through secondary 'natural' causes. Secondly, and more controversially, there are *scientific* questions being asked, and not only by believers in God, as to the precise status of the second assertion. This is evidenced by the increasing number of publications on the topic by some of the world's leading academic publishing houses.[15]

The idea that God and evolution are mutually exclusive implies that both God and evolution belong to the same category of explanation. But this is false, as we have already seen in a different context. A category mistake is being committed. Evolution purports to be a biological mechanism, and those who believe in God regard him as a personal Agent who, among other things, designs and creates mechanisms. We observed earlier that the existence of a mechanism is not in itself an argument for the non-existence of an agent who designed the mechanism.

With this in mind let us look again at Dawkins' famous description of the evolutionary blind watchmaker: 'The only watchmaker in nature is the blind forces of physics... [*sic*] Natural selection, the blind, unconscious, automatic process which Darwin discovered, and which we now know is the explanation for the existence and apparently purposeful form of all life, has no purpose in mind... If it can be said to play the role of watchmaker in nature, it is that of the blind watchmaker.'[16] Five claims are made here – two for the forces of physics and three for natural selection:

1. The forces of physics are the only watchmaker in nature.

2. The forces of physics are blind.

3. Natural selection is a blind, automatic, process with no purpose in mind.

4. Natural selection is the explanation for the existence of all life.

5. Natural selection is the explanation for the form of all life.

Of course 'natural selection' here is shorthand for the modern synthesis involving natural selection, mutation, genetic drift, etc. and not simply natural selection itself.

The first thing to say about these claims is that they take us far beyond Darwin. For the implication of Assertion 1 is that natural selection, a process certainly put on the map by Darwin (and Wallace), is reducible to the laws of physics; a claim which Darwin nowhere makes, as far as I am aware. For natural selection by definition *assumes* that life is there (or at least a system capable of self-replication) to start with. Otherwise natural selection cannot even get going as there is nothing to select from. The danger of sliding rather superficially over the transition from the non-living to the living is such an important matter that we deal with it in greater detail later.

Secondly, Dawkins ascribes creative power to the forces of physics and personifies them. These forces are the watchmaker. The anthropomorphic rhetoric of personifying forces is important here because it subtly adds a bogus credibility to an otherwise unsubstantiated thesis. We are more likely to grant that a person has creative powers than an impersonal force. Moreover, Dawkins' personified forces are blind. But what does this mean?

For, from one point of view, there is nothing controversial in describing forces or mechanisms as 'blind'. Quite obviously, most are. The strong and weak nuclear forces, electro-magnetism, and gravity have no eyes to see with, either physical or mental. And most mechanisms are blind. Think of a watch, a car, a CD player, a computer hard-disc. Moreover, they are not only blind but also unconscious; indeed, to be even more precise, they are incapable of conscious thought since they have no minds to think with. But those mechanisms, though blind *in themselves*, are all the *products of minds* that are far from being blind.

What is more, this holds even for mechanisms that involve an element of randomness in their operation. The mechanism of a self-winding watch, for example, is blind and automatic and it involves chance processes. It uses the energy from random movements of the arm to wind itself up. Yet, it would be foolish to argue that the watch had not been designed. Indeed, in terms of design, a self-winding watch is more sophisticated than an ordinary watch.

In the field of engineering, computer-implemented genetic algorithms are routinely used to optimize a particular engineering design – for example, to work out the best possible shape for an aircraft wing. It would be absurd to suggest that the fact that such evolutionary optimization algorithms are themselves blind and automatic constitutes an argument that they have not been intelligently designed. It is unfortunately all too easy to miss this point when reading Dawkins, since the subtle rhetorical effect of personifying the evolutionary process is to make the reader think that Dawkins has argued away real personal agency when he has done no such thing. In fact, at no point has he even attempted to address the question of whether or not personal agency is involved. It is a very clever sleight of mind.

The lesson here is that we need to be wary of rhetoric, since descriptions of putative evolutionary mechanisms are often loaded with words such as 'blind', 'automatic', 'random', 'chance', and 'purposeless', which, because of their ambiguity in such contexts, tend to convey the impression that the question of the involvement of an intelligent agency has been investigated and rejected when in fact nothing of the kind is the case. Using Dawkins' own terminology, one is tempted to say that he has appeared to deal with the question, but that such appearance is an illusion.

As another case in point to go along with Dawkins, consider the views of philosopher of science Daniel Dennett. He maintains that, granted that the existence of a mechanism does not *in general* logically preclude the existence of a designer, nevertheless the *particular* evolutionary mechanism that Darwin found is of such a kind that it does not, in fact, need a designer. Indeed, according to Dennett, to think that it does need a designer shows a failure to appreciate the evolutionary mechanism for what it actually is. Dennett admits that: 'automatic processes are themselves often creations of great brilliance... we can see that the inventors of the automatic transmission and the automatic door-opener were no idiots, and that their genius lay in seeing how to create something that could do something "clever" without having to think about it.'[17] He then goes on to say how it might have seemed to some people (like novelist Charles Kingsley, mentioned below) that God did his work of creation by designing an automatic design-maker.

Dennett then claims, and this is his key point, that what Darwin found was a different sort of process (natural selection), which distributed the 'designing' work over a long period of time, and conserved what had been accomplished at each stage. That is, natural selection somehow designs without either itself being designed or having any purpose in view. Dennett characterizes this process as 'mindless, motiveless, mechanicity'.[18]

At first sight the language here looks somewhat ambiguous but Dennett goes on to explain that he means that the Darwinian mechanism is mindless and motiveless, not only in the sense that it has no mind *in it*, but also in the sense that it has neither mind nor motive *behind it*. It is a mechanism that came into existence without either the direct or the indirect involvement of an intelligent agent. 'Love it or hate it,' he continues, 'phenomena like this [DNA] exhibit the heart of the power of the Darwinian idea. An impersonal, unreflective, robotic, mindless little scrap of molecular machinery is the ultimate basis of all agency, and hence meaning, and hence consciousness in the universe.'[19] To use the language of Aristotle, Dennett claims that it is the very nature of the efficient cause (evolution) that rules out the very existence of a final cause (divine intention or teleology).

Now these are all bold, rhetorically strong assertions and on inspection it appears that that is all they are. For, like Dawkins, Dennett fails to offer any solid evidence to support his claims. In his thorough investigation Alvin Plantinga gives an excoriating demolition of Dennett. He points out that Darwin's idea is only dangerous to theism – as Dennett alleges – if it is attractive and if there are good reasons for adopting it and rejecting theism.

Plantinga asks: 'But does the theory of natural selection really show what Dennett says it does – that every feature of the world, including mind itself, "*can* be the product of a blind, unforesightful, nonteleological, ultimately mechanical process of differential reproduction over long periods of time?" No.' Plantinga goes on to give his reasons and comes to the conclusion that: 'there is nothing in current evolutionary science to show or even to suggest that God did *not* thus superintend evolution.'[20]

The actual logic at issue here is well captured by the late Sir John Houghton FRS: 'The fact that we understand some of the mechanisms of the working of the universe or of living systems does not preclude the existence of a designer, any more than the possession of insight into the processes by which a watch has been put together, however automatic these processes may appear, implies there can be no watchmaker.'[21]

On the basis of the kind of reasoning advanced by Plantinga, Houghton, and others there have been and are many leading thinkers who accept:

> **Assertion 1**[**] *Guided biological evolution is compatible with belief in a Creator.*

That is, they understand the evolutionary mechanisms as the Creator's way of producing life's diversity through secondary causation via a process that he designed and supervises. Darwin himself had such people among his supporters, including the distinguished Harvard botanist Asa Gray, a Christian, who was the first person outside England to whom Darwin revealed his theory, and with whom he kept in constant touch.[22]

On 8 November 1859 Charles Kingsley wrote to Darwin that his theory of natural selection provided: 'just as noble a conception of Deity, to believe that He created primal forms capable of self-development... as to believe that He required a fresh act of intervention to supply the lacunas which He Himself had made'.[23] Though Kingsley was not a scientist, Darwin was so impressed by his words that he cited them in the second edition of *The Origin of Species*, possibly with an eye to influencing some of his more sceptical clerical readers. Kingsley's view of a 'God who was so wise that he could make all things make themselves' is re-expressed by Richard Swinburne: 'Nature... is a machine-making machine... men make not only machines, but machine-making machines. They may therefore naturally infer from nature which produces animals and plants, to a creator of nature similar to men who make machine-making machines.'[24]

The argument here is that the evolutionary viewpoint, far from invalidating the inference to intelligent origin, does nothing more than moving it back up one level, from the organisms to the processes by which those organisms have come to exist, or, if you like, from primary to secondary causation. Think of a man who, on seeing a car for the first time, supposes that it is made directly by humans only later to discover it is made in a robotic factory by robots which in turn were made by machines made by humans. His initial inference to intelligent origin was not wrong: it was his concept of the nature of the implementation of that intelligence that was inaccurate. To put it another way, direct human activity was not detectable in the robotic factory because it is the existence of the factory itself and its machines that is, ultimately, the result of intelligent human activity.

No less a person than T. H. Huxley, who figured prominently in the early Darwinian debates, seems to have been well aware of this. He reminded his contemporaries that:

> there is a wider teleology which is not touched by the doctrine of Evolution. This proposition is that the whole world... is the result of the mutual interaction, according to definite laws, of the forces possessed by the molecules of which the primitive nebulosity of the universe was composed. If this be true, it is no less certain that the existing world lay potentially in the cosmic vapour, and that a sufficient intelligence could, from a knowledge of the properties of the molecules of that vapour, have predicted say, the state of the fauna of Britain in 1869, with as much certainty as one can say what will happen to the vapour of the breath on a cold winter's day.

He concluded that the doctrine of evolution 'does not even come into contact with Theism, considered as a philosophical doctrine'.[25]

Thus, even Huxley did not think that the question of God's existence or non-existence could be settled by biology. In an 1883 letter to Charles Watts he wrote: 'Agnosticism is of the essence of science, whether ancient or modern. It simply means that a man shall not say he knows or believes that which he has no scientific grounds for professing to know or believe... Consequently agnosticism puts aside not only the greater part of popular

Agostic –

Atheistic evolution.

theology, but also the greater part of anti-theology.' It was Huxley, we recall, who invented the term 'agnostic' to describe himself.[26]

Huxley's comment on the potentiality of the 'cosmic vapour' reminds us that the theory of evolution demands the existence of a fine-tuned universe producing exactly the right kind of materials and operating according to complex laws. The fine-tuning arguments from chemistry, physics, and cosmology are, of course, left unaffected by the biological theory of evolution. It is therefore surely arguable that the anthropic fruitfulness, both of the fine-tuning of the universe at the physical level and the capacity of its processes to produce organic life by a process of evolution, provided, of course, that they did, would constitute evidence of a creative intelligence. This view is called variously *theistic evolution, evolutionary creationism,* or *evotheism* and maintains that God 'supervises' the process of evolution. One of the best known holders of this view is Francis Collins, who prefers the term *Biologos* to that of theistic evolution. This term appears to denote the exact opposite of a mindless unguided process, but rather one that involves *logos,* and, probably (certainly, in Collins' case), the *Logos* of John 1:1.[27]

Each of these terms combines two very different concepts – a worldview, theism and a natural science, evolutionary biology. The idea that it intends to convey is that this is a branch of science the understanding of which is (in part) worldview dependent. And that may be a good idea. What puzzles me somewhat is that this is also true of other scientific disciplines. Carl Sagan and Steven Weinberg approached astrophysics from an atheist standpoint, as did Francis Crick and James Watson in their approach to molecular biology. Would it therefore help to speak of atheistic astrophysics, etc? Should we redress the balance by denoting the kind of evolutionary theory espoused by atheists as atheistic evolution? What then about the theistic physics of John Polkinghorne or the atheistic chemistry of Peter Atkins?

Why not cover everything by talking about theistic science and atheistic science? But we wouldn't do that in a formal setting, although, informally, it must be said that many of us are happy to say that we are scientists who are Christians and others that they are scientists who are atheist, agnostic, etc.

It is not easy to see how to resolve this satisfactorily, although our discussion here highlights the fact that there is something uniquely odd about the terminology used to describe the perceived status of evolution.

Nevertheless, by whichever name you know it, evolutionary creationism has commended itself to many scientists, from Asa Gray and Richard Owen in Darwin's day to the present. Commenting on this fact, the late Stephen Jay Gould wrote: 'Either half of my colleagues are enormously stupid, or else the science of Darwinism is fully compatible with conventional religious beliefs – and equally compatible with atheism.'[28] Notice that Gould separates science from worldview.

In Chapter 2 we listed some examples of Christians in science who are evolutionary creationists. All of these scientists would (as I would) vigorously reject as invalid any attempt to deduce atheism from evolutionary theory. As Alister McGrath points out: 'There is a substantial logical gap between Darwinism and atheism which Dawkins seems to prefer to bridge by rhetoric, rather than evidence.'[29] Former Director of the Faraday Institute in Cambridge, molecular biologist Denis Alexander, goes even further. He says that the 'Darwinian theory of evolution, whatever may have been the various ideological uses to which it has been put since 1859, is essentially devoid of either religious or moral significance, and those who try to derive such significance from it are mistaken',[30] a conclusion with which Richard Dawkins, among others, would radically disagree.

Similarly, Stephen Jay Gould says that 'science simply cannot (by its legitimate methods) adjudicate the issue of God's possible existence. We neither affirm it nor deny it; we simply can't comment on it as scientists.'[31] Those scientists who think that there is simply no case to be made for evolutionary biology having any implications for theism or atheism maintain that there is no need to consider evolution any further in this connection, although they do not deny that science can make a contribution to the science–religion debate. For example, the theists among them tend to support the fine-tuning arguments advanced earlier. Indeed, it cannot be emphasized too strongly that *biological evolution (whatever its extent) requires a fine-tuned universe in which to occur so that no arguments about the nature or status of evolution can undermine the arguments advanced hitherto in this book.*

Not only that, but Simon Conway Morris thinks that there may well be some biological analogue of the kind of fine-tuning in physics that we discussed earlier. He cites Howard van Til's insistence that 'It is not simply the numerical values of certain parameters that must be "just-right" in order for life to develop. No, it's the entire formational economy of the universe that must be "just right".' Conway Morris concludes that: 'Not only is the universe strangely fit to purpose, but so, too, as I have argued throughout this book, is life's ability to navigate to its solutions.'[32] This certainly doesn't sound much like a blind watchmaker, but rather like a clear-sighted navigator.

In a more recent book, Conway Morris says as much about the phenomenon of evolutionary convergence: 'Indeed, as our knowledge, especially of biochemistry and protein function, continues to expand, so at least my sense of amazement can only grow. If the watchmaker is blind, he has an unerring way of finding his way around the immense labyrinths of biological space. And even if he doesn't know where he is going, does He still know?'[33] Conway Morris subsequently spells out that amazement:

> ...invariably the words tend towards adjectives of stupefaction: *astonishing, astounding, remarkable, striking, even uncanny* and *stunning*, are all stock-in-trade responses. As I have pointed out elsewhere, although pronounced by loyal Darwinians, these exclamations seem to reveal a sense of unease. This, I conjecture, is at the least reflecting a hesitancy as to evolution's having a degree of directionality and, perhaps in the more alert investigator, their worst fears of the re-emergence of a telos.[34]

For this reason, and in light of the tendency for discussions of evolution to generate more heat than light, this would be a comfortable place to stop and draw our conclusions. I now must make clear why I personally cannot indulge in that particular luxury, in spite of the perils that may lie in wait for me if I proceed any further. My position is that, to the extent that guided biological evolution has occurred, it is certainly compatible with theism. It seems clear, however, that Assertion 1 is false – which means that the requirement that A1 & A2 be both valid fails as a matter of elementary logic! [Not P=> Not (P&Q)]. Could it be even worse than that? What if Assertion 2 is also false?

14

Evolution:
Asking Hard Questions

Two important things come out of the previous chapter. Firstly, Dennett, Dawkins, and the like have not made the case for *unguided* evolution. Secondly, guided evolution is *compatible* with a creator. However, that leaves open the scientific question of the extent to which guided evolution has actually occurred. In other words, what is the status of Assertion 2 in the previous chapter: *Biological evolution accounts for the existence of all of life's complexity.*

This was a risky question to ask in the past, though not so much nowadays, since after this book was last revised, there has been an increase in the number of leading biologists who not only ask it but think it may well have a negative answer. There is an important worldview reason for the strong reaction against questioning Assertion 2. It is this: if we assume naturalism as our worldview then evolution is a philosophical necessity irrespective of any scientific considerations. We consider how distinguished philosopher Thomas Nagel, an atheist, probes the difficulties here and concludes that there are real problems with materialistic theories.

The argument that the existence of mechanism does not preclude the activity of intelligent agency seems logically compelling to many and it therefore puzzles them, especially in the light of cautionary statements such as those made by Huxley and Gould as cited above, that so many others, like Dawkins and Dennett, nonetheless still cling tenaciously to the notion that evolution implies atheism.

It would seem that among those who are convinced by the neo-Darwinian argument there are two diametrically opposed opinions. The theists argue that evolution is a process that was used by God to produce all manner of life from its original primitive form. What is more, if you take into account the sheer marvel of all that evolution has achieved, it provides evidence for the existence of God, or, at least, it is consistent with the existence of God.

The atheists, on the other hand, argue that there is no mind of any kind behind evolutionary processes, which proceed of their own accord without any input from an external mind. Indeed, the marvels they produce show that there is no need to invoke God. What is more, they are evidence for the non-existence of God. Such people dismiss theistic evolution saying that by definition evolution is a blind, unguided process and therefore theistic evolution is an oxymoron. Furthermore, they often ask: What kind of a God is it who is active in evolution but remains so undetectable that his existence is completely irrelevant in practice?

Two diametrically opposed worldview interpretations, then, of the same biological theory. Should we not just choose the one we think to be correct and leave it there? Many people do just that, since going any further has in the past tended to open a rather large can of worms. Why? Because it involved questioning whether the modern synthesis is sufficiently scientifically robust to bear all the weight that is put upon it.

At first sight, it is a perfectly reasonable question to ask since an essential part of the normal scientific method of establishing a theory is constantly to subject it to critical enquiry. We wish to see how robust the modern synthesis is, for if it cannot withstand serious probing, then it may need to be modified, or even abandoned. There have been many theories in the past that flourished for a time, but then collapsed under close questioning and, of course, the discovery of disconfirming evidence: phlogiston, caloric, and ether are classical examples.

Yet, in my experience, even doing something as revolutionary as questioning the standard 'Big Bang' model of the early universe provokes nothing like the hurricane that is unleashed against the person who dares to query the validity of certain aspects of the neo-Darwinian synthesis. It provokes Richard Dawkins so sorely that he proclaims his (rather unexpected) belief in an absolute: 'It is absolutely safe to say that if you meet somebody who claims not to believe in evolution,[1] that person is ignorant, stupid or insane (or wicked, but I'd rather not consider that).'[2] The use of the phrase 'claims not to believe' shows Dawkins' utter incredulity that anyone could really have doubts. Is there a possibility that their claim does not match what they believe? Do they understand what they are saying?

When I wrote the first edition of this book I faced the momentous decision whether or not to risk a Dawkins' Certificate of Lunacy by continuing. Why not rest content with the argument so far? Well, apart from the reason just given above, the sheer vehemence of the protest fascinated me. Why was it so strong? Furthermore, why was it only in connection with this area of intellectual endeavour that I have ever (personally) heard an eminent scientist, the Nobel laureate Christian de Duve, no less, say in a public lecture in Oxford in the late 1990s: 'You must not question evolution'?[3]

After all, scientists have dared to question even Newton and Einstein. Indeed, most of us were (rightly – dare I say?) brought up to believe that questioning standard wisdom was one of the most important ways in which science grows. All science, however well established, benefits from being periodically questioned. So why is there such a taboo on questioning evolution? Why is it that only in this area of science have I ever heard a top-level researcher say that he dare not question evolution because it was more than his job was worth? Why does this so often seem to be a no-go area? That attitude is completely antipathetic to the spirit of science. Yet Daniel Dennett indulges in it: 'To put it bluntly but fairly, anyone today who doubts that the variety of life on this planet was produced by evolution is simply ignorant – inexcusably ignorant.'[4] You are not even allowed to have any doubts – and how scientific is that?

I find this slightly, but sadly, amusing since this attitude is usually associated with certain religious hyper-fundamentalists who, if you disagree with them even slightly, will condemn you as wicked. It is an odd but recognizable psychological phenomenon that people may become like those they hate.

There is a delightful story about a leading Chinese palaeontologist Jun-Yuan Chen ran into this problem when visiting the USA in 1999. His work on the remarkable discoveries in Chengjiang of strange fossil creatures led him to question the orthodox evolutionary line. In true scholarly fashion he mentioned his criticisms in his lectures but they elicited very little response. This lack of reaction surprised him and so he eventually asked one of his hosts what was wrong. He was told that scientists in the USA did not like to hear such criticism of evolution. To this he gave the delightful reply that it seemed to him that the difference between the USA and China was: 'In China we can criticize Darwin, but not the government; in America you can criticize the government, but not Darwin.'

In spite of all the pressure to keep my questions to myself, I decided to take the risk to press forward with them. In a sense it was a double risk, since I was a mathematician and not a biologist. However, I took comfort, and still do, in the fact that, from Darwin to Dawkins, from Crick and Watson to Noble and Shapiro, biologists have gone out of their way, not only to write for their professional colleagues but also for the interested non-professional on the assumption that ordinary thinking people are quite capable of understanding their ideas.

The concomitant of that, surely, was that moderately intelligent people are entitled to bleat when they do not find the ideas put to them satisfactory. And, one might add, they are encouraged in their bleating when they come across evaluations of the modern synthesis as I did later, like the following by the distinguished biologist Lynn Margulis: 'Like a sugary snack that temporarily satisfies our appetite but deprives us of more nutritious foods, neo-Darwinism sates intellectual curiosity with abstractions bereft of actual details – whether metabolic, biochemical, ecological, or of natural history.'[5]

One scientist who has bleated is engineer turned molecular biologist Douglas Axe, whose engineering experience led to hands-on research in which he showed functional proteins were exceedingly rare. This convinced him that something was seriously amiss with the neo-Darwinian synthesis. His experience at the hands of the 'academy' (Berkeley, Caltech, and Cambridge) detailed in his book *Undeniable: How Biology Confirms Our Intuition that Life is Designed*, is well worth reading to get some idea of what is involved when a biologist criticizes a reigning paradigm in their own field. Axe writes: 'Real science is nothing like the utopian version I mentioned at the beginning of my journey. The flag of materialism... still flies proudly over the academy and people working under that banner are expected to show due respect. Any serious opposition will bring the colour guard out in full force, to the sound of blowing whistles.'[6] It has been costly for him: 'Everyone must decide for himself or herself what they can do under the shadow of the materialist flag, knowing that if they press too hard they may lose even the small opportunities they once had.'[7]

But before I take the risk of asking the question that dared not be asked let me encourage the reader not to put the book down just yet. For I have no intention of denying that natural selection has an important role to play in the variations that we see in the living world all around us, as Darwin observed. My questions have to do with whether evolution by mutation and natural selection can carry *all* the weight that is often put upon it. That it can carry *some* weight is clear. And that has implications for a theistic view of the world.

As to asking whether there are limits to that weight I regard as a legitimate task, not only of biology, but of philosophy. Philosopher Thomas Nagel says that:

> intellectual humility requires that we resist the temptation to assume that tools of the kind we now have are in principle sufficient to understand the universe as a whole. Pointing out their limits is a philosophical task, whoever engages in it, rather than part of the internal pursuit of science – though we can hope that if the limits are recognized, that may eventually lead to new forms of scientific understanding.[8]

At the time of the earlier editions of this book (2007, 2009) it was hard to get an overview of opinion on this issue. For instance, was I just one of a tiny group of sceptics whereas the vast majority of educated people simply could not see our difficulty and wondered why we were making a fuss? Thankfully, the situation has changed as has been revealed by more recent academic surveys. In particular, Dr Fern Elsdon-Baker is the principal investigator of the 2017 'Science and Religion: Exploring the Spectrum' project based at Newman University, Birmingham, England. She has written a *Guardian* article on her survey of opinion in the UK and Canada. We reproduce part of it here.[9] She starts with the observation: 'Many see the rejection of evolutionary science as a marker of religiosity or hard-line conservativism. There is a widespread assumption that religious people will find it hard to reconcile evolutionary science, and by extension science as a whole, with their religious beliefs. However, our new research turns some of this thinking on its head.'

The survey, conducted in the UK and Canada, found that only a minority in both countries found it somewhat difficult, difficult, or very difficult to accept evolutionary science in relation to their own personal beliefs (12 per cent in the UK and 20 per cent in Canada). It would therefore seem that levels of religious concerns over evolutionary science are lower than some might fear. She also says that one needs to be careful not to assume that when people say they are rejecting 'evolutionary science', they are rejecting all the sciences. Indeed, most religious people in her study did not reject evolution. She writes:

> Furthermore, doubts about evolutionary science frequently appear to be related to the perceived limitations of evolutionary science-based explanations for human origins and human consciousness... Just over half of religious or spiritual people in both countries thought human consciousness could not be explained by evolutionary processes. Astonishingly, we also found that over 1 in 3 of Canadian atheists, and nearly 1 in 5 UK atheists felt the same.
>
> It seems rejection of, or doubts about, aspects of evolution are not necessarily just an issue of religious belief versus evolutionary science.

As a lifelong atheist she nevertheless thinks that it is disingenuous and unempirical to deny that there are differences between humans and other species, suggesting that what really makes us human is the capacity to ask questions about our place in the world.

However, since, in the view of many, even a modest level of questioning of evolutionary theories is (or, at least, was) nothing short of suicidal, I assured the readers of my earlier editions of this book, should I 'naturally select' my own demise by committing intellectual suicide, I had already composed my own brief epitaph:

> Here lies the body of John Lennox.
> You ask me why he's in this box?

> He died of something worse than pox,
> On Darwinism – heterodox.

Looking back, I need not have worried so much and I am glad I stuck with my questions. I can imagine, though, that at this point a reader might say: 'You are a mathematician, not a biologist. I can understand that it makes sense for you to write about science in general and the world of mathematics and physics in particular, but isn't evolutionary biology a step too far?' For my answer I refer to Suzan Mazur's interview with evolutionary biologist

James Shapiro in which she asked him: 'Should amateurs who are seriously challenging Darwinian scenarios be welcome to the evolutionary science discourse?' Shapiro replied:

> Well I don't see how you can exclude anybody. The point
> is not who's saying something or what their credentials
> are but the value and substance of what they are saying.
> Having started off my career as an amateur with a degree
> in English rather than biology, I think sometimes that's
> an advantage because you are without prejudices. You're
> freer to understand and interpret data.[10]

So, now let me indicate why I think the feeling that we should not question evolution is so strong in the hope that this will clear the ground for a more meaningful discussion.

We start with something that we alluded to earlier which is the unusual, if not unique, relationship of evolutionary theory to philosophical and worldview assumptions.

The relationship between evolution and philosophy

Reflecting on Strickberger's admission, cited in the previous chapter, that, in his opinion at least, part of the motivation behind evolutionary theory lies in an attempt to remove God,[11] we are led to probe what relationship there might be between evolutionary theory and metaphysics. In a keynote lecture to the American Association for the Advancement of Science in 1993, Michael Ruse, a leading philosopher of biology, said that, for many people, evolution has played the role of a secular religion. Colin Patterson reminds us of Popper's caution: that even a scientific theory may become an intellectual fashion, a substitute for religion, an entrenched dogma, adding, 'this has certainly been true of evolutionary theory'.[12] Phillip Johnson, a lawyer at the University of California, Berkeley, who did much to stir up debate (and high-level debate at that) on the subject, has pointed out: 'The danger here is that a methodological premise which is useful for limited purposes has been expanded to form a metaphysical absolute.'[13]

The late Donald McKay, whose research focussed on communication networks in the brain, described the way that this happened:

'Evolution' began to be invoked in biology... as a substitute for God. ... From standing for a technical hypothesis... the term was rapidly twisted to mean an atheistic metaphysical principle whose invocation could relieve a man of any theological shivers at the spectacle of the universe. Spelt with a capital E and dishonestly decked in the prestige of the scientific theory of evolution (which in fact gave it no shred of justification), 'Evolutionism' became the name for a whole anti-religious philosophy, in which 'Evolution' played the role of a... personal deity, as the 'real force in the universe'.[14]

Similarly, in an essay entitled 'The Funeral of a Great Myth', C. S. Lewis explains that: 'we must sharply distinguish between Evolution as a biological theorem, and popular Evolutionism... which is certainly a myth'. Lewis grounds this assertion, first of all, in chronology: 'If popular evolutionism were (as it imagines itself to be) not a myth but the intellectually legitimate result of the scientific theorem on the public mind, it would arise after that theorem had become widely known.'[15] But, he goes on to say that it did not. Historically, the philosophy of evolutionism appeared long before the biological theory of evolution and it differs from what true biologists think. They hold that evolution is a hypothesis that covers more facts than any other and so should be accepted until superseded by a fresh theory that covers more facts with less assumptions. Lewis mentions a certain Professor D. M. S. Watson, according to whom evolution 'is accepted by zoologists, not because it is observed to occur... but because the only alternative, special creation, is clearly incredible'.[16] This would mean that the sole ground for believing it is not empirical but metaphysical – the dogma of an amateur metaphysician who finds special creation incredible. I do not think it has come to that.

One wonders what Lewis would have to say today. The thing about myths is that they are beguiling. Denis Noble FRS says: 'I refer to a web of interpretation as it is the whole conceptual scheme of neo-Darwinism that creates the difficulty. Each concept and metaphor reinforces the overall mindset until it is almost impossible to stand outside it and to appreciate how beguiling it is.'[17]

The logical implications of naturalism: evolution as a philosophical necessity

Lewis' observation above brings us to the heart of the matter. We argued earlier that naturalism does not follow from biological evolution (remember Assertion 1); but what about the reverse deduction? Suppose that naturalism/materialism is true. Then, *merely as a matter of sheer logical necessity*, it follows that some kind of evolutionary account must be given for life, apart altogether from any evidence which may be offered to support it. For, what other possibility can there be? If, for example, we start off with the materialistic hypothesis that all we have is matter/energy and the forces of physics, then there is only one option – matter/energy together with the forces of nature over time have produced life, that is, evolution of some sort.

The fact that, from the naturalistic and materialistic perspectives, evolution of some form or other appears as a philosophical necessity is nothing new. It was perceived centuries, indeed millennia, before Dawkins and Darwin. The ancient Greek materialist philosopher Epicurus used precisely this logic to produce an evolutionary theory from the atomic theory of Democritus in the fifth century BC. This means that, in the contemporary scientific world, we have the extraordinary situation that the theory of evolution stands in such a close relationship to naturalism that large parts of it can be deduced directly from that philosophy without the need to consider any evidence, as the ancient arguments of Lucretius plainly show.

It is very difficult to think of another scientific theory that is in a similar position. Think, for example, of trying to deduce Newton's theory of gravitation or Einstein's theory of relativity or the theory of Quantum Electrodynamics from a philosophical principle or worldview, whether materialistic, naturalistic, or, even, theistic. There is no way that it could be done. And yet, as Lucretius saw, and as anyone who thinks about it can readily see, it can be done with evolution. All we need to do is to put on an atheist cap and ask ourselves the question: How did life come to be? In a very short time we will come up with some kind of theory of evolution.

It may be argued here that this can be done with evolution because of the kind of question it is trying to answer – the question of the existence of humans, for example. In addition, unusual closeness of relationship between a scientific theory and a worldview does not, of course, determine whether that theory is true or false. It does, however, mean that there may be so much *a priori* philosophical pressure from the reigning naturalistic or materialistic paradigm, that aspects of the theory may not be subjected to the wide-ranging, rigorous, self-critical analysis which is, or should be, characteristic of all science.[18]

I am not alone in thinking that that is exactly what happened. For example, biologist Robert G. Reid in his comprehensive work *Biological Emergences: Evolution by Natural Experiment* writes: 'Since neo-Darwinists are also hypersensitive to creationism, they treat any criticism of the current paradigm as a breach of the scientific worldview that will admit the fundamentalist hordes. Consequently, questions about how selection theory can claim to be the all-sufficient explanation of evolution go unanswered or ignored.'[19] It would appear that fear of those who do not share your worldview can also be a factor in negatively influencing the quality of scientific research.

Thomas Kuhn warned of paradigms that produced a box-like structure so rigid that things did not fit into it and which were therefore often simply overlooked. If something has simply got to be true, then conflicting evidence can easily be ignored or superficially dismissed as irrelevant. To avoid this danger, Richard Feynman emphasized that one should always be careful to record all the evidence against one's theories; indeed, one should bend over backwards to consider it, since the easiest person to fool is oneself.

Sadly, Kuhn and Feynman's warnings seem often to go unheeded, with the result that the questioning of evolution, even on scientific grounds, is fraught with risk. For this, in the eyes of many, is tantamount to questioning what is, to them, sheer fact by virtue of philosophical necessity; and thus the questioner runs the risk of being classified – if not certified – as a member of the lunatic fringe. But that kind of attitude, ironically, is precisely the one that Galileo faced. There is a luminous parallel between the Aristotelianism of his day and the naturalism of our own. Galileo ran the risk of questioning Aristotle, and we all know what happened to him. We also know who was right. The question is: Will we learn anything from it? Must Darwin be protected in the same way that Aristotle was? After all, it was a clear fact, was it not, that the earth did not move?

Granted that there is powerful worldview pressure from naturalism to adopt an evolutionary paradigm, nevertheless, there are some prominent atheist philosophers and scientists who think that there is good reason to probe the claims of the modern synthesis. But now it is time for us to get down to define precisely what is meant by evolution.

Evolution: 1) change
2) Common descent
3) micro evolution
4) Macro evolution
5) artificial selection
6) molecular evolution.

15

The Nature and Scope of Evolution

'Nothing makes sense in biology except in light of evolution.'
Theodosius Dobzhansky

'Nothing makes sense in biology except in light of information.'[1]
Bernd Olaf Küppers

We explore the range of uses of the word evolution, introducing six of the most common, and making brief comments about each of them. They are: change, common descent, microevolution, macroevolution, artificial selection, and molecular evolution.

We also think about what is meant by 'fact' and 'theory' in order to discuss the distinction that is often made between the 'fact of evolution' and 'the theory, or theories of evolution'. We then further think about further aspects of *a priori* philosophical commitments on the way in which evolution is understood.

The definition of evolution

Thus far we have been using the term 'evolution' almost as if it had a single, agreed meaning. But this is manifestly not the case and as a result discussion of evolution is frequently fogged by failure to recognize that the term may be used in several different ways. Some of these usages are non-controversial, so that questioning or rejecting them might indeed evidence some kind of ignorance or stupidity (but, even then, scarcely wickedness, which, like Dawkins, I won't contemplate). What, then, do we mean by 'evolution'? We now list some uses of the term and end the chapter with some of the evidences put forward for evolution.

1. Change, development, variation

'Evolution' may be used to describe change without any implication for the kind of mechanism or intelligent input (or lack of it) involved in bringing about that change. For example, we speak of the 'evolution of the motor car', where, of course, a great deal of intelligent input is necessary. We also speak of the 'evolution of a coastline', where the natural processes of sea and wind, flora and fauna shape the coastline over time, plus possibly steps taken by engineers to prevent erosion. When people speak of the 'evolution of life' in this sense, as they sometimes do, they simply mean that life arose and has developed by some means or other which they do not specify or even know. Used in this way, the term 'evolution' is neutral, innocuous, and uncontroversial. I shall sometimes use the term in this way.

2. Common descent

Darwin's theory of evolution was framed in terms of descent with modification. This led to postulating the existence of a common ancestor for all living things. The chain of being ran in terms of gradual development for around 4.5 billion years, from unicellular organisms like bacteria, to multicellular organisms like worms, then fish, amphibians, reptiles, birds, mammals, and finally humans. However, Darwin did not himself have a viable candidate for a mechanism that would account for such modification. The modern synthesis fills out Darwin's theory by adding mutation, and a number of other things like genetic drift, to account for the modification. Arguments for common descent are usually based on the fossil record and on genetic similarities.

3. Microevolution

This term refers to variation within prescribed limits of complexity, that is quantitative variation of already existing organs or structures. Such processes were observed by Darwin and form an important part of his theory. This aspect of evolution is scarcely controversial, as such effects of natural selection, mutation, genetic drift, etc. are constantly being recorded by biologists today.[2] Classic examples with which we are all too familiar right round the world are the way in which bacteria develop resistance to antibiotics and the way in which viruses mutate. Scientists in Australia have discovered several changes in humans that have appeared over a short time. For example, some babies are born without wisdom teeth and more people have a previously rare additional artery in their forearm. Dr Teghan Lucas, of Flinders University in Adelaide, said faces are also becoming shorter, due to changes in our diet, and our smaller jaws mean there is less room for teeth.[3]

4. Macroevolution

This term refers to large-scale innovation, the coming into existence of new organs, structures, body-plans, of qualitatively new genetic material – for example, the evolution of multicellular from single-celled structures. Macroevolution thus involves a marked increase in qualitative complexity. The distinction between micro and macroevolution is (still) disputed by the gradualist thesis (Darwin and Dawkins, for example) that macroevolution is accounted for by extrapolating the processes that drive microevolution over time. For this reason, unless one is careful to make clear what exactly one means, it is quite likely that people will think that macroevolution is just microevolution writ large and extrapolated over long periods of time. I personally find myself in an ambivalent position regarding the usefulness of these terms.

5. Artificial selection

Plant and animal breeders have produced many different kinds of roses and sheep from basic stocks, by very careful selective breeding methods. Think of the huge range of the dog species. Darwin argued that what humans can do in a relatively short time, nature could surely do in a long time – hence 'natural' selection.

However, the process of selective breeding by humans involves a high degree of intelligent input and so provides no real evidence for evolution by *unguided* processes.

6. Molecular evolution

To most peoples' way of thinking, evolution presupposes the existence of self-replicating genetic material, i.e. life. However, the terms 'molecular evolution' and 'chemical evolution' are often used to describe biogenesis, the emergence of the living cell from non-living materials, by means yet to be ascertained, though many scenarios have been proposed.[4] This language usage can easily obscure the fact that the word 'evolution' here *cannot* mean the Darwinian process. We have already seen some of the difficulties in the way of a naturalistic solution to biogenesis.

The term 'evolution' also covers theories about how life developed – like the modern synthesis, according to which natural selection operates on the basis of variations that arise through mutation.

One of the claims often made is that evolution is a fact, whereas many strong opponents will say that it is 'just a theory'. For instance, Richard Dawkins writes: 'Evolution is a fact. Beyond reasonable doubt, beyond serious doubt, beyond sane, informed, intelligent doubt, beyond doubt evolution is a fact... That didn't have to be true. It is not self-evidently, tautologically, obviously true, and there was a time when most people, even educated people, thought it wasn't. It didn't have to be true, but it is.... Evolution is the only game in town, the greatest show on earth.'[5]

Harvard geneticist Richard Lewontin confidently asserts the same: 'It is time... to state clearly that evolution is fact, not theory... Birds arose from non-birds and humans from non-humans. No person who pretends to any understanding of the natural world can deny these facts any more than she or he can deny that the earth is round, rotates on its axis and revolves around the sun.'[6]

What is a fact? *The Oxford English Dictionary* (OED) informs us that 'fact' is derived from the Latin *facere* = to do. It therefore denotes 'a deed' or 'something done'. In our context it denotes (OED again): 'Something that has really occurred or is actually the case; something certainly known to be of this character; hence, a particular truth known by actual observation or authentic testimony, as opposed to what is merely inferred, or to a conjecture or fiction; a datum of experience, as distinguished from the conclusions that may be based on it.'

What is a theory? The OED tells us that the word is derived from similar-sounding Latin and Greek words that denote: a looking at, viewing, contemplation, speculation, theory. The main meanings that concern us here are:

1. A scheme or system of ideas or statements held as an explanation or account of a group of facts or phenomena. In a loose or general sense. A hypothesis that has been confirmed or established by observation or experiment, and is propounded or accepted as accounting for the known facts. A statement of what are held to be the general laws, principles, or causes of something known or observed.

2. A systematic statement of the general principles or laws of some branch of mathematics; a set of theorems forming a connected system.

3. In loose or general sense: A hypothesis proposed as an explanation; hence, a mere hypothesis, speculation, conjecture; an idea or set of ideas about something; an individual view or notion.'

The first thing to notice here is that there is an overlap between aspects of the definition of 'fact' and definition 1 of 'theory', namely: 'a particular truth known by actual observation or authentic testimony' and 'a hypothesis that has been confirmed or established by observation or experiment, and is propounded or accepted as accounting for the known facts'. As an example we take what Lewontin says (noted above): 'the earth is round, rotates on its axis and revolves around the sun'.

However, Lewontin is wrong to suggest that this example is not a theory. At least, he is half-wrong. It is a theory in senses 1 (and, indeed, 2 because of Newton's laws) but not in sense 3. There is often confusion between senses 1 and 3 not only among the general public but even among scientists.

What do some sceptics mean when they say: 'evolution is only a theory'? They usually mean sense 3. Indeed, they may not be aware of sense 1, and, in any case, they frequently don't specify what they mean by 'evolution'. For, if we look at the meanings of 'evolution' listed above, some of them clearly qualify as theory in sense 1 and also as facts. For instance, evolution in the sense of change is a fact and microevolution is a fact as they are both confirmed by repeated observation, just like the fact that the earth is round and spins on its axis. Lewontin is right at this level.

However, that particular fact is not in the same category as Lewontin's claim that: 'Birds arose from non-birds and humans from non- humans' for two simple reasons. Firstly, no one has ever observed birds arising from non-birds (whatever a non-bird might be?) or humans arising from non-humans. Secondly, the fact that the earth orbits the sun is not only a matter of observation, it is also a matter of *repeated* observation. Lewontin's claim about the origin of birds concerns an unrepeatable, unobserved, past event. To put an unobservable and unrepeatable phenomenon in the same category as an observable and repeatable one would seem to be such an elementary blunder that one cannot help wondering if Lewontin's aforementioned fear of a Divine footprint (Chapter 5) is playing a key role, and that materialistic prejudice is overriding common (scientific) sense and leading him to talk nonsense.

His admitted *a priori* commitment to materialism may well be why he regards neo-Darwinism's common descent explanation of the origin and birds and humans as a fact. Similarly, Richard Dawkins' claim that evolution in the sense that natural unguided processes led to life is the only game in town is the only possibility for all atheists. Whether there is any evidence or not that points in another direction is, strictly speaking, irrelevant. This 'evolution' simply must be: 'something that has really occurred or is actually the case' independent even of observation or experiment.

It is this, I think, that leads some scientists to distinguish between the fact of evolution and the theory of evolution – that is, theories about the mechanism of evolution. Among them, some hold that natural selection is a theory only in sense 3 and others a theory in sense 1.

It should also be noted that mathematician and biologist Peter Saunders said in 2015 in an interview with Suzan Mazur that, since neo-Darwinism is not falsifiable, it should not be thought of as a theory but rather as a paradigm in the Kuhnian sense.[7] A leading textbook, *Strickberger's Evolution*, says:

> ... the facts of evolution are the anatomical similarities and differences between organisms, the places where they live, the metabolic pathways they use, the embryological stages through which they develop, the fossil forms they leave behind and the genetic, chromosomal and molecular features that connect them. The theory of evolution accounts for the historical sequence of organisms through time. It explains their existence through processes that cause change in their genetic inheritance through time.[8]

Here, the expression 'facts of evolution' is somewhat ambiguous. It could mean the facts shown by evolution but here it clearly mean the facts, observable and unequivocal, on which theories of evolution can be based. The authors are not so much saying that evolution *is a fact* but rather are claiming that it is *based on facts*. Anatomical similarities and fossils are a fact, macroevolution and common descent are theories that attempt to account for them. The question arises: theories in which sense, 1 or 3?

It is important also to reflect on the possibility of the intrusion here of *a priori* worldview commitments. We have argued that evolutionary theory is unique in science in that some form of it is derivable directly from atheist philosophy without any scientific considerations. It is inevitable that this will prejudice atheists to such an extent that many of them will regard it as heresy to question evolution, however unscientific their attitude might appear. Loose statements like Lewontin's certainly do not help the dialogue.

However, in light of these variations in the meaning of evolution, Lewontin's and Dawkins' objections to people questioning evolution may appear somewhat more understandable – depending on what aspect is being questioned. For example, questioning evolution in senses 1, 2, or 4, could understandably lead to an accusation of stupidity or ignorance. As we have already said, no one seriously doubts the validity of things we can observe directly – like microevolution and cyclic change as examples of the operation of natural selection.

Here are some examples that are put forward as:

Evidences for evolution
Darwin's finches

One of the main factual evidences adduced by Darwin for evolution had to do with his famous observations made in the Galapagos islands of the changes in finch beak lengths. Darwin noticed that in a population of finches during periods of drought the average beak size was larger. He argued that this was a result of the fact that food had become scarce and increased the competition for survival. Birds with larger beaks were able to deal with larger nuts, for example, and had a survival advantage in comparison with birds with smaller beaks that found it harder to find food. There is a major study of these effects by Pulitzer Prize winner Jonathan Weiner.[9]

However, it turned out that the variation in average finch beak lengths, observed during the drought of 1977, was reversed by the rains of 1983 – a reversal not always mentioned in textbooks.[10] This means that what was observed was cyclical change due to natural selection, rather than permanent improvement or change into something different. It does not even amount to microevolution.

Industrial melanism

One of the main studies that has been copied from textbook to textbook and heralded as one of the main proofs of evolution has come in for criticism. It concerns industrial melanism in the peppered moth (Biston betularia).

The best evidence for evolution? Is it surprising then that some people are skeptical?

The claim is that natural selection produced a variation in the relative proportion of light moths to dark moths in a population. Light moths were more easily seen than dark ones by predators against the dark, polluted surfaces of tree trunks so that eventually the population would become dominated by dark moths. Of course, if this account were true, it would at best only be another of cyclical change: no new species of moths were created in the process since both kinds existed from the outset. Therefore it would not be controversial except insofar as it might be used as sufficient evidence for macroevolution.

However, according to Michael Majerus, a Cambridge expert on moths: 'the basic peppered moth story is wrong, inaccurate or incomplete, with respect to most of the story's component parts'.[11] In addition, there appears to be no evidence that peppered moths rest on tree trunks in the wild. Many photographs in textbooks, showing them doing so, have apparently been staged. In the *Times Higher Educational Supplement*,[12] biologist Lynn Margulis is puzzled by the fact that Steve Jones still used the peppered moth in his book update of Darwin, entitled *Almost Like A Whale*,[13] even though, according to her, he must know of the dubious nature of the research. When University of Chicago biologist Jerry Coyne learned of the difficulties with the peppered moth story, he wrote: 'My own reaction resembles the dismay attending my discovery, at the age of six, that it was my father and not Santa who brought the presents on Christmas Eve.'[14]

This reaction is interesting: why didn't Coyne, who is a scientist after all, rather say that the result raises important questions of the capacity of microevolution that I would like to explore as it might lead me to find important new ideas that I would otherwise have missed'? However, calling established theory into question is very difficult since prejudice in its favour tends to run very deep.

Coyne's reaction reminds me that many years ago while still a research student I went to a seminar on evolution that was attended by some well-known biologists. I asked the question: What is the best evidence for evolution? The only answer I was offered was the peppered moth. That was all they had to say. I then asked them why they were then surprised that some people were sceptical. No answer.

It was an enlightening experience.

Misunderstanding can easily arise, therefore, particularly when, as sometimes happens, evolution is essentially *defined* as microevolution. Take, for instance, the following statement about evolution by E. O. Wilson:

> Evolution by natural selection is perhaps the only one true law unique to biological systems, as opposed to non-living physical systems, and in recent decades it has taken on the solidity of a mathematical theorem. It states simply that if a population of organisms contains multiple hereditary variants in some trait (say, red versus blue eyes in a bird population), and if one of those variants succeeds in contributing more offspring to the next generation than the other variants, the overall composition of the population changes, and *evolution has occurred*.[15]

Wilson goes on to say that the regular appearance of novel genetic variants will mean that evolution will continue for ever. Imagine a breeding population consisting of both red-eyed and blue-eyed birds where the red-eyed birds are better adapted to the environment. This will result in the population coming to consist mainly of red-eyed birds. However, if green-eyed mutants appear that are even better adapted, the population will eventually become green-eyed. Wilson concludes: 'Evolution has thus taken two more small steps.'[16]

Quite so. But this is merely a description of microevolution ('small steps'), since we have both red-eyed birds and blue-eyed birds in the initial population, Wilson is once more simply describing the kind of uncontroversial cyclic change mentioned above in connection with Darwin's finches and the peppered moths.

Wilson, therefore, completely bypasses the question as to whether the particular (micro) evolutionary mechanism he has described can bear all the extra weight that is put upon it in any full-blown understanding of evolution. Where, for example, does he give an answer to the question as to how birds arose in the first place? Yet Wilson claims elsewhere in his article that natural selection does bear that weight. For instance: 'all biological processes arose through evolution of these[17] physicochemical systems through natural selection'; or again, humans are 'descended from animals by the same blind force that created those animals'.[18] The reader will not miss the implicit claim that biogenesis came through evolution.

The fossil record

On my travels I try to visit natural history museums whenever possible and enjoy perusing the displays. I usually pause to look at the way in which evolution is presented (examples of such images are to be found by searching on the internet for 'evolution of life through geologic time').

Such images, and those of the fossil record that accompanies them, are impressive with the effect that, to misquote Richard Dawkins, it is 'terribly, terribly tempting' to believe that they demonstrate a slow gradual from the simple to the complex making the modern synthesis really 'apparent'.

What seems apparent, however, may not always actually be what is true. The late Robert Wesson of Waterloo University, Ontario, a physicist with broad scientific interests wrote: 'Large evolutionary innovations are not well understood. None has ever been observed, and we have no idea whether any may be in progress. There is no good fossil record of any.'[19] This will surprise many people who share the widespread public impression, often gained from the aforementioned natural history museums, that one of the most powerful evidences for evolution comes from the fossil record. And yet that impression does not really correspond to all that is to be found in the scientific literature.

In Darwin's time palaeontologists were among the most formidable *opponents* of his theory. They argued that the fossil record failed to demonstrate gradual accumulation of features over geologic time. Darwin commented on this in *The Origin of Species*:

> The abrupt manner in which whole groups of species suddenly appear in certain formations has been urged by several palaeontologists – for instance by Agassiz, Pictet and Sedgwick – as a fatal objection to the belief in the transmutation of species. If numerous species, belonging to the same genera or families, have really started into life at once, the fact would be fatal to the theory of descent with slow modification through natural selection.[20]

He also wrote: 'The number of intermediate varieties, which have formerly existed on the earth, [should] be truly enormous. Why then is not every geological formation and every stratum full of such intermediate links? Geology assuredly does not reveal any such graduated organic chain; and this, perhaps is the most obvious and gravest objection which can be urged against my theory.'[21]

Swiss-American Louis Agassiz of Harvard was the leading palaeontologist of the day and a founder of the American scientific tradition.

His work on glaciers and fossil fish are regarded as classics. Adam Sedgwick was a British geologist regarded as one of the founders of modern geology. What concerned both of these men was the sudden appearance of new life forms in the Cambrian strata without any ancestral fossil evidence in the Precambrian. The Scottish geologist Sir Roderick Impey Murchison who had explored geologic strata in Wales[22] as Sedgwick had done, reported: 'The earliest signs of living things, announcing as they do a high complexity of organisation, entirely exclude the hypothesis of transmutation from lower to higher grades of being.'[23]

Some years later, in the early twentieth century, evidence of the same thing was found in the Burgess Shale in British Columbia, Canada, by the Director of the Smithsonian Institute, Charles Doolittle Walcott. He and his co-workers eventually put together a vast collection of more than 65,000 fossil specimens of a great variety of hitherto unknown creatures, some of them so bizarre that they were given appropriately bizarre names – like *Hallucigenia Sparsa*. They included specimens from around 20 out of approximately 27 phyla – the broadest classification category – that are to be seen in the fossil record. They had all appeared in a geologically short period that became known as the 'Cambrian Explosion'.

The 'explosive' nature of this event has created a considerable amount of controversy. In particular, the book, *Darwin's Doubt*,[24] by philosopher of science Stephen Meyer, which gives a detailed account of the 'Cambrian Explosion', has come in for considerable criticism by those claiming that there was in fact no explosion and the timescale is enough for the modern synthesis to account for it. Meyer addressed these criticisms in a later edition of his book. What I find disturbing is that some of the criticism aimed at Meyer is that due to his being a prominent representative of ID, his worldview colours his science. The critics, who are often in the atheist camp, are not so aware of the way their science may be coloured by their naturalistic worldview. It is noteworthy that both Agassiz and Sedgwick would have stood with Meyer on the issue of intelligent causation.

We must not allow this controversy to cause us to lose sight of what zoologist Mark Ridley wrote: 'The fossil record of evolutionary change within single evolutionary lineages is very poor. If evolution is true, species originate through changes of ancestral species: one might expect to be able to see this in the fossil record. In fact it can rarely be seen. In 1859 Darwin could not cite a single example.'[25]

What, then, is the result of the many years of intensive activity, since Darwin's time? Palaeontologist David Raup of Chicago's Field Museum of Natural History, which houses one of the largest fossil collections in the world, said in 1979: 'We are now about 120 years after Darwin and the knowledge of the fossil record has been greatly expanded. We now have a quarter of a million fossil species, but the situation hasn't changed much. The record of evolution is still surprisingly jerky and, ironically, we have even fewer examples of evolutionary transition than we had in Darwin's time.'[26]

Stephen Jay Gould, no sympathizer with ID, said, 'The extreme rarity of transitional forms in the fossil record persists as the trade secret of palaeontology.'[27] His fellow palaeontologist, Niles Eldredge, who developed the theory of punctuated equilibrium with him, added: 'When we do see the introduction of evolutionary novelty, it usually shows up with a bang, and often with no firm evidence that the fossils did not evolve elsewhere. Evolution cannot forever be going on somewhere else. Yet that's how the fossil record has struck many a forlorn palaeontologist looking to learn something about evolution.'[28]

In fact, Eldredge makes an astonishing admission: 'We palaeontologists have said that the history of life supports [the story of gradual adaptive change] knowing all the while it does not.'[29] But why? What conceivable reason could there be for members of an academic community to suppress what they know to be the truth – unless it were something which supported a worldview, which they had already decided was unacceptable?

What, then, does the fossil record reveal? Gould wrote:

> The history of most fossil species includes two features particularly inconsistent with the idea that they gradually evolved:
>
> 1. Stasis. Most species exhibit no directional change during their tenure on earth. They appear in the fossil record looking pretty much the same as when they disappear; morphological change is usually limited and directionless.
>
> 2. Sudden appearance. In any local area a species does not arise gradually by the steady transformation of its ancestors; it appears all at once and 'fully formed'.[30]

"Punctuated equilibrium"

Gould and Eldredge's reading of the fossil record as revealing short periods of rapid change, followed by long periods of stasis, led to their development of the theory of 'punctuated equilibrium'. Their idea is that the long periods of stasis are broken sporadically by sudden large macroevolutionary 'jumps'. As a spectacular example of such a jump Gould, in his bestselling book *Wonderful Life*,[31] described how all the major phyla (taxonomic ranks) we have today – plus a good many more which have become extinct – appeared very suddenly in the Cambrian Explosion. Of course, the question of what caused such sudden 'jumps' is another matter and increases the difficulties of those who wish to argue that microevolutionary processes are an adequate engine for large-scale evolution.

It is interesting and perhaps somewhat ironic that the theory of punctuated equilibrium was embraced by Marxist thinkers long before it had any basis in biology, since it seemed to fit into their dialectical way of thinking. They argued that, when thesis and antithesis clash, the new synthesis occurs rapidly in the form of a jump rather than a long, gradual process. This is another example of how worldviews and ideologies can influence science.

Simon Conway Morris FRS, of Cambridge University, is more tempered in his approach to the Cambrian Explosion than Gould, but nonetheless thinks that it took place:

> Forms transitional between species can be observed today, and can be inferred to have existed in the past. Nevertheless, the net result is very far from a seamless tapestry of form that would allow an investigator to read the Tree of Life simply by finding the intermediates – living and extinct – that in principle connect all species. On the contrary, biologists are much more impressed by the discreteness of organic form, and the general absence of intermediates.[32]

Evolutionary biologist and expert in the field of computational biology, Eugene Koonin of the National Center for Biotechnology Information (NCBI), National Institutes of Health, and a member of the National Academy of Sciences, said, in 2007, essentially the same thing as David Raup did thirty years before: 'Major transitions in biological evolution show the same pattern of sudden emergence of diverse forms at a new level of complexity. The relationships between major groups within an emergent new class of biological entities are hard to decipher and do not seem to fit the tree pattern that, following Darwin's original proposal, remains the dominant description of biological evolution.'[33]

The theory of punctuated equilibrium stands in complete contrast to the gradualist approach of the 'ultra-Darwinians', such as John Maynard Smith, Richard Dawkins, and Daniel Dennett. Indeed, the battle between the two groups has been vitriolic at times. The gradualists, as we have seen, hold that microevolution over time becomes macroevolution. They believe that the slow accumulation of tiny evolutionary steps over aeons of time can add up to a large innovatory step.

Eldredge accused them of being weak on palaeontology. His argument is that the gradualists are concerned to understand how genetic information comes to be modified over the course of time, and then they simply assert that 'evolutionary history is the outcome of natural selection working on available genetic variation'. In other words, they simply extrapolate from what they observe in the present, backwards through geological time. 'And that,' Eldredge continues,

facts

> to my palaeontological eyes is just not good enough. Simple extrapolation does not work. I found that out back in the 60s as I tried in vain to document examples of the kind of slow directional change we all thought ought to be there ever since Darwin told us that natural selection should leave precisely such a tell-tale signal... I found instead that once species appear in the fossil record they tend not to change very much at all. Species remain imperturbably, implacably resistant to change as a matter of course – often for millions of years.[34]

This verdict, which is so strikingly at odds with the popular understanding of fossils, was supported by Colin Patterson FRS: 'I will lay it on the line – there is not one such fossil [a fossil which is ancestral or transitional] for which one could make a watertight argument.'[35] It is additionally interesting that Patterson said this in connection with the Archaeopteryx, whose fossilized remains were actually under his care in the British Natural History Museum and which is often cited as an example of a transitional species between reptiles and birds. This is one reason it is important to

A ←— "c" —→ B
Intermediate

A → C ———— B
Transitional

distinguish conceptually between intermediate forms and transitional forms. An intermediate form is precisely that – a form which could, on the criteria of some given scheme of classification, be placed 'between' two entries A and B of that classification, without any necessary implication of whether it had descended from A and was an ancestor of B. An intermediate form would only be transitional if it could be *shown* to have descended from A and was an ancestor of B. To establish those relationships, of course, some mechanism would have to be exhibited that was demonstrably adequate for the task.

Now it is frequently argued in the literature that the fossil record is liable to be incomplete, in particular because soft body parts do not easily fossilize for obvious reasons. However, palaeontologists are very well aware of this and yet think nevertheless that the incompleteness of the fossil record cannot be the whole story. James Valentine, in a major study *On the Origin of Phyla*, writes: 'Many of the branches [of the Tree of Life], large as well as small, are cryptogenic (cannot be traced into ancestors). Some of these gaps are surely caused by the incompleteness of the fossil record, but that cannot be the sole reason for the cryptogenic nature of some families, many invertebrate orders, all invertebrate classes, and all metazoan phyla.'[36]

It should also be pointed out in this connection that, although soft body parts are rarely preserved, there are some spectacular recent finds of preserved sponge embryos in the Precambrian near Chengjiang in China. Their existence, according to marine palaeobiologist Paul Chien and his colleagues, creates a real problem: If the Precambrian strata are capable of preserving soft-bodied embryos of organisms why do they not also contain the precursors to the Cambrian animals? Does not the preservation of soft embryos make more likely the preservation of the fully mature animal?[37] However, palaeontologist Günther Bechly has shown in his recent detailed analysis (2020) that the case for Precambrian sponges is 'embarrassingly bad'. His conclusion runs: 'We can safely conclude that, contrary to common misconception, there exists zero compelling evidence for the existence of any genuine Precambrian fossil sponges. Unambiguous sponges only appear in the Cambrian explosion together with the other animal phyla.'[38]

Of course, interpretation of the fossil record may well be complicated by genetic considerations. Intensive studies are being made of the connection between genes and morphology, particularly the Hox genes,

Universal Common Descent (UCD)

and there are suggestions by Simon Conway Morris, for example, that once animals that have a sufficiently high degree of complexity are in existence, then relatively small genetic changes may trigger fairly large morphological changes. But he advises caution even here: 'While few doubt that the development of form is underwritten by the genes, at the moment we have almost no idea how form actually emerges from the genetic code.'[39] We shall learn more about this in Chapter 19.

What, then, shall we make of the fossil record? Surely the fact that such leading thinkers as those we have cited are publicly expressing concerns about foundational aspects of the theory, in particular about the extrapolation from the present to the past, would indicate, at the very least, that the fossils do not offer the strength of support to the neo-Darwinian theory at the macro level that is often claimed.

Genetic relatedness and universal common descent UCD

As evidence for the modern synthesis, universal common descent (UCD) is one of the most frequently cited. UCD is the theory that all living things have descended from a common ancestor. Sophisticated computational methods for comparing the structure of the DNA sequences in a collection of organisms have shown remarkable correspondences between genomes, with long stretches of DNA in different organisms being nearly identical.

It is argued that this work, which is independent of palaeontology or comparative anatomy, establishes the genetic relatedness of all living things, and enables us to place them on a common ancestral tree. This stunning triumph of molecular biology, it is claimed, forms the most overwhelming evidence for the truth of the neo-Darwinian synthesis. And, indeed, once again, when one sees it laid out, it is 'terribly, terribly tempting to believe it is true.'

However, in light of foregoing arguments, we may need to apply caution. Firstly, it is one thing to say that there is genetic relatedness; it is entirely another to claim that mutation and natural selection are the *only* cause of that relatedness – a claim that, as we have seen, has not delivered. And if no mechanism is offered the theory remains a 'relatedness of the gaps'. However, we shall see in Chapter 19 that research in systems biology has shown that that there might be completely different, non-Darwinian mechanisms that could extend the range of genetic relatedness.

It is important also to say that UCD does not affect the overall design arguments either way. Biochemist Michael Behe, who is a prominent promoter of ID, accepts UCD but is convinced that it is the genetics itself that evidences design.

On relatedness in the abstract, zoologist Mark Ridley makes an important observation that is familiar to mathematicians: 'The simple fact that species can be classified hierarchically into genera, families, and so on, is not an argument for evolution. It is possible to classify any set of objects into a hierarchy, whether their variation is evolutionary or not.'[40] Cars, for instance, can be arranged in a hierarchy. But all cars have similar parts because those parts are essential for their operation, and because they are constructed according to a common design, not because the cars have 'descended' from each other.

From this perspective, similarities in the DNA sequences could therefore logically equally well be read as evidence of common design. Indeed, from a philosophical perspective, the common ancestry might have been designed, so that the concepts are not mutually exclusive. For instance, former Human Genome Project Director, Francis Collins, suggests that, although from our perspective 'Evolution could appear to be driven by chance, from God's perspective the outcome would be entirely specified.'[41] Collins' remark here raises the important question of what exactly we mean by 'appear to be driven by chance' or 'random'. Philosopher of biology Elliott Sober, interestingly, takes this to mean that: 'There is no *physical mechanism* (either inside organisms or outside of them) that detects which mutations would be beneficial and causes those mutations to occur.'[42] This definition of randomness would appear to leave open guidance by a *mind* external to the system.

A simple thought experiment might throw some light on the situation here. Imagine a molecular biologist, based on some remote planet in five million years' time, analysing the structure of the DNA of various kinds of wheat from the early twenty-first century that archaeologists found embedded in a small fragment of rock drifting in space.

Let us suppose too that she does not know that this is a piece of the planet known as Earth after it was destroyed by collision with a comet a million years earlier. Her molecular analysis shows that the different species appear to be related in that their DNA is very similar – indeed identical for long stretches – so she puts the differences down to natural selection and random mutation although the differences do not seem yet to fit completely into any explanatory pattern hitherto understood.

A short time later, space archaeologists find a bit of text on the rock in space and they eventually manage to interpret its (to them) extremely primitive language that says, 'Professor Smith genetically altered the structure of wheat in order to increase the yield.' They bring this scrap of decoded text to the molecular biologist: 'This seems to suggest that one of your two wheat samples was not produced by an unguided natural process but involved non-random mutations, that is, it was deliberately designed.'

'Nonsense,' she says. 'This is a myth from some previously unknown primitive civilization. Look at the primitive character of its language compared with our science. That isn't real science. In any case, my research is following a very promising line and I think we shall soon be able to see that chance and necessity can readily account for what we observe. I am not prepared to believe in a "Professor Smith of the gaps" that would bring science to an end.' Yet we who live in the twenty-first century know that such a 'Smith' actually exists. Human intelligence has produced genetically modified crops. Furthermore, acknowledging that such a Smith existed, far from being a science-stopper, could open up new avenues of research into ancient civilizations.

The interest of this thought experiment lies in the fact that, even in the case where it would probably be argued that only chance and necessity are involved in producing the second strain of wheat, the fact is that intelligence was involved. That is, we cannot even rule out the involvement of external intelligence at that level. The question then arises whether, in suggesting that genetic relatedness involves input of information by an external mind, we are risking a God-of-the-gaps scenario? From the scientific point of view, the answer is no, if such an informational input is what the evidence demands.

Of course, in order to rule the involvement of supernatural intelligence in, we should rightly demand more evidence – of the kind associated with the edge of evolution and, most importantly, with the origin of life itself, as we shall see in the next chapter.

Certainly similarities, both genetic and morphological, are to be expected whatever hypothesis one adopts – whether design or common descent or a combination of both. Stephen Meyer argues that the hypothesis of common ancestry is methodologically equivalent to that of common design in the sense that any accusations of being scientific or unscientific which can be made against one, can be made equally against the other. For instance, postulating an unobserved Designer is no more unscientific than

"Evolution of the gaps"

postulating unobserved macroevolutionary steps.[43] It is surely very evident that 'evolution of the gaps' may be as widespread as 'god of the gaps'.

16

Natural Selection – Not Creative! Weeding out process

Natural selection plays a central role in the modern synthesis and in this chapter we think about exactly what it means. Colin Patterson FRS says that: 'The term natural selection is used to describe the way in which the strain in a population that produces the weaker progeny eventually gets weeded out, leaving the stronger to thrive.' Some think it is a tautology. Others capitalize it and regard it as a creative natural process.

We next consider a thought experiment that occurred to me as a mathematician to see what would happen in the limiting case where there was enough food to do away with the need for a struggle for survival. I then found that my thought experiment had been anticipated not only in correspondence between Darwin and Hooker but in a lecture given by Karl Popper at the Royal Society in London in 1986. Questions about the power of natural selection began to come thick and fast.

It is now time to examine more closely one of the central concepts that has dominated evolutionary theory for a long time: natural selection. What exactly is meant by it? It has been repeatedly pointed out that, at the level discussed in Wilson's definition, natural selection itself is essentially a self-evident phenomenon. Colin Patterson FRS, in his standard text on evolution, presents it in the form of the following deductive argument:

- all organisms must reproduce
- all organisms exhibit hereditary variations
- hereditary variations differ in their effect on reproduction
- therefore, variations with favourable effects on reproduction will succeed, those with unfavourable effects will fail, and organisms will change.[2]

As mentioned above, Patterson's definition of natural selection is as follows: '[it] is used to describe the way in which the strain in a population that produces the weaker progeny eventually gets weeded out, leaving the stronger to thrive.' He argues that, formulated this way, natural selection is, strictly speaking, not a scientific theory, but a truism. That is, if we grant the first three points above, then the fourth follows as a matter of logic. This argument is similar to that advanced by Darwin himself in the last chapter of *The Origin of Species*. Patterson observes that 'this shows that natural selection must occur but it does not say that natural selection is the only cause of evolution,[3] and when natural selection is generalized to be the explanation of all evolutionary change or of every feature of every organism, it becomes so all-embracing that it is in much the same class as Freudian psychology and astrology.'[4]

He seems to be suggesting here that natural selection fails to satisfy Popper's criterion of falsifiability, just as the Freudian statement that adult behaviour is due to trauma in childhood is not falsifiable.[5] Patterson is warning us of the danger of simply slapping the label 'natural selection' in this generalized sense on some process, and thinking that we have thereby explained that process.

Patterson's description highlights something very easily overlooked – the fact that natural selection is not creative. As he says, it is a 'weeding out process' that leaves the stronger progeny. The stronger progeny must be already there: it is not produced by natural selection. Indeed the very word 'selection' ought to alert our attention to this: selection is made from already existing entities. This is an exceedingly important point because the words 'natural selection' are often used as if they were describing a creative process. This is often indicated by capitalizing their initial letters and speaking of 'Natural Selection'.

This can mislead and research has shown that Patterson was right to be very sceptical about natural selection qualifying as the explanation of all evolutionary change – because it isn't. That there is much more to biological change we learn from the following important statement made in 2003 by Gerd Müller, Head of the Department of Theoretical Biology in the Centre for Organismal Systems Biology at the University of Vienna, an expert on EvoDevo, an increasingly influential theory integrating evolutionary theory and developmental biology that aims to fill some of the gaps in standard neo-Darwinism, a matter that we shall explore in much more detail in Chapter 19.

Speaking of various biological systems, Müller says that:

> Only a few of the processes listed above are addressed
> by the canonical neo-Darwinian theory.... Although, at
> the phenotypic level, it deals with the modification of
> existing parts, the theory is intended to explain neither
> the origin of parts, nor morphological organization, nor
> innovation. In the neo-Darwinian world the motive
> factor of morphological change is natural selection,
> which can account for the modification and loss of parts.
> But selection has *no innovative capacity*: it eliminates
> or maintains what exists. The generative and ordering
> aspects of morphological evolution are thus absent from
> evolutionary theory.[6]

Müller thus confirms what is fairly clear from the definition: natural
selection, by its very nature, does not create novelty. This contradicts
Richard Dawkins' original assertion cited earlier that natural selection
accounts for the form and existence of all living things. Such polar
opposition of views between scientists on the central thesis of the modern
neo-Darwinian synthesis raises serious questions as to the adequacy of its
scientific basis and whether it can carry the weight of explanation that is
put on it.

Now it could just be that Dawkins is using loose language here. Maybe
he thinks of the term 'natural selection' as a shorthand way of describing the
neo-Darwinian synthesis: that the hereditable variations on which natural
selection acts are random mutations in the genetic material of organisms.
However, Dawkins and others stress that natural selection is not a purely
random process, though mutation is. Dawkins is sufficiently impressed
by calculations of mathematical probabilities to reject any notion that,
say, the human eye evolved by pure chance in the time available. In his
inimitable way he writes: 'It is grindingly, creakingly, crashingly obvious
that, if Darwinism were really a theory of chance, it couldn't work. You
don't need to be a mathematician or a physicist to calculate that an eye or
a haemoglobin molecule would take from here to infinity to self-assemble
by sheer higgledy-piggledy luck.'[7]

What then is the answer? That natural selection is a law-like process
that sifts the random mutations so that evolution is a combination of

necessity and chance. Natural selection, we are told, will find a faster pathway through the space of possibilities. The idea here is, therefore, that the law-like process of natural selection increases the probabilities to acceptable levels over geological time.

Putting it simply, the essence of the argument is this. Natural selection 'favours' the strong progeny over the weak in a situation where resources are limited. It helps preserve any beneficial mutation that gives an organism a 'selective advantage'. Organisms with that mutation survive and others do not. But what do we mean by 'favours' and 'helps'? It sounds as if we are speaking of a conscious entity. It would be more accurate to say that strong progeny are more likely to survive than weak in a situation with limited resources. There is no conscious entity doing the selecting. For the same reason natural selection does not cause the mutation. It does not cause anything. The mutation occurs by chance. I must add that as a mathematician I am not alone in being unable to imagine any selective advantage for survival conveyed by a mutation that favoured abstract thought of any kind – in mathematics, art, music, etc.

Denis Alexander, former Director of the Molecular Immunology Programme and the Laboratory of Lymphocyte Signalling and Development at the Babraham Institute, Cambridge, provides a more useful definition of natural selection that he obtained by modifying one given by Francisco Ayala, a Spanish-American evolutionary biologist and philosopher. Alexander writes: 'Natural selection is the differential reproduction of alternative genetic variations, determined by the fact that some variations are beneficial because they increase the probability that the organisms having them will live longer or be more fertile than organisms having alternative variations. Over the generations beneficial variations will be preserved and multiplied; injurious or less beneficial variations will be eliminated.'[8]

The late William Provine was a distinguished philosopher and historian of biology at Cornell University. Although a convinced atheist, he was prepared to engage in very open and respectful discussion with those scientists in the ID community and elsewhere who were raising questions about Darwinism. In an afterword to the re-publication of his book in 2001 *On the Origin of Theoretical Population Genetics* he commented on the way his understanding of evolution had changed over his lifetime. However, as you read it please do not imagine that Provine ceased to believe in evolution. He did not. But he became much more nuanced in his approach and very honest about the deficiencies as he saw them, in particular, in connection with natural selection.

He says that in the period from 1959 to 1970, he, along with everyone else, thought that natural selection was the primary mechanism at every level in the evolutionary process. However, his views changed. In 2001 he wrote:

> This simple statement raises two major problems for me now. As John Endler has argued eloquently in *Natural Selection in the Wild* (1986),[9] natural selection is not a mechanism. Natural selection does not act on anything, nor does it select (for or against), force, maximize, create, modify, shape, operate, drive, favor, maintain, push, or adjust. Natural selection does nothing. Natural selection as a natural force belongs in the insubstantial category already populated by the Becker/Stahl phlogiston (Endler, 1986) or Newton's 'ether.'[10]

What then is natural selection? Provine now outlines a much more nuanced and helpful view:

> Natural selection is the necessary outcome of discernible and often quantifiable causes. Some of these causes produce heritable differences between individuals of most populations, and between populations. The possible production of offspring is immense in any species and a 'struggle for existence' occurs... resulting in organisms adapted to their environments, as long as the environments don't change too rapidly. Otherwise the same basic set of causes results in extinction of the population. Understanding natural selection as the result of specific causes requires the researcher to understand ecological settings, life histories, and development in relations to differential leaving of offspring.[11]

His point here is that it is erroneous to suggest that natural selection is a cause, since, without further elaboration, it remains an unsubstantial concept. In forthright and honest language Provine continues: 'Having natural selection select is nifty because it excuses the necessity of talking about the actual causation of natural selection. Such talk was excusable for Charles Darwin, but inexcusable for evolutionists now. Creationists have discovered our empty "natural selection" language, and the "actions" of natural selection make huge, vulnerable targets."[12]

One of the variable parameters in the natural selection context is the amount of food available. It occurred to me as a mathematician that it would be interesting to see what happens if this parameter is allowed to increase. I invite you to consider the following thought experiment.

Imagine a situation in which resources increase so that, in the limiting case, there is food for all – the strong and the weak. As resources increased, there would be less and less 'struggle for survival', until there was none, since most progeny would survive in any case. What would neo-Darwinists say to this? Would they now argue that evolution would now be less and less likely? For, in this situation, it would seem that chance would have to do all the work, whereas I understood that the neo-Darwinists had ruled that possibility out of court.

When this thought experiment occurred to me, I felt sure that it must have occurred to someone earlier. Indeed it had. In 1966, R. E. D. Clark had drawn attention to a letter that the eminent botanist Joseph Hooker wrote to Darwin in 1862. His letter apparently disturbed Darwin by saying that natural selection was not a creative process.[13] Clark had to reconstruct Hooker's argument from Darwin's reply because he thought Hooker's original letter had been lost. However, it had not been lost. Hooker's letter said:

> You must remember that it is neither crossing nor natural selection that has *made* so many divergent human individuals, but simply *Variation* [Hooker's emphasis]. Natural selection, no doubt has hastened the process, intensified it (so to speak), has regulated the lines, places etc., etc., etc., in which, and to which, the races have run and led, and the number of each and so forth; but, given a pair of individuals with power to propagate, and [an] infinite [time] span to procreate in, so that not one be lost, or that, in short, Natural Selection is not called upon to play a part *at all*, and I *maintain that after n generations you will have extreme individuals as totally unlike one another as if Natural Selection had extinguished half.*

If once you hold that natural selection can make a difference, i.e. create a character, your whole doctrine tumbles to the ground. Natural Selection is as powerless as physical causes to make a variation; the law that 'like shall *not* produce like' is at the bottom of [it] all, and is as inscrutable as life itself. This it is that Lyell and I feel you have failed to convey with force enough to us and the public: and this is the bottom of half the infidelity of the scientific world to your doctrine. You have not, as you ought, begun by attacking old false doctrines, that '*like does produce like*'. The first chapter of your book should have been devoted to this and nothing else. But there is some truth I now see in the objection to you, that you make natural selection the *Deus ex machina* for you do somehow seem to do it by neglecting to dwell on the *facts* of infinite incessant variation. Your eight children are really all *totally* unlike one another: they agree *exactly in no one property*. How is this? You answer that they display the inherited differences of different progenitors – well – but go back, and back and back in time and you are driven at last to your original pair for origin of differences, and logically you must grant, that the differences between the original [MALE] & [FEMALE] of your species were equal to the sum of the extreme differences between the most dissimilar existing individuals of your species, or that the latter varied from some inherent law that had them. Now am not I a cool fish to lecture you so glibly?[14]

Go back to origin al (handwritten margin note)

It is interesting to note the force with which Hooker writes in ascribing 'half the infidelity of the scientific world' against Darwin to his failure to deal with this argument. Darwin's reaction came in a letter (after 26 November but actually dated 20 November 1862).

But the part of your letter which fairly pitched me head over heels with astonishment; is that where you state that every single difference which we see might have occurred without any selection. I do and have always fully agreed; but you have got right round the subject and viewed it from an entirely opposite and new side, and when you took me there, I was astounded... When I say I agree, I must make proviso, that under your view, as now, each form long remains adapted to certain fixed conditions and that the conditions of life are in [the] long run changeable; and second, which is more important that each individual form is a self-fertilizing hermaphrodite, so that each hairbreadth variation is not lost by inter-crossing.

Your manner of putting [the] case would be even more striking than it is, if the mind could grapple with such numbers – it is grappling with eternity – think of each of a thousand seeds bringing forth its plant, and then each a thousand. A globe stretching to furthest fixed star would very soon be covered. I cannot even grapple with the idea even with races of dogs, cattle, pigeons or fowls; and here all must admit and see the accurate strictness of your illustration. Such men, as you and Lyell thinking that I make too much of a Deus of natural selection is conclusive against me. Yet I hardly know how I could have put in, in all parts of my Book, stronger sentences. The title, as you once pointed out, might have been better. No one ever objects to agriculturalists using the strongest language about their selection; yet every breeder knows that he does not produce the modification which he selects. My enormous difficulty for years was to understand adaptation, and this made me, I cannot but think rightly, insist so much on natural selection. God forgive me for writing at such length; but you cannot tell how much your letter has interested me, and how important it is for me with my present Book in hand to try and get clear ideas.[15]

Hooker's argument is important because it questions attempts to render probabilities of macroevolution acceptable within the time-constraints supplied by contemporary cosmology.

It is also of historical interest to see that Alfred Russell Wallace, the co-discoverer of evolution with Charles Darwin, thought that there were limits to what natural selection could achieve. Here is a fascinating passage in the final chapter of the collection *Contributions to the Theory of Natural Selection*, published in 1870:

> It will, therefore, probably excite some surprise among my readers, to find that I do not consider that all nature can be explained on the principles of which I am so ardent an advocate; and that I am now myself going to state objections, and to place limits, to the power of natural selection.' I believe, however, that there are such limits; and that just as surely as we can trace the action of natural laws in the development of organic forms, and can clearly conceive that fuller knowledge would enable us to follow step by step the whole process of that development, so surely can we trace the action of some unknown higher law, beyond and independent of all those laws of which we have any knowledge. We can trace this action more or less distinctly in many phenomena, the two most important of which are the origin of sensation or consciousness, and the development of man from the lower animals.[16]

What is of considerable interest for us in what follows is the way in which he proposes to establish the existence of this 'unknown higher law'. He writes:

> I would further remark that this enquiry is as thoroughly scientific and legitimate as that into the origin of species itself. It is an attempt to solve the inverse problem, to deduce the existence of a new power of a definite character, in order to account for facts which according to the theory of natural selection ought not to happen. Such problems are well known to science, and the search after their solution has often led to the most brilliant results. In the case of man, there are facts of the nature above alluded to, and in calling attention to them, and in inferring a cause for them, I believe that I am as strictly within the bounds of scientific investigation as I have been in any other portion of my work.[17]

One wonders what Wallace would have made of our thinking in this book.

The thought experiment mentioned above also occurred to the great philosopher of science, Karl Popper, and he gave the first Medawar Lecture about it at the Royal Society in 1986 under the title 'A New Interpretation of Darwinism'. In it he invented an imaginary world in which there was no competition for survival – long before the same idea occurred to me.

Denis Noble's account of the lecture mentions that it was attended by Nobel laureates Medawar and Perutz who must have been shocked that Popper rejected the modern synthesis by proposing that random DNA mutations were not the driver of creative evolutionary processes but that the organisms themselves were. He deduced from this that neo-Darwinism was not so much wrong as incomplete and that the central dogma which holds that the genome is responsible for all inherited characteristics in an organism is weakened by the discovery of reverse transcription. Inevitably this altered the neo-Darwinian concept of the genome as read-only to read-write and thus undermined the theory itself. Noble continued to say of Popper that:

> He was therefore deeply suspicious of sophisticated manoeuvrings and redefinitions to protect the dogma from falsification. In his 'conjectures and refutations' view of science it is better to acknowledge when a strong version of a theory has been refuted. The strong Neo-Darwinist interpretation of the Central Dogma was refuted. But he went further than this. He saw that reverse transcription could be one of the routes through which Lamarckian processes and wholesale reorganisation of genomes could occur. Again, the philosopher in him wanted to see this recognised, not hidden behind a web of clever re-interpretations.[18]

Noble's work has shown that this lecture was remarkably prescient – see Chapter 19.

There are, however, more difficulties lying in the path of deductions invoking the law-likeness of natural selection that are independent of Hooker's argument. In Chapter 18 we shall investigate, from a mathematical perspective, some of the scenarios developed by Dawkins and others to simulate the way in which they think that such law-likeness might be realized, and we find them wanting for very different reasons. Of course, Hooker's argument does not affect the sort of (microevolutionary) variations that Darwin observed.

Thus the next question one might reasonably ask is whether research has shown any evidence of a limit to what microevolution can achieve. Could it be that other cracks are appearing in the neo-Darwinian edifice?

How did life come to exist in the (1ˢᵗ place?)

17

The Edge of Evolution

In this chapter we explore the idea of whether there are determinable limits to the reach of mutation and natural selection.

Although, as we mentioned earlier, some biologists resist differentiating between microevolution and macroevolution, the terms are often used to distinguish, roughly speaking, between evolution below species level and evolution at or beyond species level, there being debate on just where the line should be drawn.[1] Resistance to this distinction often comes from those 'gradualists' like Richard Dawkins who conceive the evolutionary process as one seamless whole in the sense that macroevolution is simply what results from microevolutionary processes gradually operating over long periods of time.

Gradualism begs the key question as to whether evolution really is one seamless whole or not; whether, for example, the selection 'mechanisms' which can, say, reasonably account for variations in finch beak lengths, or the development of antibiotic resistance in bacteria, can also answer the much bigger question as to how finches and bacteria came to exist in the first place. In other words, the key question is this: Is there an 'edge' to the evolutionary capacity of the modern synthesis?

A. P. Hendry of the Quebec Centre for Biodiversity and M. T. Kinnison, Professor of Evolutionary Applications at the University of Maine, put it as follows:

> Evolution is often considered in two categories: microevolution and macroevolution. The former obviously implies a small amount of change and the latter a large amount. The difficulty comes in deciding where the boundary... should fall, whether or not they represent the same processes (acting over different timescales), and

The arrival of the fittest?

Basic Type = Kind

whether or not the dichotomy is even useful or valid... Are macroevolutionary events (large morphological changes or speciation) simply the cumulative outcome of microevolutionary mechanisms (micromutation, selection, gene flow, genetic drift) or does macroevolution require some qualitatively different mechanism? The history of this debate is long, convoluted and sometimes acrimonious.[2]

One problem here is that extrapolating from the observed to the unobserved is fraught with danger. S. F. Gibbert, J .M. Opitz, and R. A. Raff maintain that: 'Microevolution looks at adaptations that concern only the survival of the fittest, not the arrival of the fittest. As Goodwin (1995) points out: 'the origin of species – Darwin's problem – remains unsolved',[3] thus echoing the verdict of geneticist Richard Goldschmidt: 'the facts of microevolution do not suffice for an understanding of macroevolution'.[4] Convinced Darwinists John Maynard Smith and E. Szathmary took a similar line: 'There is no theoretical reason that would permit us to expect that evolutionary lines would increase in complexity with time; there is also no empirical evidence that this happens.'[5]

Siegfried Scherer, Professor of Microbiology at the Technical University in Munich, put forward the thesis that all living things can be classified in certain basic types – a classification slightly broader than that of species. A 'basic type' is defined to be a collection of living things connected either directly or indirectly through hybridization, without regard for whether the hybrids are sterile or not.[6] This definition incorporates both genetic and morphological concepts of species, and, according to Scherer, research so far indicates that: 'in the whole experimentally accessible domain of microevolution (including research in artificial breeding and in species formation), all variations have certainly remained within the confines of basic types.'[7]

Such comments lend weight to the view of biologist and philosopher Paul Erbrich: 'The mutation-selection mechanism is an optimization mechanism.'[8] That is, it enables an already existing living system to adapt selectively to changing environmental conditions much in the same way as genetic algorithms facilitate optimization in engineering. It does not, however, create anything radically new.

James Shapiro, an expert in bacterial genetics at the Department of Biochemistry and Molecular Biology in the University of Chicago, in his ground-breaking book *Evolution: A View from the 21st Century* says

[handwritten annotation at top: gradual accumulation of numerous successive slight modifications. A limited explanation at best.]

that the evidence of DNA leads him to reject the deeply ingrained notion that evolution occurs through the "gradual accumulation of numerous successive slight modifications" – to use Darwin's phrase.[9] Shapiro is an evolutionary biologist who rejects both the gradualist thesis and ID. We shall say more about his work in Chapter 19.

The late Eric Davidson, who was a leading Caltech developmental biologist held that

> Neo-Darwinism erroneously assumes that change in protein coding sequence is the basic cause of change in developmental program; and it *erroneously assumes that evolutionary change in body plan morphology occurs by a continuous process* [my italics]. All of these assumptions are basically counterfactual. This cannot be surprising, since the neo-Darwinian synthesis from which these ideas stem was a pre-molecular biology concoction focused on population genetics and adaptation natural history, neither of which have any direct mechanistic import for the genomic regulatory systems that drive embryonic development of the body plan.[10]

The evidence is rapidly mounting that the modern synthesis simply will not bear the weight that is put upon it, and, in light of what Shapiro, Davidson, and others say, we might well ask why it is that so many people still cling to the neo-Darwinian gradualist thesis. And, if top biologists are questioning that thesis in the name of science, surely it is not surprising that people like me who read their books also question it. Do I hear Kant whispering: '*Sapere Aude!*' (Dare to know!)?

A well-known French biologist once said to me: 'Darwinism – Non, Evolution – Oui!' Another French biologist whose research convinced him long ago that there was a limit to what mutation and natural selection could do and so led him to reject neo-Darwinism was Pierre Grassé of the Sorbonne in Paris, who was President of the Académie Française and editor of the definitive 28-volume work *Traité de Zoologie*. The great geneticist Theodosius Dobzhansky held Grassé in high esteem: 'Now one can disagree with Grassé, but not ignore him... his knowledge of the living world is encyclopaedic.'[11] He described Grassé's book, *L'évolution du vivant*,[12] as 'a frontal attack on all kinds of Darwinism. Its purpose is "to destroy the

The myth of evolution has deceived millions

myth of evolution, as a simple, understood and explained phenomenon", and to show that evolution is a mystery about which little is, and perhaps can be, known."[13]

In his book Grassé observed that fruit flies remain fruit flies in spite of the thousands of generations that have been bred and all the mutations that have been induced in them. In fact, the capacity for variation in the gene pool seems to run out quite early on in the process, a phenomenon called genetic homeostasis.

There appears to be a barrier beyond which selective breeding will not pass because of the onset of sterility or exhaustion of genetic variability. If there are limits even to the amount of variation the most skilled breeders can achieve, the clear implication is that natural selection is likely to achieve very much less. It is not surprising that he argued that microevolution could not bear the weight that is often put upon it.

We shall see in Chapter 18 that Sir Fred Hoyle has come to the same conclusion on the basis of mathematical calculation.

missing one part renders it inoperable   *acid-driven motor that powers the bacterial flagellum*

Irreducible complexity

The Challenge   *Key*

In his day, however, Charles Darwin regarded gradualism as the very essence of evolution. He presented a challenge to opponents of his theory of evolution when he wrote: 'If it could be demonstrated that any complex organ existed which could not possibly have been formed by numerous, successive, slight modifications, my theory would absolutely break down.'[14] The point is repeated by Richard Dawkins in *The Blind Watchmaker*,[15] who says that if such an organism is found he will 'cease to believe in Darwinism'.[16]

Such a complex organ, if it existed, is called irreducibly complex. Biochemist Michael Behe of Lehigh University, has taken up Darwin's challenge in his book *Darwin's Black Box*,[17] which has generated a great deal of discussion. His main candidate for an irreducibly complex biological entity is the tiny acid-driven motor, discovered in 1973, that powers the bacterial flagellum that we described in Chapter 8. We recall that its motor is amazingly complex, consisting of around forty protein parts including a rotor, a stator, bushings, and a drive-shaft. Behe argues that the absence of any one of these protein parts would result in complete loss of motor function. He provides a simple illustration of this concept: the humble mousetrap. All of its five or six components must be present for it to

Mousetrap

Missing a part — non-functional

How did complex structures come to be?

function. He points out that this illustrates the fact: 'that no irreducibly complex system can be produced directly (that is, by continuously improving the initial function, which continues to work by the same mechanism) by slight, successive modifications of a precursor system, because any precursor to an irreducibly complex system that is missing a part, is by definition non-functional'.[18] Behe then takes up Darwin's challenge by arguing that the flagellum is only one among many irreducibly complex molecular machines.

It is clear from the definition that establishing that any particular system is irreducibly complex involves proving a negative; this, as is well known, is notoriously difficult. Not surprisingly, therefore, Behe, who, incidentally, appears to have no quarrel with the Darwinian idea of descent with modification, has provoked a storm of controversy[19] with his claim:

> Molecular evolution is not based on scientific authority. There is no publication in the scientific literature – in prestigious journals, specialty journals, or books – that describes how molecular evolution of any real, complex, biochemical system either did occur, or even might have occurred. There are assertions that such evolution occurred, but absolutely none is supported by pertinent experiments or calculations... despite comparing sequences and mathematical modelling, molecular evolution has never addressed the question of how complex structures came to be. In effect, the theory of Darwinian molecular evolution has not published, and so it should perish.[20]

James Shapiro, cited earlier, also says that there are no detailed Darwinian accounts for the evolution of any fundamental biochemical or cellular system; only a variety of wishful speculations.[21] Even the highly critical review of Behe by Cavalier-Smith concedes Behe's point that no detailed biochemical models exist.[22]

Stephen Jay Gould, who had no known sympathy with Behe's argument either, nonetheless recognized the importance of the concept of irreducible complexity:

Restricts research to unintelligent causes!

The design was planned by intelligence!

Classical science, with its preferences for reduction to a few
controlling factors of causality, was triumphantly successful
for relatively simple systems like planetary motion and the
periodic table of the elements. But irreducibly complex
systems – that is, most of the interesting phenomena of
biology, human society and history – cannot be so explained.
We need new philosophies and models, and these must
come from a union of the humanities and the sciences as
traditionally defined.[23]

It is interesting here that Gould speaks of new philosophies and not simply
of new scientific methods, a point that is also of interest to Behe for whom
the inadequacy of the neo-Darwinian synthesis consists in the fact that it
cannot *even in principle* explain the origin of irreducible complexity.

I.D.

He argues that the existence of irreducible complexity at the
molecular machine level points unmistakably to intelligent design:

To a person who does not feel obliged to restrict his search
to unintelligent causes, the straightforward conclusion is
that many biochemical systems were designed. *They were
designed not by the laws of nature, not by chance and necessity;
rather, they were planned.* The designer knew what the
systems would look like when they were completed, then
took steps to bring the systems about. Life on earth at its
most fundamental level, in its most critical components, is
the product of intelligent activity.[24]

In addition Behe emphasizes that his conclusions are inferred naturally
from the data, and not from sacred books or sectarian beliefs. They require
no new principles of logic or science, but flow from the evidence provided
by biochemistry combined with a consideration of the way in which we
normally make design inferences.

In a further book, *The Edge of Evolution*,[25] Behe backs up his argument
on the basis research on E. coli bacteria in which no real innovative
changes were observed through 25,000 generations.[26] Behe points out that
now more than 30,000 generations of E. coli have been studied, equivalent
to about a million human years, and the net result is that evolution has
produced is, in his words:

Devolution:

Mostly devolution. Although some marginal details of some systems have changed during that thirty thousand generations, the bacterium has repeatedly thrown away chunks of its genetic patrimony, including the ability to make some of the building blocks of RNA. Apparently throwing away sophisticated but costly molecular machinery saves the bacterium energy. Nothing of remotely similar elegance has been built. The lesson of E. coli is that it's easier for evolution to break things than to make things.[27]

Key

More recent work of Richard E. Lenski et. al. extends these results to show that E. coli is still E. coli after 60,000 generations of breeding in the laboratory.[28]

This is part of the evidence that Behe adduces to argue that there is an 'edge' to (neo-Darwinian) evolution, that is, there are limits to what natural selection and mutation can do. He argues that scientists are in a much better position to ascertain those limits since the genetic basis of mutation is understood. He applies that knowledge to a particular case that has been the object of intense study – the study of malaria.

Behe points out that hundreds of different mutations conferring some resistance to malaria have occurred in the human genome and spread through our population by natural selection. These mutations, he says, have been rightly hailed as some of the best examples of Darwinian evolution but the evidence also shows that there are fundamental limits on the efficacy of random mutation. These studies have yielded unexpected results:

> 1) Darwinian processes are incoherent and highly constrained. 2) The battle of predator and prey (or parasite and host), which has often been portrayed... as a productive arms-race cycle of improvements... is in fact a destructive cycle ... 3) Like a... drunk who falls after a step or two, when more than a single tiny step is needed for an evolutionary improvement, blind random mutation is very unlikely to find it. And 4) extrapolating from the data on an enormous number of malaria parasites allows us to... estimate the limits of Darwinian evolution... .[29]

By means of a mutation involving the shift of two amino acids, malaria has developed resistance to the drug chloroquine. The odds against this happening are about one in one hundred billion, billion (1 in 10^{20}); yet it did happen, because there is a vast number of parasitic cells in an infected person's body (about a trillion) and about a billion infected people in the world each year. Behe calls mutation clusters of this degree of complexity CCC-clusters (chloroquine-complexity clusters). He calculates that we would have to wait a hundred million times ten million years, which is many hundreds of thousands of times the age of the universe, before such a mutation occurred in the very much smaller population of human beings.

He deduces that one would not expect a double CCC (that is a mutation cluster twice as complex as a CCC) to show up as the result of a Darwinian process at any stage in the history of life on earth. 'So if we do find features of life that would have required a double CCC or more, then we can infer that they likely did not arise as a result of a Darwinian process.' He then argues in detail that 'life is bursting with such features',[30] giving as just one of his impressive examples the elegant control systems, or genetic regulatory networks, which are involved in the construction of animal bodies.[31]

He draws an interesting parallel between the presumption in nineteenth-century physics that light was carried by the ether, and the Darwinian presumption that random mutation and natural selection were responsible for building the cell. He points out that testing was a problem in both cases giving rise to wild speculation:

> Nevertheless, although we would certainly have wished otherwise, in just the past fifty years nature herself has ruthlessly conducted the biological equivalent of the Michelson-Morley[32] experiment. Call it the M-H (malaria-HIV) experiment. With a billion times the firepower of the puny labs that humans run, the M-H experiment has scoured the planet looking for the ability of random mutation and natural selection to build coherent biological machinery and has found absolutely nothing.'
> Why no trace of the fabled blind watchmaker? The simplest explanation is that, like the ether, the blind watchmaker does not exist.[33]

Many readers will be aware that the Behe is a prominent defender of ID and as such has come in for a lot of criticism, some of which seems to stem, not from serious investigation of his science, but from prejudice based on what often looks like wilful misunderstanding of the scientific issues that ID raises. Thomas Nagel makes a spirited, indeed, courageous, defence of Behe and his colleagues, who he regards as serious thinkers. Nagel writes:

> Even though writers like Michael Behe and Stephen Meyer are motivated at least in part by their religious beliefs, the empirical arguments they offer against the likelihood that the origin of life and its evolutionary history can be fully explained by physics and chemistry are of great interest in themselves... . They do not deserve the scorn with which they are commonly met. It is manifestly unfair.[34]

 Bias

I heartily agree, as someone who has faced similar scorn – witness, for instance, my debates with Richard Dawkins and Peter Atkins which are available on YouTube. I might just say, however, that Nagel also is being rather unfair to the ID proponents by saying they were motivated by their religious beliefs while omitting to say anything at this point about the obvious atheist motivation of many staunch defenders of Darwinism.

However, happily, Nagel does comment on this later: 'Nevertheless, I believe the defenders of intelligent design deserve our gratitude for challenging a scientific worldview that owes some of the passion displayed by its adherents precisely to the fact that it is thought to liberate us from religion.'[35] Precisely.

We should also note that, even from a theistic or ID standpoint, research investigating the reach of natural processes is in itself a highly worthwhile area and may even be more important in the future.

As I said, Behe's work is hard science. Another approach to studying natural phenomena is to use mathematical and computer simulation. We shall now investigate a well-known attempt to do this due to Richard Dawkins.

18

The Mathematics of Evolution

In this chapter we explore essentially the same question as in Chapter 17 but from a very different perspective. DNA plays an important role in the transmission of the information necessary to build organic material and, since it is digital information, it lends itself to mathematical investigation. Richard Dawkins claims that unguided natural processes can account for the origin of biological information – no external source of information is necessary. He tries to back up this claim by tackling the age-old question of whether a typing monkey could eventually produce meaningful literature. However, his putative solution ironically not only fails to establish his claim but becomes an argument for the very thing he holds in contempt – ID. We conclude the chapter by describing the work of Sir Fred Hoyle FRS on the mathematics of evolution – work that has not received the attention it deserves.

Richard Dawkins contends that unguided natural processes can account for the origin of biological information – no external source of information is necessary. In *The Blind Watchmaker* he uses an analogy whose roots lie in an argument alleged to have been used by T. H. Huxley in his famous debate with Wilberforce in Oxford in 1860. Huxley is said to have argued that apes typing randomly, and granted long life, unlimited supplies of paper, and endless energy, would eventually type out one of Shakespeare's poems or even a whole book, by chance.[1] Well, it is hardly likely that Huxley said such a thing for the simple reason that typewriters were not available on the market until 1874.[2] But no matter. It is a nice story and, within the limit now set for the age of the universe, let alone that set for the earth, it is easy to see that it is mathematical nonsense. The eminent mathematician Gian-Carlo Rota in a book on probability (unfinished at the time of his death) wrote: 'If the monkey could type one keystroke every nanosecond, the expected waiting time until the monkey types out *Hamlet* is so long that the estimated age of the universe is insignificant by comparison... this is not a practical method for writing plays.'

The calculations are not hard to do. For example, Russell Grigg, in his article, 'Could Monkeys Type the 23rd Psalm?',[3] calculates that if a monkey types one key at random per second, the average time to produce the word 'the' is 34.72 hours. To produce something as long as the 23rd Psalm (a short Hebrew poem made up of 603 letters, verse numbers, and spaces) would take on average around 10^{1017} years. The current estimate of the age of the universe lies somewhere between four and fifteen times 10^9 years. According to Dawkins' definition, this calculation certainly makes the 23rd Psalm a complex object: it possesses 'some quality, specifiable in advance, that is highly unlikely to have been acquired by random chance alone'.[4]

Calculations of this kind have long since persuaded most scientists – Dawkins included – that purely random processes cannot account for the origin of complex information-laden systems. He cites Isaac Asimov's estimate of the probability of randomly assembling a haemoglobin molecule from amino acids.[5] Such a molecule consists of four chains of amino acids twisted together. Each of the chains consists of 146 amino acids and there are 20 different kinds of amino acid found in living beings. The number of possible ways of arranging these 20 in a chain 146 links long is 20^{146}, which is about 10^{190}. (There are only about 10^{70} protons in the entire universe.)

Sir Fred Hoyle and astrophysicist Chandra Wickramasinghe agree.

> Troops of monkeys thundering away at random on typewriters could not produce the works of Shakespeare, for the... reason that the whole observable universe is not large enough to contain the necessary monkey hordes.... The same is true for living material. The likelihood of the spontaneous formation of life from inanimate matter is one to a number with 40,000 noughts after it.... It is big enough to bury Darwin and the whole theory of evolution. There was no primeval soup... and if the beginnings of life were not random, they must therefore have been the product of purposeful intelligence.[6]

Is Mount Improbable climbable?

All seem agreed, then, that the chance origin of the constituents of life seems to be dead in the primeval soup. So how can the origin of such complexity be explained? Dawkins attempts to solve the difficulty of the origin of systems whose highly specified complexity rules out a chance origin by 'breaking the improbability up into small manageable parts, smearing out the luck needed, going round the back of Mount Improbable and crawling up the gentle slopes, inch by million-year inch.'[7]

Let's try, then, to follow Dawkins up his mountain, and try to reduce the improbability of producing, say, a haemoglobin molecule (described above) by breaking the process up into small steps. Let us say 1,000 steps to the top of the mountain, and let us look at a very simplified situation where there are only two choices at every step. One leads to something viable, and the other does not, so that natural selection will eliminate it, and each step is independent. What is the probability of finding the right path up the mountain? 1 in 2^{1000}, that is about 1 in 10^{300}. But this is smaller than the probability of the random assembly of the haemoglobin molecule in the first place. Dawkins' mountain climb is improbable in more senses than one.

Nobel Prize-winning physicist, Brian Josephson of Cambridge, points out another hidden assumption in Dawkins' attempt to climb his mountain:

> In such books as *The Blind Watchmaker*, a crucial part of the argument concerns whether there exists a continuous path, leading from the origins of life to man, each step of which is both favoured by natural selection, and small enough to have happened by chance. It appears to be presented as a matter of logical necessity that such a path exists, but actually there is no such logical necessity; rather, commonly made assumptions in evolution require the existence of such a path.[8]

The only way out of the probabilistic impasse is to try to drastically increase the probabilities, and this is precisely what Dawkins attempts in *The Blind Watchmaker*. He claims that the origin of life was far from a purely chance process, although, according to him, it must have begun with something simple enough to have arisen by chance. But then, instead of having a purely one-step 'sieving' process, like that of jumbling together all the amino acid constituents of haemoglobin and hoping to get that molecule by chance, he suggests that the process was a kind of cumulative sieving or 'selection'[9] in which the results of one sieving process are fed into the next. According to Dawkins this introduces a measure of law-likeness into the process so that it can be thought of as a combination of chance and necessity.

To illustrate this, he uses a computer simulation of a variant of Huxley's typing monkeys analogy and gives us an algorithm based on it.[10] He provides the monkeys with a target phrase, his chosen example being the Shakespearean phrase 'Methinks it is like a weasel', which is taken from Hamlet. This phrase is 28 'letters' long (we count spaces as 'letters' and we take the alphabet to consist of 26 letters and one space). So the situation is that we have 28 monkeys (one corresponding to each letter of the target sequence) sitting in a row and typing.[11] Each monkey, therefore, has a target letter in the target phrase and there is a mechanism that compares their efforts with the target phrase and retains any letter they get right.

However, this target is a precise goal, which, according to Dawkins himself, is a profoundly un-Darwinian concept! And how could blind evolution not only see that target, but compare any attempt with it, in order to select it, if it is nearer the target than the previous one? This is so far from being a conceivably realistic model of mutation and natural selection as to cast doubt on whether it explains anything at all – even the distinction between single-step and cumulative selection as Dawkins claims.[12]

The simulation fails completely even on Dawkins own terms. Mathematician David Berlinski trenchantly comments: 'The entire exercise is... an achievement in self-deception.'[13] For their plausibility Dawkins' analogies depend on introducing to his model the very features whose existence in the real world he denies.

As noted above, Dawkins actually admits that his analogy is misleading, precisely because cumulative natural selection is 'blind to a goal'. He claims that the program can be modified to take care of this point – a claim that, not surprisingly, is nowhere substantiated, since it cannot be. Indeed such a claim, even if it were true, would serve to establish the exact opposite of what Dawkins believes, since modifying a program involves applying yet more intelligence to an intelligently designed artefact – the original program.

Biomorphs are graphical computer representations of an organism, used to model evolution. In Dawkins' program for generating them the computer generates certain shapes to be displayed on the screen that the computer operator can select for their elegance, etc. However, once again his procedures involve an intelligently designed filtering principle.

Dawkins himself admits that he is here attempting to simulate artificial and not natural selection – remove the target the filtering principle, and you end up with into his model the very features whose existence in the real world he denies. What Dawkins has really shown is that sufficiently complex systems such as languages of any type, including the genetic code of DNA, are not explicable without the pre-injection of the information sought into the system.

Perry Marshall, the electrical engineer and entrepreneur responsible for the Evolution 2.0 Prize, is very familiar with genetic algorithms. Referring to the work of Stanford computer scientist John Koza who showed that a genetic algorithm (GA) is capable of designing analogue circuits that are useful, he says: 'I wonder how many people noticed that Koza's GA had to be given a very specific, narrow set of constraints and precise goals before it could work? In this regard the experiment, like Dawkins', does not resemble old-school Darwinism. It's an alternative form of design.'[14] A simpler example of what is going on here is provided by a self-winding watch. Such a device uses the random movements of wrist and arm to wind itself up. How does it do that? An intelligent watchmaker has designed a ratchet that allows a heavy flywheel to move in only one direction. Therefore, it effectively selects those movements of wrist and arm that cause the flywheel to move, while blocking others. The ratchet is a result of intelligent design. Such a mechanism, according to Dawkins, cannot be Darwinian. His blind watchmaker has no foresight. To quote Berlinski again:

> The Darwinian mechanism neither anticipates nor remembers. It gives no directions and makes no choices. What is unacceptable in evolutionary theory, what is strictly forbidden, is the appearance of a force with the power to survey time, a force that conserves a point or a property because it will be useful [like the ratchet in the watch]. Such a force is no longer Darwinian. How would a blind force know such a thing? And by what means could future usefulness be transmitted to the present?[15]

Irreducibly complex machines

But there are yet more problems with Dawkins' monkey-typing analogy, especially if we try to apply it to the origin of one of the irreducibly complex machines described by Michael Behe that we discussed earlier. The problem here is best illustrated by Elliott Sober's version of Dawkins' analogy, in which he imagines a combination lock that can be opened only by the combination METHINKSITISAWEASEL. The combination lock is composed of 19 discs placed side by side, each containing the 26 letters of the alphabet and equipped with a window through which a single letter of the alphabet can be seen. We imagine that the discs are randomly spun and a disc is stopped by some mechanism when the letter in the viewing window matches the target combination. The remaining discs are randomly spun and the process repeated. So the system is essentially that of Dawkins.

Behe points out that this system claims to provide an analogy for natural selection and which therefore requires a function. So he asks what the function is of a lock combination that is incorrect:

> Suppose that, after spinning the discs for a while, we had half the letters right, something like the sequence MDTUIFKQINIOAFERSCL in which every other letter is correct. The analogy asserts that this is an improvement over a random string of letters, and that it would somehow help us open the lock. ... If your reproductive success depended on opening the lock, you would leave no offspring. Ironically for Sober and Dawkins, a lock combination is a highly specified, irreducibly complex system which beautifully illustrates why, for such systems, function cannot be approached gradually.[16]

In Dawkins' original typing monkeys version, selection would only retain attempts at the target that had some function; which, in terms of the analogy, would mean that what the monkeys typed at every intermediate step in the process would have to form words that made sense. On such terms, by simply looking at the output of Dawkins' simulation, the process could not even start. Dawkins' ideas simply cannot begin to cope with irreducible complexity. 'Instead of an analogy for natural selection acting on random mutation, the Dawkins-Sober scenario is actually an example of the very opposite: an intelligent agent directing the construction of an irreducibly complex system.'[17]

Before leaving the typing monkeys it should also be noted in passing that the fact that a correctly typed key is retained, never to be lost again,

286 / COSMIC CHEMISTRY: DO GOD AND SCIENCE MIX?

is equivalent to making the assumption that advantageous mutations are always preserved in the population. But, as evolutionary biologist Sir Ronald Fisher showed in his foundational work, this is not the case in nature.[18] Most potentially beneficial mutations get wiped out by random effects, or by the likely much larger number of deleterious mutations. This contradicts the idea commonly held since Darwin, that natural selection would preserve the slightest beneficial variation until it took over the population. It also gives further evidence for the irreducible complexity argument – as illustrated earlier by Behe's combination lock: an 'advantageous' mutation is only advantageous if it occurs simultaneously with a large number of other 'advantageous' mutations – which is a further fatal flaw in the 'target phrase' argument for the typing monkeys model.

For multiple reasons, therefore, Dawkins' proposal turns out to be nothing but a further example of assuming what you wish to prove. Philosopher Keith Ward's comment is highly apposite: 'Dawkins' strategy for reducing amazement and incredibility just does not work. It just shifts the surprise from the spontaneous generation of a complex and highly desired result to the spontaneous existence of an efficient rule which is bound to produce the desired result in time.'[19]

Marcel-Paul Schützenberger was an eminent French mathematician and medical doctor who worked in the fields of combinatorics, formal language theory, and information theory. He was one of the participants in the Wistar Conference in 1966 that brought mathematicians together – a rare occasion – to have a discussion on 'Mathematical Challenges to the Neo-Darwinian Interpretation of Evolution'.[20] Schützenberger spoke of the attempt to simulate the Darwinian process by making random changes to computer programs at the typographical level, by letters or blocks. He calculated that we have no chance (that is, with probability less than $1/10^{1000}$): 'even to see what the modified programs would compute: it just jams'. His conclusion was that this showed that the neo-Darwinian programme was inconceivable.[21] Unfortunately, there was not a great deal of mathematical analysis of the mutation-selection paradigm in the Wistar published proceedings of the kind that Sir Fred Hoyle was later to do, as we shall see below.

Schützenberger gave an interview in 1996 in which he referred to his simulation that likened mutations to typographical errors. He said: 'evolution could not be an accumulation of such typographical errors'.[22] He went on to analyse Dawkins' model and pointed out that it is out of touch with palpable biological realities since, from a mathematical perspective, it lays entirely to the side the triple problems of complexity, functionality and their interactions'. He also said in the same interview:

> It seems to me that the union of chance mutation and selection has a certain descriptive value; in no case does the description count as an explanation. Darwinism relates ecological data to the relative abundance of species and environments. In any case, the descriptive value of Darwinian models is pretty limited. Besides, as saltationists have indicated, the gradualist thesis seems completely demented in light of the growth of paleontological knowledge. The miracles of saltationism, on the other hand, cannot discharge the mystery I have described.[23]

It looks as if Dawkins' watchmaker is not only blind, but dead. In fact, he never really existed in the first place.

Dawkins' typing monkeys constitute only one example of a whole genre of computer simulations that purport to simulate not only evolution but also the origin of life. For example, a great deal of work has been done in this area by Stuart Kauffman and his collaborators at the Santa Fe Institute. However, computers are not self-organizing entities – they are intelligently designed and their programming is an intelligent activity. Steve Fuller therefore says that the ability to simulate evolution on a computer to the satisfaction of someone like Kauffman strengthens the case for divine creation. The point is that if humans have the ability to program a computer that creates an output with profound self-organizing properties, surely God could do the same? Fuller concludes:

> In short, intelligent design becomes more and more plausible as an alternative explanation for the emergence of life as evolution theorists rely increasingly on computers to demonstrate that natural history is not merely complicated but genuinely complex. This is simply because the two positions will become harder to distinguish from each other, and the evolutionists will be playing on the intelligent design theorists' turf.

The alternative, of course, would be for evolutionists to demonstrate the existence of a von Neumann machine[24] in the wild that bears no signs of design, human or otherwise.[25]

To sum up

Dawkins' algorithmic approach to solving the problem of generating information by typing monkeys does not embody his belief that evolution is mindless and without goals. What his argument shows is that if you front-load the system with a pre-designed mechanism, it then reaches the prescribed target. Thus Dawkins' simulation is teleological and is evidence for ID not against it.

The mechanism fails for the base level of specified complexity present in DNA. In the next chapter we shall see that a radical re-thinking of biology, called systems biology, which moves beyond the modern synthesis, has led to the discovery of a veritable onion of levels of intricate complexity, one after another. *A fortiori* these additional levels could not be reached by a Dawkins' type computer simulation.

The origin of language

Dawkins' attempt to show how a short phrase could arise incrementally from unguided processes was a complete failure. But what about the origin of (human) language itself? Could it have evolved incrementally? Linguistics expert Noam Chomsky said no. In his view it: 'doesn't seem at all consistent with even the most basic facts. If you look at the literature on the evolution of language, it's all about how language could have evolved from gesture, or from throwing, or something like chewing, or whatever. None of which makes any sense.'[26]

Another linguistics expert, David Premack, is deeply sceptical about efforts to explain the origin of grammar. He writes:

> I challenge the reader to reconstruct the scenario that would confer selective fitness on recursiveness... Would it be a great advantage for one of our ancestors... to be able to remark: 'Beware of the short beast whose front hoof Bob cracked when, having forgotten his own spear

back at camp, he got in a glancing blow with the dull spear he borrowed from Jack'? Human language is an embarrassment for evolutionary theory because it is vastly more powerful than one can account for in terms of selective fitness.[27]

Chomsky also commented on the origin of the human capacity to do mathematics saying that it: 'could not have evolved by natural selection; it's impossible because everybody's got them, and nobody's ever used them, except for a very tiny fringe of people in very recent times. Plainly it developed in some other way.'[28] Quite so. That remark forms a convenient segue to consider the work of an eminent mathematician and astrophysicist.

The wit and wisdom of Sir Fred Hoyle FRS

I am sure many of my readers may feel that it is time that we had a little light relief. For that reason I turn to someone I cited earlier in this chapter, the famous mathematician and astrophysicist Sir Fred Hoyle FRS who founded the astronomy department at Cambridge and was actually one of the examiners for my degree at Cambridge. I shall describe later how I subsequently met him. Fred Hoyle was a genius but of a somewhat irascible nature that, in the opinion of some, was the reason that he was not awarded a Nobel Prize for his prediction of carbon resonance. Many people thought, and indeed do still think, that he well deserved it.

He had a great turn of mordant wit and was a good storyteller, which is to be seen, not only in his novels, but, of all places, in a book on mathematics! Entitled *The Mathematics of Evolution* it was first published in 1987 by the University of Cardiff Press in a facsimile copy of his handwritten manuscript. Only 100 copies were made of it but I managed to get hold of a copy, since I was at that time a member of the Mathematics Institute in Cardiff. Hoyle decided to revisit the text some years later, and in 1999, twelve years after the first edition, it was republished.[29]

He starts the book by reminiscing on his childhood of which he says: 'My earliest research work was in truancy from school... .'[30] He spent a lot of time in the open country getting to know the flora and fauna which one might have thought would be an inspiration to any child to take up a career in biology. But then, as he tells us, in his early teens he encountered the Darwinian theory that convinced him that biology was a deeply suspect enterprise. This had nothing to do with religious inclinations as he had given that up at an earlier date. He says: 'The criticism of the Darwinian theory given in this book arises straightforwardly from my belief that the theory is wrong, and that continued adherence to it is an impediment to discovering the correct evolutionary theory.'[31] That conviction had to do with the 'logic' of natural selection. He explains how he first encountered it:

> The theory seemed to me to run like this:
> If among the varieties of a species there is one that survives better in the environment than the other, then the variety that survives best is the one that best survives.[32]

Hoyle scathingly concluded that this 'natural selection' amounted to nothing more than a tautology and he riled people by saying that it did nothing at all. In his trenchant yet amusing style he mocked the idea of selection pointing out that no amount of selection of potatoes would turn them into rabbits, nor would selecting oaks produce bats. In fact he thought the people who believed this stuff were 'bats in the belfry'. Hoyle also ridiculed the idea that natural selection increased complexity by saying that it was surely less problematic to make a rabbit from a potato than from sludge – which was precisely what some highly qualified people believed. According to Hoyle they had to swallow this idea in blind faith since there was no evidence for its truth. That is, they had to swallow it in order to pass exams and avoid mockery by their colleagues.

In his inimical style Hoyle concludes:

> So it came about from 1860 onward that new believers became in a sense mentally ill, or, more precisely, either you became mentally ill or you quitted the subject of biology as I had done in my early teens. The trouble for young biologists was that, with everyone around them ill, it became impossible for them to think they were well unless they were ill, which again is a situation you can read all about in the columns of *Nature*.[33]

From this it is not hard to see why and how Hoyle got himself into trouble. Yet, in spite of the vehemence of his denunciation of Darwinism, he nevertheless could see that it was not entirely false, as he explains in what I think is an important statement on scientific methodology:

When ideas are based on observations, as the Darwinian theory certainly is, it is usual for those ideas to be valid at least within the range of the observations. It is when extrapolations are made outside the range of observations that troubles may arise. So the issue that presented itself was to determine just how far the theory was valid and exactly why beyond a certain point it became invalid.[34]

This fits with the evidence from biological experiment presented in Chapter 19. Hoyle eventually accepted a challenge from his botanist friend George Carson, who was also sceptical of the theory, to make a serious mathematical attempt to answer this question. That work is contained in Hoyle's book. Hoyle was a very gifted mathematician and, as a (lesser) mathematician myself, I am surprised to find that so few champions of the natural selection mutation paradigm appear to be even aware of it, let alone have read it. That is very odd, since it was the statistician R. A. Fisher, together with Sewall Wright and J. B. S. Haldane, who laid down the mathematical foundations for evolutionary theory. His book, *The Genetical Theory of Natural Selection*,[35] has been called the deepest book on evolution since Darwin. Hoyle, who knew Fisher personally, recommends it for its 'brilliant obscurity'.

Now publishers have told me that the number of readers of a book is halved for every equation that appears in it. That means that, however, tempted I may feel, I shall not reproduce much mathematics here except for the little that now follows. Hoyle made the important point that he felt that much of the appeal of the Darwinian theory lay in a simple mathematical confirmation of an obvious intuition that consists of two parts:

1. variation must exist in a population
2. the fittest members of that population have a selective advantage so that they are more likely than others to transmit their genes to the next generation.

Let us now look at this mathematically. Suppose x is the fraction of a large population that possesses a particular property P, say. Then 1-x is the proportion of the population that does not have P, but has another property, Q, say. Assume that otherwise the members of the population are all similar to each other. The initial population reproduces itself down through the generations, the old dying and making space for the young. Since change is slow, time may be represented as a continuous variable, with a unit equal to the average inter-generational interval.

We next assume that individuals in the population with properties P (favourable) and Q (not so favourable) produce offspring in the ratio 1+s to 1 and we assume that these offspring survive to reproduce in the next generation. We also regard $s > 0$ as a constant independent of x and the time t.

The relevant reader-halving equation is the simple differential equation:

$$dx/dt = sx$$

This integrates to give the solution

$$x = x_0 \exp (st),$$

where at

$$t = 0, x = x_0$$

a given initial boundary condition.

We deduce at once that the entire population will come to have the favourable property P in

$$-\ln (x_0)/ s$$

generations.

Hoyle gives an example putting

$$s = 0.01 \text{ and } x_0 = 10^{-6}$$

which gives about 1,400 generations as the time taken for the favourable property P to spread throughout the entire population.

If, on the other hand, P is disadvantageous, then $s < 0$ and P is rapidly eliminated in the order of $1/s$ generations.

So far so good. But what happens if we move towards the more realistic case where individuals with a good gene P also have a bad gene with larger $|s|$? Now the mathematics becomes much more complicated as the nature of mutations has to be factored in together with the fact that the great majority of them are harmful. After a great deal of precise mathematical work Hoyle concludes that:

> subject to the choice of a highly sophisticated reproductive
> model, the theory works at the level of varieties and

How did the 1st kind get to be?

species, just as it was found empirically to do by biologists from the mid-nineteenth century onward. But the theory does not work at broader taxonomic levels; it cannot explain the major steps in evolution. For them, something not considered in the Darwinian theory is essential.[36]

Hoyle summarizes his work as follows: 'Well as common sense would suggest, the Darwinian theory is correct in the small but not in the large. Rabbits come from other slightly different rabbits, not from either soup or potatoes. Where they come from in the first place is a problem yet to be solved, like much else of a cosmic scale.'[37]

In terms of actual calculation, Hoyle and Wickramasinghe suggested that a protobiont – a precursor of life – would need 2,000 enzymes to sustain itself and to reproduce. Yockey comments on their calculation and refines it as below.

On the assumption that each of Hoyle's 2000 enzymes has 374 bits, the same as the information content of cytochrome c, Yockey estimates that the information content of the genome of the protobiont amounts to 93,500 bytes. He then calculates the probability of generating a given message containing 93,500 eight-bit bytes as follows:

> According to the Shannon-McMillan-Breiman theorem... since cytochrome c is a long sequence, each has approximately the same probability $[2.3 \times 10^{93}]^{-1}$, and we are treating the appearance of each of the 2000 enzymes as an independent chance event. Therefore the 'probability' that all 2000 enzymes were formed by chance is the product of the separate 'probabilities': $[2.3 \times 10^{93}]^{-2000} = 10^{-186000}$. Thus we see that Hoyle's estimate of a 'probability' of 10^{-44000} that a protobiont of 2000 enzymes was created by chance is outrageously optimistic.[38]

Gregory Chaitin and the mathematics of Darwinism

We have already introduced the mathematician Gregory Chaitin as one of the fathers of the algorithmic information theory. In 2012 he published a book entitled *Proving Darwin: Making Biology Mathematical*.[39] In the spirit of Dawkins it espouses a diametrically opposite view to that of Hoyle. We shall not examine it in detail since it turns out to have several major flaws, not in the mathematics of the model but in its purported applicability to the topic. For instance, natural selection operates on populations, whereas Chaitin's simulation considers a single 'organism' only. Secondly, Chaitin's proposal is teleological, like Dawkins', which of course means that it cannot be used as evidence for *undirected* evolution. It is also totally unrealistic, as Radosław Siedliński of the Polish-Japanese Academy of Information Technology in Warsaw explains by saying that, although Chaitin is aware the procedure he constructed is uncomputable, he sets this fact aside as unproblematic which seems rather lax at first sight (Shallit 2013[40]). However:

> It ceases to be like that if we keep in mind that Chaitin is operating in the domain of pure mathematics. He does not try to create any model design for implementation in any of the existing programming languages or for execution on real computers. Chaitin knows that his model is a simplification so far reaching that only common terminology and nothing more links it to the world studied by biologists. Therefore he regards it only as a mathematical 'landmark', as well as an impetus for further studies.[41]

It certainly does not negate the strong evidence that the information content of DNA alone cannot be the result of any natural law-like processes. Furthermore, as we shall see in Chapter 19, it is now clear from research in systems biology that there is functional biological information that is not in the genes (or DNA) – epigenetic information – so there is much much more to explain. Siedliński says: 'It seems that biological information is not located in any particular place in the living system. It is rather a nonlocal property, scattered throughout the whole system. It is impossible to point to any isolated physical structure in a cell and state: "biological information is located precisely here"... .'[42]

Siedliński concludes his review of what Chaitin calls 'metabiology' by saying that a comprehensive mathematical theory of Darwinian evolution still remains a future dream.

Kozłowski (2011)[43] suggests two possible scenarios: 1) it is impossible to build a mathematical theory of evolution at all, 2) it is possible, but such a theory would be useless for any practical purposes due to the hyper-complexity of the evolving biosphere. As for metabiology, I believe it should be regarded rather as an expression of the philosophical views of its creator than a serious attempt at contributing something new and vital into the field of theoretical biology.[44]

Two further critical reviews from polar opposite philosophical perspectives are given by Ewert, Dembski, and Marks on the one hand[45] and Jeffrey Shallit on the other.[46] This shows once more just how hard it is to get a mathematical grip on biology and how controversial and misleading claims can be. Ewert, Dembski, and Marks have also written a book, *Introduction to Evolutionary Informatics*, in which they show that other attempts to use mathematics to prove Darwinism like *AVIDA* and *ev* fail.[47] Chaitin himself says: 'We shouldn't, however, expect metabiology to ever become as realistic as theoretical physics or chemistry. And why not? Because *biology is just too messy, too far removed from mathematics*.'[48]

In any case, of course, if ever a very much more sophisticated version of Chaitin's metabiology was developed, then, firstly, it wouldn't account for the hardware aspect of life and the fact that life's software contains the program for construction of its own hardware, and, secondly, it would have been developed by a mind – and a rather intelligent one at that! Another thing that Chaitin admits is that metabiology in its present form cannot address thinking and consciousness.[49]

PART 5

The Information Age

19

Systems Biology

In this chapter we outline some of the very exciting developments in a burgeoning field -- systems biology. This broad area of biology, which in general comprises the complexity within the cell including genomics, metabolomics, proteomics, lipidomics, etc., has been pioneered by Nobel laureate Barbara McClintock, Denis Noble FRS, and James Shapiro, McClintock's student and collaborator. McClintock's work was earth-shaking in its implications in that it demonstrated that an organism could actually modify its own genome in complete contradiction of established Darwinist wisdom. This work received public recognition at a meeting of the Royal Society in London in 2016 devoted to: 'New trends in evolutionary biology: biological, philosophical and social science perspectives'.

This Royal Society meeting recalls another fifty years earlier at the Wistar Institute in Philadelphia in 1966 that, as we mentioned earlier, brought mathematicians together to discuss the 'Mathematical Challenges to the Neo-Darwinian Interpretation of Evolution'. That meeting was opened by Nobel laureate Sir Peter Medawar who said:

> [T]he immediate cause of this conference is a pretty widespread sense of dissatisfaction about what has come to be thought of as the accepted evolutionary theory in the English-speaking world, the so-called neo-Darwinian Theory. ... There are objections made by fellow scientists who feel that, in the current theory, something is missing.... These objections to current neo-Darwinian theory are very widely held among biologists generally; and we must on no account, I think, make light of them. The very fact that we are having this conference is evidence that we are not making light of them.[1]

The eye is highly improbable — time restraint

Some of the interchanges at that meeting were harbingers of trouble to come for the modern synthesis, not least because of the faulty logic that its representatives displayed. As an instance of this, the mathematician D. S. Ulam argued that it was highly improbable that the eye could have evolved by the accumulation of small mutations, because the number of mutations would have to be so large and the time available for them to appear was not nearly long enough in any case. Peter Medawar and C. H. Waddington replied by saying that Ulam was doing his science backwards; the fact was that the eye had evolved and therefore the mathematical difficulties must only be apparent: 'I think you have got the question upside down'. Ernst Mayr commented that Ulam's calculations were based on assumptions that might turn out to be unfounded. Mayr concluded: 'So all I am saying is we have so much variation in all of these things that somehow or other by adjusting these figures we will come out all right. We are comforted by the fact that evolution has occurred.'[2]

David Swift, in his excellent survey *Evolution under the Microscope*, says that these comments show what operating within an accepted paradigm actually means: that the biologists at Wistar did not even consider how good or bad the mathematical arguments were:

> As far as they were concerned their paradigm was true and they rejected everything that would not fall in line with it. Rather than allow anything to challenge their own beliefs, their firm presumption was that there must be something wrong with the supposed challenge, even if they had no idea what it was. The symposium was convened specifically to consider mathematical challenges to Neo-Darwinism, but for the biologists it could be construed only as biological challenges to the maths![3]

bias
world view

Fifty years on there was to be an even greater shake-up of ideas. One of the most spectacular is the research of James Shapiro, who has convincingly demonstrated that the genome is not just a read-only memory but a read-write system so that the genome can be modified top down. He says:

> The genome has traditionally been treated as a Read-Only Memory (ROM) subject to change by copying errors and accidents. In this review, I propose that we need to

> change that perspective and understand the genome as an intricately formatted Read–Write (RW) data storage system constantly subject to cellular modifications and inscriptions. Cells operate under changing conditions and are continually modifying themselves by genome inscriptions.... Cells possess the biochemical activities that allow them to restructure DNA in the same ways that we do in laboratory genetic engineering.[4]

The mind-boggling levels of informational sophistication at the epigenetic level that have already been uncovered by such research (including its promise of many more levels to come) seem to make the inference to an intelligent source quite irresistible.

It is clear from the foregoing that reductionist attempts to explain biogenesis do not work and the modern (neo-Darwinian) synthesis has failed – not in the sense that they have not taught us useful science, but in the sense that they have not reached their stated goal of giving a satisfactory account of the genesis and evolution of life. One reason for this failure would appear to be a lack of clarity about natural selection as flagged up by William Provine (see Chapter 16). Unsurprisingly, there is also marked reluctance to grasp the incapacity of unguided natural processes to produce the 'language' encoding of DNA.

Another reason is that, for a considerable time, some scientists have felt that there is something missing. For instance, we cited earlier the distinguished University of Massachusetts academic, the late Lynn Margulis, who said that: 'Neo-Darwinism sates intellectual curiosity with abstractions bereft of actual details.' In conversation with Suzan Mazur she filled that out by saying: 'The real disagreement about what the neo-Darwinists tout, for which there's very little evidence, if any, is that random mutations accumulate and when they accumulate enough, new species originate.'[5]

Margulis' own theory, called 'symbiogenesis', is that our own mammalian nucleated (eukaryotic) cells are descended from amalgams of different strains of ancient bacteria, an idea way outside the neo-Darwinian paradigm. Her book on the topic, *Symbiosis in Cell Evolution*, was published in 1981 with a second edition in 1992. In 1995, she and co-author science writer Dorion Sagan wrote a more popular illustrated version of her ideas that bore the same title as that of Erwin Schrödinger's famous 1943 text: *What is Life?*

A further reason for failure of the modern synthesis may well be the intrusion of ideology where it does not belong. Attention to this was drawn in 2005 by physics Nobel laureate Robert Laughlin, whose research is on the properties of matter that make life possible. He felt strongly enough about it to issue a warning to scientists about the ideological nature of much contemporary biological theory due to the fact that it cannot be tested because it carries no implications:

> I call such logical dead ends anti-theories because... they stop thinking rather than stimulate it. Evolution by natural selection, for instance, which Darwin conceived as a great theory has lately come to function as an anti-theory called upon to cover up embarrassing experimental shortcomings and legitimize findings that are at best questionable and at worst not even wrong. Your protein defies the laws of mass action—evolution did it! Your complicated mess of chemical reactions turns into a chicken—evolution! The human brain works on logical principles no computer can emulate? Evolution is the cause.[6]

We also recall from Chapter 16 what EvoDevo expert Gerd Müller of the University of Vienna wrote in 2003 about the failure of the modern synthesis to give causal explanation of many biological processes: 'Only a few of the processes listed above are addressed by the canonical neo-Darwinian theory.... In the neo-Darwinian world the motive factor of morphological change is natural selection, which can account for the modification and loss of parts. But selection has *no innovative capacity*: it eliminates or maintains what exists. The generative and ordering aspects of morphological evolution are thus absent from evolutionary theory' (my italics).[7]

A great deal more has been achieved in this direction since Müller and Laughlin wrote these things. In particular, seminal contributions on the flourishing area of systems biology have been made following Nobel laureate Barbara McLintock's discovery of 'the jumping gene' – now termed a 'mobile genetic element'. Two of the major players here are Oxford physiologist Denis Noble and University of Chicago bacterial geneticist James Shapiro.

McClintock was an exceptional cytogeneticist of immense courage. Her study focussed on what happened to the chromosomes of maize plants under exposure to X-rays. The rays fragmented the chromosomes and messed up the genome which was no surprise, but what happened afterwards was a considerable shock. Sometimes, the broken pieces recombined in novel ways. In 1943 she made the startling discovery that segments of the maize chromosomes could switch places on the genome – a phenomenon called the 'jumping gene'. She had started research as a student in the 1920s and in 1953 she felt she had to stop because of intense opposition from the scientific establishment, another victim of the risk of challenging the reigning Darwinian paradigm. However, her work triumphed and she was honoured in 1983 with the Nobel Prize in Physiology or Medicine for the discovery of 'mobile genetic elements' – the first woman to win it outright. However, she was not afraid to mention in her acceptance speech the opposition she had experienced. It tells us a lot about the science community. Here is a sample of what she said about how she felt during a lengthy period when her research was ignored and dismissed:

> My understanding of the phenomenon responsible for rapid changes in gene action, including variegated expressions commonly seen in both plants and animals, was much too radical for the time.... In the interim I was not invited to give lectures or seminars, except on rare occasions, or to serve on committees or panels, or to perform other scientists' duties. Instead of causing personal difficulties, this long interval proved to be a delight. It allowed complete freedom to continue investigations without interruption, and for the pure joy they provided... .[8]

Of her work she said:

> The conclusion seems inescapable that cells are able to sense the presence in their nuclei of ruptured ends of chromosomes, and then to activate a mechanism that will bring together and then unite these ends, one with another....They make wise decisions and act upon them.

She concluded by saying:

> The examples chosen illustrate the importance of stress in instigating genome modification by mobilizing available cell mechanisms that can restructure genomes....
>
> In the future attention will undoubtedly be centred on the genome... as a highly sensitive organ of the cell, monitoring genomic activities and correcting common errors, sensing the unusual and unexpected events, and responding to them, often by restructuring the genome. We know about the components of genomes that could be made available for such restructuring. We know nothing, however, about how the cell senses danger and instigates responses to it that often are truly remarkable.[9]

Her research was revolutionary in that it totally contradicted the established wisdom of Darwinism by showing that an organism could actually *act as an agent and* modify *its own genome*. Not only that, but that the reaction of the genome to stress could trigger species formation.

Research work flowing out of this breakthrough has been proceeding ever since. In 1979 geneticist Mae-Wan Ho and mathematician and theoretical biologist Peter Saunders published a paper whose abstract says that the basic neo-Darwinian theory based on natural selection and random mutation does not adequately account for evolution. Moreover, natural selection has limited explanatory power being as it is unable to account satisfactorily for species diversity, the origin of new species, or large evolutionary changes. They state:

> The evidence suggests on the one hand that most genetic changes are irrelevant to evolution; and on the other, that a relative lack of natural selection may be the prerequisite for major evolutionary advance.
>
> Contrary to the neo-Darwinian view, we point out that the variations of the phenotype, on which natural selection could act, do not arise at random; they are produced by interactions between the organism and the environment during development.

Wow

They go on to say: 'The intrinsic dynamical structure of the epigenetic system itself, in its interaction with the environment, is the source of non-random variations which direct evolutionary change.'[10]

In an interview with Suzan Mazur thirty-six years later, in 2015, Ho, who had been awarded the Prigogine Medal the previous year, said: 'I think the Modern Synthesis has got to be completely replaced, and unfortunately those people who are very attached to neo-Darwinism won't look at the evidence. A lot of them don't know molecular genetics at all. Or like [Richard] Dawkins, they will say, I just don't believe it. They're not scientists.'[11] One of Ho's well-known quotes is: 'Life is achingly beautiful and creative once you free yourself from the mind-numbing shackles of neo-Darwinian dogma.'

Oxford physiologist Denis Noble CBE FRS, who acknowledges this work of Ho and Saunders, has made groundbreaking advances in further elucidating the epigenetic dimension. In 2014 he co-founded the 'Third Way of Evolution' with a number of other distinguished biologists. Its website, which is to be strongly recommended, states: 'The DNA record does not support the assertion that small random mutations are the main source of new and useful variations. We now know that the many different processes of variation involve well-regulated cell action on DNA molecules.'[12]

Research on these issues eventually received high-level recognition in the form of a remarkable meeting at the Royal Society in London in November 2016 where 300 scientists from around the world gathered to evaluate a potential sea change in evolutionary theory. The meeting was entitled: 'New trends in evolutionary biology: biological, philosophical and social science perspectives.' It was organized in partnership with the British Academy by Professors Denis Noble FRS, Nancy Cartwright FBA, Sir Patrick Bateson FRS, John Dupré, and Kevin Laland. Noble is renowned for his work on developing the first viable mathematical model of the human heart, thus paving the way for the invention of the pacemaker that has saved many lives.[13] Over the years I have had the privilege of attending some of his seminars on systems biology in Oxford. Like Ho, his view, as he explained before the symposium was held – to Suzan Mazur of Huff Post,[14] is that the modern synthesis needs not to be modified but replaced – an absolutely radical step. His reasons are, firstly, that a central feature of the modern synthesis was the rejection of any form of the inheritance of acquired characteristics, an idea put forward by the eighteenth-century French naturalist Jean-Baptiste Lamarck although it was mooted as far back as Hippocrates, Aristotle, and Galen. Noble points out that experiments have demonstrated the existence of acquired characteristics that can be inherited. This is entirely inimical to the modern synthesis.

Noble is careful to affirm that processes of random mutation followed by selection certainly do *something*, as has already been made clear. He insists, however, that selection-mutation is *only one process or mechanism among many others* that interact with each other. Indeed, he goes so far as to say: 'I would certainly go along with the view that gradual mutation followed by selection has not, as a matter of fact, been demonstrated to be necessarily a cause of speciation.' He continues with a much more conceptual reason for setting aside the modern synthesis and replacing it:

> I think that as a gene-centric view of evolution, the modern synthesis has got causality in biology wrong. Genes, after all, if they're defined as DNA sequences, are purely passive. DNA on its own does absolutely nothing until activated by the rest of the system through transcription factors, markers of one kind or another, interactions with the proteins. So on its own, DNA is not a cause in an active sense. I think it is better described as a passive data base which is used by the organism to enable it to make the proteins that it requires.'[15] (We have already hinted at this in Chapter 9 where we asked the chicken-egg question about DNA and the cell.)

Walker and Davies put it this way:

> DNA does not contain a blueprint for building the entire cell, but instead contains only small parts of a much larger biological algorithm, that may be roughly described as the epigenetic components of an organism. The algorithm for building an organism is therefore not only stored in a linear digital sequence (tape), but also in the current state of the entire system (e.g. epigenetic factors such as the level of gene expression... methylation patterns, chromatin architecture, nucleosome distribution, cellular phenotype, and environmental context). The algorithm itself is therefore highly delocalized, distributed

molecule to man : Molecules are not alive

inextricably throughout the very physical system whose dynamics it encodes.[16]

These insights are fascinating and open up new scientific possibilities that are beginning to break the impasse into which the modern synthesis had got itself through being so wedded to a dogmatic physical reductionism. Noble's approach to the complexities involved is integrative, involving both bottom-up and top-down causation. There is, therefore, no 'privileged' position of causality. The central dogma of molecular biology that causation only flows in one direction – from the genes upwards to the organism – is dead and buried.

Noble therefore rejects the reductionist view that he admits that he once held and which he now thinks resulted in the general sidelining of the integrative approach in the second half of the twentieth century. He expresses that reductionism in what he terms the biological mantra that insists on: 'from molecules to man'. In his view, that cannot be true for the simple reason that molecules are not alive. That does not, of course, imply that he rejects reductionism in its entirety. Nor does anyone else including me. It is, after all, a methodology that has proved itself in all manner of disciplines including my own (mathematics) as we said earlier. What brilliant successes the discovery of the double helix structure of DNA and the sequencing of the human genome have been. *The point is that reductionism, though part of the story, from which a great deal has been learned, is far from being the whole story.* James Shapiro puts it this way: 'We have this terrible dilemma in science. We need to be reductionists to get meaningful results and make observations. But when we take the observations and try to understand what they mean, then we have to stop being reductionists and become integrationists to understand how the things we've identified and singled out fit into the whole picture.'[17]

It is a pity to have even to mention it, but, in light of what happened to McClintock, I think it is worth underlining that Noble's attitude to reductionism is not motivated by crypto-theism or ID. He is purely motivated by science and a desire to get at the truth rather than bowing to dogma. Noble explains his thinking in a delightful little book called *The Music of Life: Biology Beyond the Genome*[18] which is a must-read if the reader, as I sincerely hope, wishes to get a proper sense of the revolution of thinking that is being brought about by the integrative approach of systems biology. Noble uses a vivid analogy of a huge pipe organ with 30,000 pipes

reductionist ←→ integrationists
ad

Pipe Organ – The composer what plays (writes)
The organist interprets
Systems Biology / 307

The composite of cellular from ♂ and ♀

to illustrate the function of the human genome with its 30,000 genes. He says:

> To think that the genome completely determines the organism is almost as absurd as thinking that the pipes in a large cathedral organ determine what the organist plays. Of course, it was the composer who did that in writing the score, and the organist himself who interprets it. The pipes are his passive instruments until he brings them to life in a pattern that he imposes on them, just as multi-cellular organisms use the same genome to generate all the 200 or so different types of cell in their bodies by activating different expression patterns.[19]

Elsewhere Noble says that the development of an organism involves much more than the genome:

> If there is a score for the music of life, it is not the genome, or at least, not that alone. DNA never acts outside the context of a cell. And we each inherit much more than our DNA. We inherit the egg cell from our mother with all its machinery, including mitochondria, ribosomes and other cytoplasmic components, such as the proteins that enter the nucleus to initiate DNA transcription. These proteins are, initially at least, those encoded by the mother's genes. As Brenner[20] said, 'the correct level of abstraction is the cell, and not the genome'.[21]

(This is a comment that recalls Lynn Margulis' remark that, 'Life is thus truly a cellular phenomenon.'[22])

What is more, it turns out that the non-DNA information is at least as great as that in the genome.[23] Not only that but there is increasing evidence of the transmission by a mother to the embryo adverse or favourable influences on its gene expression levels that may extend over several generations. This is clear evidence of the 'Lamarckian' inheritance of acquired characteristics that is anathema to the modern synthesis. It would be hard to over-estimate the importance of these results and the radically new perspective they bring.

cellular phenomenon

Natural genetic engineering

A seminal contribution has been made to systems biology and epigenetics by James Shapiro that is explained in his book *Evolution: A Viewpoint from the 21st Century*. One of his important discoveries is reverse transcription of RNA into DNA. We saw in Chapter 9 that RNA is used to transcribe DNA. When that process is complete the RNA can be modified. What Shapiro found was that it can sometimes happen that such modified RNA can write itself back into DNA and thus alter it.

We referred earlier to his seminal work in establishing the genome as a read-write system like that found in computers. In the abstract of his 2013 paper describing this work Shapiro says that it has been traditional to regard the genome as a read-only memory that is only subject to modification by accidents and mistakes in copying. However, he now thinks that this perspective must be changed to regard the genome as an:

> intricately formatted Read-Write (RW) data storage system constantly subject to cellular modifications and inscriptions. Cells operate under changing conditions and are continually modifying themselves by genome inscriptions. ... Research dating back to the 1930s has shown that genetic change is the result of cell-mediated processes, not simply accidents or damage to the DNA. This cell-active view of genome change applies to all scales of DNA sequence variation, from point mutations to large-scale genome rearrangements and whole genome duplications (WGDs). This conceptual change to active cell inscriptions controlling RW genome functions has profound implications for all areas of the life sciences.[24]

One of those implications is that: 'Evolutionary inscriptions are those written into the DNA sequence structure that influence taxonomic divergence. Although the traditional concept of gradual genome change in evolution assumes that these inscriptions have to accumulate within vertical lineages over long chronological periods, some evolutionary inscriptions clearly occur in a single organismal generation by cell actions outside normal vertical heredity.'

Shapiro also says that cells act in a 'cognitive way' – that is, essentially as agents. He defines what he calls natural genetic engineering as follows:

Cells possess the biochemical activities that allow them to restructure DNA in the same ways that we do in laboratory genetic engineering. Thus, the summary term 'natural genetic engineering' (NGE) is suitable for describing the constellation of activities involved in DNA (genome) biochemistry. Many of these activities are the same as ones used in DNA damage repair, but certain functions are present specifically for generating genomic novelties. The NGE toolbox is full.

His conclusion is this: 'The empirical evidence for biological action in hereditary genome changes has become so overwhelming that it is surprising how widespread the notion of accidental change still remains.'[25] And that was over five years ago.

The title of Denis Noble's book, *The Music of Life*, and his analogy of the organ with 30,000 pipes raise the question as to whether there is a composer of the music or, indeed, an organist who plays the organ. Noble's response is that the composer is evolution, which, he states is 'of course' a blind process, concluding that: 'The grand composer was even more blind than Beethoven was deaf.'[26] Noble's concept of blindness does not seem to suffer from the ambiguities that we saw were inherent in Dawkins' *The Blind Watchmaker*. Noble says, 'Just as the heart oscillates without there being a specific oscillator to drive it, so evolution works without a master plan.'[27]

I wonder, however, if this analogy is really fair? The heart seems to be an organ that functions together with other organs to an over-arching master plan. It raises the thought that a master planner, or, dare I say, organist, might well exist for the organ of life. In any case, Noble does not claim to know what precisely this 'evolution' is that he credits with these remarkable powers. For, he prefaces this chapter of his book (Chapter 8) with the following quotation: 'We don't have a theory of interactions and until we do we cannot have a theory of development or a theory of evolution.'[28] We might even add 'let alone a theory of biogenesis'. He then says that finding them must be the ultimate goal for systems biology and honestly confesses that we are 'only at the very beginning of the attempt to do that' and we have 'only a small glimmering of how it might be possible to develop such an understanding'.[29]

I sincerely hope I am not misunderstanding him at this point, since his statement is humble and honest, an attitude that scientists do not always show. However, I cannot help thinking that it sounds uncomfortably like the kind of ideological 'evolution of the gaps' usage referred to by Robert Laughlin as cited at the beginning of this chapter. Not only that, but I find it strangely inappropriate in light of the very telling analogy that Noble himself gives to help us think about it.

Moving from his wonderful genomic organ with its 30,000 gene pipes, Noble considers the Chinese writing system which has, roughly speaking, around the same number of characters. They are formed from two to three hundred basic elements in a modular system, analogous to the way in which genes are built up from a couple of thousand such modules. Both of these analogies involve fiendishly complicated systems of expression, the first in the language of music and the second in a human language. Music and literature add a virtually unlimited additional level of complexity beyond the instruments of organ or language on which they are 'played' – perhaps we could call them epi-organic and epi-linguistic. In addition they are, at both levels, products of human intelligence. Can all of this exquisite complexity – way beyond anything known to Paley – be construed as evidence of the existence of an intelligent creator? Noble mentions this possibility but then points out that 'life is full of design faults, false trails and imperfect compromises'.[30]

Now, I really do not like challenging the implications here, since Denis Noble is a scientist from whom I have learned so much and for whom I have the greatest admiration and respect. However, engineering science research, for instance, is full of design faults, false trails, and imperfect compromises. It is even possible to mistake damage subsequent to construction for design fault or compromise. None of these, however, constitute an argument against the creative intelligence of the technologists. Furthermore, further research sometimes shows that what has been thought to be a design fault and imperfect compromise is nothing of the kind. A famous instance of this is the so-called 'backwards wiring of the eye'. For light travels through a mass of neurons before it gets to the rod and cone cells that detect it and so some thought that the retinal cells were wired the wrong way round. Biologist Erez Ribak, working at the Technion in Haifa, reports in *Scientific American* on his research on that particular feature of the eye which he presented at a meeting of the American Physical Society. He writes:

> New research has uncovered a remarkable vision-enhancing function for this puzzling structure.... These

results mean that the retina of the eye has been optimised so that the sizes and densities of glial cells match the colours to which the eye is sensitive (which is in itself an optimisation process suited to our needs). This optimisation is such that colour vision during the day is enhanced, while night-time vision suffers very little. The effect also works best when the pupils are contracted at high illumination, further adding to the clarity of our colour vision.[31]

It reminds me of so-called 'junk DNA' that has turned out to be full of significant information. I think, therefore, that Noble's argument here against the existence of a divine composer is not sustainable.

Revisiting the weasel algorithm

In their paper, 'Was the Watchmaker Blind? Or Was She One-Eyed?',[32] Denis Noble and Raymond Noble revisit the Dawkins' typing monkey algorithm mentioned in Chapter 18. In the abstract they say that the usual discussion of whether evolution is blind involves choosing between the blind-watchmaker scenario where there are no goals and alternative scenarios like intelligent design or special creation that involve long-term objective external to the organism:

The arguments either way do not address the question whether there are short-term goals within rather than external to organisms. Organisms and their interacting populations have evolved mechanisms by which they can harness blind stochasticity and so generate rapid functional responses to environmental challenges. They can achieve this by re-organising their genomes and/ or their regulatory networks. Epigenetic as well as DNA changes are involved. Evolution may have no foresight, but it is at least partially directed by organisms themselves and by the populations of which they form part.

They agree with Dawkins that:

> (a) completely stochastic processes with no 'hold' or similar 'guiding' mechanism would require impossibly long periods of time for successful evolution to occur, and (b) there is no need to assume that evolution has a long-term goal. This is where both he and we part company with Intelligent Design (ID) and creationist theories. But we will nevertheless show that organisms and populations of organisms do have identifiable and empirically testable goals, and that variations on the theme of the Weasel program found experimentally in nature, show this to be true.

I find this paper extremely interesting as I agree with (a) but I would have thought that the fact that organisms can act as agents in the sense that they have identifiable and empirically testable goals within themselves is strong evidence that the whole of the biosphere of which those organisms are part shows foresight and is goal-directed. In other words, (a) could be taken as evidence for high-level teleology, the opposite of (b) without necessarily assuming an ID model! It is all a matter of interpretation and presupposition but it is nevertheless good to know that Denis Noble no longer thinks that 'evolution' is blind.

The paper ends with the following statement giving a new definition of evolution:

> Our overall conclusion is that there are several processes by which directed evolutionary change occurs—targeted mutation, gene transposition, epigenetics, cultural change, niche construction and adaptation. Evolution is an ongoing set of iterative interactions between organisms and the environment. Evolution is a continuous organic process. Directionality is introduced by the agency of organisms themselves as the one-eyed watchmakers. Evolution itself also evolves.

An example of this is given by David M Prescott: 'Hypotrichous ciliates also possess extraordinary organizational features in their micronuclear and macronuclear genomes and carry out extensive developmental manipulations of their genomic DNA. These DNA phenomena, which considerably expand our view of genetic versatility, are the subject of this review.... We can be confident that the spectacular contortions shown by ciliate genomes have played an important part in their evolution — a phenomenon that has been summed up incisively as the 'evolution of evolvability'.[33] A further example is provided by biochemist Kwang W. Jeong who points out that: 'Intracellular symbiosis is a widespread and important biological phenomenon in terms of genetic novelty, bringing about genetic changes that could be greater in magnitude than what may result from mutation, hybridization, or ploidy changes, because symbiosis draws genomes from the entire biosphere.'[34]

Cancer

Finally, research is revealing the astonishing ability of cancers to develop the capacity to metastasize beyond anything that could be achieved by random mutation. Researchers Kenneth J. Pienta, Emma U. Hammarlund, Robert Axelrod, et al. argue that metastatic cancers are incurable because tumours have the capacity to evolve resistance to all known therapies and their ability to metastasize and develop resistance 'demands an explanation beyond the slow and steady accrual of stochastic mutations.'[35]

It will be interesting to see what future research reveals as to whether these modified versions of sometimes rapid, biological developmental change, depending on where you start assessing it, has a quantifiable reach or edge at a further discontinuity like that of the origin of life itself, say the origin of animals, or of human consciousness and language. Whatever the answer to that question is, these discoveries of extra levels of epigenetic complexity in organisms would seem to make the mystery both of the origin and the development of life very much more resistant to elucidation in terms of purely naturalistic processes. The mind-boggling levels of informational sophistication and processing capacity of living organisms that have been laid bare by such work, with every indication of much more to come, make the inference to an intelligent source very tempting indeed. Remember, we not only have to account for the vast amounts of information contained in each molecular machine, but for the higher-level information management processes that control and regulate them in the whole organism. That management process would appear to have its headquarters in the human brain.

I would like to stress at this point that, although the groundbreaking work on systems biology and natural genetic engineering is providing a great deal of new information about what cells can do once they exist and how speciation may occur, it does not bring us any nearer to solving the fundamental problem of the *origin* of life and its informational base.[36] Palaeontologist Günther Bechly describes how the scientific principle of following evidence wherever it leads in fact led him to:

> doubt the materialistic paradigm of Neo-Darwinian macro-evolution via a purely mechanistic process of chance (random mutation, sexual recombination, genetic drift) and necessity (natural and sexual selection), even when supplemented with more modern concepts like symbiogenesis, multilevel (group) selection, epigenetic inheritance, evolvability, natural genetic engineering, phenotypic plasticity, and niche construction, as suggested by the proponents of an extended evolutionary synthesis ('Third Way of Evolution', 'Evolution 2.0'). None of these phenomena can sufficiently explain the origin of complex biological novelty, and some of them (e.g., natural genetic engineering, phenotypic plasticity, and evolvability) themselves require finetuning and specified information themselves.[37]

20

The Origin of Information: A Word-Based World

'In the beginning was the bit.'
Han Christian von Baeyer

'In the beginning was the Word.'
John, author of the Fourth Gospel

Our consideration of the nature of the information contained in living systems and present at many levels, together with the high-level information management functions detectable in living organisms, make plausible a design inference – that there is a cosmic Mind behind the universe. We also discuss the idea that information is a fundamental and irreducible immaterial quantity in its own right, preceding and not derived from mass/energy. We show how this resonates profoundly with biblical teaching on the nature of the Creator as the Word – a fact that, as we shall see, some scientists, like physicist John Wheeler, have even mentioned in their technical papers.

I take courage from that to explore further insights that may be gained from some of the biblical texts on origins. We noticed earlier that Genesis was speaking of a beginning to the universe millennia before science got there. Noticing that the stages of creation mentioned in Genesis are prefaced by the statement: 'And God said...' we consider whether they might just hint at the existence of a small number other singularities – in the sense of discrete inputs of information/energy from outside the open system that is the universe – in addition to the Big Bang, namely, for instance, at the origin of the various types of life – vegetation, sea, bird and animal life, and, finally human life.

We conclude with a list of the principal grounds on which a design inference might be made.

Information and the design argument

One of the main contentions of this book is that the existence of complex specified (language-like) information that is found in the genetic structure of all living things provides a formidable challenge to the notion that unguided natural processes can account for life. It makes *scientifically plausible* the suggestion that an intelligent source was ultimately responsible for life's origin. Such an inference to intelligent causation, based on the specific language-like/database character of DNA, is not simply an argument from analogy. Many classical design arguments were of that kind. In them, an attempt was made to reason back from similar effects to similar causes, so that the validity of the arguments often turned on the degree of similarity between the two situations being compared.

This circumstance was famously discussed by David Hume in his criticism of design arguments, as we have seen. But the design inference from DNA and the informational content and processing capabilities of living organisms is much stronger than its classical predecessors for the following reason, given by Stephen Meyer: 'DNA does not imply the need for an intelligent designer because it has some similarities to a software program or to a human language. It implies the need for an intelligent designer because... it possesses an identical feature (namely, information content) that intelligently designed human texts and computer languages possess.'[1] Yockey says essentially the same: 'It is important to understand that we are not reasoning by analogy. The sequence hypothesis (that the genetic code works essentially like a book) applies directly to the protein and the genetic text as well as to written language and therefore the treatment is mathematically identical.'[2]

When we say that a program needs an intelligent programmer we are not, therefore, arguing from analogy, but making an inference to the best explanation. And, as any detective knows, causes that we know are capable of producing an observed effect are a much better explanation for that effect than causes that we do not know are capable of producing any such effect and, *a fortiori*, causes that we know are not capable of doing so. Mathematician William Dembski's work, *The Design Inference*,[3] is devoted to explicating the exact nature of the kind of design inferences that we make from our experience with information-rich systems such as languages, codes, computers, machines, etc. Such design inferences are actually quite widespread in science. A few small marks on a flint are enough to tell an archaeologist that he is dealing with an artefact, and not just a piece of weathered stone. Inferences to intelligent agency are made as a matter of routine in disciplines such as archaeology, cryptography, computer science, and forensic medicine.

The search for extra-terrestrial intelligence and its implications

In recent years even natural science has shown itself prepared to make such design inferences in connection with intelligent causation, notably in the Search for Extra-Terrestrial Intelligence (SETI). The North American Space Administration, NASA, has spent millions of dollars setting up radio-telescopes monitoring millions of channels, in the hope of detecting a message containing information from intelligent beings somewhere else in the cosmos.[4]

Though some scientists regard SETI with scepticism, it clearly raises a fundamental question as to the precise scientific status of the detection of information arising from intelligence. How does one *scientifically* recognize a message emanating from an intelligent source, and distinguish it from the random background noise that emanates from the cosmos? Clearly, the only way this can be done is to compare the signals received with patterns specified in advance that are deemed to be clear and reliable indicators of intelligence, like a long sequence of prime numbers, and then to make a design inference. How much more would ETI be inferred if the complete code for Windows 10 or the blueprint for a PC were picked up in a signal from outer space. In SETI the recognition of intelligent agency is regarded as lying within the legitimate scope of natural science and can be done. The astronomer Carl Sagan thought that a single message from space would be enough to convince us that there were intelligences in the universe other than our own.

But there is a further crucial observation to be made. If we are prepared to look for scientific evidence of intelligent activity beyond our planet, why are we so hesitant about applying exactly the same thinking to what is on our planet? There seems here to be a glaring inconsistency which brings us to the nub of the question we referred to in the introduction: Is the attribution of intelligent design to the universe science? At one level, it certainly is as scientists seem quite relaxed about including forensic medicine and SETI in the realm of science. Why, then, the furore when some scientists claim that there is scientific evidence of intelligent causation in physics (small furore) or biology (large furore)? There is surely no difference in principle. Is the scientific method not applicable everywhere? And, in any case. SETI assumes the existence of ETI.

What, then, should we deduce from the vast amount of information that is contained in even the simplest living system – in a single cell, for example? Does that not give far stronger evidence of intelligent causation than did the argument from the fine-tuning of the universe, an argument which, as we have seen, convinces many physicists that we humans are meant to be here? Could it not be the real evidence of extra-terrestrial intelligence?

At the public announcement of the completion of the Human Genome Project, its director, Francis Collins, said: 'It is humbling for me and awe-inspiring to realize that we have caught the first glimpse of our own instruction book, previously known only to God.' Gene Myers, a computer scientist who worked on the genome mapping at the Maryland headquarters of Celera Genomics, said: 'We're deliciously complex at the molecular level.... We don't understand ourselves yet, which is cool. There's still a metaphysical, magical element.... What really astounds me is the architecture of life... the system is extremely complex. It's like it was designed.... There's a *huge intelligence* there. *I don't see that as being unscientific*. Others may, but not me' (my italics).

Considerations of this kind have been instrumental in altering the worldview of some eminent thinkers. Eminent observational cosmologist Allan Sandage, whom we mentioned earlier, discussing his conversion to Christianity at the age of fifty, said: 'The world is too complicated in all its parts and interconnections to be due to chance alone. I am convinced that the existence of life with all its order in each of its organisms is simply too well put together.'[5] And philosopher Anthony Flew, a world authority on David Hume, gave as the reason for his conversion to theism after over fifty years of atheism that biologists' investigation of DNA 'has shown, by the almost unbelievable complexity of the arrangements which are needed to produce life, that intelligence must have been involved'.[6]

Information as a fundamental quantity

Over recent years we have seen that physics is increasingly entertaining the hypothesis that information and intelligence are fundamental to the existence of the universe and life, and, far from being the end products of an unguided natural process starting with energy and matter, they were involved from the very beginning. Indeed, they may have been the very beginning. In an article in the *New Scientist*,[7] under the intriguing title 'In the beginning was the bit', there is an account by Hans Christian von Baeyer of the work of University of Vienna physicist Anton Zeilinger. Zeilinger, who is famous for his study of teleportation, advances the thesis that, in order to understand quantum mechanics, one has to start by associating information (in terms of bits) with so-called elementary systems in quantum mechanics which, like the spin of an electron, 'carry' one bit of information (there are only two possible outcomes from measuring spin – 'up' or 'down'). Zeilinger argues that his basic principle gains credibility by leading directly to three pillars of quantum theory – quantization itself, uncertainty, and quantum entanglement. This proposal, *that information be regarded as a fundamental quantity*, has profound implications for our understanding of the universe. It adds its weight to the design inference.

This is not a new idea. According to Paul Davies, it was first proposed in 1989 by the distinguished American physicist John Archibald Wheeler who was involved in the Manhattan Project. Wheeler said: 'Tomorrow, we will have learned to understand all of physics in the language of information.' It was he who coined the phrase 'It from bit'. He realized that the idea had been around since the first century. Just like the idea that the universe had a beginning, the notion that word plays a vital part in nature is several thousand years old – whereas science has only just recently got to them.

Wheeler is cited in the work of physicist Rolf Landauer who says that Wheeler,

> has a second and more significant relation to this discussion. Our scientific culture normally views the laws of physics as predating the actual physical universe. The laws are considered to be like a control program in a modern chemical plant; the plant is turned on after the program is installed. 'In the beginning was the Word and the Word was with God, and the Word was God' (John 1,1), attests to this belief. Word is a translation from the Greek Logos 'thought of as constituting the controlling principle of the universe'.[8]

The Greek term for 'Word' here is *Logos*, a term that was used by Stoic philosophers for the rational principle behind the universe and subsequently invested with additional meaning by Christians, who used it to describe the second person of the Trinity. The term 'Word' itself conveys to us notions of command, meaning, code, communication – thus information; as well as the creative power needed to realize what was specified by that information. The Word, therefore, is more fundamental than mass-energy. Mass-energy belongs to the category of the created. The Word does not. To Wheeler, 'Word' suggested a computer program that contains information. It certainly is at least that.

It is fascinating to note that the discoverer of the nucleic acids, the stereochemist Friedrich Miescher, at the end of the nineteenth century, had a profound insight into the language-like structures in genetic material. He wrote to colleague Wilhelm His: 'the many asymmetric carbon atoms offer such a colossal number of possible stereoisomers that all the richness and all the variety of heredity could just as well find its expression in them as do the worlds and concepts of all languages in the 24–30 letters of the alphabet.'[9] Philosopher Hans Blumenberg commenting on Mieschner' work said that it indicated that living organisms did not behave like clockwork (*Uhrwerk*) but like speechwork (*Sprachwerk*).[10] Exactly the sentiment of John 1:1. I find it very encouraging that both Wheeler and Landauer were prepared to quote this ancient text in an academic context. This is entirely in keeping with what Denis Noble did by citing a Buddhist text, *The Oxherder*, in his book *The Music of Life*.

Wheeler, Landauer, and Noble have taken insights from literary sources, which, as Noble says, 'might raise some of his readers' eyebrows'. I shall take courage from them to do the same thing myself in the next chapter on the basis of Noble's principle that: 'One can appreciate an insight from wherever it might come, whether or not one agrees with the rest of the package in which the insight can be found.'[11] My objective here is to demonstrate that science has not buried God, and no more. In order to do that I shall only refer to biblical ideas that seem relevant to that endeavour.

One of the most striking of these is that at the heart of the biblical analysis of creation, often so cavalierly, dismissed, we find the scientifically fundamental concept of information. In addition, the creation narrative was understood by the pioneers of modern science to carry the implication that the universe was contingent. That is, God could have created it any way he wished, so that if we want to understand it, we need to go and look (science), rather than impose some metaphysical prior ideology of how we think it ought to be, as was earlier the habit of Aristotle and others. Descartes (1590–1650) put it this way:

> We cannot determine by reason how big these pieces of matter are, how quickly they move or what circles they describe. God might have arranged these things in countless different ways; which way he chose rather than the rest we must find learn by observation. Therefore, we are free to make any assumptions we like about them, as long as all the consequences agree with experience.[12]

We also find in the Genesis account of creation that God instructed humans to name the animals.[13] That is the essence of biology. Naming things, or, in technical language, taxonomy, is a fundamental intellectual discipline. It brings an extra dimension into every area. The night sky becomes much more interesting when we can name the planets, stars, and galaxies – as does the living world when we can name the fish, plants, animals, and birds that we find around us. We have here a biblical mandate for doing science that is confirmed by the words from Psalm 111 verse 2 that Scottish physicist James Clerk Maxwell had engraved over the door in the old Cavendish Physics Laboratory in Cambridge: '*Magna opera Domini exquisita in omnes voluntates ejus*'. At the instigation of a then PhD student, Andrew Briggs, now Professor of Nanomaterials at Oxford, it was put up at the entrance of the new Cavendish Laboratory, this time, in English: 'The works of the Lord are great; sought out of all them that have pleasure therein'.

The pro-science thrust of these biblical texts leads me to think that there may well be more to be found in them that is of relevance to our present topic. Let me at once make clear that, like Denis Noble, I am not expecting that the reader will necessarily buy into any particular religious package. That is not my purpose. Nor, of course, am I suggesting that Genesis is a 'textbook of science'.

I might, however, just be hoping that the reader is aware of the work of historian and philosopher of science, Peter Harrison FAHA, once holder of the Chair in Science and Religion at Oxford, now an Australian Laureate Fellow and Director of the Institute for Advanced Studies in the Humanities at the University of Queensland, Australia. Harrison has refined the thesis that there is a close causal connection between the

Judaeo-Christian worldview and the rise of modern science. He argues
that a further contributing factor to the rise of science in the sixteenth and
seventeenth centuries was the methodology the Reformers developed in
their study of Scripture. The blurb's description of his seminal work *The
Bible, Protestantism and the Rise of Natural Science* says that Harrison shows
that: 'The rise of modern science is linked to the Protestant approach to
texts, an approach that spelled an end to the symbolic world of the Middle
Ages, and established the conditions for the scientific investigation and
technological exploitation of nature.'[14]

For all of these reasons, I would suggest that it may well be worthwhile
setting aside any prejudice and carefully reading what the biblical texts
have to say about the origin and structure of the physical universe. I am,
of course, aware that, unfortunately, much prejudice has been generated
against doing so because the text of Genesis has often been treated in an
off-putting manner insensitive to language, culture, genre, grammar, and
metaphor.[15] The religious text that Denis Noble cites in his book *The Music
of Life* is a Zen text, *The Oxherder*; it is one that he regards as least overlaid
with metaphysics, so that it can speak to a secular society. It talks about
down to earth things like plants, water, animals, and birds, sun and sky.
The text I wish now to cite is similarly down to earth and also speaks of
the very same familiar things, and they, it should be noticed, are things and
processes that are also of interest to science. It is the text with which the
book of Genesis begins:

> In the beginning God created the heavens and the
> earth. Now the earth was formless and empty, darkness
> was over the surface of the deep, and the Spirit of God
> was hovering over the waters. And God said, 'Let there
> be light,' and there was light. God saw that the light
> was good, and he separated the light from the darkness.
> God called the light 'day,' and the darkness he called
> 'night.' And there was evening, and there was morning –
> the first day.[16]

I encourage you to read the entire chapter at this point.

These majestic words form the introduction to the most translated,
most printed, and most read book in history. I can well remember the
profound effect they had on me on Christmas Eve, 1968, as a student at

Cambridge University, when I heard them read to the watching world on live television by the crew of Apollo 8 as they orbited the moon. The context was a triumphant achievement of science and technology that caught the imagination of millions. To celebrate that success the astronauts chose to read a text that needed no added explanation or qualification, even though it was written millennia ago. The biblical announcement of the fact of creation was as timelessly clear as it was magnificently appropriate.[17]

The literary shape of the whole passage is clear. It divides into three parts. There is an opening section (verses 1–2), followed by a sequence framework of six 'days'[18] of creative activity (verses 3–31), with a sabbath day of rest at the end (2:1–3) The creation activity is thus cast in the form of the human working week.

One of the remarkable things here, as scholars have pointed out, is that the text bears no trace of mythology. For instance the sun and moon are simply sources of light, not gods.[19] This is exceptional for a document of such antiquity from the Ancient Near East and supports a clear monotheism as distinct from the polytheism of contemporary surrounding cultures.

We notice next that in the middle part each day or stage in God's activity is introduced by the phrase: 'And God said...' and each of the first six concludes with the phrase: 'And there was evening and morning, the n day'. By this device creation is portrayed not as a single but as a sequence of speech acts, starting with the creation of the universe and reaching its conclusion with God making human beings in his image.

This narrative contrasts with that of *The Oxherder*. The latter is geared to encouraging a process of meditation to subdue the mind and achieve self-detachment and, presumably, become one with an impersonal universe. The former describes a process, a sequence of steps that lead to the creation of beings whose self-identity is to be found in a personal Creator who is distinct from the universe and whose image the humans bear.

Understanding Genesis here is facilitated by looking more closely at the particular New Testament text to which Wheeler referred:

> In the beginning was the Word, and the Word was with God, and the Word was God. He was with God in the beginning. Through him all things were made; without him nothing was made that has been made. In him was life, and the life was the light of all mankind. The

a Word-based universe.

light shines in the darkness, and the darkness has not overcome it.[20]

Here, as in Genesis, we are told that there was a beginning. Next, we read that in the beginning the Word already was. This is an *existence* statement and means that God the Word is eternal. He never *came* to exist. That paves the way for a contrasting existence statement that only becomes evident when we translate the Greek text of the next phrase more accurately. 'All things *came to be* through him and without him nothing *came to be* that *came to be*.' Of course, it carries with it the fact that all things were *made* by him, but the nuanced emphasis is on coming to exist.

The Greeks understood as well as we do that many things, including ourselves, came to be. A question that interested them was whether there existed anything that never came to be, the universe itself, for instance? The point made by John, therefore, is that God the Creator has existed eternally but the universe came to exist and is therefore certainly of finite age.

Using the term 'Word' to describe God, taken together with the idea that God speaks the universe into existence – the origin of life, for instance – resonated with Wheeler as it does with me because of what has become more and more apparent throughout this book – the central role played by 'word' in the shape of information at all levels in the sciences: physics, chemistry, bio-informatics, and computer science. When we make things, especially complex things like cars or computers or houses, we first draw up descriptions, plans – these things exist first as information before they are actualized.

In that sense, as we are increasingly learning, this is a word-based universe. What is surprising to many people is that the idea is to be found in the Bible.

I vividly recall a conversation that took place when I was working in the Mathematics Institute in the University of Wales in Cardiff. One of my colleagues there was the astrophysicist and astrobiologist Professor Chandra Wickramasinghe, who did his research under, and subsequently collaborated with, the distinguished astrophysicist Sir Fred Hoyle. On one occasion Wickramasinghe was called to give expert evidence before a judge at one of the 'creation trials' in the USA.

When he returned he called me in to his office to tell me about it. He was full of praise for the hospitality he had been shown but was disturbed to find that many of the people he met took the Bible so seriously and naïvely. I replied that I took also took it seriously also – but not naïvely. 'Surely you're not one of them,' was the reply. 'Here, why don't you show me?' As he said that he threw me a piece of chalk and gestured towards his blackboard. I wrote: 'And God said, "Let there be light"'. He roared with laughter and retorted: 'You are one of them! How can you be so naïve? Has God got a voice box and lungs, like we have?' I said: 'Now it is you who are being naïve. This is simple language, involving the metaphor of human speech, but, as is usual with metaphor, it is conveying a reality at a higher level. It is saying that there is a God and that he can and does communicate intelligibly in a way that is far superior to our speech in that it is not only informational but also creative. When I say: 'Let there be light', nothing happens! Let me put it another way for you.'

I then wrote once more on his board: 'In the beginning was the Word… and the Word was God… all things came to be through him.' He asked what it meant. I replied that the Greek for 'word' is 'logos' which conveys a wide spectrum of ideas including command, logic, reason, instruction, information… He stopped me: 'Did you say information? Are you telling me that the idea of information is to be found in the Bible?' 'It very much looks like it,' I replied. 'Well,' he said, 'if that is the case I need to change my view of the Bible. Does Fred Hoyle know about this?'

Hoyle subsequently visited Cardiff on which occasion, so far as I recall, he gave his memorable lecture in which he said that he had done the mathematics to show that biogenesis could not have happened on earth in the time that was available, so that he now thought that life must have come from outer space, carried on asteroid-like rocks. Wickramasinghe invited me to meet him. He was interested in what I had to say about information and said: 'I was not aware that this was to be found in the Bible. I thought it only went back to Shakespeare.' Sadly, I never got the opportunity to pursue it with him again.

I can imagine that some readers may be starting to wonder why I am bothering to enlist support from ancient texts, since, as we have already seen, the concept of information has already turned out to be extremely fruitful in science. I would ask them please to be patient since there are several aspects of those texts that I think provide stimulus for further exploration.

Extra singularities?

In the Genesis creation account the phrase 'And God said...' punctuates the narrative at discrete intervals. It occurs ten times, eight of which are concerned with the appearance of something new:

1. the origin of light
2. the origin of the expanse (sky) between the waters
3. the origin of the separation of sea and land
4. the origin of life – plants
5. the (origin or visibility?) of sun, moon and stars to rule day and night;
6. the origin of fish and sea creatures and birds
7. the origin of animals
8. the origin of human beings.

This is a fascinating presentation of creation as a finite sequence of speech acts, in each of which the Creator, after setting the universe going, subsequently intervened from time to time to insert a new level of creative information. It is quite striking how very *few* such discrete creation acts or events are postulated. This is not to be construed as semi-deism. Deism is the view that God starts the universe off and leaves it to its own devices. Semi-deism holds that God started the universe off and occasionally intervenes thereafter, but is not otherwise involved. However, the biblical view is that not only does God create by his word, he also 'upholds the universe by the word of his power.'[21] God is immanent in his creation at every point, supervising and guiding it towards its goal but is not to be thought of as a micro-manager, creating every species separately by constant intervention.

In fact, the narrative itself shows that is not the case. Take, for instance, the initial mention of life, where we read: 'Let the earth sprout vegetation, plants yielding seed, and fruit trees bearing fruit....' And: 'Let the waters swarm with swarms of living creatures and let birds fly above the earth....' Far from suggesting that God got involved in creating every species separately – 'Let there be a whale', 'Let there be a giraffe', 'Let there be a kingfisher', ... – there are only two commands here, each of which arguably refers to a direct injection of new information and, presumably, creative energy that triggers a new level of the world. That input seems,

The effort by some is to replace (?) total divine miracles by Darwinian miracles (?)

therefore, to be an instance of direct causation. Its content subsequently unfolds by processes at a secondary level of causation until the next input.

An interesting sidelight on the oft-repeated idea of the 'tinkering' God doing endless miracles to create each species separately was given in an interview by the French mathematician Marcel-Paul Schützenberger. He accused the modern synthesis of doing essentially the same thing by believing in 'Darwinian miracles', that is, events that should be ruled out by a Darwinian perspective in view of their improbability. He points out that to fit an elephant's trunk – presumably onto some 'proto-elephant' – it is not enough to fit a trunk but the elephant's brain needs modifying to wire up to the trunk and to do that:

> These macromutations must be coordinated by a system of genes in embryogenesis. If one considers the history of evolution, we must postulate thousands of miracles; miracles, in fact, without end.
>
> No more than the gradualists, the saltationists[22] are unable to provide an account of those miracles. The second category of miracles are directional, offering instruction to the great evolutionary progressions and trends – the elaboration of the nervous system, of course, but the internalization of the reproductive process as well, and the appearance of bone, the emergence of ears, the enrichment of various functional relationships, and so on.

He points out that there are several series of miracle here directed towards increasing the complexity and efficiency of various organisms and concludes that the notion of bricolage (tinkering), introduced by French biologist Nobel laureate Francois Jacob, sounds good but is completely bereft of explanatory power.

Clearly, replacing divine miracles that might be credible by a plethora of Darwinian miracles that are not credible is not likely to enhance the discussion!

Back, then, to those discrete direct insertions of creative information from outside the system. What, then, shall we make of them? Their effect would be that, to any purely naturalistically based science, they would appear as singularities, similar to the Big Bang creation event which appears to cosmologists as a singularity, a place where the laws of physics break down. What is more, they readily accept the Big Bang as a singularity which, incidentally, has not had a 'science stopper' effect of discouraging them from asking questions and carrying on with their research to understand the origin of the universe better.

What I wish to suggest is that there may be a few singularities *additional* to the Big Bang that scientists could look for, were they so inclined. The main ones could be the origins of the various types of life including that of plants, fish, birds, animals, and humans. The careful reader of Genesis will notice that on two of the days God is said to speak more than once: day 3 and day 6. On day 3, the phrase 'And God said...' marks the transition from non-life to life, that is, from the inorganic to the organic. On Day 6, the phrase marks the transition from animals to humans. I find this intriguing: it is almost as if the ancient writer sensed that these would one day be hot topics! Thus, we have at least three major singularities: at the origin of the universe, at the origin of life, and at the origin of human life.

The inputs we are speaking of are informational, and, most likely, also energetic, since information does not create on its own, as we have seen with DNA. That would mean that scientists might be able to discover informational/energetic and possibly other kinds of discontinuity at these 'transition' events. In one sense this would be nothing new. SETI, the Search for Extra-Terrestrial Intelligence, is an obvious example since it focuses on distinguishing between singular information-bearing signals from space and random radio noise.

In any case, as we have already seen, biology has already gone a long way towards pin-pointing informational discontinuity, or, discontinuities, in connection with the origin and evolution of life. These discontinuities are confirmed particularly convincingly by the failure of the physical reductionism characteristic of the modern synthesis to cope with the language-like complexity of digital information bearing macromolecules like DNA. They are also confirmed by discontinuities in the fossil record as at the Cambrian Explosion.

To see just how science has moved on in the past twenty years in this regard, we cite a statement by Paul Davies made in 2000: 'biologically relevant macromolecules simultaneously possess two vital properties: randomness and extreme specificity. A chaotic process could possibly achieve the former property but would have a negligible probability of achieving the latter. At first sight *this appears to make the genome an impossible object* [my italics], unattainable by either known laws or chance.' Quite so.

[handwritten annotation at top: physical reductionism cannot account for the existence of words, language, encoded information]

Nevertheless Davies continues: 'But this conclusion is too hasty. Clearly Darwinian evolution by variation and natural selection has what is needed to generate both randomness (information richness) and tightly specified biological functionality in the same system.'[23]

Even for the time when he wrote it, it is an astonishing statement. For, it is difficult to see how Davies could have thought that natural selection and mutation have that capacity since his own argument at this point indicates that they do not? For, he continues: 'The problem as far as biogenesis is concerned is that Darwinism can only operate when life (of some sort) is already going. *It cannot explain how life starts in the first place*' (my italics).[24]

Long before that, even, in 1983, theologian and biochemist Arthur Peacocke wrote: 'In no way can the concept of "information", the concept of conveying a message, be articulated in terms of the concepts of physics and chemistry, even though the latter can be shown to explain how the molecular machinery (DNA, RNA and protein) operates to carry information.'[25] In a similar vein Nobel laureate Roger Sperry said that: 'The laws of biophysics and biochemistry are not adequate to account for the cognitive sequencing of a train of thought.'[26] Quite so. Two dimensions are not enough to grasp extended solids. Or to put it more picturesquely in the inimitable language of the 1884 satire *Flatland* by William Abbott, epistemology is not adequate for Spaceland ontology.

That insight has been solidly confirmed by the more recent uncovering of higher levels of complexity than were dreamed of in the heyday of the neo-Darwinian modern synthesis. As we saw in Chapter 19, research in the burgeoning fields of systems biology, and epigenetics shows the prevalence of top-down causation and control systems involving sophisticated feedback mechanisms, where activity at the higher levels cannot be described in the language of the lower levels.

[handwritten annotation in right margin: Key]

Is information physical?

It is no accident that the central issue here can be expressed by saying that physical reductionism cannot deal with a semantic dimension: words, language, and encoded information. And, if I may suggest it, another clear reason for that is flagged up by a further biblical passage. In a famous statement about faith the author of the letter to the Hebrews says: 'By faith we understand that the universe was created by the word of God, so that what is seen was not made out of things that are visible' (11:3, ESV). The writer here claims that, since the universe was created by the Word of God, what we see – the visible universe – was not made out of things that are visible. Does he mean that it is made out of 'invisible things' – like dark matter? Or, is he saying something else? Recall that John, the author of the fourth Gospel, says that God the Word never came to be but is eternal. This means that the Word is not material, since the same text also says that material things all came to be. The implication for cosmology is that the universe came to be from nothing *physical*, but it did not come from nothing as is so often alleged. God is not physical, he is not material but he is not nothing. God is spirit.[27] By saying that the universe was not made out of visible things might the letter to the Hebrews be indicating that creative information is not material? Whether Hebrews is or is not doing this, it serves to remind us of that fact: information is immaterial.

There is some confusion about this issue stemming from a famous paper that exists in two versions with different titles, the first of which asserts the contrary to what I have just said. It is 'Information is Physical'. The second title is a little more ambiguous: 'The Physical Nature of Information'. It was written by the late German-American physicist Rolf Landauer, cited above, who worked, among other things, on the thermodynamics of information. His view was that: 'Information is not a disembodied abstract entity; it is always tied to a physical representation.'[28] However, this does not necessarily mean that information itself is physical, as the title of Landauer's paper, seems to imply. This misunderstanding has led to a great deal of unnecessary confusion that might have been avoided by careful attention to his opening statement: 'Information is inevitably tied to a physical representation and therefore to restrictions and possibilities related to the laws of physics and the parts available in the universe.'

Oxford philosopher C. G. Timpson, commenting on Landauer's work, writes:

> Pieces of information, whether every day, classical or quantum, are abstract items; while information as a quantity... is a property, so by no means a concrete thing. Yes, to have a token of a piece of information, or to write down or record an everyday item of information, one will need some physical systems, but that doesn't make what is encoded, stored, written down... physical.[29]

The carriers of information may well be visible – like paper and writing, smoke-signals, television screens, or DNA – but the information itself is not only invisible, it is immaterial. You are reading this book; photons bounce off the book and are received by your eye, converted into electrical impulses, and transmitted to your brain. Suppose you pass on some information from this book to a friend by word of mouth. The sound waves carry the information from your mouth to your friend's ear, from where they are converted into electrical impulses and transmitted into his brain. Your friend now has the information that originated in your mind, but nothing material has passed from you to your friend. The *carriers* of the information have been material, *but the information itself is not*.

The importance of this is that it deals a death blow to the idea that *physical* reductionism will solve the problem of the origin of life. The semiotics of words on a page cannot be reduced to the physics and chemistry or self-organization of the paper and ink on and with which they are written. By the same token mind, without which information cannot be recognized as such, cannot be reduced to matter. To contradict Marshall McLuhan, the medium is not the message. This serves to highlight what we have already explored to a certain extent – the central role of information in our understanding of life. The 2017 book *From Matter to Life* by Sara Walker, Paul Davies, and George Ellis is devoted to the idea that information might hold the key to unravelling life's mysteries – its nature and origin. The subtitle of the book is: *Information and Causality* which immediately recalls the 'Word' as being causally responsible for creation.

The introductory statement in the book is: 'The concept of information has penetrated almost all areas of human inquiry, from physics, chemistry and engineering through biology to the social sciences. And yet its status as a physical entity remains obscure.'[30] It is not clear whether this obscurity concerns whether information is physical or not, or whether it is the nature of its physicality that is obscure. The authors continue to say:

> Because bits of information are always instantiated in material degrees of freedom, the properties of information could, it seems, always be reduced to those of the material substrate. Nevertheless, over several decades there have been attempts to invert this interdependence and root reality in information rather than matter. This contrarian perspective is most famously associated with the name

of John Archibald Wheeler whom we have already mentioned. He famously encapsulated his proposal in the pithy dictum 'it from bit'.[31]

By that, we would add, Wheeler meant that all things physical are information-theoretic in origin. 'It from bit' means that

> every particle, every field of force, even the space-time continuum itself — derives its function, its meaning, its very existence entirely — even if in some contexts indirectly — from the apparatus-elicited answers to yes-or-no questions, binary choices, bits. It from bit symbolizes the idea that every item of the physical world has at bottom ... an immaterial source and explanation; that which we call reality arises in the last analysis from the posing of yes-no questions and the registering of equipment-evoked responses; in short, that all things physical are information-theoretic in origin and that this is a *participatory universe*.[32]

In light of this, going back to the initial statement in *From Matter to Life*, one might ask: To whom does it seem that the properties of information are reducible to those of the physical substrate? For that is not in actual fact correct as has been shown by the work of Noble and others. The second part of that initial statement turns the usual explanatory paradigm on its head in saying that information may be primary and matter derivative, which is exactly in line with Wheeler's claim and with the statement he quoted from John 1:1 written 2,000 years earlier. Wheeler clearly understood the notion that matter came to exist through the Word ('program'). Indeed, he once said that the universe appeared to be more like the expression of an idea than a physical thing. This would seem to be another example of science catching up with something that has been in ancient literature for centuries. It is noteworthy that Gregory Chaitin, mathematician and originator of algorithmic information theory expressed the same idea: 'What if information is primary and matter/energy is a secondary phenomenon?'[33]

The key idea here is that Word is primary, matter is derivative. The Word has causal power and is not to be thought of merely as passive information: it caused matter to exist. Therefore, the Word is more than information – it is the Agent that used the information. Not only that, Word caused mind to exist which gives validation to and an intelligible explanation of the existence of our mental capacities in strong contrast, as Thomas Nagel says, to that of reductionist explanation via natural processes: 'Evolutionary naturalism provides an account of our capacities that undermines their reliability and in doing so undermines itself.'[34]

Now comes my radical suggestion. I think the time has come to accept both the existence of an 'information first' universe and of additional historical informational singularities – at least at the origin of life and the origin of human consciousness. However, information first essentially implies consciousness first – not, of course, human consciousness, but the consciousness of the Mind of God. Perhaps we should re-calibrate and say, with Nobel laureate for physics, Max Planck (1858–1947): 'I regard consciousness as fundamental. I regard matter as derivative from consciousness.'

As an Irishman myself, I would also like to quote Irish physicist John Bell (1928–90), known especially for Bell's theorem. He wrote: 'As regards mind, I am fully convinced that it has a central place in the ultimate nature of reality.' For many, this will probably, at least initially, seem a step too far. But think about it. The research that has been done on the structure and function of the myriad molecular machines in the cell and on its information-processing capabilities have all been done on the assumption of apparent design. It would have made no difference if that research had been done on the assumption of real design triggered by (a series of) discrete singular informational inputs. Exactly the same can be said for work on epigenetics and systems biology.

The reductionism of the modern synthesis acted as a brake on research, excluding, as it did, essentially anything but bottom-up determinism. In physics, however, such determinism was dealt a death blow by Heisenberg's discovery of the uncertainty principle in quantum mechanics. However, the undermining of determinism in biology has taken a great deal longer. Real progress there was only made when pioneers like Denis Noble, Gerd Müller, James Shapiro, and others broke the mould and opened their minds to the hitherto unknown world of top-down causation.

I found listening to the talks at the 2016 Royal Society meeting and reading the publications of those involved immensely stimulating. However, I must confess that I was left with a feeling that I was listening to a radio that was not quite tuned in, or seeing a picture that was not quite in focus. I sensed that there was a problem, somewhat like the one encountered by the Hubble Telescope in its early days. Astronomers at the time could see enough to indicate that wonders would be discovered if only we could get the focus sharp. They were right.

I think that the ingredient missing at the Royal Society meeting, the key to sharpening the focus, would be a recognition that we really are in a word-based universe, because there is an eternal Word who caused it and holds it together. Failure to do so will, I think, forever leave the barrier between the non-living and the living insuperable. Chemist Marcos Eberlin experienced a similar reaction to mine. He felt that the explanations he was hearing lacked what is: 'the secret sauce in every engineering success – foresight, ingenuity and planning.'[35] After all, as scientists our work presupposes the rational intelligibility of the universe. I would like to remind you of part of a Keith Ward quotation I used in Chapter 4:

> To the majority of those who have reflected deeply and written about the origin and nature of the universe, it has seemed that it points beyond itself to a source which is non-physical and of great intelligence and power... They had different specific ideas of this reality, and different ways of approaching it; but that the universe is not self-explanatory, and that it requires some explanation beyond itself, was something they accepted as fairly obvious.[36]

Is there any real reason not to join them and accept that the biosphere looks designed because it really was designed; that there exists an even higher level of intelligent causation than the cell or the complete organism; that the entire biosphere is the product of and is held in existence by an overarching immaterial creative intelligence, the divine Word?

A research programme

Taking this radical approach is already stimulating much research. Firstly, research on the capacities of natural processes in the context of inorganic matter, for instance, the fascinating world of self-organization. It would be very interesting to find out how far self-organization can take us, whether there are recognizable boundaries to its reach, and, if so, how that might

Hypothesis – the universe is Word-based!

Top Down causation.

help us understand more precisely the difference between the non-living and the living. That might further lead to the development of methods of detecting the nature of the informational discontinuity between the two. Some of Lee Cronin's work in Glasgow University look very promising in this connection, as does that of biophysicists such as Professors Ard Louis in Oxford, Cees Dekker in Delft in the Netherlands, and James Tour at Rice, Texas.

Secondly, we shall surely see the ramping up of active research on systems biology, which has already revealed hitherto unimagined capacities of living organisms to change themselves by changing their genomes, sometimes very rapidly. It will be very exciting to find out about the creative genetic engineering potential of life itself – and whether it also has limits for a given level of organism complexity. Clearly those limits will be beyond the reach of the modern synthesis. But do they exist and therefore indicate that the next level is only reached by an external input of new 'software'?

I would dare to suggest another avenue of research alongside the above two. That is to develop experiments to test the hypothesis that the universe really is word-based and that there is overarching top-down causation in terms of the injection of information from outside what is an open system. This would involve working on the claim that the origin of life plus a few other events are singularities within history. Perhaps we already have enough evidence of this, but are reluctant to accept its consequences?

Yet, I am fully aware that there is still a lot of resistance to the idea of additional singularities. Physicist Paul Davies raises the God-of-the-gaps objection – the danger of using God as an explanation for (current) gaps in the scientific picture so that when science closes those gaps, God gets pushed out:

> Theologians long ago accepted that they would forever be fighting a rear-guard battle if they tried to challenge science on its own ground. Using the formation of life to prove the existence of God is a tactic that risks instant demolition, should someone succeed in making life in a test tube. And the idea that God acts in fits and starts, moving atoms around on odd occasions in competition with natural forces, is a decidedly uninspiring image of the Grand Architect.[37]

Well, such an image might well be uninspiring if it were true. But it isn't. For a start, if someone were to make life in a test tube that would simply prove that intelligence, human in this case, working on available materials, had created life. That would strengthen, not weaken the claim that it was divine intelligence that created life in the first place.

God of the gaps again:
Gaps of ignorance and gaps of principle ③

Davies' statement requires revisiting the God-of-the-gaps issue that we introduced in Chapter 6. To begin with I would underline that the inferences to an intelligent cause made in this book do not, so far as I can see, fall into the 'God-of-the-gaps' category. They are carefully based, not on ignorance of science but on knowledge of it. They are inferences to the best explanation. For instance, the supporters of the SETI programme would not find convincing the suggestion that postulating an alien intelligence as the source of an information-rich message that had been received, was tantamount to postulating an 'alien of the gaps'. No, they would regard their conclusions as scientifically valid inferences to the best explanation. And if the mathematical and information theoretical analysis is similar, would it not be consistent to postulate an intelligent source for the information-rich messages contained in DNA and not regard that as god of the gaps thinking?

The example of SETI can help us tease out at least part of the reason why it is that the impression of a god of the gaps argument is hard to dispel. It is this. Let us grant the validity of the hypothesis that underlies SETI, that is, that there exist scientific methods to recognize that a received signal has been transmitted by an intelligent source. Let us also assume that we have received such a signal. Then there remains an obvious gap in our knowledge – the identity of the intelligence involved. It does not lie at the level of the scientific determination that intelligence is involved. In other words, we are back with the same confusion about the nature of the 'intelligent design' hypothesis that we outlined in the preface.

Also, as we saw earlier, we find no difficulty whatsoever in inferring an intelligent author as the source of a piece of writing, since we know the futility, indeed absurdity, of attempting to give a reductionist explanation in terms of the physics and chemistry of paper and ink. We would never think of the author as an author of the gaps.

Key

Putting it another way, when it comes to fully explaining writing on paper, there is certainly a gap in the explanatory power of physics and chemistry. This is not a gap of ignorance, but a gap in principle; a *gap that is revealed by our knowledge, and not by our ignorance, of science*. And this is a hugely important consideration. I call a gap that is uncovered by science a gap in principle to distinguish it from gaps of ignorance that will eventually be closed by science. The failure to distinguish between them has led to a lot of rather superficial dismissal of gaps in principle as if they were gaps of ignorance.

Writing on paper or a painting on canvas exhibits what philosopher Del Ratzsch calls 'counterflow' – phenomena that nature, unaided by agent activity, could not produce. It is because we know that, even in principle, physics and chemistry cannot give an explanation of the counterflow exhibited by the writing, that we reject a purely naturalistic explanation, and we postulate an author. But it needs to be said that postulating an intelligent agent to explain writing is not falling into an 'author of the gaps' syndrome; rather it is our knowledge of the nature of the 'gap' that demands we postulate an author. Again, it is a valid inference to the best explanation – where, as always, there is the question of what 'best' means.

This idea of different kinds of gap is another way of expressing something I came across in my late teenage years when reading R. E. D. Clark's book *The Universe: Plan or Accident?* Unusually, Clark raises the question of gaps right at the beginning of his book, where he makes the point that: 'an important element in the scientific method is the focusing of attention on the things that science cannot explain, or has difficulty in explaining. In this way only can it be discovered whether known principles will cover all the facts or whether new principles remain to be discovered.'[38] In other words, science itself thrives in gaps and the scientist looks on them positively and not negatively – as opportunities to perhaps discover something radically new. He adds: 'No reasonable person is interested in gaps for their own sake. Christians of a former generation are sometimes ridiculed today for their outmoded belief in the "God of the gaps", but did they in fact, even in their wildest moments ever *really* argue that whatever could not be explained by science was due to God?'[39]

Similarly, it is (scientific) knowledge of the fact that chance and necessity cannot generate the kind of complex specified information that occurs in biology (see Chapters 10 and 11), together with knowledge that intelligent sources are the only known sources of that kind of information, that point to design as the best explanation for the existence of information-rich DNA and non-genomic information.

There is more than a whiff of suspicion that reluctance on the part of some scientists to make a design inference from the existence of information-rich biomolecules has much less to do with science than it has to do with the implications of the design inference as to the possible identity of the Designer. It is, therefore, a worldview issue, and not simply a scientific one. After all, if you will forgive the repetition, scientists seem to be perfectly happy to make scientific design inferences to human or even alien agency, so the difficulty certainly does not lie in our incapacity or reluctance to make design inferences as such.

It is at this point that some people begin to get very uneasy, atheists understandably so, since, *on principle*, they reject God's existence let alone his action. But such is the fear of being accused of God-of-the-gaps thinking that some theologians hold that nature has a sort of 'functional integrity', which means that the world is created but that it 'has no functional deficiencies, no gaps in its economy of the sort that would require God to act immediately' – that is, the universe, after creation, is essentially causally closed.[40] Thus it would appear that those holding this view are obliged to believe that at least all the information for producing all the complexity we see around us was front-loaded into the universe at the original creation and none has since been added from external sources.

However, John Polkinghorne, who emphatically rejects a god-of-the-(bad)-gaps theology, nevertheless insists that we must not 'rest content with a discussion in such soft-focus that it never begins to engage our intuitions about God's action with our knowledge of physical process'. His view is that 'if the physical world is really open, and top-down intentional causality operates within it, there must be intrinsic "gaps" ("an envelope of possibility") in the bottom-up account of nature to make room for intentional causality... We are unashamedly "people of the gaps" in this intrinsic sense and there is nothing unfitting in a "God of the gaps" in this sense either.' As to the nature of God's interaction, it is 'not energetic but informational'.[41] But why could it not be both? There is an important issue here. Clearly, if God has done some things directly, like create a universe, he is certainly responsible for some energetic action and interaction. After all, the law of conservation of energy tells us that energy is conserved. It does not tell us where that energy came from in the first place, something easily and often overlooked.

Granted that we should be careful not to fall into God-of-the-gaps of ignorance type-thinking, nevertheless, as Alvin Plantinga has pointed out, it is a matter of elementary logic that if there is a God who does anything in the world indirectly, he must ultimately do something directly. And, once we admit that God has acted directly at least once to bring the world into being, what is there to prevent him acting more than once, whether in the past or in the future? After all, the laws of the universe are not independent of God; they are (our) codifications of the regularities that He has built in to the universe. It would, therefore, be absurd to think that they constrained God so that he could never do anything special. Plantinga sums up: 'Could we not sensibly conclude, for example, that God created life, or human life, or something else specially? I do not say we *should* conclude that: I only suggest that we *could*, and should if that is what the evidence most strongly suggests.'[42] The crux of the matter is: Are we prepared to follow where the evidence leads – even if it points away from a purely naturalistic interpretation and, in effect, leads those who believe in it to abandon so-called methodological naturalism? **Conversion**

If there is a Creator, then we should find two things. Firstly, it should not surprise us if our attempts to understand the universe on naturalistic presuppositions are, *for the most part*, very successful[43] for the very simple reason that nature is there – and, incidentally, we did not put it there – whether or not we believe in a Creator.

Secondly, we are likely to find that there are relatively few gaps in principle that do not yield but rather become increasingly opaque, to any purely naturalistic methodology.[44] But those good gaps are of great significance as we can see by listing what they might be: the origin of the universe, its rational intelligibility, its fine-tuning; the origin of life; the origin of consciousness; and, finally, the origin of human life together with its rationality, concepts of truth, morality, and spirituality.

I believe that such gaps in principle are consistent with belief in a Creator in the sense that you would expect them on the hypothesis of theism. That does not mean by a long way that they are the *only* evidences that science provides for God's existence. They are *additional* to the main body of evidence that is provided by the wonder of creation as a whole. After all, serious Christian theology holds that God not only created the universe originally but also that he is constantly active in upholding it. Without him it would cease to exist. The bits of it we do understand in terms of physics and chemistry show us his glory quite independently from whatever we make of the bits we do not understand in such terms. That same theology holds that God has revealed himself in history at specific times and places.

The materialist will, by definition, reject *a priori* the possibility of the existence of 'good' gaps that point to the activity of a Creator.[45] For theists the situation is very different. They will believe, at the very least, that God caused the universe to exist and upholds it so that he is responsible for its natural processes. Then there arises the question of whether these processes are all simply to be regarded as indirectly or ultimately caused by God in that they occur in a universe for which he is ultimately responsible, or whether some of the processes or events that happen in the universe may involve some kind of direct action on God's part through which he introduces a 'software upgrade' by imparting new information to lift creation to a higher level and thus carry it further towards his purposes for it. This means that science done from a theistic perspective may be more open and therefore better than science done from an atheistic position.

Front-loading

This brings me once again to the issue of the front-loading of information. Materialistic reductionism demands it by definition, in the sense that all the ingredients needed for the subsequent evolution of the universe, life, and consciousness must have been present at the start. This view certainly has something going for it. For instance, cosmologists have shown us that all that was necessary for the formation of stars, galaxies, and planets seems to have been present at the beginning. The four fine-tuned fundamental forces of nature together with the laws of nature functioned together to produce what we see. This is already a considerable amount of front-loading, although, as we have seen, naturalism cannot deliver on the provenance of the laws of nature nor the cause of the universe's appearance from (whatever is meant by) 'nothing'.[46] Theism answers these questions by saying that 'In the beginning, God created the heavens and the earth.'

Here are several examples of scientists' who espouse front-loading. Arthur Peacocke (1924–2006), biochemist, theologian, and one-time Director of the Ian Ramsey Centre for Science and Religion in Oxford, thought that evolution was entirely consistent with an all-knowing, all-powerful God who exists throughout time, sets initial conditions and natural laws, and knows what the result will be. He thought of (neo-Darwinian) evolution as the continuous action of God in the world. Sir John Polkinghorne FRS holds a similar view: 'this is not just any old universe. Rather it is a universe which is a creation which has been endowed by its creator with just those finely tuned given laws and circumstances that will make its history fruitful. Our world and our lives are the fulfilment of a purpose.'[47]

They think that God originally endowed the universe with all the potential to 'make itself', as Charles Kingsley famously put it. Evolutionary processes did the rest without any further direct intervention by God. Denis Alexander, who has described himself as a 'Christian and a passionate Darwinian',[48] writing on the origin of life, uses an analogy to argue that it would be insulting to God to suggest that he has *not front-loaded* the universe with everything needed: 'Imagine going into an artist's studio ... and then telling the artist 'you've chosen the wrong type of paints, they're really hopeless!' I think we would all agree that would be insulting. But to confidently proclaim that the precious materials which God has brought into being in the dying moments of stars do not have the potentiality to bring about life seems to me equally insulting.'[49]

This is very unconvincing since the analogy does not correspond to the application. Firstly, I don't think anyone would imagine or say that the Creator's materials are 'the wrong type' or 'hopeless'. What I, and many others, would say is that it is not demeaning to say to the Creator that his good materials cannot bring life into existence without his additional direct intelligent input. This is no more an insult to God than it would be an insult to the artist to suggest that his paints are incapable of producing a masterpiece without his direct input. It is rather the (ludicrous) suggestion that the paints could do it on their own without him that would be a real insult! Furthermore, is it intellectually lazier to reject the idea that life is a product of the latent potential of matter and energy working according to the laws of nature, than it is to abandon the search for perpetual motion, or to attribute a magnificent painting to the creative genius of Leonardo da Vinci rather than to the latent physical and chemical capacities of paint and canvas?

That recalls Paul Davies' assertion cited a little earlier in this chapter that: 'the idea that God acts in fits and starts, moving atoms around on odd occasions in competition with natural forces, is a decidedly uninspiring image of the Grand Architect.'[50] Leonardo da Vinci can also help us here. Neither the mind nor information is a material substance. Leonardo's mind is the agency that used the information in it to cause the movement of the atoms in his hand that moved the atoms of the paintbrush that moved the atoms of paint that produced his masterpieces. None of those movements was in competition with natural forces. On the contrary, they involved natural forces directed by mind. And, since God moved atoms after creating them in order to launch the universe, it follows that Davies has got it completely wrong. It would be a very 'uninspiring image' of the Creator *not* to credit him with moving atoms at the origin of life. It would also be uninspiring to fail to credit the Creator with the creation of human beings in such a way – in his image – that their minds could move atoms too.

It seems to me, then, that there is a formidable barrier to the suggestion that everything necessary for the appearance of life was present at the origin of the universe. That barrier is the language-like information involved in all life, as distinct from non-life: DNA, genetics, epigenetics, systems biology, pathways in the cell, molecular machines, and a myriad other things. What would it mean for such information to be front-loaded in non-organic material? Our knowledge of inorganic chemistry would seem to rule out anything like this.

From a theistic perspective there seems little point in crediting God with doing something for which there is no positive evidence and a mountain of negative evidence. I suspect that the tenacity with which people refuse to face the negative evidence may well have to do with *a priori* worldview conviction that nature has been absolutely uniform from the Big Bang. I can understand naturalists sticking to this belief, but I have considerable difficulty in seeing why so many scientists who are Christians still cling to it, especially when, at the same time, they also willingly accept a whole cluster of discontinuities in the uniformity of nature associated with the incarnation, life, death, and resurrection of Christ.

James Shapiro asks a key question in light of all that we have been saying. He gives a very encouraging answer to it:

> What significance does an emerging interface between biology and information science hold for thinking about evolution? It opens up the possibility of addressing scientifically rather than ideologically the central issue so hotly contested by fundamentalists on both sides of the Creationist–Darwinist debate. Is there any guiding intelligence at work in the origin of species displaying exquisite adaptations that range from

lambda prophage repression and the Krebs cycle through the mitotic apparatus and the eye to the immune system, mimicry and social organization?'[51]

Biophysicist Dean Kenyon, co-author of a definitive textbook on the origin of life,[52] said that the more that has been learned in recent years about the chemical details of life, from molecular biology and origin-of-life studies, the less likely a strictly naturalistic explanation of origins becomes. Kenyon's studies led him to conclude that biological information had been designed:

Big question ?

> If science is based on experience, then science tells us that the message encoded in DNA must have originated from an intelligent cause. What kind of intelligent agent was it? On its own, science cannot answer this question; it must leave it to religion and philosophy. But that should not prevent science from acknowledging evidences for an intelligent cause origin wherever they may exist.[53]

The eminent entomologist E. O. Wilson thought that any scientist who could establish intelligent design within the accepted paradigm and thus prove that science and religion are compatible would achieve eternal fame, recognition for which would not be adequately expressed by combining a Nobel with a Templeton Prize: 'Every scientist would like to accomplish such an epoch-making advance. But no one has even come close, because unfortunately there is no evidence, no theory and no criteria for proof that even marginally might pass for science. There is only the residue of hoped-for default, which steadily shrinks as the science of biology expands.'[54]

I say that this surprises me, for, even if one were to discount our preceding chapters on biology because they challenged certain prevailing views on origins, how can one ignore the evidence from physics and cosmology that, far from questioning accepted science, flows out of it? Compare Wilson's attitude with that of Allan Sandage who is widely regarded as the greatest living cosmologist: 'The world is too complicated in all its parts and interconnections to be due to chance alone. I am convinced that the existence of life with all its order in each of its organisms is simply too well put together.'[55] We recall also that it was the evidence of scientific research on questions of the origin of life that led the eminent philosopher

Key

and life-long atheist Anthony Flew to believe that the nature of the complexity of DNA can only be accounted for by an intelligent Creator.[56] Wilson says there is no evidence; Sandage and Flew claim that there is. Both views cannot be right.

Front-loading subsequent to biogenesis

What then are the implications of our thinking with respect to the way in which life has developed once it was created? The first mention of life in Genesis (1:11–13) is as follows (esv):

> And God said, 'Let the earth sprout vegetation, plants yielding seed, and fruit trees bearing fruit in which is their seed, each according to its kind, on the earth.' And it was so. The earth brought forth vegetation, plants yielding seed according to their own kinds, and trees bearing fruit in which is their seed, each according to its kind. And God saw that it was good. And there was evening and there was morning, the third day.

The statement 'Let the earth sprout vegetation, plants… trees according to [their own] kind' could be interpreted as a front-loading of the potential to develop a vast variety of species. There is no record of extra inputs needed to produce them. My question is then: What would this look like through the lens of systems biology? What I mean by that is this. For a long time those people like myself who are sceptical of some of the claims made of evolution, particularly the kind envisaged by the modern synthesis, have concentrated on two main issues: the origin of life and the failure of the modern synthesis to account for macroevolution. Over time the evidence against the capacity of natural processes to account for the origin of life has become overwhelming.

However, although *the materialist neo-Darwinian synthesis* fails to account for innovation beyond the small amounts usually associated with microevolution, research in systems biology has opened up new perspectives. For instance, it has been shown that organisms are able to alter their own genomes top-down. It has also been shown that acquired characteristics may be inherited. It has turned out that some organisms are able to change themselves much more rapidly and much more extensively than was hitherto thought possible. In other words, it may be that at least some developments *beyond* the reach of microevolution may occur *by non-Darwinian means*, without additional inputs of information.

I say 'some' since, from the perspective of the Genesis account, there remain three further putative informational discontinuities: the origin of life of all kinds in the sea and air; animals of all kinds on the earth; and distinctively human life and consciousness. It is interesting that the co-founder of the theory of evolution, Darwin's contemporary Alfred Russell Wallace, also thought that there were three (slightly different) discontinuities: the origin of life; the origin of consciousness; and the origin of specifically human faculties. Wallace has been called the 'forgotten man of evolution'. In fact he worked out the theory of natural selection and sent his idea to Charles Darwin, who had been working on a similar theory. Both versions were read to members at the same meeting of the Linnean Society in 1858. Wallace therefore deserved priority and much more credit than he ever received.

In addition, we recall from Chapter 15 that there is evidence for such discontinuities from palaeontology as the fossil record shows clear breaks, particularly in the Cambrian Explosion, which might fit with the suggestion of additional discontinuities due to God's primary causation. The term 'evolution' could then be used without ambiguity for what happens in the natural course of things *between* the discontinuities, so that the absolute uniformity of nature would be replaced by a punctuated uniformity of nature. And this would fit in with a theistic worldview. I have said several times in this book that mutation and natural selection do something – they are seen to account for variation and adaptation and, as such, a theist will see this as a process designed by God. In fact, it is mentioned in the New Testament. In his famous speech to the philosophers at Athens the leading Christian missionary Paul said of God: 'And he made from one man every nation of mankind to live on all the face of the earth.'[57] Over time human beings have exhibited different kinds of variation. Paul ascribes this variation to God and therefore it is a legitimate deduction that it arose by secondary causation through the processes of selection and mutation. Earlier we quoted the following statement by Francis Collins that although from our perspective 'evolution could appear to be driven by chance, from God's perspective the outcome would be entirely specified'.[58]

Collins was thinking of the modern synthesis in its entirety which, as we have seen, has failed to deliver the whole story. Nevertheless, if we replace 'evolution' in this observation by the adaptations and variations that we can actually observe, then, of course, God was responsible for them and the statement makes sense. It is an example of chance processes (in the mathematical sense as described earlier) designed by God. To use Shapiro's terminology it might be part of natural genetic engineering. So we could say that God's construction of the biosphere involves chance processes but they are not the whole story.

Postulating additional discontinuities at the level of God's primary causation and understanding the filling of the time between as resulting from secondary causation would not alter the fact that all biological life possesses a great deal in common. It would mean, however, that the idea of 'common descent' would need modification to cope with those additional discontinuities, including that between animals and humans. One indicator of what that might be is that the sequence of phrases 'And God said...' in Genesis 1 comes to its highpoint with: 'And God said *to them*...' The humans were capable of understanding God's communication: they had the faculty of language with all that this implies. Keith Ward FBA points out that this feature distinguishes humanity from all other living things:

> There are three distinctive capacities of the human person, unique among all organisms on Earth, so far as we can tell①the capacity to be sensitive to and appreciative of information received②to be creative in responding to it, and③to learn and develop such capacities in relation to other persons in specific historical contexts. Human persons receive information, interpret it, and transmit it in a fully semantic way.[59]

Key

We have seen that one of the greatest barriers to a naturalistic explanation of biogenesis is the 'language' like information encoded in DNA. There would now seem also to be a similar barrier at a higher level where the language involved is conscious intelligent communication. In fact, my suspicion would be that the origin of life and the origin of human consciousness and linguistic capacity are at least two major additional singularities besides the origin of the universe.

I find it noteworthy that a distinguished scientist, committed to the modern synthesis, like Francis Collins, nevertheless believes that there is a supernatural discontinuity between animals and humans.

Collins, like Wallace, thinks that, in his view, there came a point in history where God specially conferred his image on a creature that had emerged from the evolutionary process. This, according to Collins, was the beginning of the human race 'made in the image of God'.

21

Brain, Mind, and the Quantum World

The concept of information has given us reason to think that the universe is word-based – a *Sprachwerk*.[1] Information is not material and words are mental concepts. Words do not exist in a vacuum. The main source of them with which we are intimately familiar is the human mind and its associated physical organ, the human brain. The human brain is thought to be the most complex entity in the entire physical universe. It functions more efficiently than current supercomputers. Yet, what really sets it apart is not that it is unbelievably complicated and information rich, but that it is the organ of consciousness and mind. Consciousness is mysterious. No one really understands it and it has defied all attempts at physical reduction – not surprisingly since such attempts destroy the very rationality we need if we are to think about it at all. This implies that the mind and the brain, though closely related, are nevertheless distinct. In considering the interaction between them we are inevitably led to consider the quantum revolution in physics that has shown that consciousness plays a fundamental role in our interaction with the physical world.

What are the implications of all of this? We have seen that the informational aspects of the world make plausible the idea of the existence of an eternal creative Word. Will the existence of the human mind add even more to the evidence that that Word is a mind, the Mind of God?

One of the greatest mysteries yet to be unravelled by science is how the human mind and brain are linked. With the mind we associate ideas of conscious thought, intention, ideas, emotions whereas the brain is a physical organ contained in the human skull. At this moment I am thinking of the next word to write. My thought activates neurones in my brain and causes various impulses to flow to my hands to cause the muscles to contract and expand so that my fingers transfer the contents of my thought onto my computer. How does that mental activity cause the physical activity? Nobody seems to know.

The human brain weighs around 1.4 kg, and, with its hundred billion neurons and trillions of synaptic connections, may well be the most complex entity in the entire physical universe. It is made up of two types of cell called neurons and glia. Neurons are have branch-like projections called axons and dendrites that gather and transmit electrochemical signals. Glial cells provide physical protection for the neurons. Glial cells – the non-neuronal cells also allow dramatically increased electrical transmission speeds. There are different varieties – notably oligodendrocytes and the utterly remarkable Schwann cells.[2] The nerve impulses rip along from node to node in an amazing added degree of sophistication.

Here is a diagram of a neuron.

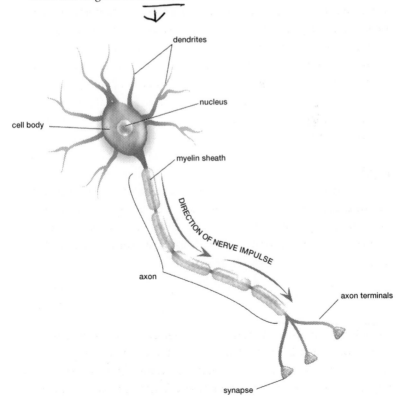

what do you want to happen?

The axons and dendrites are about 1 micrometre[3] thick but the axons can be up to two metres long reaching from brain to toes. Can we even begin to imagine what it is like to have a hundred billion of these inside our heads without even being aware of it?

Experimental evidence shows that even at the smallest unit of our cognition, there is a kind of conversation going on between individual neurons that modifies each other's behaviour. Neurons are complex nanomachines with an instruction set and the capacity to send coded messages to each other. The human brain is far more advanced and efficient, and possesses more raw computational power than the most impressive supercomputers that have ever been built. Although it is impossible to calculate precisely, it is reckoned that the human brain operates at 1 exaFLOP, which is equivalent to performing a quintillion, i.e. a billion billion (10^{18}) calculations per second. It is reported that in 2014 some Japanese scientists attempted to match the amount of processing that 1 per cent of the brain could perform in one second. It took the fourth fastest supercomputer in the world (the K Computer) forty minutes to do the same.[4] However, there is really no comparison between the brain and computers. For not only can the brain outstrip even supercomputers – at the moment – but it, or rather its possessors, are conscious whereas computers are not. That has led some scientists to say that we may have to up our thinking to the quantum level when it comes to the computational capacity of the brain. At the moment a lot of work is going into the development of quantum computers, which, if successful, would immensely increase computational power and possibly even help us make progress in our understanding of the brain. It is in the brain that we have to take into consideration the interaction between the invisible small-scale quantum level activity and the large-scale activities that seem to be connected with consciousness and are not yet well understood.

The brain plays a fundamental role in the biology of human beings and its existence and multiple levels of complexity raise many questions since the brain, physical object that it is, is also intimately connected with consciousness. I remember once having the opportunity to chat briefly to Professor Bert Sakmann of the Max Planck Institute in Heidelberg, who had won the Nobel Prize for work related on the ion channels that are involved in synaptic transmission. I asked him what his dream research result would be. His instant reply was that he would love to find out how a memory is held in the brain for half an hour.

Worldviews 1) materialism Naturalism (NOT equal)
2) theism

Think of our journey so far. We started with the reductionism of the modern synthesis and found that, although it has yielded impressive understanding of many things – the structure of DNA, proteins and genomes, for instance – it has turned out to be inadequate since causation in the living cell is not one-directional as was assumed. There is both bottom-up and top-down causation as well as feedback mechanisms in cells – a perspective that has falsified the central dogma of molecular biology. The discovery of top-down causation and feedback together with the inheritance of acquired characteristics has opened up the new discipline of systems biology where the cell takes pride of place.

Does the human brain represent yet a further level, even beyond that, especially due to its intimate, yet baffling connection with consciousness? It is here that we face a further case of reductionist thinking. At one time it was more common than it is now to distinguish between mind, self, I, and brain, although it was agreed that there was a strong dependence link between the brain and the mind. Now, however, many neuroscientists hold the reductionist physicalist view that 'you are your brain' or, equivalently, that 'the brain is the self'.

Yet, just as systems biology is pushing aside the reductionism of the modern synthesis, some neuroscientists and philosophers are re-thinking the mind-body problem and pushing back at the 'you are your brain' paradigm.[5] The key metaphysical question here is: What is the ontology of consciousness, thought, and the self? It would surely be unwise to assume without further reflection that it will be the same as the ontology of the material universe, since what we are now purporting to study is the very thing that does the studying: what we wish to know about is what it is that does the knowing and who it is that is the knower. Indeed, I wish to suggest that our answer to this question will depend, not so much on whether we are scientists or not, but on our worldview. I shall limit my comments to the two main worldviews that dominate the discussion – materialism/naturalism and theism. I shall bear in mind that a distinction is made between materialism and naturalism. According to the *Oxford Companion to Philosophy*, naturalism in metaphysics is 'most obviously akin to materialism but it does not have to be materialistic. What it insists on is that the world of nature should consist of a single sphere without incursions from outside by souls or spirits, divine or human... but it need not reject the phenomena of consciousness, nor even identify them somehow with material phenomena as the materialist must.' American philosopher John H. Randall of Columbia

What is the "nature" of ultimate reality?

University writes: 'naturalism finds itself in thoroughgoing opposition to all forms of thought which assert the existence of a supernatural or transcendent Realm of Being, and which make knowledge of that realm of fundamental importance to human living.'[6]

The particular worldview question in the frame here is: What is the nature of ultimate reality?

- For the materialist, mass/energy is the ultimate reality; it is *the given*, from which everything else derives.

- For the theist, God is the ultimate reality; he is the fundamental given, from which everything else derives.

It is worth noting that these are views that determine our approach to science, rather than their being determined by science alone – in spite of insistent claims to the contrary.

For instance, Daniel Dennett asserts what his materialist worldview demands, namely that the mind: '*is* the brain, or, more specifically, a system of organization within the brain that has evolved in much the way our immune system or digestive system has evolved.'[7] Dennett holds that the self is an illusion, a 'centre of narrative fiction' in the sense that language creates the idea of a self that is having these experiences.

Francis Crick, similarly, thinks that: 'You, your joys and your sorrows, your memories and your ambitions, your sense of personal identity and free will are in fact no more than the behaviour of a vast assembly of nerve cells and their associated molecules.'[8] This statement, although written by a scientist, is not a scientific result but an expression of the author's metaphysical pre-commitment to a reductionist materialistic worldview. If Dennett and Crick were right, what should we say of human love and fear? Are they meaningless neural behaviour patterns? Or what shall we make of the concepts of beauty and truth? Is a Rembrandt painting nothing but molecules of paint scattered on canvas? Crick seems to think so. But if that is the case, by what means could we recognize it? After all, if the concept of truth itself is a product of 'nothing more than the behaviour of a vast assembly of nerve cells' how, in the name of logic, would we know what the words 'nerve cells' meant, let alone the fact that our brain was composed of them?

As Fraser Watts has pointed out,[9] Crick himself seems to realize that there must be more to it than this, for he radically modifies his 'astonishing' hypothesis by weakening it to the almost innocuous statement: 'You are *largely* the behaviour of a vast population of neurones'[10] (my italics). But such a drastically modified hypothesis is prosaic and completely fails to astonish. Come to think of it, even if the astonishing hypothesis were true how would it astonish? For how could we begin to know or understand it? And what meaning would 'astonishment' have? The idea is intrinsically incoherent at all levels. Crick's modification of it indicates that he may well have suspected the problem himself – though he has not corrected it, so far as I am aware.

John Locke made this point a long time ago in a very interesting context that has relevance to the discussion of a universe from nothing: 'If, then, there must be something eternal, let us see what sort of Being it must be. And to that it is very obvious to Reason, that it must necessarily be a cogitative Being. For it is as impossible to conceive that ever bare *point* incogitative Matter should produce a thinking intelligent Being, as that nothing should of itself produce Matter.'[11] Neither Dennett nor Crick has shown that Locke was wrong. Careful examination shows that they do not even address these questions as distinct from making unsubstantiated assertions.

Neuroscience has certainly made impressive and valuable strides in correlating mental activity (the 'I' –story) with electrochemical activity in the cerebral cortex (the brain-story), mapping various regions of the brain that respond to mental stimuli and even using external electrical stimuli to stimulate the growth of new neural pathways in the cortex. However, *correlation* of mind-states with brain-states is one thing, claiming that they are no more than, or *identical with*, brain-states is quite another.[12] For instance, my brain state can be the subject of a PET[13] scan, my mind state cannot; my mind-state is 'about something' my brain state is not about anything; my brain state can be spatially located but my mind-state cannot. A neuroscientist can tell me what is going on in my brain – to a certain extent. I can tell him what is in my mind. Can he tell me anything about what is in my mind? *The New York Times* reports that a computational neuroscientist at the University of California, Berkeley, Dr Jack Gallant, has constructed an artificial intelligence system working on a large database that stores patterns of brain activation of people in fMRI machines labelled with what film clips they are viewing. A volunteer is then given something new to look at and the brain activation pattern is fed into the AI system that searches for similar patterns in its database and produces an image based on the film clips associated with those patterns. *The Times* says: 'The reconstructed images move with a dreamlike fluidity. In their imperfection, they evoke expressionist art. (And a few reconstructed images seem downright wrong.) But where they succeed, they represent an astonishing achievement: a machine translating patterns of brain activity into a moving image understandable by other people — a machine that can read the brain.'[14]

The relationship 'being identical with' is symmetrical. Thus, if pain is composed of nothing but C-fibre firings, then C-fibre firings have to be the very same elements that constitute pain. Colin McGinn argues that this leads, ironically, to the strange consequence that materialism fails: 'to respect the intrinsic objectivity of physical properties' and ends up contradicting its own basic presuppositions by denying the objectivity of matter.[15]

Not only that, but the assumption that the mind is the brain is incapable, even in principle, of dealing with consciousness, since it invalidates the very rationality that is necessary to do any science at all. Crick's reductionism is, therefore, intellectually suicidal. Physicist John Polkinghorne explains that its fatal flaw lies in replacing thought by electro-chemical events that are incapable of rational discourse. He says that they are neither right nor wrong but simply happen:

> If we are caught in the reductionist trap we have no means of judging intellectual truth. The very assertions of the reductionist himself are nothing but blips in the neural network of his brain. The world of rational discourse dissolves into the absurd chatter of firing synapses. Quite frankly, that cannot be right and none of us believes it to be so.[16]

'Suicidal' is the right word. For there is a patent self-contradiction running through all attempts, however sophisticated they may appear, to derive rationality from irrationality. When stripped down to their bare bones, they all seem uncannily like futile attempts to lift oneself by one's bootstraps, or to construct a perpetual motion machine. After all, it is the use of the human mind that has led people to adopt ontological reductionism, which, in turn, carries with it the corollary that there is no reason to trust our minds when they tell us about anything at all; and in particular, that such reductionism is true.

Cognitive scientist David Chalmers is one of those who started off as a materialist but then began to have doubts. In a chapter of *The Conscious Mind*, intriguingly entitled 'The Irreducibility of Consciousness', he writes: 'Many people, including a past self of mine, have thought that they could simultaneously take consciousness seriously and remain a materialist. This is not possible... those who want to come to grips with the phenomenon must embrace a form of dualism. One might say: You can't have your materialist cake and eat your consciousness too.'[17] Chalmers says that there may be 'systematic reasons to think there will always be a gulf between the physical and the mental'.[18] He therefore argues that we may have to regard the mental as what he calls a 'nonreductive primitive' – that is a fundamental building block of reality just as much as matter and energy, space and time. After all, as Denis Noble says: 'Suppose we really succeeded in "reducing" rational behaviour to molecular and cellular causation. In that case we would no longer be able meaningfully to express the truth of what we had succeeded in doing. In any event, the question does not arise. No such reduction is conceivable.'[19] Indeed, the fact that there is a yawning gap between matter and mind is well recognized and was called 'the explanatory gap' by philosopher Joseph Levine in a paper in 1983 entitled 'Materialism and Qualia: The explanatory gap'. This is a further very important example of what I earlier called a 'good' gap – one revealed by science.

Human consciousness introduces completely new dimensions beyond anything we have considered up to now – the dimensions of thinking, understanding, knowing, seeing, perceiving beauty and morality, enjoying, purposing, planning for the future, imagining, engaging with others, and a limitless range of things that combine together to bring meaning into life. These are by far and away the most important aspects of human life and convey a sense that consciousness must somehow play a primary role in the universe. It is ironic that physical reductionism is used to try to bury God when in fact what it succeeds in doing is interring rational thought and science.

These arguments are extensions of what has come to be known as 'Darwin's Doubt'. He once wrote expressing concern about the reliability of the human mind: 'With me, the horrid doubt always arises whether the convictions of man's mind, which has been developed from the mind of the lower animals, are of any value or at all trustworthy.'[20] This statement calling in question the reliability of human cognitive abilities is of great importance in the appraisal of evolution's capacity to develop mind. Thomas Nagel gets to the heart of the matter: 'But if the mental is not itself merely physical it cannot be fully explained by physical science... Materialism requires reductionism; therefore the failure of reductionism requires an alternative to materialism.'[21] This means that if Dawkins is right, that we are the product of mindless unguided natural processes, then he has given us strong reason to doubt the reliability of human cognitive faculties and therefore inevitably to doubt the validity of any belief that they produce – including Dawkins' own science and his atheism. His biology and his belief in naturalism would therefore appear to be at war with each other in a conflict that has nothing at all to do with God.[22]

That is, such reductionism undermines the foundations of the very rationality that is needed to construct or understand or believe in any kind of argument whatsoever – let alone a scientific one. Thomas Nagel confirms this assessment: 'Evolutionary naturalism implies that we shouldn't take any of our convictions seriously, including the scientific world picture on which evolutionary naturalism itself depends.'[23] Atheist philosopher and expert on European thought John Gray makes the same point about the modern synthesis: 'Modern humanism is the faith that through science humankind can know the truth and so be free. But if Darwin's theory of natural selection is true this is impossible. The human mind serves evolutionary success, not truth.'[24] Philosopher, historian, and archaeologist R. A. Collingwood was evidently right when he said that materialism has the characteristic of 'writing itself a large cheque on income it had not yet received'.

Surveying the literature, Plantinga writes, 'Nietzsche, Nagel, Stroud, Churchland and Darwin, non-theists all, seem to concur: (naturalistic) evolution gives one a reason to doubt that human cognitive faculties produce for the most part true beliefs.'[25]

Plantinga's supportive approach involves analysing what a belief looks like from a materialistic/naturalistic perspective. He considers the alternatives: reductive materialism and non-reductive materialism. In the reductive view a belief is an electrochemical or neurophysiological (NP) event or structure. In the non-reductive view a belief is caused by an NP event. However, a belief must have content – a belief that p, for some proposition p. Plantinga says that it is essentially impossible to see how a material structure or event could have content in the way that a belief does. Also, on an evolutionary hypothesis, when and how did neural structures develop the capacity to contain beliefs? What is more, why should we think that such beliefs are true? Plantinga concludes that there is no reason – that, in fact, a naturalist who accepts evolution must give up the assumption that his or her cognitive faculties are reliable. Plantinga, of course, believes that they are for the most part reliable – his point is that the combination of naturalism and evolution acts as a dangerous acid as a defeater for that belief. I strongly recommend my readers to look carefully at his work.[26]

Perhaps the best summary of this view is due to C. S. Lewis:

> Unless human reasoning is valid no science can be true... If Ultimate Reality is not material, not to take this into account in our context is to neglect the most important fact of all. Yet the supernatural dimension has not only been forgotten, it has been ruled out of court by many... The Naturalists have been engaged in thinking about Nature. They have not attended to the fact that they were thinking. The moment one attends to this it is obvious that one's own thinking cannot be merely a natural event, and therefore something other than Nature exists.[27]

In addition, Denis Noble warns that: 'for some scientists reductionism functions as a security blanket. It avoids the need to ask too many questions, to stare into the abyss of fundamental uncertainty... We need to take on board the reality that causation and explanation do not always run upwards from lower to higher levels.'[28] In the preceding chapter we saw the evidence from Noble's work on systems biology that reductionism is not by any means the whole story. We should also take Noble's comments seriously in connection with the problem of consciousness. He writes: 'The idea that the person can be identified with his/her brain is now deep in our culture. I suspect that it will take a shock to shake people out of it. Nevertheless it is instructive to try.'[29] Noble also suggests that the self is not a neural object but that it is an 'integrative concept, occasionally a fragile one. It is also a necessary construct. It is one of the greatest symphonies of the music of life.'[30]

Keith Ward FBA also warns against simplistic attempts to explain consciousness:

The eternal Mind of God. ~

if we are not simply to give up all attempt at explanation, and say that consciousness is just a random by-product of the evolutionary process, we must look for a different type of explanation… which is now increasingly being forced on our attention. That is, a cosmic holistic explanation, in which the development of the parts is explained by their contribution to the existence of an integrated totality.

Taken together, these considerations suggest the idea of a primordial consciousness that is ontologically prior to all physical realities, that contains the 'coded' information for constructing any possible universe….[31]

In other words, the eternal Mind of God that has not arisen from matter but is both prior to it and independent of it.

Quantum mechanics[32]

Writing about the mind/brain question David Chalmers says, 'Perhaps quantum mechanics might play a role in characterising the psychophysical link, but quantum theory alone cannot tell us why consciousness exists.'[33]

Surveying the literature it seems that distinguished quantum physicist Henry Stapp, who worked at various times with Heisenberg, Pauli, and Wheeler, has made some of the most important contributions to this debate and we shall therefore refer to his work in what follows. He writes:

Although many neuro-scientists and neuro-philosophers do not explicitly specify that they are assuming the validity of classical physics, which they know to be false in the regime of the behaviours of the ions and molecules that play a key role in the dynamics of the conscious brain, they nevertheless endeavour to conceptualize the dynamics of the conscious brain in essentially classical terms: they have closed their minds to the huge practical and conceptual advantages wrought by the twentieth century advances in physics.[34]

Could this possibly partly be because QM provides us with a strong case for making the distinction between brain and mind?

QM, one of the most important scientific achievements in the twentieth century, is a theory that no one claims to understand fully, even though it has received spectacularly detailed confirmation in practice. It introduces us to a seething world of fleeting elementary particles behaving in the strangest of ways. It even leads us to ask what, exactly, do we mean by the material world? For, as our understanding of physics has advanced, the concept of 'matter' has become more and more ephemeral and complicated. We have moved a long way from previous naïve ideas of hard 'stuff' like a wooden table that we once may have imagined it to be. First, there is the mass/energy equivalence discovered by Einstein in 1905 and governed by his famous equation $E = mc^2$ where E is energy, m is mass and c is the velocity of light, 299,792 kilometres per second. As physicist Paul Davies puts it:

> [The] increasing application of the information concept to nature has prompted a curious conjecture. Normally we think of the world as composed of simple, clod-like, material particles, and information as a derived phenomenon attached to special, organized states of matter. But maybe it is the other way around: perhaps the universe is really a frolic of primal information, and material objects a complex secondary manifestation.[35]

And that frolic is subject to QM.

It may be in part because QM is not easy that many scientists have failed to grasp that it has completely overturned classical views of the ontology of matter. In the classical world of Newtonian physics up to the end of the nineteenth century scientists in the main held that they were studying a reality that existed 'out there' – a universe that consisted of space, time, and particles. The classical universe was described by Newton's laws of motion and Clerk-Maxwell's equations for electromagnetism and seemed to many like a vast clockwork machine that, from a theological perspective (which Newton held), ran on the fixed laws that had been prescribed for it by its Creator. Ideas of position and motion were clear: you could simultaneously see where a bicycle was and what it was doing – you could measure its velocity. Your only handicap was the precision of your measuring instruments. More precisely, the (classical) laws describe how the universe works *when left to itself*, that is, provided it is an isolated and closed system, not subject to external causal influence of any kind.

To many people this meant determinism. Laplace said that one ought to view the current state of the universe

> as the effect of its previous state and as the cause of the one which is to follow. Given for one instant a mind which could comprehend all the forces by which nature is animated and the respected situations of the beings that compose it – a mind sufficiently vast to subject these data to analysis – it would embrace in the same formula the movements of the greatest bodies of the universe and those of the lightest atom; for it, nothing would be uncertain and the future, as the past, would be present to its eyes.[36]

This is full causal closure and, of course, it excludes divine action. It also destroys human freedom and with it the rational base for human moral responsibility.

This mechanistic deterministic view proved to be incorrect at its core. It was turned upside down, or, perhaps better, the right way up, by the QM understanding of the sub-atomic world of electrons, neutrons, protons, and other elementary particles that are the fundamental building blocks of matter. A key issue was that classical mechanics could not account for the stability of the atom. Rutherford's planetary model of the atom faced the problem that the electrons orbiting the nucleus should radiate, and therefore lose energy, and eventually spiral into the nucleus so that the atom collapses. But it doesn't collapse. Niels Bohr solved the problem with his brilliant insight that the energy of electrons was quantized so that they could not spiral into the nucleus. The classical age was over.

Werner Heisenberg showed that you cannot simultaneously measure where an electron is and what it is doing. His famous 'indeterminacy' or 'uncertainty principle' says that the more accurately you measure position the less accurately you can measure momentum and vice versa. In addition, you cannot tell precisely where an electron is but you can calculate the probability that it is in a particular place. We do not get a unique prediction of outcomes but only a distribution of probabilities of possible outcomes. QM introduces an unavoidable *probabilistic* fuzziness into the universe. At its heart is the famous Schrödinger wave function which is a mathematical abstraction that contains all the accessible information about the quantum particle with which it is associated. You get that information by performing an operation on the wave function. For instance, by squaring it you get the probability of finding the particle at a particular location in space.[37]

More precisely, on one particular (and popular) interpretation of QM, the Copenhagen Interpretation, the fuzziness of indeterminism only holds when measurements are being made. The wave function does not tell us anything about where an electron is until we do an observation. This is one of the strangest results of QM. Whereas in the classical world the observer has no effect on what it observed, in the quantum world, observation and measurement do affect what is being observed and measured. Observation becomes an interplay of mind and matter and involves non-material causation. The universe revealed by QM is not a materialistic universe. It involves psycho-physical effects. John Wheeler called it a 'participatory universe', and, as such, it presents us with a new perception of reality. Werner Heisenberg, wrote: 'the natural laws formulated mathematically in quantum theory no longer deal with the elemental particles themselves but with our knowledge of them.' In other words, in his view the theory is more epistemological than ontological.[38] It is, therefore, a theory of information and thus it fits in with our considerations in the previous chapter.

Stapp puts it this way:

> The classical theory presumes that all aspects of nature can be explained purely in terms of the action of matter upon matter. But the quantum world differs in a fundamental way from that core precept of materialism. This huge structural difference in the real (that is, quantum) world between the matter–matter interaction and the matter–mind interaction makes manifest the extreme naïveté of trying to comprehend the connection between mind and matter within a materialistic framework.[39]

QM is highly mathematical and an interesting sidelight on the relationship of mathematics to consciousness is given by Sir Roger Penrose OM FRS, one of the most brilliant mathematicians of his generation. In his fascinating book *The Emperor's New Mind* he says that:

> Mathematical truth is *not* something that we ascertain merely by use of an algorithm. I believe also that our

> *consciousness* is a crucial ingredient in our comprehension
> of mathematical truth. We must 'see' the truth of a
> mathematical argument to be convinced of its validity.
> This 'seeing' is the very essence of consciousness. It must
> be present whenever we directly perceive mathematical
> truth. When we convince ourselves of the validity of
> Gödel's theorem we not only 'see' it, but by doing so we
> reveal the very non-algorithmic nature of the 'seeing'
> process itself.[40]

Thus the seeing process cannot be the product of a computer-like brain whose computations would be algorithmic. This constitutes a further argument for the inequivalence of brain and mind and the demise of materialism.

> It would be hard to overstate the importance of QM for
> that demise. Paul Davies and John Gribbin explain how
> quantum theory totally transformed the earlier conviction
> that the world at the atomic level was simply a scaled-down
> version of the macro world of everyday life. That view had
> to be discarded and with it the deterministic Newtonian
> machine that was replaced by a shadowy and paradoxical
> conjunction of waves and particles, governed by the laws
> of chance, rather than the rigid rules of causality. An
> extension of the quantum theory goes beyond even this; it
> paints a picture in which solid matter dissolves away, to be
> replaced by weird excitations and vibrations of invisible
> field energy. Quantum physics undermines materialism
> because it reveals that matter has far less 'substance' than
> we might believe. But another development goes even
> further by demolishing Newton's image of matter as inert
> lumps. This development is the theory of chaos, which has
> recently gained widespread attention.[41]

Sometimes it is thought that QM has to do with the exceedingly small – the atomic and subatomic levels – and so has no implications for macroscopic objects like the human brain. However, Stapp shows that this is not the case, since it is not clear that classical approximation will work due to the processes in nerves that control our brains being at the ionic level. Schwartz, Stapp, and Beauregard (2005)[42] show that quantum mechanics must be used at the fundamental level in the treatment of the dynamical processes occurring in human brains. Stapp goes on to say: 'The classical approximation can, for special reasons, be adequate for many purposes, but the applicability of the classical approximation to brain dynamics is neither automatic nor universally guaranteed. According to contemporary basic physics, quantum mechanics must be used as a matter of basic principle, with the classical approximation usable in those special cases where it can be justified.'[43]

Let us pause to take stock and grasp the revolutionary implications that QM has for our big-picture worldview. In his essay on 'Minds and Values in the Quantum Universe', Stapp writes:

> Information, from the quantum theoretical perspective, is carried by the physical structure that communicates the potentialities created by earlier psycho-physical events to the later one. This communication of potentialities is an essential part of the process that creates the unfolding and actualization in space and time of the growing sequence of events that constitutes the history of the actual universe. Information resides also in the psychologically described and physically described aspects of these events themselves, and is created by these events.[44]

He explains how quantum theory opens the door to and indeed demands free choices made by the human players, which all leads to a situation that: 'is concordant with the idea of a powerful God that creates the universe and its laws to get things started, but then bequeaths part of this power to beings created in his own image, at least with regard to their power to make physically efficacious decisions on the basis of reasons and evaluations.'[45] Stapp sees no way that science can show that this religious understanding of quantum theory is wrong or even unlikely. He also thinks that science cannot produce

> strong evidence in support of an alternative picture of the nature of those 'free choices'. These choices *seem to be* rooted in reasons that are rooted in feelings pertaining to

value or worth. Thus it can be argued that quantum theory provides an opening for an idea of nature and of our role within it that is in general accord with certain religious concepts, but that, by contrast, is quite incompatible with the precepts of mechanistic deterministic classical physics. Thus the replacement of classical mechanics by quantum mechanics opens the door to religious possibilities that formerly were rationally excluded.[46]

Stapp, who, incidentally, shows little sympathy for religious ideas or ID, nevertheless concludes that QM has major implications for our thinking about ourselves as human beings:

This conception of nature, in which the consequences of our choices enter not only directly in our immediate neighbourhood but also *indirectly and immediately* in far flung places, alters the image of a human being relative to the one spawned by classical physics. It changes this image in a way that must tend to reduce a sense of powerlessness, separation and isolation, and to enhance the sense of responsibility and of *belonging*.[47]

It seems remarkable that, although QM is nearly a century old, relatively few people seem to grasp that it has demolished the materialist worldview with its mechanistic determinism. Physicist Stephen Barr writes that: 'the argument against materialism based on quantum theory is a strong one, and has certainly not been refuted. The line of argument is rather subtle. It is also not well known, even among most practicing physicists. But, if it is correct, it would be the most important philosophical implication to come from any scientific discovery.'[48] Perhaps this is one of the most uncomfortable aspects of QM. It shows that scientists cannot avoid the clear philosophical implication of their science that materialism cannot stand. For, this is not a question of *religion* triumphing over materialism, it is *science* triumphing over materialism and re-opening the door to perceiving the Mind of God.

Epilogue: Beyond Scier
But Not Beyond Reason

We now list some of the evidence that I believe makes plausible, as an inference to the best explanation, that the universe and life in it appear to be products of a divine Mind because that is precisely what they are. Since no explanation that does not involve a mind seems to work, it is surely perfectly rational to accept an explanation that does. Since every explanation that does not involve a mind seems to fail in principle, it is surely perfectly rational and consistent to accept an explanation that does. To establish purely scientifically that mind must have been involved would surely lead to winning the Mind 2.0 Prize – if anyone should offer to fund it! There is a strong case that science and God together form a rational conjunctive explanation.[1] The notion that they are alternative conflicting explanations stems from failure to distinguish between different kinds of explanation – mechanism and agency.

Here is the evidence as I see it.

- The failure to produce credible non-theistic natural explanations for the origin of life and the lack of any evidence that life is reducible to physics and chemistry.
- The failure to recognize worldview bias in the misuse of the modern synthesis as an engine of atheism.
- The scientific failure of the modern synthesis in consequence of the inadequacy of natural selection and mutation to bear the weight that has been placed on them in the past and which is still placed on them by those who are unaware of recent developments.
- The scientific fruitfulness of the concept of a Creator and the influence of the biblical worldview on the rise of modern science.
- The rational intelligibility of the universe that facilitates the doing of science. The 'unreasonable' effectiveness of mathematics. All pointing to, or at least consistent with, the existence of a rational mind behind the universe.

- The fact that space-time had a beginning and the implications that this demands a cause. The rational fitness of the theistic answer to the question: why is there something rather than nothing.

- The precision of the fine tuning of the universe for life that supports an inference to purposeful creation.

- The limits to scientific explanation on the one hand, and, on the other hand, the existence of other equally valid modes of rational enquiry and explanation such as history, philosophy, and theology that indicate that there must be 'something more'.

- The fact that there is no evidence for the existence of a primeval soup much different in its concentrations of amino acids from those in the ocean of today. In any event, all the various scenarios that have been put forward to explain how life emerged from this hypothetical primeval soup have serious drawbacks.

- The fact that information is one of the main things that distinguish life from non-life. The language-like nature of the information content of DNA and the existence of a sophisticated coding system that uses the information in DNA to construct proteins.

- The existence of a vast variety of protein nanomachines exhibiting spectacular engineering sophistication involving incalculable informational input.

- The fact that cells not only contain information but are information processors. The mind-boggling complexity of the information management and control systems within cells.

- The existence of epigenetic levels of information and control above and beyond the information contained in DNA and the additional level of information contained in the geometric folding of proteins.

- The machinery involved in heredity and the fact that information additional to that contained in DNA is transmitted between the generations.

- The extra levels of information processing implied by the discovery that organisms can modify their own genomes.

- The 'chicken and egg' circularity found in living systems makes best sense if there was foresight in the construction of those systems and if they were constructed together.

- The ideas of Medawar on the conservation of information, as developed by Chaitin, give a precise way to express the strong impression that the information content of life could not be generated naturalistically.

- Penrose's argument that thinking (in mathematics, say) is non-algorithmic.
- C. S. Lewis' argument that thinking cannot be a purely natural process if our thoughts are to be regarded as valid.
- The incompatibility of quantum mechanics with materialism.

Where Does All of This Leave Us?
Niels Bohr
'I therefore suggested that the very existence of life might be taken as a basic fact in biology in the same sense as the quantum of action has to be regarded in atomic physics as a fundamental element irreducible to classical physical concepts.'[2]

Sara Imari Walker and Paul C. W. Davies
'We point out a curious philosophical implication of the algorithmic perspective: if the origin of life is identified with the transition from trivial to non-trivial information processing – e.g. from something akin to a Turing machine capable of a single (or limited set of) computation(s) to a universal Turing machine capable of constructing any computable object (within a universality class) – then a precise point of transition from non-life to life may actually be undecidable in the logical sense. This would likely have very important philosophical implications, particularly in our interpretation of life as a predictable outcome of physical law.'[3]

James Tour
'We synthetic chemists should state the obvious. The appearance of life on earth is a mystery. We are nowhere near solving this problem. The proposals offered thus far to explain life's origin make no scientific sense.'[4]

These are cautious attitudes that are to be expected from scientists aware of the limitations of their field. They are rightly concerned that there is a danger of forcing science to say what it cannot say. However, it is one thing to say that life is unknowable from the natural sciences, or undecidable by human reasoning from physics and chemistry. It is quite another to say that it is unknowable or undecidable by human reasoning full stop, since science is only part of rational discourse. After all, the fact that I am a mathematician is undecidable from physics and chemistry, but is (I would

[Handwritten margin note at top: "The origin of life being caused by Intelligence!"]

sincerely hope) decidable by human reason. It is knowable by my mind and other minds.

Chapter 24 of Perry Marshall's book *Evolution 2.0* is entitled 'Beyond "God of the Gaps": A New Paradigm for Biology'.[5] Like me, he dislikes a god of the gaps. Like everyone else he regards the biggest gap as that between the non-living and the living: 'Our newest scientific models have not successfully crossed this chasm. And the only hard evidence I have ever been able to find regarding this gap... pointed to the Origin of life being caused by an act of intelligence.' A little further on he says: 'In all my exploration, I have never found evidence that life can come from nonlife.' Between those two statements we find another: 'I'm all for filling that gap; that's why I'm offering the Evolution 2.0 Prize.' Marshall says that in order to progress, 'biology must draw upon an additional level of scientific principles beyond traditional physics, including linguistics, information theory, and signal processing. Perhaps even art, music and architecture.' Yes, but what about philosophy and theology? I say that because Marshall goes on to ask whether life is a miracle, saying if that were true 'it might be impossible to test that theory in the lab' and adds, 'Nevertheless we must all respect any scientists who have confidence that the gap will be bridged, they are only doing their job after all.'

I have a niggling feeling that Marshall, whose book is a fascinating read, may nevertheless be missing something here. For it might just be possible to test in a lab the theory that the origin of life does involve an intelligent input. In which case, why not balance things by encouraging a research effort to establish *scientifically* that Mind must have been involved? That would mean offering a Mind 2.0 Prize for the person that achieves it.

In the end, the burning question is: Does science teach us that matter produces mind, or that Mind produces matter? The answer will have to be determined by following Socrates' advice and examining the evidence and seeing where it leads, however threatening this may turn out to be to our preconceived notions. Thomas H. Huxley put it this way: 'Sit down before fact as a little child, be prepared to give up every preconceived notion, follow humbly wherever and to whatever abysses nature leads, or you shall learn nothing.'[6]

I have argued in the foregoing that the results of the natural sciences – cosmology, physics, chemistry, and biology – give strong support for the intuition that there is a supernatural Mind/Logos behind the universe and life. In this connection, it is worth mentioning an unusual argument

Matter produce mind
or mind produced matter?
Epilogue: Beyond Science But Not Beyond Reason / 369

used by the eminent German philosopher, the late Robert Spämann.[7] He cites the work of musicologist, Helga Thöne, who discovered in the Violin Partita in D-minor by J. S. Bach a remarkable double coding. She found that if you apply to the music a formal scheme of numbers corresponding to letters of the alphabet[8] there appears the following ancient proverb: 'Ex Deo nascimur, in Christo morimur, per Spiritum Sanctum reviviscimus'.[9] Clearly one does not have to know about this hidden text in order to enjoy the sonata. It has been enjoyed for hundreds of years without people having any idea that the message was there. But it was Bach's genius to encode a completely different kind of message in music that, in itself, judged solely by the criteria of musicology, is wonderful music. Spämann, writing in the days before the advent of systems biology, takes the following lesson from Bach's encoding: 'You can describe the evolutionary process, if you so decide, in purely naturalistic terms. But the text that then appears when you see a person, when you see a beautiful act or a beautiful picture can only be read if you use a completely different code.'[10] Spämann goes on to imagine a musicologist saying that the music explained itself completely, that it was simply chance that the message popped out so that it is enough to interpret the music purely as music without thinking about any text. Would that not strain our credulity? Of course it would. We would not for a moment accept that the text just happened to be there by chance.

It is the same with science. You can, if you wish, restrict yourself to a purely naturalistic science. Remember, though, that if you do, it is no good appealing to David Hume as we saw in Chapter 6. Also, if you do, you cannot hope to explain the text that appears. A musicologist, as musicologist, can explain how the music was composed; but only if she ignores the text. At a higher level, naturalism fails to account for the 'text' that is a human person with all the rich tapestry of her life, conversation, and thought.

The philosopher, Thomas Nagel, once set down what he would really like to find: 'The hope is not to discover a foundation that makes our knowledge unassailably secure but to find a way of understanding ourselves that is not radically self-undermining, and that does not require us to deny the obvious. The aim would be to offer a plausible picture of how we fit into the world.'[11] That sounds very reasonable and it reflects the motivation and spirit in which I have tried to write this book.

Although there are many questions that the natural sciences as such cannot address, nevertheless the universe contains rationally accessible clues as to its provenance. Its rational intelligibility, for instance, points

Purpose of

towards the existence of a Mind that was responsible both for the universe and for our minds. It is for this reason that we are able to do science and to discover the beautiful mathematical structures that underlie observable phenomena. Not only that, but our increasing insight into the fine-tuning of the universe increases the sense that we are meant to be here. All of this constitutes a rational *argument from design*. However, it works even more strongly as an *argument to design*. That is, if we believe *on other grounds* that there is a Mind behind the universe, that there is a God, then we might well expect to find that the universe is rationally intelligible, that it is fine-tuned for life, that life is based on information, etc. Since that is what we have found, it strengthens the evidence for the existence of God considerably by a process of cumulative evidence.

Key

In addition, if there really is a Mind behind the universe, and if that Mind intends us to be here, the really big question is: Why are we here? What is the purpose of our existence? It is this question above all that exercises the human heart. As we have seen, scientific analysis of the universe cannot give us the answer, any more than scientific analysis of Aunt Matilda's cake could tell us why she had made it. Scientific probing of the cake may tell us that it is good for humans; even that it was highly likely to have been designed specifically with humans in mind, since it is fine-tuned to their nutritional requirements. In other words, science may be able to point towards the conclusion that there is a purpose behind the cake; but precisely what that purpose is, science cannot tell us. It would be absurd to look for it within the cake. Only Aunt Matilda can reveal it to us.

The natural sciences are not embarrassed by their inability at this point. They simply recognize that they are not equipped to answer such questions. It would therefore be a serious logical error only to look within the ingredients of the universe – its material, structures, and processes – in order to find out what its purpose is and what we are here for. The ultimate answer, if there is one, will have to come from outside the universe, from something or someone who stands in a similar relationship to the universe as Aunt Matilda does to her cake.

But how shall we find out? We have argued that there is evidence that there is a Mind behind the universe, a Mind that intended us to be here. And we have minds. It is, therefore, not illogical that one of the major reasons why we have been given minds is not only that we should be able to explore our fascinating universe home, but also that we should be able to understand and even get to know the Giver of that home. After all, we humans are capable of giving expression to the thoughts of our minds and communicating them to others. It would therefore be very surprising if the Mind from which we are derived should be any less capable of self-expression and communication than we are. This leads us at once to the question: Is there any serious and credible evidence that that Mind has ever spoken into our world?

Many ancient cosmologies populated the universe with gods of every kind. These deities were usually thought to emerge from the primeval material chaos of the universe, so that they were ultimately part of the basic stuff of the universe itself. They cannot be the answer to our question since we are, by definition, looking for a Mind that exists independently of the universe. The Greek philosopher Aristotle in his *First Way* formulated the concept of an 'Unmoved Mover', which, though changeless itself, imparted change to other things. Regarding as absurd the idea that the principle of change should be inside the universe, he believed that this Unmoved Mover was in some sense outside the universe. However, Aristotle's Unmoved Mover was much too remote and abstract to have been interested in speaking into the world. This reminds me of a statement by Lord Jonathan Sacks we cited earlier: 'The meaning of a system lies outside the system.' He also said that: 'Science takes things apart to see how they work. Religion puts things together to see what they mean. Without going into neuroscientific detail, the first is a predominantly left-brain activity, the second is associated with the right hemisphere.'[12]

Long before Aristotle, the book of Genesis was penned. It starts, as we have mentioned, with the words: 'In the beginning, God created the heavens and the earth' (1:1). This statement stands in complete contrast with the other mythical cosmogonies of the time – like the Babylonian, in which the gods were part of the stuff of the universe, and where the world was made out of a god. Genesis claims that there is a Creator God who exists independently of the universe, a claim that is foundational to Judaism, Christianity, and Islam. As we have seen, the apostle John puts it this way: 'In the beginning was the Word, and the Word was with God, and the Word was God. He was in the beginning with God. All things were made through him, and without him was not anything made that was made. In him was life, and the life was the light of men (John 1:1-5 ESV).

This analysis bears close attention in light of Polkinghorne's remark, cited above, that God's input was 'informational', although there Polkinghorne was thinking more of the original creation. We have already considered the implications of this biblical statement for the priority of the concept of information over matter. And there are further implications. In Greek the word translated 'Word' is *Logos*, which, as we said earlier, was often used by Greek philosophers for the rational principle that governs the universe. Here we have the theological explanation for the rational intelligibility of the universe, for the fine-tuning of its physical constants and its word-like biological complexity. It is the product of a Mind – the divine *Logos*. What lies behind the universe is much more than a rational principle. It is God, the Creator himself. It is no abstraction, or even impersonal force, that lies behind the universe. God, the Creator, is a person. And just as Aunt Matilda is not part of her cake, neither is God part of the universe.

If the ultimate reality behind the universe is a personal God, this has very far-reaching implications for the human search for truth, since it opens up new possibilities for knowing ultimate reality other than the (scientific) study of things. For, persons communicate in a way that things do not. Persons can reveal themselves in speech and thereby communicate information about themselves that the most sophisticated scanner applied to their brains could not reveal. Being persons ourselves, we can get to know other persons. Therefore, the next logical question to ask is: If the Creator is personal, has he spoken directly, as distinct from what we can learn of him indirectly through the structures of the universe? Has he revealed himself? For if there is a God, and he has spoken, then what he has said will be of utmost importance in our search for truth.

Here we once again encounter the biblical claim that God has spoken in the most profound and direct way possible. He, the Word who is a person, has become human, to demonstrate fully that the ultimate truth behind the universe is personal. 'The Word became flesh and made his dwelling among us. We have seen his glory, the glory of the one and only Son, who came from the Father, full of grace and truth' (John 1:14).

This statement is highly specific. It asserts that, at a certain time and place, God the Creator encoded himself in humanity. It is, of course, a staggering claim to supernatural activity of the highest order. Yet, as we have taken care to point out earlier, science has not and cannot eliminate the supernatural.

As with so much else beyond the competence of science, this does not mean that there is no rational evidence for them. Indeed, presenting that evidence would take us far beyond the scope of this present book into matters both of history, literature, and experience that I have discussed in other books.[13] I shall, however, say a few things. Arthur Schawlow, who won the Nobel Prize for his work on laser spectroscopy, once said: 'We are fortunate to have the Bible and especially the New Testament, which tells us so much about God in widely accessible human terms.'[14]

Throughout this book I have tried to remain as objective as possible, though I am aware that this is impossible. All of us are influenced by our worldviews, whoever we are. I am passionate about science and the insights it gives us about the incredible creativity of God, and gives further objective evidence on which faith in him rests. Furthermore, it is the existence of a rational creator that validates science since it grounds the conviction necessary for doing science that the universe is rational intelligible. Indeed, scientific investigation and utilization of its findings seem to be encouraged by the Bible, in that it places human beings as stewards of nature and having minds that reflect the fact that they are made in the image of God.

I regard science as an input into my relationship with the God who created the universe that science studies – just like music may be involved in a musician's relationship with God who is a musician. All true science is God's science and therefore I am not conflicted at the intellectual level. I have no fear, as some do, of what science might throw at me. To put it another way, God is the God of the whole show – of what science has revealed as well as what it has not yet revealed and even of what it cannot in principle reveal. I find this attitude liberating in terms of my relationship with science: in particular, it frees me from limiting science to a narrow naturalistic paradigm.

How did I get there in my own life's journey? Sufficient to say here that I came to believe in God before I understood the arguments contained in this book. God was a living reality to me before I met arguments from design, although, in my restless curiosity I met them earlier than most. Yet such arguments were not the initial source of my faith in God, they were rather the confirmation of its validity and they have combined to strengthen that faith immeasurably. My parents were Christians and their Christianity was credible as it was lived out in lives of real integrity and consistency. This was for me the first convincing evidence of the truth of the Christian faith. In addition, far from forcing their Christian convictions on me, they loved me enough to encourage me to think for myself, read about other worldviews and make up my own mind – a rather unusual attitude in Northern Ireland in those days. They guided me to literature providing historical evidence, for example, for the authenticity of the New Testament documents and for the credibility of the resurrection of Jesus from a scientific and historical perspective. I found Christianity supremely rational and intellectually stimulating and mind-expanding. Not only that, but its personal message was unique: not only was there a God but also that I could have a personal relationship with God through Jesus Christ, not by my merit but by trusting him. I took the step of committing my life to him as Saviour and Lord and for over sixty years I have experienced what he promised – forgiveness, peace with God, a new quality of life, and a new power to live it, all received as a free gift. That is, I have found that Christianity, like much in science, is testable.

Now I realize that these things need to be unpacked in detail and I have done that elsewhere.[15] Sufficient to say here these convictions have been central to my life since then, and, far from hindering my science and intellectual inquiry, they have profoundly inspired it. Far from science having buried God, all I have found in science, indeed, the very fact that we can do science, confirms the existence of God in whom, in my case, I already believed because of the evidences for the life, death, and resurrection of Jesus Christ.

We have had a long journey together and, as we come to its end, my final comment is this: inevitably, not only those of us who do science, but all of us, have to choose the presupposition with which we start. There are not many options – essentially just two. Either human intelligence ultimately owes its origin to mindless matter; or there is a Creator. It is strange that some people claim that it is their intelligence that leads them to prefer the first to the second.

Faith is the evidence

Two options:

As people, our ability to be alive and to think

① due to being created my mindless matter

② due to the mind of The Creator God of the Bible.

Notes

Chapter 1: Introduction

1. Albert Einstein, *Ideas and Opinions* (New York: Dell Publishing, 1954), p. 11.
2. Ludwig Wittgenstein, *Notebooks 1914–1916*, 2nd ed, G. E. M. Anscombe (trans.) (Chicago, IL: University of Chicago Press, 1979), p. 74.
3. Stephen Hawking and Leonard Mlodinow, *The Grand Design* (London: Bantam Press, 2010).
4. Peter Atkins, 'The Limitless Power of Science' in *Nature's Imagination: The Frontiers of Scientific Vision*, ed. John Cornwell (Oxford: Oxford University Press, 1995), p. 125.
5. Baruch A. Shalev, *100 Years of Nobel Prizes*, 3rd ed. (Los Angeles: Atlantic, 2005).
6. G. Galilei, *Dialogues Concerning the Two Chief Systems of the World*, trans. S. Drake (Berkeley: The University of California Press, 1953).

Chapter 2: Matters of Evidence and Faith

1. Peter Atkins, 'Will science ever fail?', *New Scientist*, 8 August 1992, pp. 32–35.
2. Richard Dawkins, 'Is science a religion?', *The Humanist*, Jan/Feb 1997, pp. 26–39.
3. Richard Dawkins, *The God Delusion* (London: Bantam Press, 2006), p. 5.
4. 'Science Extra', *The Daily Telegraph*, 11 September, 1989.
5. William James, *The Will to Believe* (New York: Dover Publications, 1956), p. 51.
6. John 20:31.
7. Romans 1:20.
8. Francis Collins, *The Language of God* (New York: Free Press, 2006), p. 164.
9. John Haught, *God and the New Atheists* (Louisville, KT and Westminster: John Knox Press, 2008), p. 62.
10. Alister McGrath, *Dawkins' God* (Oxford: Blackwell), 2004.
11. Richard Dawkins, *A Devil's Chaplain* (London: Weidenfeld and Nicholson, 2003), p. 248
12. Alvin Plantinga, *Where the Conflict Really Lies: Science, Religion, & Naturalism* (Oxford: OUP, 2012), p. xi.
13. 3 April 1997, 386, pp. 435–36.
14. Larry Witham, *Where Darwin Meets the Bible* (Oxford: OUP, 2002), p. 272.
15. *Scientific American*, September 1999, pp. 88–93.
16. M. Stirrat and R. E. Cornwell, 'Eminent scientists reject the supernatural: a survey of the Fellows of the Royal Society', *Evolution Education Outreach* 6, article no. 33, 2013. See https://doi.org/10.1186/1936-6434-6-33
17. D. Ruth, 'Misconceptions of science and religion found in new study', 16 February 2014, http://news.rice.edu/2014/02/16/misconceptions-of-science-and-religion-found-in-new-study/
18. John Houghton, *The Search for God: Can Science Help?* (Oxford: Lion Hudson, 1995) p. 59.
19. In *God and the Scientists*, compiled by Mike Poole, CPO, 1997.
20. Peter Atkins, *Nature's Imagination: The Frontiers of Scientific Vision*, John Cornwell (ed.) (Oxford: OUP, 1995), p. 132.

Chapter 3: A Historical Perspective: The Forgotten Roots of Science and Arguments from Design

1. Melvin Calvin, *Chemical Evolution* (Oxford: Clarendon Press, 1969), p. 258.
2. Werner Jaeger, *The Theology of the Early Greek Philosophers* (Oxford: OUP, 1967 [paperback]), pp. 16–17.
3. https://plato.stanford.edu/entries/teleological-arguments/
4. This emptying of the natural world of gods, demons, and spirits is often called the de-deification of the universe.
5. Deuteronomy 17:3.
6. Jeremiah 8:2.
7. See, for example, Edward G. Newing, 'Religions of pre-literary societies', in *The World's Religions*, Sir Norman Anderson (ed.) (London: IVP, 1975, 4th edn), p. 38.
8. Cited in Anthony Kenny, *A Brief History of Western Philosophy* (Oxford: Blackwell, 1998).
9. 'Atom' from Greek *'atomos'* meaning something that cannot be cut.
10. *The Feynman Lectures on Physics*, Robert Leighton and Matthew Sands (eds.) (London: Basic Books, 2011), vol. 1.
11. Plato, *Three Dialogues: Protagoras, Philebus, and Gorgias*, trans. Benjamin Jowett (New York: Cosimo

Classics, 2011), p. 73.

12. Brian Morley, 'Western Concepts of God', Internet Encyclopedia of Philosophy, https://iep.utm.edu/god-west/

13. The term is said by some to come from Academos, the name of the man who previously owned the site on which the Academy was built.

14. For an account of mathematics in the Academy see *A History of Mathematics* by Uta C. Merzbach and Carl B. Boyer (Hoboken, NJ: John Wiley, 2011), p. 74ff.

15. *The Epicurus Reader*, Brad Inwood and L.P. Gerson (trans.) (Indianapolis, IN: Hackett, 1994), 10.104.

16. Benjamin Wiker, *Moral Darwinism* (Downers Grove, IL: IVP, 2002).

17. It is worth noting that Paul made essentially the same point to an audience that consisted of both Epicurean and Stoic philosophers in Athens – see Acts 17.

18. *Fortune*, F. C. Babitt, in Moralia (trans.), vol. 2, Loeb Classical Library (Cambridge, MA: Harvard University Press, 1928), p. 87.

19. 'How Has Jewish Thought Influenced Science?', *Moment*, Jan–Feb 2014, https://momentmag.com/jewish-thought-influenced-science/

20. Thomas Aquinas, *Summa Theologica*, Article 3, Question 2.

21. Keith Ward, *Why There Almost Certainly is a God* (Oxford: Lion Hudson, 2008), p. 104.

22. Isaac Newton, *Opticks* (1704) (New York: Dover, 1979), p. 400.

23. Carlo Rovelli, *Reality is Not What it Seems* (London: Penguin Random House, 2016), p. 36.

24. Alfred North Whitehead, *Science and the Modern World* (London: Macmillan, 1925), p. 19.

25. C. S. Lewis, *Miracles*, Signature Classics Edition (London: Collins, 2016), p. 169.

26. 'Science and Society in East and West', *The Great Titration* (London, Allen and Unwin, 1969).

27. T. F. Torrance, *Theological Science* (Edinburgh: T & T Clark, 1996), p. 57.

28. Torrance, *Theological Science*, p. 58.

29. Torrance, *Theological Science*, p. 58.

30. John Brooke, *Science & Religion: Some Historical Perspectives* (Cambridge: CUP, 1991), p. 19.

31. Peter Harrison, *The Bible, Protestantism and the Rise of Science* (Cambridge: CUP, 1998).

32. For detailed investigation of the current ramifications of determinism, see my book *Determined to Believe?* (Oxford: Lion Hudson), 2017.

33. Henry Stapp, *Mindful Universe: Quantum Mechanics and the Participating Observer* (Berlin-Heidelberg: Springer, 2007), pp. 5–6.

34. Peter Harrison, *The Territories of Science and Religion* (Chicago and London: University of Chicago Press, 2015), pp. 172–73.

35. Dava Sobel, *Galileo's Daughter* (London: Fourth Estate, 1999).

36. Arthur Koestler, *The Sleepwalkers: A History of Man's Changing Vision of the Universe* (London: Penguin, 1989, p. 358).

37. Paul Marston, *Great Astronomers in European History* (Bristol: Canopus Publishing for UCLAN, 2014), Chapter 6.

38. The reader interested in more detail should consult the excellent chapter on Galileo in *Reconstructing Nature*, John Brooke and Geoffrey Cantor (Edinburgh: T&T Clark, 1998).

39. Galileo made reference to this in his famous letter to the Grand Duchess Christina of Tuscany (1615) when he upbraided those who failed to realize that 'under the surface meaning this [biblical] passage may contain a different sense'.

40. For a more detailed investigation of these issues see my *Seven Days that Divide the World* (Grand Rapids: Zondervan, 2nd ed., 2021).

41. Marston, *Great Astronomers*, Chapter 6.

42. See, for example J. H. Brooke, 'The Wilberforce–Huxley Debate: Why Did It Happen?' in *Science and Christian Belief*, 2001, 13, pp. 127–41.

43. See 'Wilberforce and Huxley, A Legendary Encounter', by J. R. Lucas in *The Historical Journal*, 22 (2), 1979, pp. 313–30.

44. J. H. Brooke, *Science and Religion: Some Historical Perspectives* (Cambridge: CUP, 1991), p. 71.

45. See David M. Knight and Matthew D. Eddy, *Science and Beliefs: From Natural Philosophy to Natural Science 1700–1900* (London: Ashgate, 2005).

46. C. Russell, 'The Conflict Metaphor and its Social Origins', *Science and Christian Belief*, 1989, 1, 3, 26.

47. Michael Poole, *Beliefs and Values in Science Education* (Buckingham: Open University Press, 1995), p. 125.

48. That debate (and other material) may be found on my website johnlennox.org.

49. *The Nature of the Gods*, H. C. P. McGregor (trans.) (London: Penguin, 1972), p. 163.

50. William Paley, *Natural Theology; or Evidences of the Existence and Attributes of the Deity*, 18th ed. rev., (Edinburgh: Lackington, Allen and Co, and James Sawers, 1818), pp. 12–14.

51. Paley, *Natural Theology*, pp. 12–14.

52. Paley, *Natural Theology*, p. 473.
53. Stephen Jay Gould, *The Structure of Evolutionary Theory* (Cambridge, MA: Harvard University Press, 2002), p. 230.
54. Nora Barlow (ed.), *The Autobiography of Charles Darwin, 1809–1882: with original omissions restored* (New York: W. W. Norton, 1969), p. 87.
55. Bertrand Russell, *History of Western Philosophy* (London: Routledge, 2000), p. 570. Russell also notes the limitations of the design argument in demonstrating the full range of God's attributes.
56. That Paley was well aware of what Hume had written, we have already seen.
57. David Hume, *An Enquiry Concerning Human Understanding* (1748), J. C. Gaskin (ed.) (Oxford: OUP, 1998).
58. Hume, *An Enquiry*, p. 46.
59. *Debating Design*, William Dembski and Michael Ruse (eds.) (Cambridge: CUP, 2004), p. 107.
60. E. Sober, *Philosophy of Biology* (Boulder: CO, Westview Press, 1993), p. 34.
61. Del Ratzsch, 'Teleological Arguments for God's Existence', *Stanford Encyclopedia of Philosophy* 2005, revised 2019. https://plato.stanford.edu/entries/teleological-arguments/
62. In May 2019, researchers, in a milestone effort, reported the creation of a new synthetic (possibly artificial) form of viable life, a variant of the bacteria Escherichia coli, by reducing the natural number of 64 codons in the bacterial genome to 59 codons instead, in order to encode 20 amino acids. (For further information see Carl Zimmer, 'Scientists Created Bacteria With a Synthetic Genome. Is This Artificial Life?', *The New York Times*, 15 May 2019.)
63. Perhaps this was in part responsible for Newman's reaction?
64. There are scientists who hold the reductionist view that living organisms are nothing but machines. They, one might suppose, should therefore have no objection to the original mechanistic version of the design argument.
65. Del Ratzsch, 'Teleological Arguments'.
66. John Polkinghorne, 'Where is Natural Theology today?', *Science and Christian Belief* 18 (2), 2006, pp. 169–79.
67. BBC Radio 4 interview, 10 December 2004.
68. Del Ratzsch, *Science and its Limits* (Downers Grove, IL: IVP, 2000), p. 113.
69. For a detailed discussion of different views of the biblical creation narrative see my book *Seven Days that Divide the World* (Grand Rapids, MI: Zondervan, 2nd ed., 2021).
70. *Kitzmiller*, IL, 400 F.Supp.2d 707, 746.
71. Thomas Nagel, 'Public Education and Intelligent Design', *Philosophy & Public Affairs*, Wiley InterScience, vol. 36 (2), 2008.
72. Nagel, 'Public Education', p. 190.
73. Nagel, 'Public Education', pp. 196–97.
74. Nagel, 'Public Education', p. 196.
75. Nagel, 'Public Education', p. 202.
76. Nagel, 'Public Education', p. 199.

Chapter 4: Science, its Presuppositions, Scope, and Methodology

1. Richard Feynman, *The Meaning of it All* (London: Penguin, 2007), pp. 4–5.
2. Richard Feynman, *The Pleasure of Finding Things Out* (Cambridge, MA: Perseus Books, 1999), p. 255.
3. https://sciencecouncil.org/about-science/our-definition-of-science/
4. For these and many other examples see R. E. D. Clark, *Science and Christian Belief* (London, The English Universities Press, 1960), Chapter III.
5. 'The Evolution of the Physicist's Picture of Nature', *Scientific American*, 208 (5), 1963.
6. Feynman, *Meaning*, pp. 26–27.
7. Their suggestions have resulted in the so-called 'Science Wars'.
8. It is nevertheless important, especially in those areas of science in which the influence of worldview is most likely, for scientists to make a regular health check on the extent to which they are, in the words of Steve Woolgar, 'not engaged in the passive description of pre-existing facts in the world, but are actively engaged in formulating or constructing the character of that world' (*Science: The Very Idea* [New York: Routledge, 1988; republished 1993]).
9. Please note that this kind of induction should not be confused with induction in mathematics. That is a different concept.
10. Michael Ruse, *Darwinism Defended* (Reading: Addison-Wesley, 1982), p. 322.
11. A distinction is sometimes made between abduction and inference to the best explanation. The original sense of 'abduction' in the work of C. S. Peirce is more concerned with the generation of hypotheses, whereas it is now often used in the sense of the justification of hypotheses (and so as

equivalent to inference to the best explanation as I have done).
12. Explanatory essay.
13. http://www.newtonproject.ox.ac.uk/view/texts/normalized/NATP00056
14. Isaac Newton, *Philosophical Writings*, IV *Correspondence with Richard Bentley* (1692–93). https://www.cambridge.org/core/books/isaac-newton-philosophical-writings/correspondence-with-richard-bentley-16923/91E19809F0AACC2C3FDE14DF7501EC65
15. *Science and Religion* (Carlisle: Paternoster Periodicals, 1996).
16. Austin Farrer, *A Science of God* (London: Geoffrey Bles, 1966), pp. 29, 30.
17. Edward P. Tryton, 'Is the Universe a Vacuum Fluctuation?' *Nature*, 246, 1973, p. 396.
18. Keith Ward, *Why There Almost Certainly is a God* (Oxford: Lion Hudson, 2008), p. 23.
19. Notice Dawkins uses the faith word 'believes'. Like all of us, Dawkins is a person of faith in many things, though in his case, it is in naturalism and not in God.
20. Peter Atkins, *Creation Revisited* (Harmondsworth: Penguin, 1994), p. 143.
21. Ward, *Why There Almost Certainly*, p. 49.
22. Stephen Hawking, *A Brief History of Time: From the Big Bang to Black Holes* (London: Bantam Press, 1988), p. 174.
23. Reported by Clive Cookson, 'Scientists who glimpsed God', *Financial Times*, 29 April 1995, p. 20.
24. In an idealized situation, of course!
25. William Paley, *Natural Theology*, p. 7.
26. *New York Times*, 12 March 1991, p. B9.
27. 'Das Unverstaendliche am Universum ist im Grunde, dass wir es verstehen'.
28. Keith Ward, *God, Chance and Necessity* (Oxford: One World Publications, 1996), p. 1.
29. Albert Einstein, *Letters to Solovine* (New York: Philosophical Library, 1987), p. 131.
30. Paul Davies, *The Mind of God* (London: Simon and Schuster, 1992), p. 150.
31. For example, the use made in the study of electromagnetic waves (and hence in electronics) of the abstract pure mathematical construction of a number system, in which the number -1 has a square root.
32. E. P. Wigner, 'The unreasonable effectiveness of mathematics', *Communications in Pure and Applied Mathematics*, 13 (1960), pp. 1–14.
33. Roger Penrose, *The Emperor's New Mind* (London: Vintage, 1991), p. 430.
34. John Polkinghorne, *Reason and Reality* (London: SPCK, 1991), p. 76.
35. Davies, *Mind of God*, p. 81.
36. John Haught, *God and the New Atheists* (Louisville, Westminster: John Knox Press, 2008), p. 47.
37. Haught, *God and the New Atheists*, p. 48.
38. Ward, *God, Chance and Necessity*, pp. 55–56.
39. ABC Television 20/20, 1989.
40. J. J. C. Smart and J. J. Haldane, *Atheism and Theism* (Oxford: Blackwell, 1996), p. 92.
41. *The Structure of Scientific Revolutions*, 2nd ed. (Chicago, IL University of Chicago Press, 1970).
42. A paradigm need not be as all-encompassing as a worldview, but it is often the case that they are closely related, if not identical.
43. Thomas Nagel, *Mortal Questions* (Cambridge: CUP, 1979), p. xi.
44. As reported by Associated Press, 9 December 2004.
45. For a nuanced contemporary discussion of the relationships between science and religion see Mikael Stenmark, *How to Relate Science and Religion* (Grand Rapids, MI: Eerdmans 2004).
46. 'Why' questions connected with function as distinct from purpose are usually regarded as within the provenance of science.
47. Erwin Schrödinger, Nature and the Greeks (Cambridge: CUP, 1954).
48. P. B. Medawar, *Advice to a Young Scientist* (London: Harper and Row, 1979), p. 31; see also his book *The Limits of Science* (Oxford: OUP, 1984), p. 66.
49. P. B. Medawar, *The Limits of Science* (Oxford: OUP, 1984), p. 92.
50. Francis Collins, *The Language of God* (New York: The Free Press), 2006.
51. Bertrand Russell, *History of Western Philosophy* (London: Routledge, 2000), p.13.
52. Feynman, *Meaning*, pp. 16–17.
53. Feynman, *Meaning*, p. 43.
54. Austin Farrer, *A Science of God?* (London: Geoffrey Bles, 1966), p. 29.
55. Atkins, *Creation Revisited*, p. 1.
56. Atkins, *Creation Revisited*, pp. 127–28.

Chapter 5: Worldviews and Their Relation to Science: Naturalism and its Shortcomings

1. Alvin Plantinga, *Where the Conflict Really Lies* (Oxford: OUP, 2012), p. ix.

2. Ted Honderich (ed.), *The Oxford Companion to Philosophy* (Oxford: OUP, 1995), p. 530.
3. Ted Honderich (ed.), *Oxford Companion*, p. 604.
4. E. O. Wilson, 'Intelligent Evolution', *Harvard Magazine*, November 2005.
5. Wilson, 'Intelligent Evolution'.
6. Wilson, 'Intelligent Evolution'.
7. Power Lamprecht Sterling, *The Metaphysics of Naturalism* (New York: Appleton-Century-Crofts, 1960), p. 160.
8. Genesis 1:1.
9. Wilson, 'Intelligent Evolution'.
10. 'The Big Bang, Stephen Hawking, and God', in *Science: Christian Perspectives for the New Millennium* (Addison, TX and Norcross, GA: CLM and RZIM Publishers, 2003).
11. In *Darwinism, Design and Public Education*, John Angus Campbell and Stephen C. Meyer (East Lansing: Michigan State University Press, 2003) p. 195.
12. Christian de Duve, *Life Evolving* (New York: OUP, 2002), p. 284.
13. Kitzmiller et al. vs. Dover Area School District (2005).
14. Paul Kurtz, *Philosophical Essays in Pragmatic Naturalism* (Buffalo, NY: Prometheus Books, 1990), p.12.
15. George Klein, *The Atheist and the Holy City* (Cambridge, MA: MIT Press, 1990), p. 203.
16. Richard Lewontin's review of Carl Sagan's book *The Demon Haunted World: Science as a Candle in the Dark* in *New York Review of Books*, 9 January 1997.
17. One cannot help applaud Lewontin's openness here: he is neither unaware of his worldview commitment nor does he seek to hide it.
18. Richard Lewontin's review of Carl Sagan's book, 1997.
19. Which is, presumably, why questions about religious convictions are not normally asked by interviewing committees for scientific positions – though it is not completely unknown.
20. Richard Dawkins, *The Blind Watchmaker* (London: Longmans, 1986), p. 1.
21. Timothy Lenoir, *Strategy of Life* (Chicago, IL: University of Chicago Press, 1982), p. ix.
22. Ernan McMullin, 'Plantinga's Defence of Special Creation', *Christian Scholar's Review*, 1991, p. 57.
23. Meaning 'Decision problem'.
24. Freeman Dyson, 'The Scientist as Rebel', in *Nature's Imagination: The Frontiers of Scientific Vision*, John Cornwell (ed.) (Oxford: OUP, 1995), p. 8.
25. Francis Crick, *Of Molecules and Man* (Washington: University of Washington Press, 1966), p. 10.
26. Dawkins, *Blind Watchmaker*, p. 15.
27. Jacques Monod, *Chance and Necessity* (New York: Knopf, 1972).
28. Ernst Mayr, 'The place of biology in the sciences and its conceptual structure', in *The Growth of Biological Thought* (Cambridge, MA, London: Harvard University Press, 1982), pp. 21–82.
29. Thomas Nagel, *Mind and Cosmos* (Oxford: OUP, 2012), p. 5
30. Karl Popper, 'Scientific Reduction and the Essential Incompleteness of All Science', in *Studies in the Philosophy of Biology, Reduction and Related Problems*, F. J. Ayala and T. Dobzhansky (eds.) (London: Macmillan, 1974).
31. In his *The Tacit Dimension* (New York: Doubleday, 1966).
32. Some may think that I am cheating here. For instance, they might argue that although the semiotics of the letters cannot be given an explanation in terms of physics and chemistry *directly*, nevertheless my argument fails since in the end the human authors of the writing can ultimately be explained in terms of physics and chemistry. However, this simply begs the question that lies at the heart of our consideration: Does such a reductionist explanation for human beings actually exist?
33. Arthur Peacocke, *The Experiment of Life* (Toronto: University of Toronto Press, 1983), p. 54.
34. BBC Christmas Lectures Study Guide (London: BBC, 1991).
35. C. S. Lewis, *Mere Christianity* (New York: HarperOne, 2001), p. 22.
36. Stephen Hawking and Leonard Mlodinow, *The Grand Design* (London: Bantam Press, 2010), p. 5.
37. P. A. Schilpp (ed.), *Albert Einstein: Philosopher-Scientist, The Library of Living Philosophers* (Evanston, IL: Open Court, 1949), p. 684.
38. Albert Einstein, 'Physics and Reality', *Journal of the Franklin Institute*, 221 (3), p. 349, 1936, https://doi.org/10.1016/S0016-0032(36)91047-5.
39. Peter Atkins in *Nature's Imagination: Frontiers of Scientific Vision*, John Cornwell (ed.) (Oxford: OUP, 1995), p. 125.
40. Atkins, *On Being* (Oxford: University Press, 2011), p. xiii.
41. On YouTube see 'Duelling Professors' (https://www.youtube.com/watch?v=5gMS7WTHnho) and my 'Unbelievable' debate with Atkins at the University of Southampton (https://www.youtube.com/watch?v=fSYwCaFkYno). And it really was unbelievable!
42. Mikael Stenmark, 'Scientism' in: J. Wentzel Vrede van Huyssteen (ed.), *Encyclopedia of Science and Religion*, 2nd ed. (Detroit: Thomson Gale, 2003), p. 783.

43. Ian Hutchinson, *Monopolising Knowledge* (Belmont, Mass.: Fias Publishing), 2011.
44. *The Oxford Handbook of Religion and Science* (Oxford: OUP, 2006), p. 762.
45. See my chapter 'Scientific Fundamentalism' in *Fundamentalisms: Threats and Ideologies in the Modern World*, ed. James Dunn (London, I. B. Tauris, 2015).
46. Bertrand Russell, *Religion and Science*, Ch. IX 'Science of Ethics', 1935, p. 243.
47. Bertrand Russell, *History of Western Philosophy* (London: Routledge, 2000), p. 789.

Chapter 6: Theism and its Relationship to Science: God of the Gaps, Complexity of God, and Miracles

1. 189.R.4.47, f. 6, Trinity College Library, Cambridge, UK. Published online 2007. See http://www.newtonproject.ox.ac.uk/view/texts/normalized/THEM00256
2. See Perry Marshall, *Evolution 2.0*, Chapter 24 (Dallas, TX: BenBella Books, 2015).
3. I ask the reader to pardon this infelicity – the inventor of the internal combustion engine was not Henry Ford but another American, George Brayton, in 1872.
4. Richard Swinburne, *Is There a God?* (Oxford: Oxford University Press, 1996), p. 68.
5. Psalm 111:2.
6. Richard Dawkins, *The God Delusion* (London: Bantam Press, 2006), p.147
7. Richard Dawkins, *The Blind Watchmaker* (London: Longmans, 1986), p.141.
8. I am well aware of the view in philosophical theology that God is 'simple' but I do not refer to this view here since, in normal discussion, mind is usually regarded as more 'complex' than matter, although admittedly it is hard to pin down precisely what that means.
9. Another important criterion is consistency – both logical consistency and consistency with evidence.
10. Dawkins, *God Delusion*, p. 169ff.
11. See the discussion on the concept of a multiverse in Chapter 4.
12. Augustine, in *On the Literal Meaning of Genesis*.
13. Francis Crick, *Life Itself* (New York: Simon and Schuster, 1981), p. 88.
14. Dawkins, *God Delusion*, p. 187.
15. Ian Hutchinson, 'Can a scientist believe in the resurrection? Three hypotheses', 25 March 2016; http://www.veritas.org/can-scientist-believe-resurrection-three-hypotheses/; http://augustinecollective.org/can-a-scientist-believe/
16. Francis Collins, *The Language of God*, pp. 51–52.
17. See 'An Enquiry Concerning Human Understanding' with 'A letter from a Gentleman to his friend in Edinburgh' and Hume's 'Abstract of a Treatise on Human Nature'(Indiana: Hackett Publishing Co, 1993) 10.1, pp. 76–77.
18. David Hume, *An Enquiry Concerning Human Understanding*, 4.1, p. 15. This is an example of the so-called 'Problem of Induction'.
19. Hume, *An Enquiry* 4.1.
20. Anthony Flew, *There is a God* (New York: Harper One, 2007), pp. 57–58.
21. Christopher Hitchens, *God is Not Great* (London: Atlantic Books, 2007), p. 141.
22. Hume, *An Enquiry*, p. 79.
23. Ian Hutchinson, 'Can a scientist believe'.
24. See C S Lewis, *Miracles*, Signature Classics Edition (London: Collins, 2016), p. 62.
25. Alvin Plantinga, *Where the Conflict Really Lies* (Oxford: OUP, 2011), particularly Chapter 4.
26. In this connection one thinks of the words of Wittgenstein: 'The great delusion of modernity is that the laws of nature explain the universe for us. The laws of nature describe the universe, they describe the regularities. But they explain nothing.'
27. This should be compared with Hume's comments on regularities that we referred to earlier. Von Wachter's argument is very different.
28. Daniel von Wachter, 'Miracles Are Not Violations of the Laws of Nature Because the Laws Do Not Entail Regularity', *European Journal for the Philosophy of Religion*, 7 (4), 2015, p. 43.
29. Von Wachter, 'Miracles', p. 55.
30. We shall consider the important implications of quantum mechanics in Chapter 21.
31. Von Wachter, 'Miracles', pp. 56–57.
32. Lewis, *Miracles*, p. 63.
33. Lewis, *Miracles*, p. 73.
34. For more on Hume's argument that miracles are so improbable that any purported evidence for them could not outweigh the evidence for regularity see Jon Earman, *Hume's Abject Failure* (Oxford: OUP, 2000).
35. From the introduction to *The Natural History of Religion*, Introduction by John M. Robertson (London: A. and H. Bradlaugh Bonner, 1889).

36. David Hume, *Dialogues Concerning Natural Religion* 2nd ed., Richard Popkin (ed.) (Indianapolis, IN: Hackett, 1998).

37. That is, reasons which have to do with the convictions, beliefs, and principles we already have, before we bring them to bear on a situation.

38. Thomas Nagel, *Mind and Cosmos* (Oxford: OUP, 2012), p. 28.

39. James Shapiro, *Evolution: A View from the 21st Century* (Upper Saddle River, NJ: FT Press Science, 2011).

40. Suzan Mazur conducted an interesting interview with Shapiro in *The Paradigm Shifters* (New York: Caswell Books, 2015).

41. Suzan Mazur, *The Altenberg 16* (Berkeley, CA: North Atlantic Books, 2010).

42. Shaprio, *Evolution*, Kindle loc. 292–93

43. Jacques Monod and Austryn Wainhouse (trans.), *Chance and Necessity: An Essay on the Natural Philosophy of Modern Biology* (London: Collins 1971).

44. In a 1926 letter to Max Born (one of the pioneers of quantum mechanics).

45. Pierre Simon Laplace, *A Philosophical Essay on Probabilities*, 6th ed., F. W. Truscott and F. L Emory (trans.) (New York: Dover, 1961), p. 4.

46. We shall explore the implication of quantum mechanics in Chapter 21.

47. Francis Collins, *The Language of God*, p. 205.

48. Taken from the Australian Broadcasting Commission Science Unit broadcast on 10 June 1976 of a tribute to Monod which was entitled *The Secret of Life*.

Chapter 7: Understanding the Universe: The Beginning and Fine Tuning

1. *The Meaning of Evolution* (New Haven, CT: Yale UP, 1949), p. 344.

2. 'Energy in the Universe', *Scientific American*, 224, 1971, p. 50.

3. Paul Davies, *The Mind of God* (London: Simon and Schuster, 1992), p. 232.

4. See *The Timaeus*.

5. Friedrich Engels, *Ludwig Feuerbach* (New York: International Publishers, 1974), p. 21.

6. Stephen Hawking, *A Brief History of Time: From the Big Bang to Black Holes* (London: Bantam Press, 1988), p. 46.

7. 'The End of the World: From the Standpoint of Mathematical Physics', *Nature*, 127, 1931, p. 450.

8. *Nature*, 259, 1976, pp. 15–16.

9. *Nature*, 340, 1989, p. 425.

10. Jonathan Sacks, *The Great Partnership* (London: Hodder and Stoughton, 2011), p. 9.

11. The expression 'quantum vacuum' can be misleading for someone not familiar with the terminology of physics. For the word 'vacuum' tends to convey the idea that nothing is there at all. A quantum vacuum is a term physicists use for a quantum field in its ground or lowest energy state. It is certainly not 'nothing'.

12. That is, they use complex numbers in order to cope with the fact that in their model the geometry of space-time involves two 'time' dimensions treated in the same way as the spatial dimensions.

13. Hawking, *A Brief History of Time*, p. 139.

14. Neil Turok of Cambridge is currently challenging the standard model by suggesting that the Big Bang at the start of our universe is only one of many. His view implies a return to the eternity of space-time. The debate is not over yet!

15. Second edition (Oxford: Lion Hudson, 2021).

16. Lawrence Krauss, *A Universe from Nothing* (London: Simon & Schuster, 2012), pp. 65–70.

17. John Horgan, 'Physicist George Ellis Knocks Physicists for Knocking Philosophy, Falsification, Free Will', *Scientific American* blog, 22 July 2014, https://blogs.scientificamerican.com/cross-check/physicist-george-ellis-knocks-physicists-for-knocking-philosophy-falsification-free-will/

18. Stephen Hawking and Leonard Mlodinow, *The Grand Design: New Answers to the Ultimate Questions of Life* (London: Bantam, 2010), p. 180. I analyse this statement in detail in *God and Stephen Hawking: Whose Design is it Anyway?* (Oxford: Lion Hudson), 2021.

19. Peter Atkins, *Creation Revisited* (Harmondsworth: Penguin, 1994), p. 143.

20. Keith Ward, *God, Chance and Necessity* (Oxford: One World Publications, 1996), p. 49.

21. Charles H. Townes, *Making Waves*, American Physical Society, 1995, page unknown.

22. Fred Hoyle, *Annual Review of Astronomy and Astrophysics*, 20, 1982, p. 16.

23. Paul Davies, *God and the New Physics* (London: J. M. Dent and Sons, 1983).

24. Hugh Ross, *The Creator and the Cosmos* (Colorado Springs, CO: Navpress, 1995), p. 117.

25. See A. H. Guth, 'Inflationary Universe', *Physical Review* D, 23, 1981, p. 348.

26. Roger Penrose, *The Emperor's New Mind* (Oxford: Oxford University Press, 1989), p. 344.

27. Penrose, *Emperor's New Mind*, p. 344.

28. Paul Davies, *The Cosmic Blueprint* (New York: Simon and Schuster, 1988), p. 203.

29. Hugh Ross, *The Creator and the Cosmos*, pp. 138–39.

30. Guillermo Gonzalez and Jay W. Richards, *The Privileged Planet* (Washington DC: Regnery, 2004).

31. Gonzalez and Richards, *Privileged Planet*, p. xiii.

32. Gonzalez and Richards, *Privileged Planet*, p. 335.

33. *Cosmos, Bios and Theos*, Henry Margenau and Roy Varghese (eds.) (La Salle, IL: Open Court, 1992), p. 83.

34. For example, Barrow and Tipler, *The Anthropic Cosmological Principle* (Oxford: OUP, 1988), p. 566.

35. Richard Dawkins, *The God Delusion* (London: Bantam Press, 2006), p. 164.

36. John Leslie, *Universes* (London: Routledge, 1989), p. 14. See also the discussion in A. McGrath, *The Foundations of Dialogue in Science and Religion* (Blackwell: Oxford, 1998), p. 114 ff.

37. David Deutsch, *The Fabric of Reality* (London: Penguin, 1997).

38. Martin Rees, *Just Six Numbers* (London: Weidenfeld and Nicholson, 1999).

39. John Polkinghorne, *One World* (London: SPCK, 1986), p. 80.

40. Richard Swinburne, *Is There a God?* (Oxford: OUP, 1995), p. 68.

41. E. Harrison, *Masks of the Universe* (New York: Macmillan, 1985), pp. 252, 263.

42. In Denis Brian, *Genius Talk* (New York: Plenum, 1995).

43. Christian de Duve, *Life Evolving* (New York: OUP, 2002), p. 299.

44. Martin Rees, *Our Cosmic Habitat* (London: Phoenix, 2003), p. 164.

45. For a very comprehensive in-depth survey of this whole field see Rodney Holder, *The Multiverse, God and Everything* (Farnham: Ashgate Press, 2008).

46. In Malcolm Browne, *New York Times*, 'Clues to the Universe's Origin Expected', 12 March 1978, p. 1.

47. Lemaître called his original idea the 'hypothesis of the primeval atom'.

48. The reader interested in learning more about the issues raised in this chapter is referred to my updated and revised book, *God and Stephen Hawking 2e* (Oxford: Lion Hudson: 2021).

Chapter 8: The Wonder of the Living World

1. Though mules cannot reproduce.

2. Michael Denton, *Evolution: A Theory in Crisis* (Bethesda, MD: Adler & Adler, 1986), p. 250.

3. Denton, *Evolution*, p. 250.

4. Jacques Manod, *Chance and Necessity* (London: Collins, 1972), p. 134, as cited by Denton.

5. Bruce Alberts, 'The Cell as a Collection of Protein Machines', *Cell*, 92, 1998, p. 291. For a vivid, imaginative account of what it is like inside a cell, see Bill Bryson, *A Short History of Nearly Everything* (London: Black Swan, 2004), Chapter 24.

6. See the account in: Jasmine A. Nirody, Yi-Ren Sun and Chien-Jung Lo, 'The biophysicist's guide to the bacterial flagellar motor', *Advances in Physics X*, 2:2, 2017, pp. 324–43, DOI: 10.1080/23746149.2017.1289120.

7. The interested reader can find a useful diagram for reference at https://www.pnas.org/content/115/51/12845. Additionally, I would strongly encourage the reader to stop reading for a few minutes and watch a spectacular simulation of the walking kinesin on the internet: https://www.youtube.com/watch?v=y-uuk4Pr2i8

8. Adenosine triphosphate (ATP) is an organic compound found in all living organisms. It is an energy source for many processes in living cells, e.g. muscle contraction, nerve impulse propagation, and chemical synthesis.

9. The term amino acid is short for α-amino (alpha-amino) carboxylic acid.

10. 'How scientists are creating life-like cells from scratch', Nature, 563, 172–75, 7 November 2018, doi: https://doi.org/10.1038/d41586-018-07289-x

11. For a full list of the amino acids that can be obtained in such experiments, and a detailed discussion of the whole 'origin of life' question, see *The Mystery of Life's Origin*, Charles B. Thaxton, Walter L. Bradley and Roger L. Olsen (Dallas, TX: Lewis and Stanley, 1992), p. 38.

12. See, for example, Thaxton et al., *Mystery of Life's Origins*, pp. 73–94.

13. For an account of how the Miller-Urey experiment has been misrepresented in recent literature, see *Icons of Evolution* by Jonathan Wells (Washington: Regnery, 2000).

14. *Science*, October 2008.

15. Jeremy England is highly critical of Dan Brown's use of this work in his novel *Origin*. I discuss it in my book *2084: Artificial Intelligence and the Future of Humanity* (Grand Rapids, MI: Zondervan, 2020).

16. Hubert Yockey, *Information Theory and Molecular Biology* (Cambridge: CUP, 1992), p. 238.

17. This, it should be noted, does not take account of the fact that they need to be put in a specific order – a circumstance that we discuss in the next section.

18. For some recent work on abiogenesis that mentions chirality, see Tomonori Totani, 'Emergence of life in an inflationary universe', *Scientific Reports*, vol. 10, article no. 1671, 2020.

19. Paul Davies, *The Fifth Miracle* (London: Allen Lane, Penguin Press, 1998), p. 60.
20. Brian Miller, in 'Hot Wired', with Jeremy England, *Inference*, 5 (2), May 2020.
21. Davies, *Fifth Miracle*, p. 61.
22. A. G. Cairns-Smith, *The Life Puzzle* (Edinburgh: Oliver and Boyd, 1971), p. 95.
23. It is known that some sites in the amino acid chain of a protein can be occupied by more than one possible amino acid, and so the calculation must be modified to take this into account. Biochemists Reidhaar-Olson and Sauer have done these calculations, and reckoned that the probability may possibly be increased to 1 in 10^{65} which, in their opinion, is still 'vanishingly small' (*Proteins: Structure, Function and Genetics*, 7, 1990, pp. 306–316). Of course, if we factor in the requirement for L-acids and peptide bonds the probability drops to 1 in 10^{125}.
24. Yockey, *Information Theory*, pp. 254–57.
25. Fred Hoyle, *The Intelligent Universe* (London: Michael Joseph, 1983), p. 19.
26. *De Natura Deorum*, H. Rackham (trans.) (Cambridge, MA: Harvard University Press, 1933).

Chapter 9: The Genetic Code

1. Sara Imari Walker and Paul C. W. Davies, *The Algorithmic Origins of Life*, arXiv.org:1207.4803v2, 2012, p. 2.
2. Richard Dawkins, *The Blind Watchmaker* (London: Longmans, 1986), p. 112. Shades of Aristotle! He saw that a living organism could not be explained in terms of material causes alone: the substances of which it was made could not explain its complexity. In Aristotle's view it needed what he called *eidos* or 'form'. And, as the word itself implies, it is in-form-ation that gives to substance its form.
3. It is ironic that the Enlightenment by and large rejected the concept of the universe as machine especially in biological contexts. Now the language of information technology is de rigueur in molecular biology.
4. Marcos Eberlin, *Foresight* (Seattle, WA: Discovery Institute Press, 2019), p. 14. Another good description is to be found in Nessa Carey, *The Epigenetics Revolution* (London: Icon Books, 2011), and in any good biology textbook.
5. For a clear tabular description of this analogy, see Bernd Olaf Küppers, *The Computability of the World* (Cham, Switzerland: Springer International AG, 2018), p. 99.
6. *Evolution: A View from the 21st Century* (Upper Saddle River, NJ: FT Press Science, 2011), Kindle version loc. 781–82.
7. We speak of *the* human genome as if there were only one. But of course this is incorrect – genetic fingerprinting depends on the fact that human genomes are essentially unique. It is probably true to say that if I compare my DNA with someone else's there will be about 99.9 per cent in common. Differences will consist in part in the accumulation of single nucleotide polymorphisms (SNPs or Snips as they are commonly called), which result from a single nucleotide being miscopied in the process of DNA replication.
8. A report has been issued in *Nature* (447, 891–916, 14 June 2007) of the pilot project of the thorough Encode investigation of a targeted 1% of the human genome that provides 'convincing evidence that the genome is pervasively transcribed' so that there would appear to be very little 'junk' DNA after all.
9. An enzyme is a particular kind of protein that acts as a catalyst that regulates the rate at which echemical reactions proceed in living organisms without itself being altered in the process.
10. John Maynard Smith and Eörs Szathmáry, *The Major Transitions in Evolution* (Oxford and New York: Freeman, 1995), p. 81; see also Nature, 374, 1995, pp. 227–32.
11. Cited from Whitfield, 'Born in a watery commune', *Nature*, 427, pp. 674–76.
12. Robert Shapiro, 'A simpler origin for life', *Scientific American*, 12 February 2007. https://www.scientificamerican.com/article/a-simpler-origin-for-life/
13. Denis Noble, *Music of Life: Biology Beyond the Genome* (Oxford, OUP, 2006), p. 45.
14. Eberlin, *Foresight*, p. 138.
15. 'Using statistical methods to model the fine-tuning of molecular machines and systems', *Journal of Theoretical Biology*, 501, 2020, 110352.
16. 'Using statistical methods to model the fine-tuning of molecular machines and systems', *Journal of Theoretical Biology*, 501, 2020, 110352.
17. See an example of this process at https://www.entandaudiologynews.com/features/ent-features/post/the-structure-and-function-of-dna (1 November 2014).
18. See, for example, https://www.youtube.com/watch?v=5MfSYnItYvg
19. Robert Shapiro, 'A simpler origin for life'.
20. We shall have occasion to analyse this analogy in detail in Chapter 18.
21. Robert Shapiro, 'A simpler origin for life'.
22. Alvin Powell, 'NYU chemist Robert Shapiro decries RNA-first possibility, *The Harvard Gazette*, 23 October 2008. See https://news.harvard.edu/gazette/story/2008/10/nyu-chemist-robert-shapiro-

decries-rna-first-possibility/
23. See Noble, *The Music of Life*, p. 5.
24. James Shapiro, *Evolution*, p. 28.
25. There is an excellent account of the story of this research in Nessa Carey's book *The Epigenetic Revolution* (London: Icon Books, 2011).
26. Steve Jones, *The Language of the Genes*, revised edition (London: Harper Collins, 2000), p. 35. Jones is being somewhat disingenuous here. There are different ways of characterizing this claim. Perhaps the most reasonable way is to indicate that the 98 per cent refers to protein coding DNA – a fraction (as we have already pointed out) of the total. See the following attempt to provide a more critical view http://citeseerx.ist.psu.edu/viewdoc/download?doi=10.1.1.364.5839&rep=rep1&type=pdf
27. Noble, *The Music of Life*, p. 31.
28. Bill Gates, *The Road Ahead* (Boulder, CO: Blue Penguin, 1996), p. 228.
29. Werner R. Loewenstein, *The Touchstone of Life* (London: Penguin, 2000), p. 64.
30. Douglas Hofstadter, *Gödel, Escher, Bach: An Eternal Golden Braid* (London: Penguin, 1979), p. 548.

Chapter 10: A Matter of Information

1. The same applies every time we look up a dictionary to see if our 'Scrabble' word is really a word in the English language.
2. Recent research into the human genome has shown that the situation is even more complicated than this.
3. There is a delightfully entertaining discussion of this important concept in the book *The Advent of the Algorithm* by David Berlinski (New York: Harcourt Inc., 2000).

Chapter 11: Algorithmic Information Theory

1. By contrast with the main thrust of the Shannon theory of information, which is essentially statistical in character.
2. Leslie Orgel, *The Origins of Life* (New York: Wiley, 1973).
3. Paul Davies, *The Fifth Miracle* (London: Allen Lane, Penguin Press, 1998).
4. 20 January 1999.
5. 'Ungrammatical' does not sound like quite the right word for it. Bickerton probably means 'meaningless'.
6. Derek Bickerton, *Language and Species* (Chicago, IL: University of Chicago Press, 1990), pp. 57–58.
7. In this connection, see D. D. Axe, 'Extreme functional sensitivity to conservative amino acid changes on enzyme exteriors', *Journal of Molecular Biology*, 301, 585–96.
8. Gregory Chaitin, *Exploring Randomness* (New York: Springer, 2000), pp. 163.
9. Notices of the AMS 48 (9): 992–96, 2001.
10. Paul Davies: *The Fifth Miracle* (London: Allen-Lane Science, 1998), p. 254–56.
11. Paul Davies, in *Many Worlds*, Steven Dick (ed.) (Philadelphia, PN and London: The Templeton Press, 2000), p. 21.
12. Although that particular approach is increasingly being seen as a non-starter at this level as we shall discuss in the chapter on evolution.
13. Davies, *Many Worlds*, pp. 21–22.
14. 'Information, Algorithms and the Unknowable Nature of Life's Origin', *The Princeton Theological Review*, 8 (4), November 2001.
15. N. Bohr, 'Light and life', *Nature*, 308, 1933, pp. 421–23, 456–59.
16. See, for example, K. Karamanos, I. Kotsireas et al, 'Statistical compressibility analysis of DNA sequences by generalized entropy-like quantities: Towards algorithmic laws for Biology?', *WSEAS Transactions on Systems* 5(11), November 2006. All the DNA sequences examined were found to be essentially incompressible.
17. Gregory Chaitin, *The Unknowable* (Singapore: Springer, 1999), p. 97.
18. 'Randomness and Mathematical Proof', *Scientific American* 232 (5) May 1975, pp. 47–52. Chaitin's result is Theorem LB in G. Chaitin, 'Incompleteness Theorems for Random Reals', *Advances in Applied Mathematics*, 8 (4), June 1987, pp. 119–46.
19. Lambalgen (example 1.2.5) gives this as an application of a corollary (1.2.4) of the recursion theoretic version of Chaitin's theorem, mentioned in the main text (Lambalgen Theorem 1.2.3 in Chaitin, *The Unknowable*).
20. 'Algorithmic Information Theory', *Journal of Symbolic Logic*, 54 (4) 1989, pp. 1389–1400, Theorem 1.2.6, p. 1393.
21. There are many other variants on the theme, as a web search will show.

22. Or maybe not, since free energy would be a huge bonus in a world beset by diminishing resources!
23. Leon Brillouin, *Science and Information Theory*, 2nd ed. (New York: Academic Press, 1962).
24. P. B. Medawar, *The Limits of Science* (Oxford: OUP, 1984), p. 79.
25. Medawar, *Limits of Science*, p. 79.
26. Medawar, *Limits of Science*, p. 79.
27. See Hao Wang's article in *Nature's Imagination: The Frontiers of Scientific Vision*, John Cornwell (ed.) (Oxford: OUP, 1995), p. 173.
28. See Wladyslaw Kozaczuk, Jerzy Straszak, *Enigma: How the Poles Broke the Nazi Code* (New York: Hippocrene Books Inc., 2004), and Dermot Turing, *X, Y & Z: The Real Story of How Enigma Was Broken* (Stroud: The History Press, 2018).
29. Yockey, *Information Theory and Molecular Biology*, p. 280.
30. Bernd Olaf Küppers, *Der Semantische Aspekt von Information und seine evolutionsbiologische Bedeutung*, Nova Acta Leopoldina, NF 72, Nr. 294, 1996, 195–219, p. 216 (translation mine).
31. Küppers, *Der Semantische Aspekt*, p. 216.
32. Küppers, *Der Semantische Aspekt*, p. 217.
33. Latin for 'Creation from nothing'.
34. Küppers, *Der Semantische Aspekt*, p. 217.
35. What is Life? Daniel Sander Hoffmann im Gespräch mit Bernd-Olaf Küppers, *Episteme* 124, 2002.
36. Paul Davies, *The Demon in the Machine* (Chicago, IL: Chicago University Press, 2019), p. 110.
37. Michael Denton, 'Evolution: A Theory in Crisis Revisited', *Inference*, part 3, 1 (3), July 2015. Italics mine. All three of Denton's articles in this series are highly recommended.

Chapter 12: Life's Solution: Self-Organization?

1. Paul Davies, *The Fifth Miracle* (London: Allen Lane, Penguin Press, 1998), p. 122.
2. Michael Polyani, 'Life's Irreducible Structure', *Science*, 160, 1968, p. 1309.
3. H. Yockey, 'A Calculation of the Probability of Spontaneous Biogenesis by Information Theory', *Journal of Theoretical Biology*, 67 (3), 7 August 1977, pp. 377–98.
4. 'The Selective Chemist', pre-conference paper for 'Fitness of the Cosmos for Life: Biochemistry and Fine-Tuning' Conference, Harvard University, 11–12 October, 2003.
5. Ilya Prigogine and Isabelle Stengers, *Order out of Chaos* (London: Fontana, 1985).
6. Stuart Kauffman, *The Origins of Order* (Oxford: OUP, 1993).
7. John Horgan, *The End of Science* (London: Abacus, 1998), p. 139.
8. Other mixtures produce different colour changes. For example, if the ferroin is replaced by sulphuric acid the change is between yellow and colourless.
9. https://scipython.com/blog/simulating-the-belousov-zhabotinsky-reaction/
10. Robert Shapiro, 'A simpler origin for life', *Scientific American*, 25 June 2007, pp. 24–31.
11. For a recent account, see Michael Lockwood, *The Labyrinth of Time* (Oxford: OUP, 2005), p. 261ff.
12. Haralampos N. Miras, Cole Mathis, Weimin Xuan, De-Liang Long, Robert Pow and Leroy Cronin, 'Spontaneous Formation of Autocatalytic Sets with Self-Replicating Inorganic Metal Oxide Clusters', Chem Rxiv, 14 August 2019.
13. Leslie Orgel, 'The implausibility of metabolic cycles on the prebiotic earth', *PLoS Biology*, (1) 22 January 2008: e18.
14. A monomer is a molecule that forms the basic unit for polymers, which are the building blocks of proteins. Monomers bind to other monomers to form repeating chain molecules through a process known as polymerization. Monomers may be either natural or synthetic in origin.
15. Orgel, 'implausibility of metabolic cycles', e18.
16. Stephen C. Meyer, *The Return of the God Hypothesis*, (Seattle, WA: Discovery Institute Center for the Renewal of Science and Culture, 1998), p. 37.
17. See also Dean Overman, *A Case Against Accident and Self-Organization*, (Lanham, MD: Rowman & Littlefield, 2001), Part IV and 7.3.
18. Leslie Orgel, 'The Origin of Life: A Review of Facts and Speculations', *Trends in Biochemical Sciences*, 23, 1998, pp. 491–500.
19. Cited in Leslie Orgel, 'The Origin of life: More Questions than Answers', *Interdisciplinary Science Reviews*, 1988, 13, p. 348.
20. Francis Crick, *Life Itself* (New York: Simon and Schuster, 1981), p. 88.
21. Stuart Kauffman, *At Home in the Universe* (London: Viking, 1995), p. 31.
22. Francis Collins, *The Language of God* (New York: Free Press, 2006), p. 90.
23. James Tour, 'An Open Letter to My Colleagues', *Inference*, 2017, 3 (2), 2017.
24. Sara Imari Walker and Paul C. W. Davies, *The Algorithmic Origins of Life*, arXiv.org:1207.4803v2, 2012, p. 5.

Chapter 13: Life's Solution: Evolution?

1. Richard Dawkins, *The Blind Watchmaker* (London: Longman, 1986), p. 1.
2. Jacques Monod, *Chance and Necessity* (New York: Knopf, 1972), p. 21.
3. Francis Crick, 'Lessons from Biology', *Natural History*, vol. 97, 1988, p. 36.
4. Daniel Dennett, *Darwin's Dangerous Idea* (London: Penguin, 1996), p. 50.
5. Note, however, that this is correctly described by Dennett as an *idea*, not a *scientific discovery*.
6. Dawkins, *Blind Watchmaker*, p. 14.
7. Stephen Jay Gould, *Darwin's Legacy*, Charles L. Hamrum (ed.) (New York: Harper & Row Publishers, 1983), pp. 6–7.
8. *The Works of Robert G. Ingersoll*, vol. II (New York: The Dresden Publishing Co/C. P. Farrell, 1901), p. 357.
9. Julian Huxley, *Essays of a Humanist* (London: Penguin, 1964 [1969 reprint]), pp. 82–83.
10. Monroe Strickberger, *Evolution*, 2nd ed. (Sudbury: Jones and Bartlett, 1996), p. 62.
11. Douglas Futuyma, *Evolutionary Biology*, 2nd ed. (Sunderland, MA: Sinauer, 1986), p. 3.
12. William Provine, *Evolution and the Foundation of Ethics*, MBL Science, Marine Biological Laboratory, Woods Hole, MS, (3) 1, 25–29.
13. Dennett, *Darwin's Dangerous Idea*, p. 18.
14. Richard Dawkins, *The Selfish Gene* (Oxford: OUP, 1976), p. 1.
15. See, for example, *Intelligent Design Creationism and its Critics*, Robert T. Pennock (ed.) (Cambridge, MA: MIT Press, 2001).
16. Dawkins, *Blind Watchmaker*, p. 14.
17. Dennett, *Darwin's Dangerous Idea*, p. 67.
18. Dennett, *Darwin's Dangerous Idea*, p. 76.
19. Dennett, *Darwin's Dangerous Idea*, p. 203.
20. Alvin Plantinga, *Where the Conflict Really Lies* (Oxford: OUP, 2011), p. 33ff.
21. John Houghton, *The Search for God: Can Science Help?* (Oxford: Lion Hudson, 1995), p. 54.
22. See David N. Livingstone, *Darwin's Forgotten Defenders* (Edinburgh: Scottish Academic Press, 1987).
23. Cambridge Darwin Correspondence, https://www.darwinproject.ac.uk/letter/?docId=letters/DCP-LETT-2534.xml;query=charles%20kingsley;brand=default
24. Richard Swinburne, *The Existence of God* (Oxford: OUP, 1991), pp. 135–36.
25. *The Academy*, vol. 1 (London: John Murray, 1869), pp. 13–14.
26. We shall not elaborate on the fact that the Latin origin equivalent of 'agnostic' is 'ignoramus'.
27. Stoic philosophers used 'logos' to denote the rational principle behind the universe. John elevates its use to describe the creative Word of God, who is God.
28. Stephen Jay Gould, 'Impeaching a Self-appointed Judge', *Scientific American*, 267, (1) 1992, pp. 118–21.
29. Alister McGrath, *Dawkins' God* (Oxford: Blackwell, 2005), p. 81.
30. Denis Alexander, *Rebuilding the Matrix* (Oxford: Lion Hudson, 2001), p. 291.
31. Gould, 'Impeaching a Self-appointed Judge', pp. 118–21.
32. Simon Conway Morris, *Life's Solution* (Cambridge: CUP, 2003), p. 327.
33. *The Deep Structure of Biology*, Simon Conway Morris (ed.) (West Conshohocken, PA: Templeton Foundation Press, 2008), p. 46.
34. Morris (ed.), *The Deep Structure of Biology*, p. 50.

Chapter 14: Evolution: Asking Hard Questions

1. He means, of course, evolution understood as an unguided process.
2. 'Put Your Money on Evolution', *The New York Times Review of Books*, 9 April 1989, pp. 34–35.
3. To their credit, many in the audience reacted with suppressed yet audible incredulity.
4. Daniel Dennett, *Darwin's Dangerous Idea* (London: Penguin, 1996), p. 46.
5. Lynn Margulis and Dorian Sagan, *Acquiring Genomes: A Theory of the Origins of Species* (New York: Basic Books, 2002).
6. Douglas Axe, *Undeniable: How Biology Confirms Our Intuition that Life is Designed*, (New York: HarperOne, 2016), p. 58.
7. Axe, *Undeniable*, p. 265.
8. Thomas Nagel, *Mind and Cosmos* (Oxford: OUP, 2012), p. 3.
9. 'Questioning Evolution is neither Science Denial nor the preserve of Creationists', *The Guardian*, 5 September 2017. https://www.theguardian.com/science/political-science/2017/sep/05/questioning-evolution-is-neither-science-denial-nor-the-preserve-of-creationists
10. Suzan Mazur, *The Paradigm Shifters* (New York: Caswell Books, 2015), p. 19.
11. We would emphasize here that the question of the motivation behind a theory is not the same as the question of the truth or falsity of that theory – a point that will be made subsequently. We are not trying

here to prejudice the answer to the latter question by considering the former. What we are trying to do is to tease out a complex relationship.

12. Colin Patterson, *Evolution*, 2nd ed. (London: Natural History Museum, 1999), p. 120.
13. Philip Johnson, *Objections Sustained* (Downers Grove, IL: IVP, 1998), p. 73.
14. Donald McKay, *The Clockwork Image* (London: IVP, 1974), p. 52.
15. C. S. Lewis, *Christian Reflections* (London: Geoffrey Bles, 1967), pp. 82–93.
16. Lewis, *Christian Reflections*, pp. 82–93.
17. Cited by Mazur, *Paradigm Shifters*, p. 3.
18. Furthermore, the logic of the relationship is often reversed by sleight of hand, so that the inference from naturalism to evolution becomes 'science (evolution) proves the naturalistic worldview' – a further deception.
19. Robert G. Reid, *Biological Emergences: Evolution by Natural Experiment* (Cambridge Mass: London, MIT Press, 2007).

Chapter 15: The Nature and Scope of Evolution

1. 'What is Life?', Daniel Sander Hoffmann im Gespräch mit Bernd-Olaf Küppers', *Episteme* 124, 2002.
2. This means, of course, that Richard Dawkins' dichotomy of 'God or evolution, but not both' is far too simplistic. Microevolutionary processes are agreed to occur by all sides and so, from a theistic perspective, the world God created is a world in which natural selection processes have a role.
3. https://www.independent.co.uk/news/science/wisdom-teeth-evolution-humans-flinders-university-processed-food-b907634.html
4. For example, the major university text on *Evolution* by Peter Skelton (ed.) (Harlow: Addison Wesley, 1993), p. 854.
5. Richard Dawkins, *The Greatest Show on Earth: The Evidence for Evolution* (London: Black Swan, 2010), p. 426.
6. Cited by Futuyma in *Science on Trial* (Sunderland, MA: Sinauer, 1995), p. 161.
7. Suzan Mazur, *The Paradigm Shifters* (New York: Caswell Books, 2015), p. 55.
8. Brian K. Hall and Benedikt Hallgrimsson, *Strickberger's Evolution*, 5th ed. (Burlington, MA: Jones and Bartlett Learning, 2014), p. 12.
9. Jonathan Weiner, *The Beak of the Finch* (London: Cape, 1994).
10. A detailed analysis of the significance of the finch beak story for the theory of evolution and the way in which it is handled in textbooks, can be found in biologist Jonathan Wells' book, *Icons of Evolution* (Washington: Regnery, 2000), Chapter 8.
11. Michael Majerus, *Melanism: Evolution in Action* (Oxford: OUP, 1998), p. 171.
12. 27 November 2000.
13. Steve Jones, *Almost Like a Whale* (London: Anchor, 2000), p. 93.
14. 'Not black and white', *Nature*, 396, 1998, pp. 35–36. A detailed analysis of the peppered moth story can again be found in Wells' *Icons*, and a fascinating account of the dramatic history of the personalities involved in the story of Kettlewell's original work on the peppered moth is to be found in Judith Hooper's eminently readable book *Of Moths and Men: Intrigue, Tragedy and the Peppered Moth* (London: Fourth Estate, 2002).
15. 'Intelligent Evolution', *Harvard Magazine*, November 2005.
16. 'Intelligent Evolution', *Harvard Magazine*, November 2005.
17. Wilson does not say what these systems are.
18. 'Intelligent Evolution', *Harvard Magazine*, November 2005.
19. Robert Wesson, *Beyond Natural Selection* (Cambridge: MIT Press, 1991), p. 206.
20. Charles Darwin, *On the Origin of Species*, World's Classic Edition (Oxford: OUP, 2008), p. 302.
21. Darwin, *Origin of Species*, p. 227.
22. 'Cambria' is the Latinized form of the Welsh word for Wales, 'Cymru'.
23. Sir Roderick Impey Murchison, *Siluria* (1854) (Cambridge: CUP [reprint 2014])), p. 469.
24. Stephen Meyer, *Darwin's Doubt* (New York: HarperOne, 2013).
25. Mark Ridley, *The Problems of Evolution* (Oxford: OUP, 1985), p. 11.
26. David Raup, 'Conflicts Between Darwin and Palaeontology', Field Museum of Natural History Bulletin, January 1979, p. 25.
27. Stephen Jay Gould, 'Evolution's Erratic Pace', *Natural History*, 86, 1977.
28. Niles Eldredge, *Time Frames: The Evolution of Punctuated Equilibria* (Princeton, NJ: Princeton University Press, 1985), pp. 144–45.
29. Eldredge, *Time Frames*, pp. 144–45.
30. See 'The Episodic Nature of Evolutionary Change' in *The Panda's Thumb* (New York: W. W. Norton, 1985, page unknown).

31. Stephen Jay Gould, *Wonderful Life* (New York: Norton, 1989).
32. Simon Conway Morris, *The Crucible of Creation* (Oxford: OUP, 1998), p. 4.
33. Eugene V. Koonin, 'The Biological Big Bang for the Major Transitions in Evolution', *Biology Direct*, 2, 2007, pp. 1–17.
34. Niles Eldredge, *Reinventing Darwin* (New York: Phoenix, 1996), p. 3.
35. Cited by Pervical Davis and Dean H. Kenyon in *Of Pandas and People* (Dallas, TX: Haughton Publishing Co., 1989), p. 106.
36. James Valentine, *On the Origin of Phyla* (Chicago, IL: University of Chicago Press, 2004), p. 35.
37. Paul Chien, J. Y. Chen, C. W. Li and Frederick Leung, 'SEM Observation of Precambrian Sponge Embryos from Southern China Revealing Ultrastructures including Yolk Granules, Secretion Granules, Cytoskeleton and Nuclei', paper presented to North American Paleontological Convention, University of California, Berkeley, 26 June – 1 July 2001.
38. https://evolutionnews.wpengine.com/2020/05/the-myth-of-precambrian-sponges/
39. Simon Conway Morris, *Crucible of Creation*, p. 8.
40. *New Scientist*, 90, 1981, pp. 830–32.
41. Francis Collins, *The Language of God* (New York: Free Press, 2006), p. 205.
42. 'Evolution without metaphysics?' in J. Kvanvig (ed.), *Oxford Studies in Philosophy of Religion*, vol. 3, 2011.
43. 'The Methodological Equivalence of Design and Descent', in *The Creation Hypothesis*, J. P. Moreland (ed.) (Downers Grove, IL: IVP, 1994), pp. 67–112.

Chapter 16: Natural Selection

1. Colin Patterson, *Evolution*, 2nd ed. (London: National History Museum, 1995), p. 118.
2. Patterson, *Evolution*, p. 118.
3. In the preface to his book Patterson says that, although he believes in evolution in the sense of common ancestry, he is no longer certain that natural selection is the complete explanation. Nor, indeed was Darwin. In the first edition of *The Origin of Species* he says: 'I am convinced that natural selection has been the main but not the exclusive means of modification.'
4. Patterson, *Evolution*, p. vii.
5. In fact, Popper himself went as far as calling the theory of evolution 'a metaphysical research programme'.
6. G. B. Müller, 'Homology: The Evolution of Morphological Organization' in G. B. Müller and S. A. Newman (eds.), *Origination of Organismal Form. Beyond the Gene in Developmental and Evolutionary Biology* (Harvard, MA: MIT Press, Vienna Series in Theoretical Biology, 2003), p. 51.
7. Richard Dawkins, *Climbing Mount Improbable* (New York: Norton, 1996), p. 67.
8. Denis Alexander, *Creation or Evolution: Do We Have to Choose?* (Oxford: Lion Hudson, 2008), p.81.
9. Princeton, NJ: Princeton University Press, 1986.
10. Chicago, IL: University of Chicago Press 1971 [Afterword 2001], pp. 199–200.
11. William Provine, *The Origins of Theoretical Population Genetics* (Chicago, IL: University of Chicago Press, 1971, reissued in 2001), p. 199.
12. Provine, *Origins of Theoretical Population Genetics*, pp. 199–200.
13. R. E. D. Clark, *Darwin Before and After* (Chicago, IL: Moody Press, 1967), pp. 88–89.
14. Letter from J. D. Hooker to Charles Darwin, 26 November 1862, Letter 3831, CUL DAR 101:77–78, 61–62. Darwin Correspondence Project, 'Letter no. 3831', accessed on 12 February 2021, https://www.darwinproject.ac.uk/letter/DCP-LETT-3831.xml.
15. Letter from Darwin to Hooker, after 26 November 1862, Letter 3834, CUL DAR 115:172. Darwin Correspondence Project, "Letter no. 3834," accessed on 12 February 2021, https://www.darwinproject.ac.uk/letter/DCP-LETT-3834.xml
16. From Ch. 10 'The limits of natural selection', Alfred Russell Wallace in *Contributions to the Theory of Natural Selection*, 1870, p. 119.
17. Wallace, *Contributions*, p. 119.
18. Denis Noble, *Dance to the Tune of Life: Biological Relativity* (Cambridge: CUP, 2017), p. 199.

Chapter 17: The Edge of Evolution

1. See, for example, *Evolution*, Peter Skelton (ed.) (Harlow: Addison Wesley, 1993).
2. A. P. Hendry and M. T. Kinnison, 'An introduction to microevolution: rate, pattern, process', *Genetica*, 112–113, 2001, 1–8.
3. 'Resynthesizing Evolutionary and Developmental Biology', *Developmental Biology*, 173, 1996, p. 361.
4. Richard Goldschmidt, *The Material Basis of Evolution* (Yale, CT: Yale University Press, 1940), p. 8.
5. 'The Major Evolutionary Transitions', *Nature*, 374, 1995, pp. 227–32.

6. Siegfried Scherer, *Evolution – Ein kritisches Lehrbuch* (Giessen: Weyel Biologie, Weyel Lehrmittelverlag, 1998), p. 34.
7. Scherer, *Evolution*, p. 46, translation mine.
8. Paul Erbrich, *Zufall* (Stuttgart: Kohlhammer, 1988), p. 217, translation mine.
9. James Shapiro, *Evolution: A View from the 21st Century* (Upper Saddle River NJ: FT Press Science, 2011), p. 126.
10. Eric Davidson, 'Evolutionary Bioscience as Regulatory Systems Biology', *Developmental Biology*, 357 (1), 2011: 35–40. Published online 12 February 2011, doi: 10.1016/j.ydbio.2011.02.004.
11. Theodosius Dobzhansky, 'Darwinian or "Oriented Evolution"?', *Evolution*, 29 June 1975, 376–78.
12. Paris: Albin Michel, 1973, p. 130.
13. Dobzhansky, 'Darwinian', 376–78 .
14. *The Origin of Species*, 6th ed. (New York: New York University Press, 1988), p. 154.
15. Dawkins, *Blind Watchmaker* (London: Longmans, 1986), p. 91.
16. It should be noted that some people have claimed that Darwin's theory is unfalsifiable in the sense of Popper: Darwin's concept of irreducible complexity shows otherwise.
17. Michael Behe, *Darwin's Black Box* (New York: Simon and Schuster, 1996).
18. Behe, *Black Box*, p. 39.
19. See, for example, *Intelligent Design, Creationism and its Critics*, Robert T. Pennock, (ed.) (Cambridge, MA: MIT Press, 2001).
20. Behe, *Black Box*, p. 186.
21. James Shapiro, *National Review*, 62–65, 16 September 1996.
22. T. Cavalier-Smith, 1997, 'The Blind Biochemist', *Trends in Ecology and Evolution* 12, 1997, pp. 162–63.
23. Stephen Jay Gould's review of Mark C. Taylor's *The Moment of Complexity: Emerging Network Culture* in *The London Review of Books*, 357 (1), 2011, 22 February 2002, p. 5.
24. Behe, *Black Box*, p. 193.
25. Behe, *The Edge of Evolution: The Search for the Limits of Darwinism* (New York: Free Press, 2007).
26. D. Papadopoulos et al., *Proceedings of the National Academy of Sciences of the USA*, (96), 1999, 3807.
27. Behe, *Edge of Evolution*, p. 16.
28. Benjamin H. Good, Michael J. McDonald, Jeffrey E. Barrick, Richard E. Lenski and Michael M. Desai, 'The Dynamics of Molecular Evolution Over 60,000 Generations', *Nature*, 551, 2017, pp. 45–50.
29. Behe, *Edge of Evolution*, p. 19.
30. Behe, *Edge of Evolution*, p. 63.
31. Behe, *Edge of Evolution*, p. 195.
32. In 1887 Albert Michelson and Edward Morley conducted a classic experiment to detect the presence of the ether. They found nothing.
33. Behe, *Edge of Evolution*, p. 164.
34. Thomas Nagel, *Mind and Cosmos* (Oxford: OUP, 2012), p. 10.
35. Nagel, *Mind and Chaos*, p. 12.

Chapter 18: The Mathematics of Evolution

1. As reported by Sir James Jeans, *The Mysterious Universe* (New York: Macmillan, 1930), p. 4. Jeans gives no reference.
2. Nevertheless what is certain is that Eddington did use such an analogy to indicate the improbability of a gas, once dispersed throughout a vessel, returning spontaneously to occupy just one half of the vessel: 'If I let my fingers wander idly over the keys of a typewriter it might happen that my screed made an intelligible sentence. If an army of monkeys were strumming on typewriters they might write all the books in the British Museum. The chance of their doing so is decidedly more favourable than the chance of the molecules returning to one half of the vessel' (Arthur S. Eddington, *The Nature of the Physical World*, Gifford Lectures, 1927 [New York: Macmillan], 1929, p. 72).
3. Russell Grigg, 'Could Monkeys Type the 23rd Psalm?', *Interchange*, 50, 1993, pp. 25–31.
4. Richard Dawkins, *The Blind Watchmaker* (London: Longmans, 1986), p. 9. The interested reader might find some entertainment by reading the Wikipedia entry on The Infinite Monkey Theorem.
5. Dawkins, *The Blind Watchmaker*, p. 45.
6. Sir Fred Hoyle and Chandra Wickramasinghe, *Evolution From Space* (New York: Simon and Schuster, 1984, p. 176). See also the last chapter of their book, *Cosmic Life Force* (London: Dent, 1988).
7. Richard Dawkins, *Climbing Mount Improbable* (London: Penguin, 2006), p. 68.
8. 'Letter to the Editor', *The Independent*, 12 January 1997.
9. Remember that we are talking about the origin of life, so the word 'selection' needs to be treated with care – it does not assume that there exist mutating replicators.
10. It is rather ironic that Dawkins, who decries the use of analogies on the part of those making design

inferences, is quite happy to employ them to reject the design inference.
11. Dawkins' original version has only one monkey but this slight variant may make it easier to imagine.
12. Dawkins, *Blind Watchmaker*, p. 50.
13. David Berlinksi, *The Deniable Darwin* (Seattle, WA: Discovery Institute, 2010), p. 60.
14. Perry Marshall, *Evolution 2.0* (Dallas, TX: BenBella Books, 2015), p. 222.
15. Berlinksi, *Deniable Darwin*, p. 58.
16. Behe, *Darwin's Black Box*, p. 221.
17. Behe, *Darwin's Black Box*, p. 221.
18. Ronald Fisher, *The Genetical Theory of Natural Selection*, second revised ed. (New York: Dover, 1958).
19. Keith Ward, *God, Chance and Necessity* (Oxford: One World Publications, 1996), p. 108.
20. Later published by Wistar Institute Press, Philadelphia, 1967.
21. *Mathematical Challenges to the Neo-Darwinian Interpretation of Evolution* (Philadelphia, PA: Wistar Institute Press, 1967), pp. 74– 75.
22. 'The Miracle of Darwinism', *Origins and Design*, 17 (2), 1996, pp. 10–15.
23. 'Miracle of Darwinism', pp. 10–15.
24. In 1949 Johann von Neumann, who made seminal contributions to many fields including the foundations of computer science, proposed the construction of self-replicating machines. These are called von Neumann machines.
25. Steve Fuller, *Science Vs. Religion* (Cambridge: Polity, 2007), p. 89.
26. Noam Chomsky, *The Science of Language: Interviews with James McGilvray* (Cambridge: CUP, 2012), p. 49.
27. Cited by Steven Pinker, *Language, Cognition, and Human Nature: Selected Articles*, 1st ed. (Oxford: OUP, 2013), p. 146.
28. Chomsky, *Science of Language*, p. 15.
29. Fred Hoyle, *The Mathematics of Evolution* (Memphis, TN: Acorn Enterprises, 1999).
30. Hoyle, *Mathematics of Evolution*, p. 1.
31. Hoyle, *Mathematics of Evolution*, p. xv
32. Hoyle, *Mathematics of Evolution*, pp. 2–4
33. Hoyle, *Mathematics of Evolution*, p. 2.
34. Hoyle, *Mathematics of Evolution*, p. 5.
35. R. A. Fisher, *The Genetical Theory of Natural Selection* (Oxford: Clarendon Press, 1930).
36. Hoyle, Mathematics of Evolution, p. 10.
37. Hoyle, Mathematics of Evolution, p. 6.
38. H. Yockey, 'Origin of life on earth and Shannon's theory of communication', *Computers and Chemistry* 24, 2000, pp. 105-123.
39. Gregory Chaitin, *Proving Darwin: Making Biology Mathematical* (New York: Pantheon Books, 2012).
40. J. Shallit, 'Review of Chaitin's Proving Darwin: Making Biology Mathematical', *Reports of the National Center for Science Education*, 33 (1), 2013.
41. Radosław Siedliński, 'Turing Machines and Evolution: A Critique of Gregory Chaitin's Metabiology', *Studies in Logic, Grammar and Rhetoric*, 48 (61), 2016, p. 141.
42. Siedliński, 'Turing Machines and Evolution', p. 146.
43. J. Kozłowski, 'Czy teorię ewolucji można zmatematyzować?' 'Ewolucja życia i ewolucja wszechświata', J. Mączka, P. Polak (ed.)(Kraków: Copernicus Center Press, 2011), pp. 75–84.
44. Siedliński, 'Turing Machines and Evolution', p. 148.
45. W. Ewert, W. A. Dembski, R. J. Marks II, 'Active Information in Metabiology', *BIO-Complexity*, 2013 (4), pp. 1–10.
46. Shallit, *National Center for Science Education*, 33 (1), 2013.
47. W. Ewert W, W. A. Dembski, R. J. Marks II, *Introduction to Evolutionary Informatics* (Singapore: World Scientific, 2017).
48. Chaitin, *Proving Darwin*, p. 68.
49. Chaitin, *Proving Darwin*, p. 21.

Chapter 19: Systems Biology

1. *Mathematical Challenges to the Neo-Darwinian Interpretation of Evolution*, P. S. Moorhead and M. M. Kaplan (eds.) (Philadelphia, PA: Wistar Institute, 1967), pp. 29–30.
2. *Mathematical Challenges*, Moorhead and Kaplan (eds.), pp. 29–30.
3. David Swift, *Evolution under the Microscope* (Stirling: Leighton Academic Press, 2002), p. 371.
4. James Shapiro, 'How Life Changes Itself: The Read-Write (RW) Genome', *Physics of Life Reviews* 10, 2013, pp. 287–323.
5. Suzan Mazur, *The Altenberg 16* (Berkley, CA: North Atlantic Books, 2010), p. 279.

6. Robert Laughlin, *A Different Universe: Reinventing Physics from the Bottom Down* (New York: Basic Books, 2005), pp. 168–69.
7. G. B. Müller, 'Homology: The Evolution of Morphological Organization' in Müller G.B. and Newman S.A. (eds.), *Origination of Organismal Form. Beyond the Gene in Developmental and Evolutionary Biology* (Harvard, MA: MIT Press, Vienna Series in Theoretical Biology, 2003), p. 51.
8. Barbara McClintock – Banquet speech, 10 December 1983. NobelPrize.org. Nobel Media AB 2021. https://www.nobelprize.org/prizes/medicine/1983/mcclintock/speech/
9. https://www.nobelprize.org/uploads/2018/06/mcclintock-lecture.pdf
10. 'Beyond Neo-Darwinism: The Epigenetic Approach to Evolution', *Journal of Theoretical Biology*, 78 (4), 1979, pp. 573–91.
11. Mazur, *Altenberg 16*, p. 44.
12. https://www.thethirdwayofevolution.com/
13. Noble's description of this work in Ch. 5 of *The Music of Life* makes fascinating reading, as does also his interview with Suzan Mazur in *The Paradigm Shifters* (New York: Caswell Books, 2015).
14. 'Replace the Modern Synthesis (Neo-Darwinism): An Interview with Denis Noble', 5 April 2014 (updated 9 July 2014).
15. 'An Interview with Denis Noble', 5 April 2014.
16. Sara Imari Walker and Paul C. W. Davies, *The Algorithmic Origins of Life*, arXiv.org:1207.4803v2, 2012, p. 7.
17. Interview with Mazur, *The Paradigm Shifters*, p. 23.
18. Denis Noble, *The Music of Life* (Oxford: OUP, 2006).
19. Denis Noble, 'A theory of biological relativity: no privileged level of causation', presentation at the Royal Society Interface Focus, London, 6 February 2012, 2(1): 55–64. Published online 9 November 2011. doi: 10.1098/rsfs.2011.0067
20. Sydney Brenner, a South African biologist, shared the 2002 Nobel Prize for Physiology or Medicine.
21. Noble, *Music of Life*, p. 41.
22. Lynn Margulis, *What is Life?* (Berkeley, CA: University of California Press, 1995), p. 66.
23. Denis Noble, 'Digital and Analogue Information in Organisms', in *From Matter to Life*, Walker, Davies and Ellis (eds.) (Cambridge: CUP, 2017), p. 116.
24. 'How Life Changes Itself: The Read–Write (RW) Genome', *Physics of Life Reviews* 10, 2013, pp. 287–323.
25. For a very readable informal description see Suzan Mazur, *The Paradigm Shifters*, p. 14ff.
26. Noble, *Music of Life*, p. 112.
27. Noble, *Music of Life*, p. 109.
28. Noble, *Music of Life*, p. 101.
29. Noble, *Music of Life*, p. 112.
30. Noble, *Music of Life*, p. 111.
31. 18 March 2015 https://www.scientificamerican.com/article/the-purpose-of-our-eyes-strange-wiring-is-unveiled/ (reprinted from: *The Conversation* (UK), 13 March 2015).
32. Denis Noble and Raymond Noble, 'Was the Watchmaker Blind? Or Was She One-Eyed?', *Biology*, 2017, 6, 47; doi:10.3390/biology6040047.
33. 'Genome Gymnastics: Unique Modes of DNA Evolution and Processing in Ciliates', *Nature Review Genetics*, December 2000:1(3): pp. 191–98.
34. 'Genetic and Physiological Interactions in the Amoeba-Bacteria Symbiosis', *Journal of Eukaryotic Microbiology*, 51 (5), 2004, pp. 502–508.
35. 'Convergent Evolution, Evolving Evolvability, and the Origins of Lethal Cancer', Kenneth J. Pienta, Emma U. Hammarlund, Robert Axelrod et al, *Molecular Cancer Research*, first published online 31 March 2020.
36. For an interesting perspective on the extended evolutionary synthesis and systems biology, etc, it is worth looking at Ch. 8 of *Theistic Evolution*, J. P. Moreland, Stephen C. Meyer, et al. (eds.) (Wheaton IL: Crossway, 1917).
37. https://www.bechly.at/anti-darwinism-1/

Chapter 20: The Origin of Information: A Word-Based World

1. Stephen Meyer, 'DNA and Other Things', *First Things*, April 2000.
2. 'Self-Organization, Origin of Life Scenarios and Information Theory', *Journal of Theoretical Biology*, 91, 1981, pp. 13–31.
3. William Dembski, *The Design Inference* (Cambridge: CUP, 1998).
4. One cannot help quoting the non-attributed humorous remark to the effect that one of the main evidences that there is intelligent life out there is that it has not tried to contact us!
5. 'A Scientist Reflects on Religious Belief', *Truth* 1, 1985, p. 54.

6. As reported by Associated Press Report, 9 December 2004.

7. 17 February 2001.

8. R. Landauer, 'The physical nature of information', *Physics Letters A*, 217, 1996, p. 192.

9. Miescher, F. *Letter to W. His* of 17 December 1892. In: *Histochemische und physiologische Arbeiten*, Bd. 1 (Leipzig: Vogel, 1897).

10. H. Blumenberg, *Die Lesbarkeit der Welt* (Frankfurt am Main: Suhrkamp, 2000), p. 395f.

11. Denis Noble, *The Music of Life* (Oxford: OUP, 2006), p. 140.

12. *Principles of Philosophy* 3.46, Elizabeth Anscombe and Philip T. Geach (trans.), *Descartes: Philosophical Writings* (London: Nelson, 1969), p. 225.

13. Genesis 2:19.

14. Cambridge: CUP, 1998.

15. This is not the place to discuss matters of biblical interpretation any further. The reader interested in pursuing my views on it might have a look at my book *Seven Days That Divide the World* (Grand Rapids, MI: Zondervan, 2011).

16. Genesis 1:1–5.

17. Taken from the first chapter of my book *Seven Days that Divide the World*.

18. Placed in inverted commas since I am aware that interpretations differ. That is not relevant to my purpose here.

19. For the significance of this, see the previous reference.

20. John 1:1–5.

21. Hebrews 1:3 (ESV).

22. Those who believe that evolution took place not gradually but in large jumps or saltations.

23. Paul Davies in *Many Worlds: The New Universe, Extra-Terrestrial Life, and the Theological Implications*, Steven J. Dick (ed.) (Philadelphia, PA and London: Templeton Foundation Press, 2000), p. 21.

24. Paul Davies, *Many Worlds*, pp. 21–22.

25. Arthur Peacocke, *The Experiment of Life* (Toronto: University of Toronto Press, 1983), p. 54.

26. R. W. Sperry, 'Psychology's Mentalist Paradigm and the Religion/Science Tension', *American Psychologist*, August 1988, p. 609.

27. John 4:24.

28. R. Landauer, 'Information is physical', *Physics Today*, 23–29 May 1991 and 'The physical nature of information', *Physics Letters A*, 217, 1996, pp. 188–193.

29. C. G. Timpson, *Quantum Information Theory and the Foundations of Quantum Mechanics* (Oxford: OUP, 2010).

30. Sara Imari Walker, Paul C. W. Davis and George F. R. Ellis, *From Matter to Life* (Cambridge: CUP, 2017), p.1.

31. Walker et al., *From Matter to Life*, p. 1

32. John Archibald Wheeler, *A Journey Into Gravity and Spacetime*, Scientific American Library (New York: W. H. Freeman, 1990).

33. Gregory Chaitin, *The Unknowable* (New York: Springer Verlag Singapore Pte., 1999), p. 106.

34. Thomas Nagel, *Mind and Cosmos: Why the Materialist Neo-Darwinian Conception of Nature is Almost Certainly False* (Oxford: OUP, 2012), p. 27.

35. Marcos Eberlin, *Foresight* (Seattle, WA: Discovery Institute Press, 2019), p. 141.

36. Keith Ward, *God, Chance and Necessity* (Oxford: One World Publications, 1996), p. 1.

37. Paul Davies, 'E.T. and God', *Atlantic Monthly*, September 2003. See https://www.theatlantic.com/magazine/archive/2003/09/et-and-god/376856/

38. R. E. D. Clark, *The Universe: Plan or Accident?* (Paternoster Press, 1961 [3rd rev.]), p. 8.

39. Clark, *The Universe*, p. 8.

40. See, for example, H. J. van Till, 'When Faith and Reason Co-operate', *Christian Scholar's Review*, 21, 1991, p. 42.

41. 'The Laws of Nature and the Laws of Physics' in *Quantum Cosmology and the Laws of Nature: Scientific Perspectives on Divine Action*, Robert John Russell, Nancey Murphy and C.J. Isham (eds.), second ed. (Vatican City and Berkeley, CA: The Vatican Observatory and The Center for Theology and Natural Sciences, 1999), p. 438.

42. 'Should Methodological Naturalism Constrain Science' in *Christian Perspectives for the New Millennium*, Scott B. Luley, Paul Copan and Stan W. Wallace (eds.) (Addison TX: CLM/RZIM Pubel., 2003).

43. As I have said earlier, when we are investigating the laws and mechanisms of the universe, for the most part it makes little difference whether we suppose that there is real design or assume only apparent design.

44. It is to be observed that even the Genesis account limits the number of such special events. Furthermore, the creation sequence ends with the sabbath on which God ceases from the direct activities involved in the process of creation (see Genesis 1).

45. Just as they may also reject arguments, like the fine-tuning arguments, or elegance arguments from mainstream science.

46. See my book *God and Stephen Hawking* 2nd ed (Oxford: Lion Hudson, 2021), for detailed discussion of this point.
47. 'So finely tuned a universe of atoms, stars, quanta & God', Commonweal Foundation, 1996. https://jesuslightworker.files.wordpress.com/2017/08/polkinghornesofinelytuned.pdf, p. 6.
48. 'Theology of Evolution', *The Guardian*, 12 September 2008.
49. Denis Alexander, *Creation or Evolution*, p. 33.
50. Davies, 'E.T. and God'. See https://www.theatlantic.com/magazine/archive/2003/09/et-and-god/376856/
51. 'A Third Way', *Boston Review*, Feb/March 1997, p. 33.
52. D. H. Kenyon and G. Steinman, *Biochemical Predestination*, (New York: McGraw-Hill, 1969).
53. P. Davis and D. H Kenyon, *Of Pandas and People: The Central Question of Biological Origins* (Dallas, TX: Haughton Publishing Co., 1989), p. 7.
54. 'Intelligent Evolution', *Harvard Magazine*, November 2005.
55. 'A Scientist Reflects on Christian Belief', *Truth* 1, 1985, p.54.
56. BBC Radio 4 interview, 10 December 2004.
57. Acts 17:26.
58. Francis Collins, *The Language of God* (New York: Free Press, 2006), p. 205.
59. Keith Ward in *Information and the Nature of Reality*, Paul Davies and Niels Henrik Gregersen (eds.) (Cambridge: CUP, 2010), p. 296

Chapter 21: Brain, Mind, and the Quantum World

1. German for a 'product, work, creation of speech'.
2. For a good image – see https://www.shutterstock.com/image-vector/oligodendrocytes-unlike-schwann-cells-form-segments-235121179
3. A millionth of a metre or a thousandth of a millimetre.
4. Science ABC, https://www.scienceabc.com/humans/the-human-brain-vs-supercomputers-which-one-wins.html
5. See Sharon Dirckx, *Am I Just My Brain?* (London: Good Book Company, 2019).
6. 'The Nature of Naturalism', in Yervant H. Krikorian (ed.) *Naturalism and the Human Spirit* (New York: Columbia University Press, 1945), p. 358.
7. Daniel Dennett, *Breaking the Spell* (London: Penguin, 2007), p.107.
8. Francis Crick, *The Astonishing Hypothesis: The Scientific Search for the Soul* (Simon & Schuster, 1994), p. 3.
9. 'You're Nothing but a Pack of Neurones', *Journal of Consciousness Studies*, 1 (2), 1984, pp. 275–79.
10. Crick, *Astonishing Hypothesis*, p. 93.
11. *An Essay Concerning Human Understanding*, (1690), IV, x, 10.
12. And causation is yet another. There is sometimes a danger of confusing correlation with causation.
13. Positron Emission Tomography that detects increase in blood-flow due to the demand for oxygen by active neurones thus giving a map of 'hotspots' in the brain.
14. 'The Brain Implants That Could Change Humanity', by Moises Velasquez-Manoff, *Opinion*, 28 August 2020.
15. In *Explanations*, John Cornwell (ed.) (Oxford: OUP, 2004), p. 163.
16. John Polkinghorne, *One World* (London: SPCK, 1986), pp.92–93.
17. David Chalmers, *The Conscious Mind* (Oxford: OUP, 1996), p. 168.
18. Chalmers, *Conscious Mind*, p. 47.
19. *The Music of Life: Biology beyond the Genome* (Oxford: OUP, 2006), p. 126.
20. Charles Darwin, *Letter to William Graham*, 3 July 1881.
21. Thomas Nagel, *Mind and Cosmos* (Oxford: OUP, 2012), p. 14.
22. I have been under the impression that something like this was said by Alvin Plantinga, but no reference has been found. It would, however, seem to be a fair summary of Plantinga's view as expressed in the next reference.
23. Nagel, *Mind and Cosmos*, p. 27.
24. John Gray, *Straw Dogs* (London: Granta Books, 2003), p. 26.
25. Alvin Plantinga, *Where the Conflict Really Lies: Science, Religion, and Naturalism* (Oxford: OUP, 2011), p. 316.
26. Plantinga, *Where the Conflict*, ch. 10.
27. C. S. Lewis, *Miracles* (New York: Touchstone, 1996), p. 23.
28. Noble, *The Music of Life* (Oxford: OUP, 2006), p. 66.
29. Noble, *Music of Life*, p. 131.
30. Noble, *Music of Life*, p. 133.
31. *Information and the Nature of Reality*, Paul Davies and Niels Henrik Gregersen (eds.) (Cambridge: CUP, 2010), p. 289.
32. An excellent, informed and entertaining introduction to quantum mechanics is to be found in the book by Philip Ball, *Beyond Weird: Why Everything You Thought about Quantum Mechanics is Different* (London: The

Bodley Head, 2018).

33. Chalmers, *Conscious Mind*, p. 333.
34. Henry Stapp, *Mind Matter and Quantum Mechanics* (Berlin-Heidelberg: Springer, 2009), p. 205.
35. Paul Davies, 'Bit before it?', *New Scientist*, 30 January 1999, p. 3.
36. Pierre Laplace, *A Philosophical Essay on Probabilities*, F. W. Truscott and E. L. Emory (trans.) (New York: Dover, [1812] 1951), p. 4.
37. More accurately, what you get is a probability density, which gives the probability of finding the particle in a small fixed-size interval about the point in question. The probability of finding the particle at a precise point is zero.
38. See Ball, *Beyond Weird*, p. 54ff.
39. Henry P. Stapp, *Quantum Theory and Free Will* (Cham, Switzerland: Springer Nature, 2017), p. 9.
40. *The Emperor's New Mind: Concerning Computers, Minds and the Laws of Physics* (London: Vintage, 1990), pp. 540–541. This book contains a great deal of material relevant to the current chapter.
41. Paul Davies and John Gribbin, *The Matter Myth*, Ch. 1 'The Death of Materialism' (New York: Simon and Schuster, 1992).
42. J. Schwartz, H. Stapp, and M. Beauregard, 'Quantum physics in neuroscience and psychology: a neurophysical model of mind/brain interaction', *Philosophical Transactions of the Royal Society*, B: 360(1458), 2005, pp. 1309-27. [http://www-physics.lbl.gov/-stapp/stappfiles.html]
43. Henry P. Stapp, 'Quantum Interactive Dualism – An Alternative to Materialism', *Journal of Consciousness Studies* 12 (11), pp. 43–49.
44. Henry P. Stapp in *Information and the Nature of Reality*, Paul Davies and Niels Henrik Gregersen (eds.) (Cambridge: CUP, 2020), p. 116.
45. Stapp in *Information and Nature*, p. 117.
46. Stapp in *Information and Nature*, pp. 117–118.
47. Stapp in *Information and Nature*, p. 118.
48. *Modern Physics and Ancient Faith* (Notre Dame, IN: University Press, Part 1, 3 'The fifth twist', 2003).

Epilogue: Beyond Science But Not Beyond Reason

1. For information on research on conjunctive explanations CESAR see https://www.conjunctive-explanations.org/people.html
2. As reported by Max Delbrück in *Light and Life III*, Lecture given at the Centennial of the e Carlsberg Laboratory, Copenhagen, 27 September 1976. See also Niels Bohr, 1933, 'Light and Life', *Nature* 308, pp. 421–423, 456–459.
3. Sara Imari Walker and Paul C. W. Davies, *The Algorithmic Origins of Life*, arXiv.org:1207.4803v2, 2012, p. 8.
4. 'An open letter to my colleagues', *Inference*, 3 (2). This article is strongly recommended and can be found at Inference Online.
5. Perry Marshall, *Evolution 2.0* (Dallas, TX: BenBella Books, 2015), pp. 211–19.
6. T. H. Huxley, letter to Charles Kingsley, 23 September 1860, Leonard Huxley (ed.), *Life and Letters of Thomas Henry Huxley*, vol. 1 (1900, reprinted 1979), p. 235.
7. Robert Spämann, *Das unsterbliche Gerücht: Die Frage nach Gott und die Taeuschung der Moderne* (Stuttgart: Klett-Cotta, 2007), p. 63.
8. Similar to the gematria of the classical world where a boy, using a simple letter/number code might inscribe on a wall: 'I love the girl whose number is 467'. A famous biblical example is the enumber 666.
9. 'In God we are born, in Christ we die, through the Holy Spirit we are made alive'.
10. Robert Spämann, *Fantastische Annahmen*. Interview, *Wirtshaftswoche*, 7 August 2008.
11. 'An intelligently designed response,' Editorial, *Nature Methods*, 4 (12), 2007, p. 983.
12. Jonathan Sacks, *The Great Partnership* (London: Hodder and Stoughton, 2011), pp. 2–3.
13. *Gunning for God* and *Can Science Explain Everything?*
14. Cited by Henry Margenau and Roy Varghese, *Cosmos, Bios, Theos* (La Salle, IL: Open Court Publishing, 1992), p. 107.
15. See my *Gunning for God* (Oxford: Lion Hudson, 2011).

Index

Printed in the United States
by Baker & Taylor Publisher Services